Dyer County, Tennessee, Wills

Volume A: 1853-1893

Transcribed by:

The Works Progress Administration
1938

> *Notice*
>
> This book has been reproduced from carbon-copies of the original transcriptions of court records by the Works Progress Administration (WPA) in 1930s. In many instances, the resulting text is light, the documents are physically flawed, and foxing (or discoloration) occurs. The pages of this reprint have been digitally enhanced and, where possible, the flaws eliminated in order to provide clarity of content and a pleasant reading experience.

Dyer County, Tennessee, Wills
Volume A: 1853-1893

Originally transcribed by:

The Works Progress Administration (WPA)
1938

Reprinted by:

Janaway Publishing, Inc.
732 Kelsey Ct.
Santa Maria, CA 93454
(805) 925-1038
www.JanawayGenealogy.com

2006, 2013

ISBN: 978-1-59641-057-2

Made in the United States of America

DYER COUNTY, TENNESSEE WILLS
VOLUME A: 1853-1893

transcribed by Ms. Agnes Lambert and Mrs. Mary N. Gilmore for
the Works Progress Administration, 1938
reprinted by Byron Sistler & Associates, 1998

Please note: This book has two indexes: the first is a transcription of the original testator index from the will book, and the second is an every name index prepared by the WPA. The index page numbers refer to the original page numbers (in parentheses along the left edge of the text) and not those of the typed publication itself (in the upper right corner of each page).

The transcript this book was printed from is a carbon copy typed on onion skin paper over 60 years ago. The print quality varied throughout the work--this would seem to be due to the wear on the carbon paper. We have made an effort to make all the print as legible as possible. This is a second generation copy of the original, and there will be a few places where the writing cannot be made out.

We would like to thank Jean Sugg and Chuck Sherrill of the TN State Library and Archives for their kind loan of the original book.

Byron Sistler & Associates

TENNESSEE

DYER COUNTY

RECORD OF WILLS VOL. A
1853 - 1893

HISTORICAL RECORDS PROJECT
Official Project No. 465-44-3-115

COPIED UNDER WORKS PROGRESS ADMINISTRATION

MRS. JOHN TROTWOOD MOORE
STATE LIBRARIAN & ARCHIVIST, SPONSOR

MRS. ELIZABETH D. COPPEDGE
DIRECTOR OF WOMEN'S & PROFESSIONAL PROJECTS

MRS. PENELOPE JOHNSON ALLEN
STATE SUPERVISOR

MRS. KATHLEEN W. CARADINE
SUPERVISOR THIRD DISTRICT

COPIED BY
MISS AGNES LAMBERT

TYPED BY
MRS. MARY N. GILMORE

Dec. 21, 1938

ORIGINAL TESTATOR INDEX

DYER COUNTY

RECORD OF WILLS VOL. A
1853 - 1893

ORIGINAL INDEX

Note: Page numbers in this index refer to those of the original volume from which this copy was made. These numbers are carried in the body of the manuscript within parentheses, as (p 124)

A

Akin William H. Last Will - Nuncupative 31
Antwine William Sr. Last Will & Testament 32 & 33
Akin Stephen B. - Last will & Testament 129
Algea, John F. Last will & Testament 85-6-7
Anderson James D - Last will & Testament 142 & 143
Archibald J. G. - Last will & Testament 287

B

Baird, David - Last will & Testament 108 & 109
Barnett A. M. - Last will & Testament 127 & 128
Blake, B. T. - Last will & Testament 143 & 144 & 145
Bradshaw Edward - Last will & Testament 147 & 148
Brockman Martha - Last will & Testament 159
Benton Thana H. - Last will & Testament 350
Boon Frankin E - Last will & Testament 388
Bracken M. T. - Last will & Testament 426
Benton Clem - Last will & Testament 447
Bowen R. D. - Last will & Testament 465

B Cont'd

Borum Mrs. Ann C. - Last will & Testament 474

C

Chambers Geo. W. Nuncupative Will of 36
Cunningham James H. Last Will 68 & 69
Curtis C. N. Last Will 70 & 71
Connell Thomas F. Last Will 66 & 67
Cherry Henry Last Will 119
Cocke George W. Last Will 130 & 31
Canada Abraham Last Will 137 & 138
Chamberlain Willis Last Will 166 & 7
Carroll M. B. Last Will 174 & 175
Chambers James Last Will 177 & 178
Cunningham James B. Last Will 184 & 85 and 186
Caldwell Mary - Last will & Testament om page 196
Cocker J. C. - Last will & Testament on page 218
Canada Anna - Last will & Testament on page 215
Cribbs Cullen G.-Last will & Testament on page 220 & 21
Critchfield Richard - Last will & Testament om page 238
Charlie Clay - Last will & Testament 252 & 53

ORIGINAL TESTATOR INDEX

C Cont'd & D

Dearmore Wm. Last will & Testament 60, 61, & 62
Dickey Margaret Last will & Testament 168 & 9 & 170
Dunston James Last will & Testament 170 & 171
Duncan Stephen Last will & Testament 216 - 217
Chamberlain D. A. Last will & Testament 273 - 276
Carrells John M. Last will & Testament 302 - 303
Doyle W. C. Last will & Testament 310 - 11
Clark Hendersons Last will & Testament 314
Cearley Luke Last will & Testament 337
Drane Robert Last will & Testament 399
Chitwood Stiphen 439
Dunivant J. G. 445
Clark Jesse 452

E

Edwards Mary Last will & Testament 116 & 117
Ellis Joseph W. Last will & Testament 117 & 118
Echols J. W. Last will & Testament 155 & 6 & 7
Enochs Alfred Last will & Testament 263 - 270 inclusive

F

Fields James Page 41 - 44
Fielder Samuel - Last will & Testament 51 & 5 D.
W. P. S. Fielder - Last Will & Testament 57. 58. & 59.
Fochee Sidney Last Will & Testament 74 & 75
Ford, Thomas, Nuncupative Will 110
Fombanks Suffield Last will and Testament 112 & 113
Fielder Susannah W. Last will & Testament 125 & 126

F Cont'd

Fowlkes Henry Last will and Testament 135 & 6 & 7
Fullerton A. J. Last will and Testament 154 & 5
Freeman Asbury Last will and Testament 160
Fowlkes George A. Last will and Testament 182 & 183
Frosh Sucinthy Last will and Testament 260
Fumbanks Mary A. Last will and Testament 360
Ferris Miss M. L. E. Last will and Testament 374
Fuller Hezekiah Last will and Testament 381
Fumbanks Sam 424
Fuller Wm. 428

G

Gooch G. R. Last Will and Testament 133 & 4
Griffen Margaret E. Last Will and Testament 148 & 9
Gause G. W. 149 & 50
Gentry Nicholas Last Will and Testament 175 & 6
Gleaves W. B. Last Will and Testament 80 & 81
Gaulden M. O. B. Last Will and Testament 366

G & H

Hall Jesse, Last will &c 34 & 5
Hodge Andrew Last will &c 47 &8
Henderson Richard Last will &c 78 & 79
Hodge Elizabeth - Last will & testament 94 & 95
W. B. Gleaves will 80 & 81
Henderson Samuel C. Last will & Testament 111
Howe F. M. 131
Hendricks Daniel 138 - 39
Hall Wilson Last will & testament 162 & 63
Hall W. C. Last will and Testament 172
Henderson R. G. Last will and Testament 189 & 190
Hart John M. Last will & Testament 197 & 198

ORIGINAL TESTATOR INDEX

G & H Cont'd.

Huguely John Last will and Testament 200
Haskins Edward Last will and Testament 204
Hart John M. Last will and Testament 197
Hainbrick Elizabeth T. Last will and Testament 233
Howard Char A. Last will and Testament 289
Harris Jesse Last will and Testament 304
Harris Isaac A. Last will and Testament Page 309
Harris Allen Last will and Testament Page 339
Hughes Wm. J. Last will and Testament Page 335
Hobday John Last will and Testament Page 372
Hendricks W. C. Last will and Testament Page 376
Hood Mrs. Martha T. Last will and Testament Page 396 & 7
Hamilton Richard L. Last will and Testament Page 468
Hendricks Temperance Last will and Testament Page 483
Harwell Thos. D. Last will and Testament Page 491

J

Justice Rev. Allen A. Last will & Testament 102 & 103
Jordon E. B. Last will & Testament 209
Johnson Thomas H. Last will & Testament 228
(Joe)
Johnston Robert E. 456

L

Ledsinger C. H. Last will and Testament 163 & 4 & 5 & 6
Ledsinger P. C. Last will and Testament 284
Light J. A. Last will and Testament 277

L Cont'd

Light M. J. Last will and Testament 323
Lanier W. H. Last will and Testament 370
Lanier Thos. W. Last will and Testament 384 & 5

K

Kohuman John - Last will & Testament 482

M

Miller Rebecca - Last will Record 38
McGinnis John S. - Last will & Testament 45 & 46
Martin William Last will & Testament 72 & 73
McCarrol Narcissa Last Will & Testament 89 & 90
McCulloch Alexander Last Will & Testament 120 & 121
Moore Robert A. Last Will & Testament 173 - 174
Mills, John Last Will & Testament 146
Mitchell Thomas C. Last Will & Testament 179-180-181
Menzies William P. Last Will & Testament 224 - 225
McCoy James Last Will & Testament 230
Manning Charity Last Will & Testament 281
Mann McKnight Last Will & Testament 321
Joseph Michell Last Will & Testament 330
Enos McKnight Last Will & Testament 341 ck sig
Miller Louisa Last Will & Testament 364
Miller Thomas Last Will & Testament 348
Shelton William N. Last Will & Testament 340
Morris Mrs. S. D. C. Last Will & Testament 432-435

O

O'Neil A. P. - Last will & Testament 114 & 115

ORIGINAL TESTATOR INDEX

O Cont'd

Old Thomas - Last will & Testament 242

O & P

Payne John (Page) 39
Perry Noah last will & Testament 83
Parker Daniel C. Sr. Last will & Testament 63, 4, & 5
Parker William - Last will & Testament 93
Prichard Wm. R. Last will & Testament 122
Privett Millie Last will & Testament 132 & 3
Parrish David Last will & Testament 158
Powers Ephraum Last will & Testament 201
Parks Faustina B. Last will & Testament 219
Pace Jackson Last will & Testament 203
Parke A. S. Last will & Testament 255 & 256
Parke Adaline Last will & Testament 283
Palmer E. L. Last will & Testament 300
Parr R. C. Last will & Testament 307
Olds Jolly Last will & Testament 319
Pate Miss Nannie O. Last will & Testament 386
Penner Mrs. Sallie R. Last will & Testament 340
Parks Hamilton Last will & Testament 411 to 418
Pate Charles H. Last will & Testament 454
Parker D. E. Last will & Testament 485

R

Robinson B. Last Will & Testament 53 & 54
Rodgers Jno. W. Last Will & Testament 126 & 127
Robinson Burril Last Will & Testament 145 & 146

R Cont'd

Roberts Mary A. Last Will & Testament 305

S

Jesse Swanner - Last Will & Testament 55 & 56
Sanders F. L. Last Will & Testament 76 & 77
Smith Mrs. Ann Last Will & Testament 151
Sudbury Shadrack R. - Last will & Testament page 91 & 92
Smith James L. Last will & Testament page 106
Shaw Samuel B. Last will & Testament page 187
Stallings Sarah Ann Last will & Testament page 192
Stallings Cannah Last will & Testament page 193
Sawyer Joshua Last will & Testament page 212
Smither Virginia S. Last will & Testament page 210
Smith Tabitha C. Last will & Testament page 226
Stallcup A. B. Last will & Testament page 235
Slater F. A. Last will & Testament page 245
Spencer G. E. Last will & Testament page 257, 258 & 9
Sawyers Willis Last will & Testament page 312
Shellton W. N. Last will & Testament page 340
Scott W. L. Last will & Testament page 362
Sorrell L. W. Last will & Testament page 358
Steven C. C. Last will & Testament page 355
Stoker Francis Last will & Testament page 353
Sampson T. G. Last will & Testament page 344
Shelton William N. Last will & Testament page 340
Stevens A. M. Last will & Testament page 402

ORIGINAL TESTATOR INDEX

S Cont'd

Smith E. W. Last will & Testament page 406 & 7
Shelley Sallie H. Last will & Testament page 436
Scott H. P. Last will & Testament page 466
Simpson W. H. Last will & Testament page 479
Sorrell J. O. Last will & Testament page 478

T

Talley Thomas J. Last will testament pages 96 to 99
Tinsley James G. Last will & testament pages 101 to 102
Telford Samuel Last will & testament page 240
Tipton Ruth B. Last will & testament 261
Turney H. S. W. Last will & testament 272
Tarkington Mary H. Last will & testament page 325
Thompson Mary Last will & testament page 346
Tatum N. P. Last will & testament page 462

W

Witt B. T. page 420 &c
Wilkins Charlott - Last will & testament page 88
Williams Thomas H. - Last will & testament page 99 & 100
Williams Joanna B. - Last will & testament page 105
Warren Lewis-Last will & testament page 107
Williams Redding Last will & testament page 123 & 4
Wilkins Mary E. Last will & testament 167 & 68
Wilkins Archy - Last will & testament page 139 & 140
Whittenton N. A. - Last will & testament page 141 & 142

W Cont'd

Whitten Stephen D. - Last will & testament page 151 & 2 & 3
Wingate Isaac - Last will & testament page 49
Wellsberger Hiram - Last will & testament page 104
Walker Agnes-Last will & testament page 188
Waddis Wm K. - Last will & testament page 191
Walker Malissa C. - Last will & testament page 214
Waits Deloss S. - Last will & testament page 211
Weakley, David C. - Last will & testament page 207
White Crawford E. - Last will & testament page 202
Woods E. - Last will & testament page 223
Wilson P. E. - Last will & testament page 248 & 249
Watkins P. M. - Last will & testament page 250 & 251
Webb Fannie P. - Last will & Testament pages 298 299
Willis Emma S. - page 327
White Susan G. - Last will & Testament page 328
Wilson Timothy - Testament pages 378 & 9
Witt B. T. 420 &c
Woodard W. M. 418
Waddy Mrs. Ann 449
Watson Thomas Dec'd 480
White Miles 291

Y

Yancey James H. - Last will & Testament 243 & 244
Yancy S. A. E.-Last will & Testament 409 - 410
Young Thos. - Last will & Testament 470, 471, 472, 473

ORIGINAL TESTATOR INDEX

Z

Zimmerman J. J. Last will
   & Testament 161
Zarecor J. C. Last will &
   Testament 451

(SEE ERRATA for correction)

DYER COUNTY

RECORD OF WILLS VOL. A
1853 - 1893

NEW INDEX

Note: Page numbers in this index refer to those of the original volume from which this copy was made. These numbers are carried in the body of the manuscript within parentheses, as (p 124)

A

Aaron, (slave), 94
Abagail, (slave), 72
Abbey, (slave), 63
Abbott, John, 171
Abe Lincoln Mutual Life & Accident Society, 355
Acree, Sallie O., 391
Adams, George W., 48
Adams, Sarah, 51
Adams Street, (Newbern) 449
Adcock, Americus, 92
Adcox, Elizabeth, 59
Airguith Street, 290
Akin, Abner A., 128
Akin, Catherine A., 129
Akin, Joseph D., 31
Akin, S. B., 129
Akin, Stephen B., 129
Akin, T. H., 129
Akin, Thomas H., 31, 34, 35
Akin, Thos. A., 129
Akin, William H., 31
Albritton, Arbella, 319
Albritton, David, 319
Albritton, Edwin, 319
Albritton, Eugine, 319
Albritton, F., 114, 115
Albritton, Wm. Hodge, 319
Algea, Abner H., 85, 86
Algea, J. F., 85
Algea, J. S. B., 85, 86
Algea, James G., 86, 248
Algea, John F., 85, 86, 87
Algea, Robert H., 85
Algea, Robt. H., 85, 86
Algea, Sarah, 86
Algea, Sarah E., 248
Alice, 258

A cont'd

Allen, E. M., 362
Allen, E. W., 363
Allen, Nelson, 94
Amanda, (slave), 65, 85
American Tract Society, 415
Anders, Margaret Rebecca, 235
Anderson, James D., 142, 143
Anderson, John E., 142
Anderson, M. L., 327
Andrew, (slave), 63
Antwine, John A., 32
Antwine, William, 32
Antwine, William Sr., 32, 33
Applewhite, R. H., 370
Applewhite, Ramsey, 370
Applewhite, Thomas, 384
Applewhite, Wm. H., 339
Archibald, Ellen Viola, 287
Archibald, J. G., 288
Archibald, John G., 287, 288
Archibald, S. W., 129
Archibald, Samuel W., 287
Archibald, Sarah F., 287
Archibald, Thomas A., 287
Archibald, Thomas C., 287
Archibald, William P., 287
Arendall, J. T., 489, 490
Arkansas, 140
Armstrong, J. N., 374, 375
Arnold, W. B., 137
Arnold, William, 138
Atkins, Jas. M., 255
Atkins, Lavinia Ruth, 261

B

Bacaen, Susan, 39
Bailey, David, 132
Bailey, Mary Ann, 235

B Cont'd

Bain, Fannie E., 452
Baird, A. R., 109
Baird, Andrew R., 109
Baird, David, 108, 109
Baird, Elizabeth, 108, 109
Baird, J. W., 109
Baird, Martha, 108
Baird, Mary, 108, 109
Baird, Rebecca, 108, 109
Baird, William, 108, 109
Baker, Bettie, 317
Baker, Cora Lee, 412, 415
Baker, Ed, 317
Baker, H. L., 317
Baker, James W., 317
Baker, Jas. W., 441, 443
Baker, M. W., 141, 142
Baker, Pauline, 317
Baker, S. P., 140
Ballentine, Harriet Amandy, 235, 236
Baltimore, 290, 291, 293, 297
Baltimore & Ohio Railroad, 294
Baptist Church, 321
Barker, Joseph, 140
Barkley, S. C., 151
Barlow (tract of land), 414
Barnett, A. M., 127, 128
Barnett, Caroline, 127, 128
Barnett, Charles, 127
Barnett, Finis, 127
Barnett, John, 127
Bean, Jane (col), 483
Bean, Jeff (col), 483
Beauford, Mary A., 41
Beaver, R. L., 491
Beaver, R. S., 473
Beggs, M. M., 149
Belair, Avenue, 291
Bell County, 95
Bell, David, 319
Bell, J. E., 130
Bell, John E., 114, 115, 480
Bell, Mary A., 105
Bell, W. E., 425
Benthall, William, 49, 50
Benton, 136
Benton (tract of land), 136, 452
Benton, A., 64, 121

B Cont'd

Benton, Abner, 64
Benton, Benjamin Estice, 120
Benton, Clem, 447, 448
Benton, Dollie, 350
Benton, Eliza Ann, 447
Benton, Fannie May, 350
Benton, Joseph, 447
Benton, Julia, 447
Benton, Lulia, 447
Benton, M. E., 350, 351
Benton, Marcenus E., 350
Benton, Mariah, 447
Benton, Mary, 350, 447
Benton, Mary E., 350
Benton, Nathaniel, 120, 121
Benton, Richard, 447
Benton, T. H. (clerk), 133, 135, 137, 140, 142, 146, 148, 149, 151, 153, 157, 159, 161, 168, 170, 171, 281, 351, 352
Benton, Thomas Dr., 447
Benton, Thomas H., 350, 351
Benton, Thos. H., 135, 150, 155, 158, 163, 167, 228, 317, 350, 352 (Clerk)
Berry, 486
Berry, Mary, 290
Bessent, Martha, 158
Bessent, Rebecca, 483
Bettis, Drusilla, 123
Bettis, G. W., 123
Betty, (slave), 130
Beveraly, Peter R., 265
Bill, (slave), 63
Binkley, R. C., 487
Birmingham, L. W., 250
Black, Sid B., 212, 213
Blackemore, Rebecca, 337
Blackwell, Berry, 176
Blake, (tract of land), 309
Blake, B. F., 144, 145
Blake, Benjamin, 143
Blake, Moses, 143, 144
*)Blakemore, Rebecca, 337
*(Blake, T. B., 143
Blankenship, G. W., 200
Bloomingdale, (land), 314
Bloomingdale, C. B., 439
Bloomingdale, E., 462, 442
Bloomingdale, Everett, 439, 441, 442
Blount, Willie, 261
Boatright, Mary Elisa, 273, 274, 275

B Cont'd

Bob, (slave), 76, 181
Boggors, Susan, 350
Boling, F. M., 190, 192
Bolton Street, 291
Bone, James T., 217
Boon, 486
Boon, F. E., 388
Boon, F. E. (Mrs.), 388
Boon, Frankie E., 388, 389
Boon, J. F., 426
Borum, Ann C. (Mrs.), 474, 475
Borum, Mattie V., 474
Boston & Maine Railroad, 328
Bowen, Clifford, 437
Bowen, David, 84
Bowen, H. J., 465
Bowen, J. L., 465
Bowen, Nora, 437
Bowen, Pearl, 437
Bowen, R. D., 465, 466
Bowen, R. J., 465
Bracken, Annie M., 426
Bracken, Georgiana, 402
Bracken, J. M., 402, 403, 404, 405
Bracken, M. T., 426, 427
Bradley, Polly, 314
Bradshaw, C. S., 463
Bradshaw, Edward, 147, 148
Bradshaw, James E., 147
Bradshaw, James T., 147
Bradshaw, Jessie E., 147
Bradshaw, Robert B., 147
Bradshaw, Samuel B., 147
Bradshaw, Thomas E., 147
Brady, S. H., 397, 398
Brandon, Scott, 447
Brewer, James H., 68
Brewer, John M., 68
Brewer, Lean, 424
Brewer, Lucretia, 261
Brockman, Martha, 159
Brown, C. F., 399
Brown, D. W., 238
Brown, Elizabeth, 51
Brown, Frank, 265
Brown, J. Harmon, 294, 295
Brown, James L., 281
Brown, Mary Adilaide, 281
Brown, S. C., 136
Brown, Thompson, 346
Bryan, F. B., 378, 379

B Cont'd

Buchannon, T. C., 298
Buck, Amanda, 38
Bunnell, W. A., 386, 387
Burbank, Emma, 329
Burbank, P. M., 328
Burchett, Dr., 439
Burges, Richard, 78
Burnette, Elsey, 32
Burnim, David, 274
Burns, I. T. (Dr.), 283
Burton, Martin G., 42, 43

C

Cairo Illinois, 355
Caldwell, James P., 196
Caldwell, Mary, 195, 196, 197, 199
Caldwell, Robert M., 196
Caldwell, Robert P., 181
Caldwell, William, 196
California, (San Bernadino), 485
Calvin, Jessie, 452
Campbell, R. H., 307, 350, 351, 441
Campbell, Robert, 89
Canada, A., 137
Canada, Abraham, 137, 138
Canada, Anna, 215, 216
Canada, Annie, 137
Canada, Eliza Ann, 137
Canada, Isaac, 137
Canada, J., 137
Cane Point, 330
Capell, 315
Carnett, Sarah E., 470
Carvett, Sarah E., 470
Caroline (slave), 78
Carrell, Abner Cooper, 302
Carrell, Albert, 302
Carrell, Franklin, 302
Carrell, J. M., 302
Carrell, John D., 302
Carrell, John M., 302, 303
Carrell, Julia, 302
Carrell, Saban, 302
Carrell, Susannah Margaret Elizabeth, 302, 303
Carroll, C. F., 174
*Carroll, John K., 294
Carroll, M. B., 174, 175
Carthel, Helen, 488
Carthel, J. E., 488, 489

Carroll County, 221, 485

C Cont'd

Carthel, Mattie R. (Mrs.) 486
Carthel, Robena, 488
Cawthorn, J. L., 461
Cearley, George W., 337
Cearley, Luke, 337
Cearley, William B., 337
Chaffin, Temperance, 138
Chamberlain, Carrie C., 273, 274
Chamberlain, D. A., 273, 274, 275, 276
Chamberlain, Dempsey A., 166
Chamberlain, John S., 273, 274
Chamberlain, Kisih E., 273
Chamberlain, Kissih E., 274
Chamberlain, Sarah F., 274
Chamberlain, Sarah Frances, 273
Chamberlain, Willis, 166, 167
Chamberlain, Winnie, 166
Chambers, Alexander, 36
Chambers, George W., 36, 37
Chambers, James, 177, 178
Chambers, Jasper N., 36
Chambers, John G., 36
Chambers, Josias, 177
Chambers, Mary A., 177
Chambers, Robert T., 177
Chambers, Williams S., 177
Chana, (slave), 60
Chappel, Martha, 290
Charles, (slave), 130
Charlton, J. H., 451
Cherry, A. E., 119
Cherry, A. M. F., 119
Cherry, D. H., 119
Cherry, E. S., 119
Cherry, G. W., 119
Cherry, Henry, 119
Cherry, R. A., 119
Chestnut Bluff, 110
Childs, J. F., 134, 135, 144
Chitwood, Angeren, 441, 442
Chitwood, Bastie, 441
Chitwood, Bostic, 441
Chitwood, Bostwick, 442
Chitwood, Charley, 441
Chitwood, Creed, 440

C Cont'd

Chitwood, Dora, 441, 442
Chitwood, E., 462
Chitwood, Edmond, 140, 440
Chitwood, G., 168, 350, 351, 372, 373
Chitwood, Green, 440
Chitwood, Joe, 440
Chitwood, Joseph, 167
Chitwood, Jos., 75
Chitwood, Josiah, 440
Chitwood, L. H., 444
Chitwood, Len, 440, 441, 442
Chitwood, Levin, 441, 442
Chitwood, Pick, 442
Chitwood, S. A., 462, 463
Chitwood, Stephen, 60, 441, 442, 443, 444
Chitwood, Stephen D., 439
Chitwood, Tilda Ann, 462
Chitwood, William, 442
Cibble, Sarah M. S., 121
Citizens Bank, 487
Claiborne, C. L., 431
Clark, C. P., 315, 316, 452, 453
Clark, Charles P., 314, 316, 318
Clark, H., 315, 316, 317, 249
Clark, Henderson, 314, 317
Clark, Jessie, 134, 135, 228, 316, 318, 452, 453
Clark, Lide, 399
Clark, R. H., 491
Clark, S. J., 465
Clay, Charles, 252, 253
Clay, Charlie, 253, 254,
Clay County, 436
Clay, Henry, 252, 253
Clay Lick (land), 219
Clay, Minerva, 252
Clements, L. J., 231, 232
Clements, Sarah J., 155
Cobb, Christian S., 113
Cobb, Jacob, 112, 360, 361
Cobb, Martha Ann, 112, 360
Cochran, J. M., 472
Cochran, S. W., 296
Cocke, A., 130
Cocke, Alonzo, 130
Cocke, F. J., 130
Cocke, George, 131
Cocke, George W., 130
Cocke, Mary Ann R., 130
Coffman, Lovell, 95

C Cont'd

Coffman, Mary E., 125
Coker, 462, 485
Coker, C. J., 218
Coker, N., 226, 249, 278, 279, 392, 393
Coker, Napoleon, 218
Cole, William Avery, 312
Columbia Co. Arkansas, 139
Connell, Mrs., 66
Connell, Thomas J., 66, 67
Coon Creek, 485, 486, 487
Coop, Frances A., 125
Coop, William A. H., 125
Cooper, Ella, 479
Cooper, J. H., 128
Cooper, James H., 128
Cooper, Robert, 447
Coover, W. S., 422
Cope, Daisy, 483
Cope, Delia, 483
Cope, Ira, 483
Cotham, C., 470
Cotton, Amanda, 315
Cotton, Daniel, 315
Cotton, Emily, 315, 316
Cotton, Harry, 315
Cotton, Tom, 315, 316
Cox, (store house), 414
Cox, Manuel, 68
Cozart, Gilbert, 160
Cozart, Jasper, 160
Craig, D. M., 133
Craig, David M., 132
Craig, J. I., 172
Craig, John I., 172
Craig, Mary I., 196
Crenshaw, Mary I., 41
Crews, Joseph A., 107
Cribbs, C. G., 220
Cribbs, Cullen G., 220, 221, 222
Cribbs, Elizabeth, 72, 73
Cribbs, Elizabeth C., 72, 220, 221
Cribbs, H. E. C., 220
Cribbs, J., 220
Cribbs, John J., 72
Cribbs, Louella, 312
Cribbs, Martha, 73
Cribbs, Martha Jane, 72
Cribbs, Parthena, J. E., 220
Cribbs, Sarah H., 220
Critchfield, R. C., 238

C Cont'd

Critchfield, Richard, 238
Croaker Creek, 470
Crockett County, 314
Crow, John, 265
Crow, R. S., 146
Crutchen, Henry, 263
Cumberland Presbyterian Church, 197, 198
Cumberland University (Theological Dept.) 396
Cummings, Wm., 60
Cunningham, J. B., 185, 186
Cunningham, James B., 184, 185, 186
Cunningham, James H., 68
Cunningham, Jas. B., 186
Cunningham, Joe, 184
Cunningham, Joe Hamie, 185
Cunningham, Jo. H., 412
Cunningham, Mary Jane, 412
Cunningham, Mary W., 185
Cunningham, Mattie Lou, 184
Curtis, C. N., 70, 71
Curtis, E. B., 70, 71
Curtis, Elizabeth Paris, 70
Curtis, Harriet, 70
Curtis, Louisianna, 70
Curtis, Sarah Drucilla, 70
Curtis, Sarah F., 70

D

Daniel, Martha, 470
Daniel, Willis, 312
Davis, A. G., 456, 491
Davis Co., North Carolina, 483
Davis, J. H., 243, 275
Davis, J. J., 92
Davis, J. P., 84
Davis, John, 40
Davis, John J., 39
Davis, John P., 192
Davis, Mary, 32
Davis, Mary M., 166
Davis, Nathaniel, 80
Davis, R. H., 88
Davis, R. J., 131
Davis, R. P., 472
Davis, S. A. E., 88
Davis, Sarah Ann, 80

D Cont'd)

Davis, W. H., 274
Davis, Willie, 277
Dawson, (city), 479
Dawson, A. C. (Mrs.), 315
Dawson, Amanda C., 314, 316, 317
Dawson, Henderson, 452, 453
Dawson, W. A., 316
Dean, Alfred, 32, 33
Dean, W. M., 260, 349, 364, 365, 480, 481
Dearmore, Aycenia, 61
Dearmore, Elizabeth, 60, 61
Dearmore, Martha Ann, 61
Dearmore, Susan Elizabeth, 61
Dearmore, William, 60
Dearmore, William James, 61
Dearmore, Wm., 62
Dearmore, Wm. James, 60
Dekalb County, 272
Denson, 470
Depoyster, Elizabeth, 155
Dickerson, Arch, 336
Dickerson (Farm), 284
Dickey, Asa, 461
Dickey, Daniel, 93
Dickey, Isaac, 93
Dickey, James, 93
Dickey, John, 93
Dickey, Jon. F., 287
Dickey, M. H., 461
Dickey, Margaret, 168, 169, 170
Dickey, Martha, 93
Dickey, R. J., 401
Dickey, S. A., 362, 363
Dickey, Thomas, 93
Dickey, W. C., 269, 270
Dickey, Willie, 93
Dickinson, Margaret, 366
Dickson, A. F., 371
Dickson County, 219
Doak, Martha A., 223
Doak, Martha Ann, 169
Doak, W. E., 169
Doc, (slave), 63
Dodson, Elias, 79
Dorsey Lane, 291
Dougherty & Phillips, 411, 413
Douglass, Guy, 105, 143,

D Cont'd

144, 269, 270, 289, 309, 339, 381, 416, 417, 445
Douglass, Guy (Mrs.), 144
Douglass, Martha (Mrs., 143
Doyle, Belle, 311
Doyle, Ella, 207
Doyle, H. P., (Deputy Clerk) 172, 174, 175, 184, 188, 464, 466, 467, 469, 476, 476 - 480, 491
Doyle, Hick P., 178, 181, 186, 189, 310, 311
Doyle, J. H., 121
Doyle, James H., 36
Doyle, Jennie, 310, 311
Doyle, Jennie Sr., 310
Doyle, John Carroll, 310
Doyle, W. C. (Deputy Clerk) 31, - 37, 105 - 111, 115, 144, 145, 153, 156, 212, 218, 311, 321, 381
Doyle, William C., 310
Drane, Clyde, 399, 400
Drane, Ella F., 399
Drane, John M., 188, 189
Drane, Louisa P., 188, 189
Drane, Nellie, 399, 400
Drane, R. M., 399, 400
Drane, Robert M., 399
Drane, Robt. M., 401
Drane, Robt. M. Jr., 399
Draper, W. S., 473
Duncan, Cynthea Ann, 154
Duncan, Cynthianna, 216
Duncan, James S., 216
Duncan, John A., 216
Duncan, Louisa, 216
Duncan, Margaret C., 216
Duncan, Mary I., 216
Duncan, P. W., 332, 333
Duncan, Stephen, 216, 217
Duncan, Tyrsa A., 216
Duncan, William C., 216
Dunevant, Mary B., 196
Dunivant, F. A., 445
Dunivant, Harriet, 312
Dunivant, J. B., 445
Dunivant, J. G., 445, 446
Dunivant, J. H., 445
Dunivant, M. F., 445
Dunivant, M. F. Miss, 445
Dunivant, W. I., 445
Dunlap, 348
Dunnevant, J. G., 161

D Cont'd

Dunston, Caroline Jane, 170
Dunston, James, 170, 171
Dunston, Rebecca, 170
Dwyer, Owen, 296
Dwyer, W. G., 343
Dyersburg Bldg. & Loan Association, 468

E

Earl, Vida, 388
Eatherby, B. H., 255
Eatherby, Benj. H., 219
Eaton, 314
Echols, Benjamin, 155
Echols, J. W., 155, 156, 157
Echols, Joseph W., 155
Echols, Mary Jane, 149
Edney, Nancy, 39
Edwards, Alva, 116
Edwards, David K., 116
Edwards, Edward, 134
Edwards, Eliza, 134
Edwards, Elizabeth Ann, 116
Edwards, George R., 51
Edwards, James W., 116
Edwards, Jane, 51
Edwards, Mary, 116
Edwards, Mary Jemima, 116
Edwards, P. N., 324
Edwards, William G., 116
Elbert, (slave), 79
Elisha, (slave), 85
Eliza, (slave), 63, 108, 156
Elkins, Lucy M., 250
Elkins, R., 250
Ellick, (slave), 63
Ellis, Almedia, 117
Ellis, Charlotte Green, 117
Ellis, David T., 117
Ellis, Frances J., 117
Ellis, George Washington, 117
Ellis, Joseph W., 117, 118
Ellis, Mandy P., 117
Ellis, Margarett Eveline, 117
Ellis, Nancy, 117
Ellis, Richard Ethalany, 117

E Cont'd

Ellis, S. S., 468, 469
Ellis, William H., 117
Ellis, William W., 117
Emiling, (slave), 83
Emmety, (slave), 130
English, A. D., 458
English, Katie Wade, 458, 459, 461
Enochs, A., 161, 269
Enochs, Adaline S., 265, 269
Enochs, Alfred, 161, 263, 264, 267, 268, 269, 270
Enochs, Ann E., 382
Enochs, Eliza, 267
Enochs, Eliza R., 266, 268
Enochs, George, 267
Enochs, George A., 266
Enochs, George Alfred, 268
Enochs, Harriet E., 266
Enochs, J. W., 429, 430
Enochs, James W., 266, 382
Enochs, John, 264, 266
Enochs, Joseph, 263, 264
Enochs, Joseph W., 266, 267, 269
Enochs, Malisa T., 265
Enochs, Mary F., 263, 264, 267
Enochs, Matthew P., 264, 265
Enochs, Robert, 267
Enochs, Robert H., 266, 268
Enochs, William S., 226
Ensor Street, 291
Eramus, (slave), 63
Everett, Elizabeth C., 162
Exchange Bank, 489

F

Falcum, Narissus, 376
Falcum, Narsisous, 376
Falcum, Narsissus, 376
Farmer, J. L., 54, 119
Farmer, Sarah Frances, 92
Farris, A. G., 374
Farris, Elizabeth C., 374
Farris, M. L. E. Miss, 374
Farris, M. L. E. Mrs., 375
Farris, Mary Lou Emma, 374
Farris, W. J., 203
Farris, William Walter, 374
Fayg, Thomas J. C., 51, 52
Fays, John B., 220

F Cont'd

Featherston, C. E., 462
Featherston, W. S., 462
Ferguson, A. G., 64, 66, 67
Ferguson, Albert G., 64, 65, 127
Ferguson, H. F., 83
Ferrell, Calvin, 204
Ferrell, Edwin, 132, 133
Ferrell, J. M., 166, 167
Ferrell, Nancy, 166
Ferris, M. L. E., 375
Ferris, W. J., 374
Fielder, A. M. J., 58
Fielder, A. T., 58, 59, 172, 173, 174
Fielder, Alfred T., 95, 125
Fielder, B. F. W, 58
Fielder, Benjamin T., 51, 125
Fielder, J. F. B., 58
Fielder, John R., 125
Fielder, John S., 51
Fielder, L. B., 57, 59
Fielder, Leonard L., 51
Fielder, M. A. F., 58
Fielder, M. V. P., 58
Fielder, S. M. L., 58
Fielder, Samuel, 51, 52
Fielder, Samuel C., 51
Fielder, Susannah, 125
Fielder, Susannah W., 126
Fielder, W. P. S., 57, 58, 59
Fielder, William P. S., 124
Fields, Elizabeth, 138
Fields, James, 41, 42, 43, 44
Fields, John, 42
Fields, John T., 42
Fields, Julia, 41, 42
Fields, Peter G., 42, 44
Fields, Sarah V., 41
Fields, William B., 42
Finch, G. A., 407, 408
Finch, Thomas J., 122
Finley, 258
Finley, Allen, 131
Finley, Simpson & Jackson, 257
Fites, Isabella C., 78
Fitzhugh, H. A., 476
Fitzhugh, J. B., 476

F Cont'd

Fitzhugh, John L., 230, 231
Fitzhugh, M. B., 476
Fitzhugh, M. R., 476
Fitzhugh, O. P., 476
Fitzhugh, Sallie V., 230, 231
Fitzhugh, T. H., 476, 477
Fitzhugh, T. J., 476
Fitzhugh, Thomas H., 477
Fitzhugh, Thos. H., 476
Florida, 310
Fochee, George Washington, 74
Fochee, Jno. Henry, 74
Fochee, Joseph Perryman, 74
Fochee, Mary Ann Meldria, 74
Fochee, Mary Hays, 74
Fochee, Sidney, 74, 75
Fochee, Thos. Vaughen, 74
Fochee, William Lya, 74
Forcum, Narcis, 483
Ford, A. P., 482
Ford, Amy, 110
Ford, Julia, 110
Ford, Mary, 110
Ford, Peter, 444
Ford, Thomas, 110
Forked Deer River, 486
Fort Avenue, 291
Foster, J. A., 388, 389
Foster, John R., 111
Foust, Catherine Mrs., 312
Fowlkes, 485, 486
Fowlkes, Asa, 136, 233, 302, 303, 400, 401
Fowlkes, George A., 135, 136, 163, 182, 183, 184
Fowlkes, George Anna, 182
Fowlkes, Glenn, 284
Fowlkes, H. B., 66
Fowlkes, H. L., 66, 67, 77, 136, 174, 175, 285, 302, 303, 401
Fowlkes, Henry, 135, 137
Fowlkes, Henry L., 285
Fowlkes, J. H., 261, 401
Fowlkes, Jane, 424
Fowlkes, Jenny, 182
Fowlkes, Mary, 93
Fowlkes, Nancy, 136
Fowlkes, Otho, 284
Fowlkes, Parsha, 323
Fowlkes, S. O. H., 261

F Cont'd

Fowlkes, Scrapie, 323
Fowlkes, Septema Olivia Hull, 261
Fowlkes Station, 476
Fowlkes, Thomas, 46
Fowlkes, Thomas H., 61, 75
Fowlkes, Thos. H., 74, 439
Fowlkes, W. P., 424
Fowlkes, Wm. P., 305
Fowlkes, Zenobia Frances, 163, 182, 183
Fox, W. Tazewell, 293, 294
Frank, (slave), 86
Franklin, Margaret J., 85
Franklin, W. H., 85, 169, 170, 223
Frazier, T. J., 73, 75
Freeman, Almeda, 160
Freeman, Asbury, 160
Freeman, Ashbury, 160
Freeman, James P., 160
Freeman, Nancy J., 160
Frick, George P., 291
Frick, J. Swan, 293, 294
Friendship, 173, 190, 252, 314
Frost, Lucinthy, 260
Frost, W., 365, 481
Frost, Wilson, 260, 364, 365, 368, 369
Fryar, Martha A., 207
Fryer, R. N., 384, 385
Fulford, Lou, 483
Fuller, Ema H., 381
Fuller, George R., 383
Fuller, Geo. B., 429, 430
Fuller, H., 339, 383
Fuller, Hezekiah, 381, 383
Fuller, John T., 381, 382
Fuller, Lenora, 428, 429
Fuller, Louisa Harriet, 428, 429
Fuller, Mary A., 428
Fuller, Mary Elizabeth, 428
Fuller, Nancy, 381, 382
Fuller, Nannie S., 381
Fuller, Stacy Ann Rebecca, 428
Fuller, William, 428
Fuller, William A., 381, 382
Fuller, William M., 428
Fuller, Wm., 429, 430, 431
Fullerton, A J., 154, 155
Fullerton, Hugh, 154

F Cont'd

Fullerton, James A., 154
Fullerton, Mary Ann, 154, 155
Fumbanks, Allen, 424
Fumbanks, Andrew Lewis, 112
Fumbanks, Emily, 424
Fumbanks, Henry, 424
Fumbanks, Jack, 424
Fumbanks, John Calvin, 112
Fumbanks, Judy, 424
Fumbanks, Liza Edney, 424
Fumbanks, Mary Ann, 112, 360
Fumbanks, Sam, 424
Fumbanks, Samuel, 424, 425
Fumbanks, Suffield, 112, 113

G

Garden Street, 290, 291
Gardner, 314
Gardner, Dr., 258
Gardner, J. B., 358
Gardner, John, 258, 259
Gardner, Sarah, 449
Garrett, William E., 147
Gauldin, Amanda W., 147
Gauldin, Drury, 366
Gauldin, J. W., 366
Gauldin, M. O. B., 45, 100, 103, 339, 366, 367
Gauldin, M. Dennis, 339
Gauldin, Margaret F., 366
Gause, Frederick B., 150
Gause, G. W., 149, 150
Gause, James Ezra, 150
Gause, Mary A. Mrs., 150
Gause, Thomas Richard, 150
Gentry, Charles, 175
Gentry, Emiline, 39
Gentry, Eunice, 175, 176
Gentry, Mary Ann, 175
Gentry, N. C., 176
Gentry, Nicholas C., 175, 176
George, (slave), 63, 78
Gibson County, 169, 278, 283, 314, 362, 411, 413, 486
Gillespie, Girzah E., 78
Gillespie, Graham, 143
Gleaves, Louisa P., 80
Gleaves, W. B., 82
Gleaves, William B., 80, 82
Gooch, G. R., 133
Gooch, Nancy, 134, 135

G Cont'd

Gooch, Narcissa, 212
Gooch, S. J., 134
Gooch, Sarah J., 133, 134
Gooch, W. C., 134
Gooch, W. H., 213
Government Cemetery, 290
Gran, (slave), 63
Grayson Street, 291
Greaves, Mary Alice Mrs., 149, 150
Green, Benjamin, 471
Green, Francis, 396
Green, Harris C., 487
Green, Hattie, 489
Green, Henry Arthur, 488
Green, J. R., 397
Green, Margaret, 470, 471
Green, T. A., 472, 473
Green, Tom, 373
Greer, A., 169
Greer, Sarah Jane, 169
Gregory, G. W., 268, 269, 270, 449
Gregory, John, 169
Gregory, Latina, 169
Griffin, A., 49, 68
Griffin, Margaret E., 148, 149
Griffin, S., 201
Griffin, Timothy, 201
Grills, A. J., 418, 419
Grimms, Clarence, 289

H

Hale, 135
Hale, J. C., 215
Hale, Jno. C., 215
Hale, Maratha, 76
Hale, Nancy P., 76
Hall, C. P., 34
Hall, C. T., 34
Hall, Clarissa C., 147
Hall, E. M., 337, 353
Hall, Elias, 301, 441
Hall, Elizabeth, 34
Hall, Elizabeth C., 216
Hall, J. A., 213, 442
Hall, James, 162
Hall, Jessie, 34, 35
Hall, Robt. A., 34
Hall, S. S., 34
Hall, Sarah, 162
Hall, W. C., 172

H Cont'd

Hall, W. J., 192, 193, 194
Hall, William C., 172
Hall, Wilson, 162, 163
Hallett, A. B. Miss, 143
Hallit, Lucy, 143
Hallum, Rainey, 203
Ham, Daniel, 406
Hambrick, Elizabeth T., 233, 234
Hambrick, Frances M., 233
Hambrick, Tabitha, 233
Hamilton, Biffle, 468
Hamilton, James H. & Son, 399
Hamilton, Jas. H., 416
Hamilton, John H., 417
Hamilton, L. (Deputy Clerk), 337
Hamilton, L. D. (Depty. Clerk) 310, 322, 324, 327, 329, 338, 347, 349, 351, 352, 354, 356, 357
Hamilton, Lillie, 468
Hamilton, Loms (D. C.), 338
Hamilton, M. C., 416, 417, 468, 469
Hamilton, Richard L., 468, 469
Hamilton, T. L., 240, 241
Hamner, W. F., 465
Hampson, Joseph, 291
Hampton, William (Land), 266
Hancock, 486
Hanks, H. T., 106
Hanks, Hugh T., 106
Haralson, W. H., 51, 52
Harbut, (slave), 63
Hardin, Joab, 219
Hardin, Martin, 49
Hargis, L. D., 392
Harmon, B. H., 189, 192, 193, 194
Harrell, J. K. P., 205
Harrell, T. M., 103
Harrett, (slave), 73, 85
Harris, A., 309
Harris, A. G., 45, 46, 93, 100, 309
Harris, Allen, 45, 46, 339, 340, 381
Harris, Allen Dr., 339
Harris, Bright, 339, 406
Harris, D. A., 93
Harris, Daniel, 407
Harris, I. A., 309

H Cont'd

Harris, Isaac A., 309
Harris, J. B., 255
Harris, J. P., 255, 256, 339, 407, 487
Harris, J. K. Polk, 226
Harris, J. Polk, 406
Harris, Jessie, 304
Harris, Louise Ann, 83
Harris, Martha, 304
Harris, Mary A., 226
Harris, Mary Ann, 63, 64, 93, 406, 407
Harris, Mollie A., 406
Harris, S. J., 339
Harris, Stonewall, 406
Harris, Stonewall J., 339
Harris, Thomas J., 263
Harris, (slave), 94
Hart, Andrew, 131, 142, 258, 259
Hart, D. J., 197
Hart, Elizabeth, 140
Hart, John M., 197, 198
Hart, M. J., 197, 198, 226, 407, 408
Hart, Milton J., 197
Hart, R. L., 197
Hart, W. P., 197
Harton, B. F., 156, 238
Harwell, J. P., 491
Harwell, L. B., 491
Harwell, Martha Jane, 491
Harwell, Thomas D., 201, 491
Harwell, Thos. D., 491
Harwell, Thos. T., 491
Haskins, Aron, 204
Haskins, Creed, 204, 205
Haskins, Ed, 205
Haskins, Edward, 204, 206, 381
Haskins, Eliza Carter, 204, 205
Haskins, Harriet, 204
Haskins, Harriet Jane, 204, 205
Haskins, J. C., 381
Haskins, John C., 204
Haskins, Lucy M., 204
Hassel, 315
Hassel, J. W., 145, 146, 176, 353, 354
Hassel, Jas. T., 278, 279

H Cont'd

Hassel, Misses, 143
Hassell, Sally Ann, 158
Hassell, W. C., 213
Hawks & White, 485
Hayes, 485
Hayes, W. R., 454
Haynes, J. N., 93
Headen, H. H., 413
Heard, Sarah, 470
Heart, Andrew, 258
Heath, Lera, 203
Heath, Richard, 109
Henderson, E. A., 111
Henderson, Ezekiel A., 78
Henderson, Jain, 78
Henderson, James F., 78
Henderson, John O., 78
Henderson, Martha, 111
Henderson, Matilda Isabella, 79
Henderson, R. G., 111, 189, 190
Henderson, Richard, 78, 79
Henderson, Richard Burges, 78
Henderson, Rufus, 79
Henderson, Rufus G., 78
Henderson, Samuel C., 78, 79, 111
Henderson, William R., 78
Hendricks, A. C., 483
Hendricks, D. R., 163
Hendricks, Daniel, 138, 139
Hendricks, J. C., 343
Hendricks, M. R., 169, 170
Hendricks, Temperance, 483, 484
Hendricks, U. C., 377, 483
Hendricks, Uriah C., 138
Hendricks, Williams R., 138
Hendrix, A. C., 376
Hendrix, G. M., 376
Hendrix, J. C., 376
Hendrix, James, 74
Hendrix, M. R., 376
Hendrix, Temperance, 376, 483
Hendrix, U. C., 376
Hendrix, W. L., 377
Henry, Mollie, 452
Henry, Patrick, 440
Henry, (slave), 63, 73
Henshaw, Addison, 251

H Cont'd

Heotell, Robt. Colines, 283
Herrin, Ellen, 203
Herrin, J. R., 203
Herron, 414
Hickman, J. C., 166, 167
Hicks, Ben, 264
Hicks, John, 142
Hill, E. G., 43
Hill, George W., 381, 382
Hill, M. R., 66, 180, 181
Hill, Sarah E., 381, 382
Hillsman, B. F., 197
Hinton, R. L., 84
Hobday, John, 372
Hobday, S. M., 372
Hobday, T. C., 372
Hobday & son, 372
Hodge, Andrew, 47, 48
Hodge, Columbus L. A., 47
Hodge, Elizabeth, 94, 95
Hodge, Franklin W., 47
Hodge, George, 47
Hodge, Henry C., 47
Hodge, Josephus, 47
Hodge, Louisa C., 47
Hodge, Marcus Lafayette, 47
Hodge, Mary Susan, 47
Hodge, Nancy E., 47
Hodge, Robert, 47
Hodge, W. A., 435
Hodge, William A., 47
Hoffman, Louisa A., 291
Hoffman Street, 290, 291
Holeman, Sally, 32
Hollowell, Soloman S., 172
Hood, M. S., 396, 397
Hood, Martha S., 240, 397
Hood, Martha S. Mrs., 396, 398
Hood, Mary T., 480
Hood, (land), 257, 424
Hough, Henry, 315
Howard, C. A., 289
Howard, Charles A., 289
Howard, John, 269
Howard, Steven, 107
Howard, W. J. F., 289
Howe, F. M., 131
Howell, A. W., 243
Howell, Ben, 192

H Cont'd

Howell, E. G., 409
Howell, Elva Green, 243
Howell, Jno. B., 454
Hudson, W. A., 174, 175
Hughes, Bettie C., 335
Hughes, Emma L., 335
Hughes, James S., 335
Hughes, Jas. S., 335
Hughes, Margaret Frances, 480
Hughes, Permelia J., 335, 336
Hughes, W. J., 335, 336
Hughes, William J., 335
Hughey, Dr., 258
Huguely, John, 200
Huguely, Martha, 200
Huguely, S. E., 200
Huguely, W. J., 200
Humphreys, Geo. S., 452
Humphreys, Henderson, 452
Humphreys, Macie, 452
Hunter, Joe, 364
Hurley, Moses P., 230
Hurt, George, 284

I

Illinois, 155, 156
Ingle, John A., 294, 295
Ingram, Julia, 41
Ingram & Johnson, 264
Insurance Co. (United Order of the Golden Cross, 457
Iowa, 290, 291
Irvin, John, 131
Isbell, (slave), 63, 85

J

Jack, (slave), 63, 130
Jackson, Martha C., 428, 429
Jackson, William, 266
James, Mary J., 78
James, (slave), 63
Jane, (slave), 78, 91
Jerry, (slave), 78
Jerry, Old, (slave), 78
Jetton, W. A., 327
Jim, (slave), 85
Jimbo, (slave), 76
Joe, (slave), 108, 109
Johnson Co., North Carolina, 132

J Cont'd

Johnson, John A., 32, 33
Johnson, Manuel, 431
Johnson, Mary Elizabeth, 429
Johnson, Minerva W., 228
Johnson, R. E., 381
Johnson, Robert, 54, 110
Johnson Street, 291
Johnson, Thos. H., 141, 142, 228, 229
Johnson, W. G., 32
Johnson & Ingram, 264
Johnston, 414
Johnston, Daniel B., 458, 459, 461
Johnston, J. F., 323
Johnston, James F., 458, 459, 461
Johnston, Lucy M., 456, 460
Johnston, Pettie, 323
Johnston, Robert E., 456, 460, 461
Johnston, Robert F., 458, 459, 461
Johnston, W. E., 400, 401
Johnston, Walter E., 458, 459, 461
Johnston, William E., 458, 459, 460, 461
Johnston, Wm. E., 324
Joiner, Sarah Abergail, 452
Joiner, W. T., 452
Jones, A., 108
Jones, A. B., 314
Jones, Anna, 346
Jones, E., 343
Jones, Henry, 119
Jones, J. Ira, 383
Jones, Matthew, 314
Jones, Robert F., 346
Jones, S. M., 274, 275
Jones, Thomas W., 175, 180
Jones, Wm. B., 330, 485
Jordon, (slave), 83
Jordon, Elizabeth B., 149, 209
Jordon, Thomas A., 209
Joseph, (slave), 108
Judal, Goddin, 132
Justice, A. A., 103
Justice, Allen A., 102, 103

K

Kate, (slave), 120
Kee, C. L., 358
Kellare, Rebecca, 483
Kentucky, 470
Kerley, Luke, 231
Killaugh, William, 223
King, 411, 413
King, Caroline, 112
King, Ed. M., 402, 403, 404, 405
King, Elmira, 112
King, J. H., 478
King, James M., 159
King, Jethro, 112, 337
King, M. O., 430, 431
King, Magdeline, 112
King, Marshall, 315
King, Mary, 402
King, Mary E., 470
King, Michail O., 429
King, Nathan, 159, 432, 433, 434
King, Rufus, 365
King, Saluda, 432
King, Thomas Stats, 159
King, W. R., 201
King, Wm. M., 342
King, Zylpha, 159
Kinkead, Harriet M., 145
Kinked, Robert, 145
Kirk, E. P., 148, 300
Kirk, Elijah P., 147
Kittimus, Louis, 296
Knights & Ladies of Honor Insurance Co., 426
Knights of Honor Ins. Co., 356, 399
Knott, Kate Mrs., 437
Kohnman, Ida, 482
Kohnman, John, 482
Koonce, J. M., 447

L

Lacks, Elizabeth S., 147
Lafayette, (slave), 105
Lake County, 298
Lake Providence, La., 36
Lane, George, 274
Lanier, Henry E., 370
Lanier, O. E., 370
Lanier, P. G., 370
Lanier, P. T., 384
Lanier, Pricilla D., 370
Lanier, T. W., 384

L Cont'd

Lanier, Thos. W., 384, 385
Lanier, W. H., 370, 371
Lanier, Walter Everett, 370
Lanier, William, 45
Lanier, Wm. Olly, 370
Larkin, (slave), 63
Latta, 315
Latta, Lucy E., 152
Latta, S. R., 43, 153, 155, 165, 249, 281, 305, 311, 315, 328, 329, 344, 345, 474, 482
Latta, Samuel, 152
Latta, Samuel R., 126
Lauderdale, J. W., 311
Lauderdale, John W., 310, 426
Lauderdale, W., 261
Lauderdale & Westbrook, 204
Laurale Street, 291
Lavender, G. W., 307
Leach, Margaret, 483
Lebanon, Tennessee, 396
Ledsinger, C. H., 163, 166
Ledsinger, Charles H., 163, 165
Ledsinger, Chas. H., 117
Ledsinger, Gilbert, 284, 285
Ledsinger, James Z., 163, 164
Ledsinger, Jeff, 284, 285
Ledsinger, John P., 163
Ledsinger, Margaret E., 163, 165
Ledsinger, Nancy T., 163, 165
Ledsinger, Nettie, 284, 285
Ledsinger, P. C., 44, 160, 164, 274, 284, 285, 286
Ledsinger, Pemberton, 65
Ledsinger, Pemberton C., 42
Ledsinger, Robert, 164
Ledsinger, Robert W., 163, 164
Ledsinger, Thomas L., 163

L Cont'd

Ledsinger, Wilmina, 41
Leeroy, Mary Ann, 155, 156, 157
Legget, Nancy, 123
Leonard, W. G., 397, 398
Lewis Creek, 277, 278, 279
Lewis (slave), 60, 63, 83
Light, 485
Light, Addie, 279
Light, Adie, 278
Light, Charlie, 277, 278, 279
Light, J. A., 277, 278, 279, 280
Light, J. D., 34
Light, Joel A., 278, 279
Light, John D., 31
Light, Martha, 278
Light, Martha W., 277
Light, Mary J., 323, 324
Light, Mattie, 278, 279
Light, S. D., 279
Light, Sarah, 278
Light, Susan, 278, 279
Light, Susan Adie, 277
Linden Avenue, 290
Linden Street, 291
Linsay, G. W., 294
Lock, (slave), 93
Locke, Sallie L., 362
Louis Creek, 485
Louisville, Ky., 350
Love, C. I., 298
Love, Chas. I., 298, 299
Love, Elizabeth D., 298
Love, John, 238
Love, Richard, 298, 299
Low, Alice Humpreys, 452
Low, J. W., 452
Low, J. W. Jr., 452
Lucy, (slave), 120
Lulls, Dr., 283
Lunsford, Wyatt, 173, 174
Lutitia, (slave), 63

M

Mabry, Catherine B., 196
Mackleymoresville, 277
Maddney, Wm., 79
Madison, (slave), 73
Mahon, Pheby, 93
Mahon, W. J., 98, 106
Main Street, Newbern, 412, 449, 457

M Cont'd

Manda, (slave), 102
Mangrove, Blanch, 436
Manier, Lemiel, 80
Manier, Mary, 80
Manley, Charity, 281, 282
Manley, J. A. C., 205, 206
Marchant, William, 132
Marchant, Wm., 132
Margaret, (slave), 63
Margove, G. W., 436
Marietta & Cincinnati Rail-Road, 290, 292
Marina, (slave), 83
Marshall, M. M., 310, 324, 355, 357, 403, 404, 454
Marshall, Mary L., 355, 356
Martha, (slave), 63
Martin, Adaline, 72, 73
Martin, John, 73
Martin, John J., 72
Martin, Julia F., 72, 73
Martin, Magie F., 325, 326
Martin, T. B., 326
Martin, T. P., 325
Martin, Thomas W., 72, 73
Martin, Thomas Wm., 73
Martin, Victoria, 72
Martin, Victoria S., 73
Martin, William, 61, 72, 73
Martinville, 406, 407
Martinville (Virginia) 226
Mary, (slave), 78, 85, 91, 130
Mary Ann, (slave), 79
Maryland, 290, 297
Mason Alley, 291
Matthews, B. D., 321
Matthews, Lizzie, 321
Matthews, Lucy, 321
Matthews, Mary Freer, 321
Matthews, (slave), 94
Mayberry, Polly, 346
McCarrol, James, 89
McCarrol, Narcissa, 89, 90
McClanahan, B., 155
McClanahan, David, 278
McClanahan, S. B., 279
McClanahan, Sam B., 213
McClemen Co. Texas, 95
McClerkin, L. C., 218, 261, 328, 329
McClerkin, Luther C., 321

M Cont'd

McCorkle, Anderson J., 169
McCorkle, D. P., 86, 168
McCorkle, David P., 169
McCorkle, Finis A., 169
McCorkle, H. R. A., 362
McCorkle, Hiram R. A., 240
McCorkle, James S., 399
McCorkle, John, 362
McCorkle, John E., 168, 223, 377
McCorkle, Jno. E., 345, 363, 419, 451
McCorkle, N. R. A., 362
McCorkle, S. S., 418, 419
McCorkle & Tipton, 419
McCoy, Henry, 231
McCoy, James Henry, 230, 231
McCoy, Lugenie, 230, 231
McCoy, W. M., 232
McCoy, William M., 231
McCracken, R. P., 202, 205, 206, 207, 208
McCulloch, Alexander, 120, 121
McCulloch, Benjamin, 121
McCulloch, Francis F., 120, 121
McCulloch, Henry Estice, 121
McCulloch, James, 120
McCulloch, James C., 121
McCulloch, John A., 121
McCullough, James, 346
McDanell, 95
McDanell, J. N., 342
McDavid, J. S., 137
McDavid, John S., 137
MdDearmon, G. W., 213
McDonald, J. N., 342
McElmurry, 315
McGaughey, Fannie Mrs., 335
McGaughey, R. H., 64, 137, 144, 145, 210, 248, 251
McGaughey, Richard H., 64, 65
McGee, H. J., 466
McGeeley, Pheby, 93
McGinnis, Augustus, 45
McGinnis, Elizabeth Jane, 45
McGinnis, John M., 211
McGinnis, John S., 45
McGinnis, Leonor Ann, 45
McGinnis, Martha, 46
McGinnis, Sarah Permelia, 45
McIntosh, 487
McKee, 413, 470
McKing, V., 264

M Cont'd

McKnight, A. A., 341, 342, 343
McKnight, Andrew Reed, 321
McKnight, E., 343
McKnight, Enos, 341, 342, 343
McKnight, Ida, 321
McKnight, Lizzie, 321
McKnight, Mary, 321, 322
McKnight, Rosanna, 341, 342
McKnight, S. A., 213
McKnight, Samanna, 321
McKnight, Samuel A. Jr., 321
McKnight, Samuel A. Sr., 321
McLanahan, David, 277
McLemore, J. J., 472
McLemore & Valux, 204
McLemoresville, 278
McMacken Street, 291
McNail, R. H., 139
McNeal, James Jr., 293, 294
Memphis, 296
Menzies, Robert G., 225
Menzies, Sallie E., 225
Menzies, Sarah E., 224
Menzies, W. P., 224, 225
Menzies, William P., 183, 224, 225
Michell, B. O., 331, 332, 333
Michell, Crawford (col.), 330, 331
Michell, Heloise, 332
Michell, Heloise V., 330
Michell, Hugo, 331
Michell, Joseph, 330, 332, 333, 334
Michell, Joseph O., 331
Michell, Joseph Olive, 331
Michell, Jos., 331, 332
Michell, Jos. O., 331
Michell, Louis M., 331, 332, 334
Michell, Louis Morean, 331
Michell, Napoleon, 331
Michell, Philix, 331
Michell, Stephen C., 330, 331

M Cont'd

Michell, Susan, 331
Middle Tennessee, 479
Miles White Beneficial Society, 293
Miller, Ann, 73
Miller, Bettie, 364
Miller, Franklin, 80
Miller, G. B., 213
Miller, George, 48, 195, 197, 199
Miller, Jno. C., 365
Miller, Joseph, 38, 73
Miller, Louisa, 348, 349, 364, 365
Miller, M. J., 209
Miller, Martha J. Mrs., 149
Miller, Mary J., 150
Miller, Nancy, 32
Miller, Rebecca, 38
Miller, Susan, 38
Miller, T. C., 365
Miller, T. G., 368
Miller, T. J., 348, 369
Miller, Thomas, 38, 158, 195, 197, 260, 348, 349
Miller, Thos., 199
Miller, W. C., 364
Miller, W. H. H., 283
Miller, W. J., 435
Mills, Eliza Jane, 147
Mills, John, 146
Milly, (slave), 78
Mississippi Cty, 315
Missouri, 315
Mitchell, J. C., 343
Mitchell, Mary Ann, 120
Mitchell Point, 277
Mitchell, Thomas C., 179, 180, 181
Mitchell, William L., 121
Monroe Street, 291
Moore, 487
Moore, F. C., 449, 450
Moore, Frank, 491
Moore, J. B., 197
Moore, J. S., 173
Moore, John, 252
Moore, Joseph H., 113
Moore, Jo. M., 173
Moore, L. J., 116, 491
Moore, Maneza, 123
Moore, Mary, 252, 253
Moore, Nancy, 346
Moore, R. A., 173

M Cont'd

Moore, R. B., 197, 198
Moore, Robert A., 173, 174
Morris, A. B. Mrs., 144
Morris, A. J., 432, 433, 435
Morris, J. B., 314
Morris, John Nathan, 432
Morris, Lucy, 97
Morris, Mary Jewel, 433
Morris, S. D. C., 433, 434, 435
Morris, S. D. C., Mrs., 432
Morris, Susan Delaney Celestial, 432, 434
Morrison, M. A., 250
Moss, Ann E., 250
Moss, C. C., 134, 137, 296, 345, 353
Moss, Chas. C., 82, 135, 250
Moss, J. H., 119
Moss, Jno. H., 176
Motherell, John, 182
Mulheren, 487
Mulherene, George R., 63
Murphy, A., 315
Murray, 411
Murry, Elizabeth Ann, 95
Murry, George, 94, 95
Murry, Sarah Ann, 95
Murry, Susan Mrs., 397
Musher Street, 291

N

Nancy, (slave), 97
Nash, Thomas, 102
Nash, Thos., 101
Nash, W. B., 327
Nash, W. F., 116
Nashville, Tennessee, 397
Neal, J. R., 314
Neal, Tom W., 482
Ned, (slave), 60, 120
Neil, U. C., 410
Nelson, (slave), 63
Newbern, 184, 309, 397, 399, 412, 414, 449, 457, 468
Newbern, Tennessee, 143, 204, 396, 411
Newby, Martha, 292
Newby, Miles White, 292

N Cont'd

New York Life Insurance Co., 335
Nicholas, C., 332, 333
Nicholas, Margaret, 51
Nicholas, (slave), 63
Nix, E. C., 470
Nix, Moses, 470
Nixon, Cornelia, 474
Nixon, J. H., 253, 254
Nixon, John, 474
Nolen, C. L., 350, 351, 441, 444
Norment, Giles, 314
Norment, W. G., 133
Norsworthy, 414
North Carolina, 134, 189, 483
Northington, Mary E., 390
Norton, James, 165
Norton, John W., 165
Norton, Leonora, 165
Nunn, Betty, 348
Nunn, Buck, 348, 364
Nunn, Isaac A., 124
Nunn, J. A., 124
Nunn, J. H., 242
Nunn, James H., 145
Nunn, John, 348, 364

O

Oakley, Mary, 170
Obion County, 315, 411, 412, 413
Obion River, 154, 182
O'Conner, Mary, 248
Odell, J. A., 382
Olds, Amanda, 319
Olds, Elizabeth, 242
Olds, Jolly, 319, 320
Olds, Thomas, 242
Olds, Thos., 319
Olds, Williams, 319
Olive, J. A., 159
O'Neil, A. P., 114, 115
O'Neil, Alfred P., 114
O'Neil, Henry W., 114
O'Neil, Margaret, 114
O'Neil, U. C., 409
Orphan's Home, St. Louis, 436

P

Pace, Jackson, 203

P Cont'd

Pace, M. R., 468, 469
Pace, M. R. & Co., 468
Paducah & Memphis Railroad, 230
Palmer, Charles D., 300
Palmer, Edward J., 300
Palmer, E. L., 300, 301
Palmer, Edward L., 300, 301
Palmer, Henry A., 300
Palmer, R. L. (D. Clerk), 300, 431, 436, 446, 448, 452, 453
Palmer, Reuben L., 300
Palmore, J. R., 337
Parish, Elias, 92
Parish, Lane, 290
Parker, D. E., 151, 198, 406, 408, 485, 489, 490
Parker, Daniel, 151
Parker, Daniel Burney, 488
Parker, Daniel E., 64, 93, 166, 197, 198, 226, 272, 406
Parker, Daniel E. Jr., 63, 64, 65
Parker, Daniel E. Sr., 63, 65
Parker, Daniel G., 485
Parker, Francis, 93
Parker, G. W., 399
Parker, Isaach, 93
Parker, J. B., 124
Parker, J. N., 393, 394, 488, 489, 490
Parker, James B., 124
Parker, John, 93
Parker, John N., 486
Parker, Jno. N., 398, 479
Parker, Martha, 63, 93, 226
Parker, Nannie, 488, 489
Parker, Nannie G. Mrs., 487
Parker, R. T., 197
Parker, Robena T., Mrs., 485
Parker, Sam'l G., 321, 322
Parker, William, 63, 93
Parks, A. L., 185
Parks, A. S., 256, 412, 415

P Cont'd

Parks, Adaline, 283
Parks, Andrew, 185
Parks, Andrew S., 184, 186, 255, 412
Parks, B. R., 411, 413, 415, 416, 417, 418, 255, 256
Parks, E. E., 411, 415, 417
Parks, Edward, 283
Parks, F. B., 219
Parks, Faustina, 412
Parks, Faustina B., 219
Parks, Geo., 240, 241, 283
Parks, H., 61, 207, 416, 255, 256, 396, 397, 398, 449
Parks, H. Jr., 253, 254, 350, 413, 414, 415, 416, 433
Parks, Hamilton, 208, 255, 396, 411, 412, 417, 418
Parks, Hamilton Jr., 186, 219, 397, 398, 417, 418
Parks, Hamilton Rev., 417
Parks, Harris, 412
Parks, J. L. Smith, 219
Parks, M. E. Mrs., 406
Parks, Martha E., 255
Parks, Rebecca, 411
Parks, Robert H., 411, 412, 414
Parks, Smith, 86, 103, 144, 163, 181, 186, 191, 202, 205, 207, 217, 240, 255, 283, 287, 301, 346, 347, 374, 383, 396, 397, 398, 411, 412, 414, 415, 429, 430, 442, 443
Parks, William, 103, 216
Parks, Wm. G., 411, 415
Parr, J. W., 245, 308, 350, 351
Parr, James Wesley, 307
Parr, Mira P., 328
Parr, R. C., 104, 307, 308
Parr, R. C. Dr., 328
Parrish, David, 158
Parrish, Elias, 158
Parrish, James Bond, 158
Parrish, Mariel, 158
Parrish, Nelson, 39
Parrish, W. H., 158
Parrish, Wm. N., 158
Pate, Chas. H., 454, 455
Pate, Elizabeth Moore, 340
Pate, G. W., 386
Pate, J. C., 158

P Cont'd

Pate, Jno. C., 386
Pate, Julia A., 454
Pate, Julia A. Mrs., 455
Pate, Nancy Mrs., 386
Pate, Nannie O. Miss, 386, 387
Pate, Sallie Mrs., 386
Pate, Wm., 298
Patsy, (slave), 108, 109
Patterson, H. F., 197
Patton, William, 217
Paul, J. A. (D. Clerk), 456
Payne, America, 39
Payne, Burton, 39
Payne, George, 39
Payne, John, 39, 40
Payne, John Jr., 39
Payne, Robert, 39
Payne, S. J., 442, 443
Payne, Susan, 39
Payne, Thos., 39
Payne, William, 39
Peacock, R. W., 98
Peel, Martha, 216
Peel, Riley, 485
Pen & Harbor, 470
Pendleton, E. B., 224, 225
Pendleton, Eugene B., 224, 225
Pennett, (slave), 63
Pennsylvania Central Railroad, 328
Perry, Adalad, 83
Perry, Adline, 83
Perry, Buckhanna, 83
Perry County, 470
Perry, Franklin, 83
Perry, Franklin P., 83
Perry, G. F., 54
Perry, J. F., 145, 146
Perry, James H., 83, 84
Perry, J. F., 242, 319, 320, 360, 361
Perry, J. S., 424
Perry, John, 83
Perry, Jno. A., 83
Perry, Marcela, 83
Perry, Margaret, 83
Perry, Margaret E., 390
Perry, Margaret Louisa, 83
Perry, N. T., 190, 192

P Cont'd

Perry, Noah, 83, 84
Perry, Noah T., 83
Perry, Sarah Frances, 83
Perry, Simon, 83
Perry, Simon S., 83
Perry, Willy, 83
Petts, I. G. (tract), 314
Phely, (slave), 86
Philis, (slave), 78
Pierce, 291
Pierce, A. G., 118, 137
Pierce, Adelade, 121
Pierce, Albert G., 118, 121
Pierce, Alexander McCullock, 120, 121
Pierce, D. P., 118
Pierce, David P., 118
Pierce, G. W. Jr., 424, 425
Pierce, Jessie, 374
Pierce, Richard J., 36
Pierce, Sam J., 424
Pierce, Sam'l J., 425
Pinner, B. E., 390
Pinner, J. C., 390, 391, 474
Pinner, Joseph, 395
Pinner, Joseph C., 393
Pinner, Sallie R., 390, 394
Pinner, Sallie R. Mrs., 393
Pinner, Sally R., 392
Pinner, W. W., 390
Pinner, (slave), 63
Pitts, A. L., 343
Pitts, J. G., 314
Planters Bank of Tennessee, 330
Pope, John, 302
Porter, H. C., 268, 399
Porter, Nathaniel, 109
Poston, Harriet, 32
Powell, 480
Powell, C. B., 55
Powell, J. B., 56, 125
Powell, James, 74
Powell, James B., 126
Powell, Martha Ann, 196
Powell, R. P., 487
Powell, Roberta W., 146
Powell, Thad L., 331
Powers, Ephraim Jr., 201
Powers, Ephraim Sr., 201
Powers, John, 201
Powers, Wealthy, 201
Pricella, (slave), 63
Prichard, 285

P Cont'd

Prichard, A. B., 372
Prichard, B. F., 257
Prichard, Benjaman, 215
Prichard, George W., 122
Prichard, J. R., 215
Prichard, Joe, 122
Prichard, John R., 215
Prichard, Jos., 73, 168
Prichard, Louisa A., 122
Prichard, Mary F., 122
Prichard, Robert, 215
Prichard, Sarah A., 122
Prichard, Wm. R., 111
Pritchard, 284
Pritchard, G. W., 485, 486
Privitt, Mary Ann, 132
Privitt, Milly, 132, 133
Pulaski Street, 291
Purcell, Emily A., 136
Purcell, Henry, 66
Purcell, Henry Thomas, 136
Purcell, J. H., 336, 366
Purcell, J. H. Dr., 66
Purcell, Rebecca, 136

Q

Quick, A., 314

R

Rachel, (slave), 63, 94
Rainey, J. G., 224
Rainey, Jessie G., 224, 225
Rawles, Allen, 386
Rawles, I. N., 386, 387
Rawles, Reuben, 48
Ray, A. L., 442, 444
Ray, Alex, 441
Ray, Alex L., 442
Ray, J. E. R., 296
Raysville Indiana, 292
Redd, Mrs., 485
Reddick, Delphia, 122
Reddick, Ella Ora, 148
Reddick, Joseph T., 123
Reddick, Mary Etta, 148
Reddick, Nancy Louisa, 148
Reddick, Nympheas, 148
Reddick, Sarah E., 148
Reeves, Elizabeth J., 169

R Cont'd

Reeves, Wyatt, 169
Rice, G. S., 125
Rice, S., 95
Rice, Sol D., 324
Rice, W. P., 70, 71
Richard, (slave), 105
Richardson, M. V., 104
Richardson, T. E., 42, 77, 248
Richardson, Thos. E., 43
Richmond, Elvira C., 147
Richmond, Virginia, 449
Richmond, Zennysa F., 147
Riddick, Mary E., 83
Ridens, Rachel Elizabeth, 170
Roan Creek, 470
Robert, (slave), 78
Roberts, F. D., 271, 272
Roberts, Frank D., 305
Roberts, J. F., 305
Roberts, John E., 213
Roberts, Mary A., 305, 306
Roberts, Robt. L., 305
Roberts Street, 291
Roberts, W. D., 305, 306, 388, 447, 488
Robertson, B., 53
Robertson, Burrell, 53
Robertson, Burril, 145
Robertson, J. T., 467
Robinson, Burrell, 54, 145, 146
Robinson, Burwell, 54
Robinson, Harriet, 54
Robinson, Lucintha, 54
Robinson, Melvina, 353
Robinson, Penelope, 54
Robinson, Stephen, 54
Robinson, Stephen M., 145
Robinson, William, 54
Rodgers, J. W., 126
Rodgers, John W., 126, 127
Rodgers, Sarah Jane, 126
Ro Ellen, 485, 486
Rogers, A., 192
Rogers, James C., 136
Rook, Tennie, 209
Roonce, Rachel, 32
Rouse, Harriet, 145
Rucker, Martha, 39
Russell, Mary, 399
Rutherford, 107
Rutherford County, 346

S

Sampson, F. G., 137, 153, 212, 225, 231, 232, 261, 320, 344, 345
Sampson, Frank G., 344
Sampson, Maggie, 210
Sampson, R. W. Mrs., 344
Sampson, Rebecca, 344
Sampson, W. B., 211, 225, 340, 341, 426, 451
*Sampson, Wat B., 213
  [Sampson, Wat, 212, 383]
San Bernadino, 485
Sarah, (slave), 102
Saulsberry, James, 304
Saunders, Elisha, 470
Saunders, Eliza J., 76
Saunders, Ferdinand L., 76
Saunders, G. M., 82
Saunders, John, 470
Sawyer, Dennis F., 212
Sawyer, John, 312
Sawyer, Joshua, 212, 213
Sawyer, Monroe, 212, 213
Sawyer, Quintin T., 212
Sawyer, Stephen, 312
Sawyer, William, 140, 312
Sawyer, Wm., 372, 373
Sawyer, Willis, 312, 313
Scobey, W. J., 237
Scobey, William J., 236
Scoby, F. E., 451
Scott, Fannie, 402
Scott, G. A., 467
Scott, Geo. E., 402, 403, 404, 405
Scott, H. P., 467
Scott, H. P. Jr., 467
Scott, H. P., Sr., 466
Scott, J. M., 392
Scott, Lemuel, 362
Scott, Mary Jane, 466
Scott, R. D., 467
Scott, R. H., 362
Scott, W. L., 362, 363
Seals, Martha A., 117
Seay, E. T., 143
Segraves, Harriet E., 265
Senter, J. M., 437, 438
Senter, M. M., 437, 438
Shannon, J. J., 470
Shannon, Nancy, 470
Sharp, Anthony, 485, 486
Sharp & Turney, 485, 486

S Cont'd

Shaw, Craig N., 187
Shaw, David A., 187
Shaw, E. R., 171
Shaw, Martha O., 187
Shaw, Sam B., 188
Shaw, Samuel B., 187
Shaw, Thomas J., 187
Shearon, Joseph, 107
Shelley, J. Blanch, 436, 437
Shelley, Sallie H., 436, 437, 438
Shelley, W. B., 436
Shelton, John A., 38, 260, 348
Shelton, Lucinda, 39
Shelton, Nancy, 342
Shelton, Nelson, 340
Shelton, Nelson P., 38
Shelton, Thomas, 101, 102
Shelton, W. N., 340, 341
Shelton, William N., 340
Sherrod, J. M., 186
Sherrod, James M., 185
Shumate, J., 460
Shumate, Q., 460
Simons, D. C., 429, 430
Simpson, 258
Simpson, Chamblin, 479
Simpson, W. H., 479
Sims, Anna A., 177
Sims, Mareena, 177
Sinclair, 180
Sinclair, John F., 80, 70, 180, 181
Singleton, T. S., 55, 56
Singleton, William, 119
Skeffington, John, 144, 145, 474
Skeffington, M. A., 311
Skeffington, Mary Amelia, 474
Slater, F. A., 245, 246
Slater, Josephine, 245
Slater, T. L., 245
Slater, Thomas L., 245
Sloan, Issabella S., 207
Smith, 487
Smith, Ann, 151
Smith, B. F., 463
Smith, Betty, 424
Smith, Dr., 314
Smith, E. T., 243, 327
Smith, E. W., 407, 465

S Cont'd

Smith, Elizabeth, 407
Smith, Elizabeth Mrs., 406
Smith, Elizabeth W., 226, 408
Smith, Elizabeth Woodbridge, 151
Smith, G. W., 265
Smith, Henry G., 296
Smith, J. B., 92
Smith, J. L., 106
Smith, J. W., 210
Smith, James L., 106
Smith, James M., 226, 406, 407
Smith, Jo., 285
Smith, Jos., 278
Smith, Joseph, 183, 233
Smith, Joseph G., 434
Smith, Joseph T., 433
Smith, Lindy, 424
Smith, Mary Ann, 106
Smith, Rebecca, 257, 258
Smith, T. C., 226
Smith, Tabitha Caroline, 151, 226, 227
Smith, Tommie E. Mrs., 433
Smith, V. L., 210
Smith, Virginia L., 210
Smith, W. J., 163
Smith, W. W., 433, 434
Snow, 154
Sorrell, A. C., 358
Sorrell, Dollie, 478
Sorrell, Elvica T., 358
Sorrell, J. O., 478
Sorrell, L. W., 358, 359
Sorrell, Mentie, 478
Sorrell, N. C., 358, 359
Sorrell, Sarah L., 358
Sorrell, W. A., 478
Spence, Adar, 257, 258
Spence, G. E., 257, 258, 259
Spence, George, 140
Spence, George E., 257
Spence, Geo. E., 259
Spence, Louisa, 258
Spence, Lucinda, 257
Spencer, 412
Spraggins, 487
Stalcup, Mrs., 319
Stallcup, A. B., 235, 236, 237

S Cont'd

Stallcup, Adelaid, 235
Stallcup, Alexander B., 115, 235
Stallcup, Beauford, 235, 236
Stallcup, Elizabeth Frances, 235
Stallcup, Richard Johnson, 235, 236
Stallcup, Wm. J., 235, 236
Stallings heirs, 480
Stallings, Cannah, 192, 194
Stallings, E. G., 119
Stallings, Elizabeth, 83
Stallings, L. P., 84
Stallings, Mary A., 364
Stallings, Milla Jones, 83
Stallings, Missouri B., 260
Stallings, Sarah Ann, 192, 193
Stallings, W. B., 119
Stanfield, Catherine, 117
Stanley, Austin, 95
Stanley, George A., 95
Staritt, Emeline, 72, 73
Staritt, Wm. S., 72
Stephenson, W. R., 304
Stevens, A. M., 402, 403, 404, 405
Stevens, A. R., 355, 356
Stevens, A. More, 393, 394
Stevens, Alf, 355
Stevens, C. C., 355, 357
Stevens, Chas. C., 355, 357
St. John Street, 321
Stockton, J. T., 203
Stockton, R. G., 374, 375
Stokes, Clinton, 353
Stokes, Creek, 471
Stokes, Frances, 353
Stokes, L. H., 353
Straughn, R. N., 489, 490
Strayhorn, J. K., 178
Stutts, 479
Sudbury, J. W., 91, 92
Sudbury, Jerimiah, 91, 92
Sudbury, John B., 91, 92
Sudbury, Sarah Frances, 91
Sudbury, Shadrach R., 91, 92
Sudbury, Susan, 91
Sudsberry, John B., 39, 40
Sugg, E. G., 150
Sugg, W. P., 150
Summers, F., 452, 453
Summers, Frank, 403, 405

These three pages represent index pages 23-28 of the original WPA book. We've transcribed and condensed these entries for this edition.

Summers, Frank Dr., 402, 404
Summers, Myra 402
Swain, Cenelope 53
Swanner, Avinella, 55
Swanner, James W. 55
Swanner, Jessie 55, 56
Swanner, Louis F. 55
Swanner, Louiza 55
Swanner, Louvinia C. 55
Swearenger, James 441
Swearenger, Jas. 443
Swift, A. W. 59
Swift, John D. 312, 313
Talley, George W. 98
Talley, Permelia 96, 98
Talley, Thomas J. 96, 98
Talley, Thos. J. 98
Tanner, C. B. 245, 246
Tansil, Alice 258
Tansil, Allis, 257
Tansil, Allis 257
Tarkington, A. W. 325
Tarkington, Helen I. 325
Tarkington, Helen Isabella 325
Tarkington, M. H. 325, 326
Tarkington, Mary H. 325, 326
Tarkington, W. D. 478
Tarkington, Wm. D. 325
Tarply, J. P. 319, 320
Tarply, Mr. 319
Tarrant, Elizabeth 120
Tarrant, R. M. (clerk), 44, 52, 54, 56, 59, 62, 67, 84, 160
Tatum, A. B. 462
Tatum, G. M. 462, 463
Tatum, J. S. 462
Tatum, N. P. 140, 462, 463, 464
Tatum, Nat P. 462
Taylor, Catherine 154
Taylor, Crawford 154
Taylor, Eddie C. 491
Taylor, Francis E. 226
Taylor, George W. 148
Taylor, J. F. 418, 419
Taylor, M. M. 331, 332, 333
Taylor, Mary Ann 266
Taylor, Mollie 214
Taylor, William 214, 265, 267
Taylor, Wm. 274, 275, 276
Taylor, Wm. D. 187?, 188
Telford, Catherine 240
Telford, Samuel 240, 241
Temb. (slave) 130
Tennessee River 470
Tennessee (slave) 94
Tenney, J. W. 388, 389, 434
Terrell, 485

Terry, Lucinda 147
Terry, May 93
Texas 95, 120, 341, 397
Thomas, B. L. 403, 404
Thomas, Hiram J. 168
Thomas, J. P. 169
Thomas (slave) 78
Thompson, J. M. 147, 213
Thompson, L. C. 213, 236
Thompson, Louisa 366
Thompson, Mary 346-347
Thompson, Moses 346
Thompson, Robert 346
Thurmond, 480
Tigrett, A. B. 401, 414, 415, 417
Tigrett, L. A. 415
Tigrett, Lutie 415
Tigrett, Lutie A. 414
Tillis, Dr. 283
Timmons, Nancy 155-56
Tinley, J. D. Dr. 331
Tinley, J. G. 102
Tinley, James G. 101, 102
Tinsley, Frances Mason 101
Tinsley, G. B. 144, 185, 186, 205
Tipton, J. C. 261
Tipton, Jonathan Caswell 261
Tipton, Mary 277
Tipton, Mary P. 278
Tipton, P. L. 277
Tipton, P. M. 278
Tipton, Preston 277
Tipton, Rebecca A. 261
Tipton, Ruth B. 261, 262
Tipton, Sarah A. 277
Tipton, W. B. 261
Tipton & McCorkle 419
Todd, James N. 126
Tom (slave) 63
Townsend, Cora Mrs. 445
Townsend, T. P. 324
Trenton 169, 277, 278, 486, 489
Trout, Ann 138
Trout, Susan A. 169, 223
Trout, Thomas 418
Trout, W. G. 213
Trout, Wiley S. 169
Trower, W. B. 51
Trower, Wesley B. 52
Troy, Taylor 274
Trueblood, Jason 290
Trueblood, Mary 290
Trueblood, Miles W. 290
Trueblood, Miriam 290
Tucker, D. G. 378, 379
Tucker, Daniel G. 161
Tucker, J. G. 89, 309, 378

Tucker, R. W. 89
Turnage, Emily 260
Turnage, Sam (col.) 364
Turner, 414
Turner, Martha 388
Turney, 485
Turney, H. L. W. 187, 188, 213, 218, , 221, 222, 271, 272
Turney, Mary 272
Turney, J. B. 434, 476, 477
Turney & Sharp, 485, 486
Turnley, J. B. 476
United Order, of Golden Cross Ins. Co. 457
Vail, Roan H. 36, 37
Vail, Wm. C. 115
Vandergiff, May 123
Van Eaton, Alice 483, 484
Van Eaton, B. L. 483, 484
Vann, J. C. 382
Vann, Jo. C. 381, 382, 383
Vann, Susan M. 381, 382, 383
Vaughn, H. W. 98
Vaughn, T. H. 467
Vana, (slave) 86
Vernon, Charley 315
Vernon, E. R. 155, 165, 310, 393
Vernon, E. R. (M.D.) 392
Vernon, Lillie 465
Viar, George 47
Viar, George 477
Viar, Geo. 476
Viney, (slave) 63
Vinyard, Nancie 452
Virginia, 147, 406
Waddie, Ann 191
Waddie, John Wm. 191
Waddie, Joseph Kimbro 191
Waddie, W. K. 191
Waddie, Wm. K. 190, 192
Waddy, Ann 449
Waddy, Ann Mrs. 449, 450
Waddy, John W. 449
Waddy, Joseph K. 449
Wadlington, M. A. 457
Wagster, Wm. C. 187
Waits, Charles F. 211
Waits, D. S. 211
Waits, Deloss S. 211
Waldron, Chas. 487
Waldron, Mary S. 339
Waldron, Mollie 487
Walk, Mary Jane 158
Walker, 485
Walker, A. H. 368
Walker, Agnes 188, 189
Walker, D. L. 358, 359

Walker, Dr. 258
Walker, G. W. 92, 340, 341, 368
Walker, J. H. 368
Walker, James 220
Walker, Malissa C. 188, 214
Walker, Mary 248
Walker, Mary Ann 93
Walker, Mary F. 147
Walker, Mathew P. 188
Walker, Myra 248
Walker, P. C. 128
Walker, Phil 462
Walker, Rebecca 368, 369
Walker, Samuel 65, 93
Walker, T. J. Dr. 227
Walker, Wm. W. 248
Wallace, Jo. S. 213
Wann, (slave) 130
Ward, Buck 285
Ward, Elva Jane 116
Ward, Thomas 171?
Ward, W. B. 70
Warren, Lewis 107
Warren, N. C. 181
Warren, Newton G. 179
Warren, P. H. 301, 312, 313
Warren, Susan G. 179
Warren, Wm. A. 470
Warren, Wm. Simon 107
Waterford, 486
Watkins, B. B. 250, 271, 272, 356, 357, , 392, 393, 394, 403, 404
Watkins, Florence 250
Watkins, Lorenzo 98, 250
Watkins, Lucindo 250
Watkins, P. M. 250, 251
Watkins, Permely M. 251
Watkins, W. M. (D. Clerk) 73, 156, 180, 184, 190, 194, 195, 204, 207, 209
Watkins, W. M. (D. Clerk) 212, 248, 250, 251
Watkins, Will M. (clerk) 99, 100, 102, 103, 104, 107, 109, 110, 111, 144
Watkins, Will M. (clerk) 173-188, 191, 192, 193
Watkins, William M. (clerk) 181, 189, , 192, 197, 216
Watkins, Wm. M. (D. clerk) 48, 50, 62, 65, 67, 69, 71, 315
Watkins, Willie 250
Watkins, Z. (clerk) 243, 245, 246, 249, 256, 257, 280, 282, 286, 288
Watkins, Z. (clerk) 289, 297, 299, 301, 303, 304, 306, 306, 345, 361
Watkins, Z. (clerk) 365, 367
Watkins, Z. G. 345, 355, 356

Watkins, Zack (clerk) 190-195, 198, 200-203, 206, 208, 209, 211
Watkins, Zack (clerk) 214, 215, 216, 219, 222, 223, 225, 226, 227
Watkins, Zack (clerk) 229, 232, 234, 236, 237, 239, 241, 242, 244, 248
Watkins, Zack (clerk) 250, 251, 254, 259, 260, 262, 270, 271, 276?
Watkins, Zack (clerk) 308, 311, 313, 318, 320, 326, 327, 329, 330
Watkins, Zack (clerk) 334, 336, 338, 340, 341, 343, 347, 349, 351
Watkins, Zack (clerk) 352, 354, 357, 359
Watson, Elizabeth Ann 480
Watson, Ella 209
Watson, Emma Callus 480
Watson, John Lewis 480
Watson, Martha Narcissa 480-481
Watson, Matilda Florence 480
Watson, Nancy Hellen 480
Watson, Narcissa 480, 481
Watson, Thomas 480, 481
Watson, Thos. 481
Watson, W. H. 346, 347
Weakley, D. C. 207, 208
Weakley, David C. 207
Weakley, David _. 207
Weakley, Elizabeth 207
Weakley, Elizabeth L. 207
Weakley, M. H. P. 207
Weakley, Wm. S. 207
Wear, Lavinia 261
Webb, Fannie P. 298, 299
Webb, Fannie Peyton 298
Webb, Fannie Sue 298
Webb, G. B. 462
Webb, J. E. 487
Webb, J. L. 253, 254
Webb, John McKanny 298
Webb, Julia Elizabeth 298
Webb, M. B. 462
Webb, Robt. Wilson 298
Webb, Sue Green 298
Webb, W. J. 298
Webb, Wm. Burton 298
Weil, Moses 327
Weimer, P. J. 426, 427
Welborn, M. A. 487
Welch, W. G. 272
Wells, T. L. 356, 357, 403, 404
Wellsburger, Anna 104
Wellsburger, Hiram 104
Westbrook, Martha A. 99
Westbrook & Lauderdale, 204
West Point MS, 436

Wheeler, W. T. 258, 259
White, C. B. R. 325, 326
White, C. E. 139, 202
White, Crawford E. 202
White, Edward H. 113
White, Frances 290, 291, 292, 293, 295, 296
White, Frances A. 291, 292
White, Frances J. 202
White, L. C.? 366, 367
White, Margaret H. 290
White, Miles 290-296
White, N. C. 274
White, Rebecca 292
White, Richard J. 291, 292
White, Sara Elizabeth, 291, 292
White, Susan G. 328, 329
White, Wm. 470
White & Hawks, 378
Whiteside, Alice Mrs. 437
Whitson, Elizabeth 41
Whitten, James 153
Whitten, Mary 151, 152
Whitten, Massella 152
Whitten, Narcissa 152
Whitten, S. D. (clerk) 115, 118, 121, 122, 124, 126, 127, 128, 129
Whitten, S. D. (clerk) 153
Whitten, Stephen D. (clerk) 113, 117, 119, 151, 153
Whittenton, E. M. 141
Whittenton, N. A. 141, 142
Wilcox, B. L. 98
Wilkerson, R. B. 400, 401
Wilkerson, W. L. (clk.) 369, 371, 373, 375, 377, 379, 385, 387, 389
Wilkerson, W. L. (clk.) 395, 418, 425, , 431, 435, 436, 446, 448, 452
Wilkerson, W. L. (clk.) 453
Wilkerson, Will L. (clk.) 402, 411, 419, 423, 439
Wilkerson, William L. (clk.) 383, 409
Wilkerson & Drane, 399
Wilkins, A. 75
Wilkins, Angeline 167
Wilkins, Archibald 139, 140
Wilkins, Charlote 88
Wilkins, Christine C. 140
Wilkins, Emerson Etheridge 140, 167
Wilkins, John A. 180, 181
Wilkins, John N. 88
Wilkins, Josephine 140, 167
Wilkins, Lucy B. 167
Wilkins, Lucy Belle 140
Wilkins, Malinda 140
Wilkins, Margaret A. 140
Wilkins, Mary 140

Wilkins, Mary E. 167, 168
Wilkins, N. B. 88
Wilkins, Newton B. 88
Wilkins, Wm. Penn 140
William, (slave) 63, 94
Williams, 136
Williams, Alexander 165
Williams, Amanda 123
Williams, B. M. 321, 322
Williams, Calvin 123
Williams, Celia 123
Williams, E. J. 437
Williams, E. J. Mrs. 437
Williams, Eliza P. 85
Williams, Emily 123
Williams, Florence Mrs. 335
Williams, George M. 105
Williams, James 123
Williams, Jas. 123
Williams, Joanna B. 105
Williams, L. A. 472
Williams, L. M. 99, 205
Williams, Louis M. 99, 437
Williams, Mary E. 165
Williams, Mattie Lou 415
Williams, Mollie Lou 412
Williams, Peter W. 105
Williams, Reading 110
Williams, Redding 123
Williams, S. A. 472, 473
Williams, Susan L. 99, 105
Williams, Thomas H. 99, 100
Williams, Walter 123
Williamson, D. J. 137
Williamson, J. F. 371, 384, 385
Williamson, Jessie F. 449
Williamson, W. C. 413
Willis, Emma S. 327
Willis, J. W. 449, 450
Wilson, Asa 378
Wilson, Ida 378
Wilson, J. G. H. 34, 35
Wilson, John W. 248, 249
Wilson, Jno. W. 248
Wilson, John W. & Co. 248
Wilson, Minnie 378
Wilson, P. E. 153, 248, 249, 315
Wilson, Peter E. 153, 248, 249
Wilson, Ray 378
Wilson, Susan W. E. 248
Wilson, T. 378, 379
Wilson, Timothy 378, 379
Winchester St., Memphis 487
Winford, W. C. 422
Wingate, Elinor B. 49
Wingate, Fredrick 49
Wingate, Isaac 49, 50

Wingate Mary F. 49,
Wingate Mary F. 49, Nancy C. 49
Wingate Mary F. 49, Sarah A. E. 49
Wingate Mary F. 49, Susan E. 49
Winny, (slave) 63
Witt, Albert Sidney 420, 421
Witt, B. T. 420, 422, 423, 440
Witt, C. H. 422, 423
Witt, Carter Harrison 421
Witt, Clayton Hamilton 421, 422
Witt, Elviras Isabella 420, 421
Witt, Lillie Maude 420, 421
Witt, Martha Emaline 420, 421
Witt, Mary Isabella 420, 421
Witt, Robert Algie 420, 421
Witt, Thomas Josephus 421
Witt, W. B. 422, 423
Witt, Wm. B. 422
Witt, Wm. Butler 421, 422
Wood, S. A. 307
Wood, Stephen 93
Woodard, Martha 418
Woodard, W. M. 418, 419
Woodruff, C. F. 161
Woods, Cora Alice 169
Woods, E. 223
Woods, Eliazor 223
Woods, John Quincy 223
Woods, J. R. 397
Woods, Lucinda 223, 396, 397
Woods, W. T. 169, 223
Woody, Lula 362
Woollen, G.? P. (D. Clk.) 483, 484, 485, 490
Wright, Elijah 274
Wright, Geo. 440
Wright, John 315
Wright, John M. 146
Wright, John W. 81
Wyatt, Eliza 377
Wyatt, H. L. 376-377
Wyatt, Harriett 485
Wyatt, Hattie 376
Wyatt, I. N. Col. 413, 415
Wyatt, J. N. 186, 202
Wyatt, P. V. 415
Wyatt, Parina V. 413, 415
Wynne, Adaline S. 214
Wynne, H. V. C. 269, 270, 289, 466
Wynne, J. G. 382
Wynne, Mary T. Mrs. 445
Wynne, V. G. 314
Wynnis, John 265
Yancy, J. H. 243, 409
Yancy, James H. 243, 244
Yancy, John Hartwell 243
Yancy, S. A. E. 409, 410

Yancy, Sarah Ann Elizabeth 243
Yancy, T. J. 409, 410
Yancy, Tom 277
Yancy, Thomas Joshua 243
Yancy, Thos. 279
Yancy, (slave) 78
Yates, J. J. 360, 361, 409, 410
Yeargin, Mary Ann 156
York, J. B. 348, 349, 480
York, John H. 252, 253, 254
York, Jnc. B. 365
York, S. A. 58
York, Sarah A. 125
Yorkville, 223, 283
Young, B. F. 471, 473
Young, Benjamin F. 471
Young, Charles 470
Young, E. J. 471
Young, Elizabeth 471, 472
Young, J. S. 470
Young, John S. 470
Young, Manerva 471
Young, Moody 470
Young, Sam 470, 473
Young, T. W. 472, 473
Young, Thomas 472, 473
Young, Thomas W. 470
Young, Thos. 470, 472
Young, Thos. W. 471
Zarecor, George 451
Zarecor, J. C. 451
Zarecor, Wm. 283
Zimmerman, J. J. 161

ERRATA FOR INDEX

Carroll Co. omitted pages 221, 485
Sampson, Wat omitted pp. 212, 383
Valux & McLemore omitted p. 204
Walker, Dave omitted page 480

TENNESSEE

DYER COUNTY

RECORD OF WILLS "A"
1853 - 1893

(P.31)

Nuncupative Will of William A. Atkins dec'd Set up & Established at the October Court 1853 and ordered to be recorded	State of Tennessee - Dyer County The following is the nuncupative will of William H. Atkins Dec'd Vis as follows.

John D. Light & Thomas H. Atkins & Joseph D. Atkins all being present in the dwelling house of the said William H. Atkins in his last sickness, one or two days before his death which took place the 13th August 1853 he being then in his right mind, he called on the said J. D. Light, in the presence of the said Thomas & Joseph Atkins, and desired the said Light to take charge of his personal property, & sell such as the widow could spare to pay his debts, and allow her to keep the ballance to raise & school his children. The said William H. Atkins died within two days after making the above declaration, without altering in any way to their knowledge the above request, or altering his opinions.

The said John D. Light being willing to execute the above nuncupative will, presents the same for probate. The above being in substance what took place as above states, is reduced to writing by Our request and in Our presence, this the Third day of October 1853.

         John D. Light
         Thomas H. Atkins
         Joseph D. Atkins

MONDAY OCTOBER 3rd 1853

State of Tennessee) This day the within paper writing pur-
Dyer County Court) porting to be the Nuncupative will of
        William H. Atkins dec'd was produced here in April Court by John D. Light, the executor named therein and offered for Probate. Whereupon came John D. Light Thomas H. Atkins & Joseph D. Atkins subscribing witnesses thereunto who after being first sworn disposed and said that they were acquainted with said W. H. Atkins in his lifetime, and that they were present during his last illness and heard him direct the disposition of his property as set forth in said paper writing. That he requested them to bear witness to the same and made his requests and gave directions as set forth in said paper writing in the form of a will and was of sound mind and disposing memory and capable of making a will.

 It is therefore ordered by the Court that said paper writing be set up and established as the Nuncupative will of said William H. Atkins deceased, and recorded by the Clerk.

Attest: Recorded Oct. 26, 1853   Robert M. Tarrant - Clerk
W. C. Doyle   by W. C. Doyle - Deputy

(p.32)

William Antwine's Last will of Testament

Proven and set up at the November Court 1853

I, William Antwine Senr. of the County of Dyer and State of Tennessee do make and publish this my Last will and Testament hereby revoking and making void all former wills by me at any time heretofore made. First I direct that my body be decently intered, in a manner suitable to my condition in life, and as to such worldly Estate as it has pleased God to trust me with, I dispose of the same, as follows. To wit- I direct that all my just debts be paid and my funeral expences as soon as possible, out of my moneys that I may die possessed of or may first come to the hands of Executor from any portion of my Estate real or personal.

Secondly: I give and bequeath to my son John A. Antwine one feather bed & bed clothe, and five dollars in money. Thirdly: I give and bequeath to my son William Atwine five dollars, in money.

Fourthly: I give and bequeath to my daughter Rachel Koonce one feather bed and bed clothe.

Fifthly, I direct that the remainder of my property be sold and the proceeds of the same be equally divided between my six Daughters to wit, Nancy Miller, Rachel Koonce, Elsey Barnett, Sally Holeman, Mary Davis, Hamet Poston

I do hereby make and appoint my beloved son Jno. A. Antwine Executor of this my Last will and Testament.

In witness whereof I William Antwine Sr. the Testator have to this will written on one half sheet of paper, set my hand and seal, this the 30th day of June in the year of Our Lord one Thousand, Eight hundred and Fifty three.

Signed, Sealed and Published in the presence of us who have Subscribed in the presence of the Testator & each other

William X Atwine (Seal)
his mark

Alfred Dean
W. G. Johnson
Jon. A. Johnson

See next page

(p.33)

State of Tennessee) December Term, 1853
Dyer County Court)

This day a paper writing purporting to be the Last Will and Testament of William Antwine Sr. deceased was produced here in Open Court and the execution thereof duly proven by the oath of John A. Johnson and Alfred Dean, subscribing witnesses hereto - who testified that they were personally (p.33 cont'd)· acquainted with the testator - that he signed and published the said paper as his last will and Testament - in their presence - for the purposes therein set forth - and requested them specially to bear witness thereto - that they signed it in his presence - at his request and that he was of sound and desposing memory at the time of executing said will.

It is therefore ordered by the Court that said paper writing be set up as the Last will and testament of the said William Antwine Sr. dec'd - that the same be recorded &c.

Attest   R. M. Terrant, Clk.

(p.34)
Last Will
   of
Testament
   of
Jesse Hall, dec'd
   Set up & established
January Term County Court 1854

I Jesse Hall do make and publish this as my last will and testament, hereby revoking and making void all other wills by me at any time made.

First I direct that my funeral expenses and all my debts be paid as soon after my death as possible, out of any moneys that I may die possession of or may first come into the hands of my executors.

Secondly: I give and bequeath to my son S. S. Hall the tract of land he now lives on, and all the appertences thereunto belonging.

Also to my son C. P. Hall the tract of land he now lives on and all the appertenances thereunto belonging.

Also to my son Robt. A. Hall the tract of land that I. D. Light now lives on, to be in his posession as soon as said Light lease is out - and all the ballance of my land I make and bequeath to my wife Elizabeth Hall, together with all my property of all description, and all money that may be left in the hands of my executor after paying all my debts, to do as she thinks best with, in deviding with all the balance of my children.

Lastly: I do hereby nominate and I appoint C. P. & S. S. Hall my Executors.

In witness whereof I do to this my will set my hand and seal, This December 9th 1853.

                                         his
                              Jesse X Hall (Seal)
                                        mark

Signed, Sealed and Published in
our presence and we have subscribed our names hereunto, in
the presence of the Testator -
This December 9th 1853
   J. G. H. Wilson   Thomas H. Atkins) Witnesses

(P.35)
State of Tennessee) January Term 1854
Dyer County Court)

This day the within paper writing purporting to be the Last Will and Testament of Jesse Hall deceased, was presented here in court for probate.

Whereupon came J. G. H. Wilson and Thos. H. Atkins subscribing witnesses thereto, who being duly sworn dispose that they were personally acquainted with the said Jesse Hall in his lifetime, that he signed and acknowledged the execution of said paper writing to be his last will and Testament, in their presence for the purposes therein set forth; That he was of sound and disposing memory, that he requested them to witness the same; and that they signed their names thereto in the presence of the Testator and in the presence of one another.

It is therefore ordered, adjudged and decreed by the Court that said paper writing be set up and established as the Last will and Testament of the said Jesse Hall deceased and recorded by the clerk.
Attest;
           Robert M. Tarrant, Clerk
           by W. C. Doyle, Deputy.

(P.36)
Nuncupative Will   ) Nuncupative Will
 of   (of
George W. Chambers.   ) George W. Chambers
Set up April Term 1854   (
Recorded April 11th, 1854)

"It is my desire that my Brother Alexander Chambers shall have all my land in Dyer County, with it's improvements, tenements, and appurtenances.

It is my desire further that my brother John G. Chambers shall have my mare and saddle -

It is my desire further that my Brother Jasper N. Chambers shall have my black colt.

This will was made by George W. Chambers at Lake Providence, in the State of Louisiana and the same day he died (about the __ day of May last) in our presence and he especially requested us to bear witness to it - He died at Lake Providence, in a few hours after his desire was made known as above.

In witness of which we have hereunto subscribed our names this 5th day of January 1852.

           Roan H. Vail
           Richard (his X mark) J. Pierce

State of Tennessee) March Term 1852
Dyer County Court)

      I James H. Doyle Clerk of the County Court

(P.36 Cont'd) of said County do hereby certify that Roan H. Vail appearance in open Court this day, and proven in part the execution of the foregoing Nuncupative will of George W. Chambers deceased.

          James H. Doyle, Clerk
          by W. C. Doyle, D. C.

State of Tennessee) Apil Term. 1854

     This day a paper writing purporting to be the Nuncupative will of George W. Chambers was produced here in open court for Probate. Whereupon came Richard J. Price (P.37) the other witness thereto, who after being first duly sworn desposed and said that he was personally acquainted with said George W. Chambers that he called himself and R. H. Vail to bear witness to the disposition he desired should be made of his effects that he was of sound mind; that his desire was made known to them shortly before his death - and that the other facts set forth in said Nuncupative will are true as he understood them.

  It is therefore ordered by the Court that said Nuncapative will be set up and established as the Last will of said George W. Chambers dec'd - and recorded by the clerk.
Attest
          R. M. Tarrant, Clerk
          By W. C Doyle, Deputy.

(P.38)
Last Will   ) State of Tennessee, Dyer County, May
 &   (13th, 1851
Testament   ) I, Rebecca Miller being weak of body,
 of   (but of a Sound mind do by these present
Rebecca Miller   ) make my last will and Testament as
Deceased, Set up Feb.(follows viz; first I will to pay my
Term 1855   ) Son Joseph Miller my Buro, 2nd I will
          to my Son Thomas Miller my cuppord,
3rd To Rebecca Walker one half geese and all of my wearing clothes; fourth I will to Amanda Buck my Saddle and bed and five sheets, four quilts and one comfort four covelets, one emaud as cumberpin, three other counterpanes one blanket and Six Sets pillow slips, also the one other doulls half of my geese and all of my Turkeys, also one other domestic sheet. I hereby nominate and appoint my Son Thomas Miller my Executor.

            her
         Rebecca X Miller (seal)
            mark

Signed and Sealed in the presents of us.
John A. Shelton
Nelson P. Shelton

State of Tennessee) February Term 1855
Dyer County   )

(P.38 Cont'd) This day a paper purporting to be the last will & testament of Mrs. Rebecca Miller was produced here into Court and John A. Shelton and Nelson P. Shelton the subscribing witnesses thereto were called here into open Court and being first duly sworn depose and say that they were personally acquainted with the testator, that she signed and acknowledged and published the said will in their presents on the day it bears date and they witnessed the same in her presence at her request and in the presence of each other and that she was of sound and disposing mind at the time of making said will; to best of their knowledge & belief it is therefore ordered by the Court that the said paper writing be set up & established as the last will of said Rebecca Miller and Recorded.

Attest.   R. M. Tarrant, Clerk.

(P.39)

Last Will	State of Tennessee
&	Dyer County
Testament	I, John Payne of the County of Dyer and
of	State of Tennessee being sick of body, but
John Payne	sound mind and memory being desirious to
Deseased Set up	settle my worldly affairs do on this the
at the M̶a̶r̶c̶h̶ April	Twenty Seventh day of February Anno Domini
Term 1855	Eighteen hundred and fifty five, make this
	my last will and Testament as follows. Viz.,

I will first that all my just debts be paid and the ballance of my property be divided as follows -
Viz - To Mary Russell deceased, Nancy Edney, William Payne, Thos. Payne, John Payne Jr. Martha Rucker, Susan Bacaen, Emiline Gentry, and Robert Payne I have given their propotion of all my Estate all the ballance of my estate I give and bequeath to my beloved wife Susan Payne to have and hold the same during her natural life or widowhood and at her death or marriage I will that all my Remaining Estate be divided among my last children all follows viz; George Payne Lucinda Shelton Elizabeth Adcox Burton Payne and America Payne, I will that at the marriage of my two last named children that my wife Susan Payne give to the said two children the same amount that I have given to the last children, I also will that one hundred dollars be given to Martha Ruckers children to be appropriated towards their education, I also will that two hundred dollars be given to Burton Payne in consequence of his having no Education, I will that after said appropriation be made, the remaining potion of my Estate be equally divided between the George Payne Lousinda Shelton, Elizabeth Adcox Burton Payne and America Payne, and I hereby appoint Nelson Parrish sole executor of this last Will and Testament, hereby revoking all former wills by me made. Signed with my hand and seal this day and date above mentioned.

Signed in the presence of John Payne   (seal)
John J. Davis and of John B. Sudberry.

(P.40)
State of Tennessee)   April Term 1855
Dyer County Court)

(P.40 Cont'd) This day a paper purporting to be the last will and Testament of John Payne Deceased was produced here in open Court, and John J. Davis and John B. Sudbury the subscribing witnesses thereto were called here into open court and being first duly sworn depose and say that they were personally acquainted with the testator and that he signed and published said will in their presence on the same day it bears date and that they witnessed the same in his presence, at his request, and in the presence of each other and that he was of sound mind, desposing memory at the time of making said will to the best of their knowledge and belief; it is therefore ordered by the court that the said paper writing be set up and established as the last will & testament of the said John Payne deceased, and that it be recorded.
Attest

                            R. M. Tarrant Clk.

(P.41)
Last Will & Testament of James Fields, Deceased
Set up April Term 1855

State of Tennessee
Dyer County

In the Name of Almighty God a moni; I James Fields of the County of Dyer and State of Tennessee, well knowing the uncertainty of mortal life, the certainty of Death and being of sound and desposing mind & memory do make, ordain, and publish this my last will and testament, in the manner and form following, hereby revoking and making null and void all other wills and testaments heretofore made & published by me (that is to say) all of my just debts I desire to be paid as soon after my death as possible.

Item: To my beloved wife, Julia Fields I give and bequeath all of my property real and personal consisting of lands, negros, stock in Plank Road, horses &c,&c for and during the term of her natural life. And if at any time my said wife shall deem it to her interest, or think it advisable or necessary to sell or dispose of any of said property, either real or personal in order to increase the value, or protect the same, or to provide for her own wants, She is hereby authorised and empowered to do so, without being liable to account to any one there for. And it is my wish and desire that the whole of said property, and all of my business shall be under her guidance and controll, and that my executors here in after to be appointed shall be governed by her in the execution of this my last will and testament.

    And whereas I am largely interested in the completion of Dyersburg & Mississippi River Plank Road and Turnpike it is my wish, and I direct that my wife and my executors see that my views in this respect be carried out, and that my contract with the state of Tennessee be faithfully complied with & that my business in this respect be conducted in the same manner as if I were living.

Item: To each of my daughters "to wit" Elizabeth Whitson, Mary A. Beauford, Julia A. Ingram, Mary I. Crenshaw, Wilmina Ledsinger

(P.41 Cont'd) and Sarah V. Fields, I direct my wife to pay as soon after my death, as she can with convenience such an amount of money including what had already been advanced to them in negroes &c. as will (P.42) make the sum of two thousand dollars, the said money & property to be settled upon my said daughters for life, remainder to the heirs of their bodies, and not to be subject to the control or liable in any manner whatever to the debts or liabilities of their present or any future husbands they may have.

Item: If my business successes as I anticipate, I direct that my wife or executors shall pay as soon as they can without embarrassing my affairs to American Bible Revision Association the sum of one Thousand Dollars.

Item: It is my will & desire that all my property both real & personal here in not specifically desposed of shall on the death of my said wife Julia Fields or sooner if she desires it be equally divided between all of my children share & share alike, and the property that may be alloted to my aforesaid mentioned daughters in said divisions, I give and bequeath to them and the heirs of their bodies and as in the ___ of the _____, it is not to be subject the present or future debts or liabilities of their present or any future husbands they may have, nor in any wise subject to their control. Lastly, I do hereby nominate and appoint my three sons John T. Fields, Peter G. Fields, and William B. Fields executors of this my last will and testament and I wish and direct that they shall not be required to give any bond or security for the discharge of their duty as executors aforesaid; for testamony whereof I have hereunto set my hand and appraised my seal the thirteenth day of September in the year of our Lord one thousand eight hundred fifty three and of the 77th year of the Independence of the United States of America.

           James Fields (seal)

Signed, Sealed and published in our presence and we have subscribed our names hereto in the presence of its testator and of eachother this 30th day of September Amo Domini 1853.

           Martian G. Burton
           T. E. Richardson

A Codicil to said will and testament of James Fields, Having heretofore made and published my last will and testament, do make and publish this as a codicil thereto, First I do hereby nominate and appoint Pemberton C. Ledsinger an additional Executor of my last will (P.43) and testament, without revoking but confirming the appointment of my three sons. Lastly it is my desire that this codicil be attached to and constituted a part of my will to all interests and purposes.

 In testamony whereof I have hereunto set my hand and affirmed my seal 11th day of April A. D. one thousand eight

(P.43 Cont'd)   hundred and fifty four and of American Independence 78th.

              James Fields (seal)

Signed, sealed and published in our presence and we have hereunto subscribed our names in the presence of the testator and of each other this 11th day of April A. D., 1854.

              S. R. Latta
              E. G. Hill

State of Tennessee) April Term 1855
Dyer County Court)

   This day paper writing purporting to be the last will & testament of James Fields, deceased, was produced here in open court, and Nathan G. Burton and Thos. E. Richardson the subscribing witnesses thereto were called here into open Court, & being first duly sworn, despose and say that they were personally acquainted with the testator and that he signed and published said will in their presents on the same day it bears date and that they witnessed the same in his presents, at his request and in the presents of eachother & that he was of sound mind and disposposing memory at the time of making said will to the best of their knowledge and belief, it is therefore ordered by the Court that said Will or paper writing be set up and established as the last will and testament of the same James Fields deceased and to be recorded also a paper writing purporting to be a codicil to the last will and testament of the said James Fields was produced here into open court and S. R. Latta & E. G. Hill the subscribing witnesses thereto were called here into open Court and being first duly sworn, depose and say that they were acquainted personally with the testator and that he signed and published in their presents said codicil to said will and the same day it bears date and that they witnessed the same in his presence at his request and in the presence of each other and that he was of sound mind (P.44) and disposing memory at the time of making said codicil to said will to the best of their knowledge & belief. It is therefore ordered by the Court that the paper writing purporting to be a codicil to the last will & testament of James Fields be set up and established as such and Recorded.

Attest   R. M. Tarrant Clk.

State of Tennessee)
Dyer County Court) April Term 1855

   This day P. C. Ledsinger, John T. Fields, and Peter G. Fields came here into open court and were duly sworn as Executors of the last will and testament of James Fields, deceased.

Attest   R. M. Tarrant, Clk.

(p.45)

John S. McGinnis
    Last Will
      &
Testament
Proven and set up at
   April term 1856
	In the Name of God, Amen.
	
	    I, J. S. McGinnis of the County of Dyer & State of Tennessee do make & publish this my last will and testament hereby revoking and making void all wills

by me at any time made. First, I direct that my funeral expenses be paid and that as savingly as possible for the benefit of my little minors and all my debts be paid on demand so as to save interest out of any money that I may die possessed of as may first come into the hands of my executors.

    Secondly; I give and bequeath to my four youngest children, Sarah Pemelia Elizabeth Jane, Leonor Ann & Augustus. Money or means to school them as far as James & John has advanced my oldest sons and then an equal division is my request, my wife having her lawful share and all if she wants it untill death or marriage.

    I do hereby nominate & appoint Martha McGinnis my executor in witness whereof I date this my will, set my hand and seal this 29th day of April 1854.

                                           J. S. McGinnis.

State of Tennessee)   April Term 1856
Dyer County   )
    This day came into open Court A. G. Harris Adm. of John S. McGinnis dec'd. and offered for probate a will of the said McGinnia found by said Administrator among the papers of the said deceased & thereupon came also Allen Harris, M. O. B. Gauldin & William Lanier who being duly sworn testify to the Court that they were well acquainted with the handwriting of said McGinnis dec'd. that the will here produced is all in the handwriting of the sd. dec'd., thereupon on motion it is ordered that said will be admitted to probate ~~and~~ & that the same be entered of Record. Thereupon appeared in open (P.46) Court Martha McGinnis appointed Executrix by said will and resigned her position as Executrix, and on motion A. G. Harris was appointed administrator of John S. McGinnis, Cum testa mento annedo.

    Whereupon came the said A. G. Harris here into Court with Allen Harris and Thomas H. Fowlkes as his securities and entered into Bond in the penal sum of Six thousand Dollars, conditioned ~~and payable~~ as administrator aforesaid and was duly qualified.

Attest   Robert M. Tarrant Clerk.

(P.47)

Andrew Hodge Last will & Testament Proven and set up at the April Court 1856	State of Tennessee Dyer County A written will and testament I Andrew Hodges do make and publish

(P.47 Cont'd) this as my last will and Testament hereby revoking and make void all other wills by me at any time made.

First - I direct that my funeral expenses and all my debts be paid as soon after my death as possible out of any monies that I may die possessed of or may first come into the hands of executors.

Secondly - I give and bequeath to my wife Louisa C. Hodge one hundred acres of land including the improvements on the corner tract of land induring her widowhood and then to go to my eight heirs Franklin W. Hodge, & Josephes Hodges & Columbus A. Hodge & Henry C. Hodge & Nancy E. Hodge & William A. Hodge & Marcus Lafayette Hodge & Mary Susan Hodge, and the balance of my land to go to my eight heirs as they become of age. Also I direct that a young negro woman be bought of part of the money that is coming off my Fathers estate Robert Hodge. I also direct that my wife Louisa C. Hodge have the use of said negro woman during her widow-hood without paying any hire for her and then to go to my heirs her and her increase I also if there is not money enough in hand to pay my debts, that enough of my personal property be sold to pay my debts such as wife Louisa C. Hodge can spare best & I then Andrew Hodge do will and bequeath to my wife Louisa C. Hodge the balance of my personal property during her widowhood and then to go to my eight heirs, to wit; Franklin W. Hodge, and Josephus Hodge and Columbus T. A. Hodge and Henry C. Hodge, Nancy E. Hodge, Marcus Lafayette Hodge, Mary Susan Hodge, William A. Hodge. I Andrew Hodge do direct that the money or property that is coming to me from my uncle George Hodge estate at the death of his widow, be first to the use of educating my children if necessary, and if not put out on interest and equally divided among the above named heirs, I also direct that the balance of the money coming from my Fathers estate after buying a negro woman above mentioned, be put to the use of educating the (P.48) above mentioned heirs, I also appoint George Miller as my Executor to settle up my business. In witness whereof I do to this my last will set my hand and seal this 9th of January 1854.

Test   Andrew Hodge (seal)

George W. Adams
Reuben Rawles

State of Tennessee)   April Term 1856
Dyer County Court)

This day a paper writing purporting to be the last will and testament of Andrew Hodge dec'd was produced in open Court and the execution thereof duly proven by the oaths of George W. Adams and Reuben Rawles subscribing witnesses thereto - who testified that they were personally acquainted with the Testator, that he signed and published the said paper as his last will and testament in their presence for the purpose there in set forth and requested them specially to bear witness there to - that they signed it in his presence and at his request - and that he was of sound and disposing memory

(P.48 Cont'd) at the time of executing said will.

It is therefore ordered by the Court that the said paper writing be set up as the last will and Testament of the said Andrew Hodge dec'd that the same be recorded.

          Robert M. Tarrant Clerk
       By Wm. M. Watkins Deputy Clerk.

(P.49)

Isaac Wingate Last Will & Testament Proven and Set up 3rd September 1855	State of Tennessee Dyer County I, Isaac Wingate do make and publish this as my last will and testament hereby revoking and making void all other wills by me at any time made.

        First; I desire that my funeral expenses and all of my just debts be paid as soon after my death as possible out of any moneys that I may die possessed of, or may first come into the hands of my executor.

 2nd I give and bequeath to my son Fredrick Wingate my Dapple Grey Filley three years old past together with bridle saddle and martingales.

 3rd I wish all of my perishable and personal estate to be sold and applied as follows and schooling of my three youngest daughters Elenor B. Wingate Susan E. Wingate, and Mary F. Wingate and 2nd I wish the balance of the proceeds of said perishable & personal estate to be equally divided between all my Children (Viz) Nancy C. Wingate, Frederick Wingate Sarah A. E. Wingate Elinor B. Wingate Susan E. Wingate, and Mary F. Wingate when said Mary F. Wingate comes of age to transact for herself.

 4th I wish my real estate to be cultivated by my children for all of their benefit equally until my youngest child come of Lawful age and then to be equally divided between all of my children or lawfully heirs, and lastly I do hereby nominate and appoint Asa Griffin my executor to execute this my last will and testament. In witness whereof I do to this my will set my hand and seal this 21st day of August 1855.

              Isaac Wingate (seal)

Signed sealed & published in our presence and we have subscribed our names hereto in the presence of the testator the day and year above written.

              Martin Hardin
              William Benthall

(P.50)
State of Tennessee) September Term 1855
Dyer County Court)

(13)

(P.50 Cont'd) This day a paper writing purporting to be the last will & testament of Isaac Wingate, deceased and produced here in open court and the execution there of duly proven by the oaths of Martin Hardin and William Benthall subscribing witnesses thereto who testified that they were personally acquainted with the testator that he signed and published the said paper as his last will and testament in their presence for the purpose therein set forth, and requested them specially to bear witness there to, that they signed it in his presence and at his request, and that he was of sound and disposing memory at the time of executing said will.

It is therefore ordered by the Court that the said paper writing be set up as the last will and testament of the said Isaac Wingate desceased, that the same be recorded.

Attest   R. M. Tarrant Clerk.
                                     By Wm. M. Watkins Deputy

(P.51)
Samuel Fielder   I Samuel Fielder being of sound and
   Last Will   disposing mind and memory, but of
      &   feeble health do make and constitute
Testament   this my last will and Testament utterly revoking all others.
Proven and set up at the
July Court 1856   In the first place it is my will and desire that when it pleases God to take me hence that my Executors hereinafter named see that I am buried in a desent Christian like manner and that all of my just debts if any be paid. In the second place I wish it to be understood that on the 7th day of January 1815 I did advance in property to my daughter Elizabeth Brown which will make her equal in amount to those of my other children which I shall provide for in this will, and will exclude her from any share whatever in this my last will and testament. I also did advance in property to my son Benjamine T. Fielder on the 14th day of Febry 1815 which will make him equeal in amount to those of my other children which I shall provide for in this will and will exclude him from any share whatever in this my last will and testament.

In the third place I give and bequeath unto my children Sarah Adams, Leonard S. Fielder, Margaret Nicholson, John I. Fielder, and Jane Edwards, all of the estate which I may have at my death after the payment of my debts equally to be divided among them my last named and aforesaid children.

I here by constitute George R. Edwards and Samuel C. Fielder Executors of this my last will and testament.

In witness whereof I have hereunto set my hand and seal this 1st day of October 1851.
                                           Samuel Fielder (seal)
Attest
W. B. Trower
W. H. Haralson

(P.51 Cont'd)
State of Missouri)   February 18th, 1854
County of Pike   )

    Be it remembered that on this Eighteenth day of February 1854 Wesley Trower and William H. Harrison the subscribing witnesses to the within Will appeared before me, Thomas J. C. Fayg judge of the Probate Court for said County (P.52) of Pike and being duly sworn by me on their oaths say that they saw the within named Testator sign the within instrument of writing which he published as his last will and testament. That said Testator was at the time of sound mind and over the age of Twenty one years and that these deponents attested said will as witnesses there to by subscribing their names to the same in the presence and at the request of said Testator and in the presence of each other.

                       Wesley B. Trower
                       W. H. Haralson

State of Missouri)   I Thomas J. C. Fayg Judge and exoffice
County of Pike   )   clerk of the probate Court for said County
of Pike hereby certify that the above and foregoing affidavid was subscribed and sworn to before me this Eighteenth day of February 1854 which is deemed by me sufficient proof to establish the within will of Samuel Fielder Deceased In testimony whereof I have hereunto signed my name and affixed the seal of said court at office this the day and date last above written.

                (Probate Court seal Pike County
                      Missouri)

                    Thomas I. C. Fayg
                    Judge of Probate

State Tennessee)   July Term 1856,
Dyer County Court)

    This day a paper writing purporting to the Last will & testament of Samuel Feilder deceased, was produced here in open Court and duly proven by the oaths of Wesley B. Trower & W. H. Haralson subscribing witnesses there to who testified that they are personally acquainted with the Testator that he signed and published the last will & testament in their presence for the purpose therein set forth and requested them specially to bear witness thereto that they signed it in his presence and at his request and that he was of sound and disposing memory at the time of executing said will.

    It is therefore ordered by the court that the said paper writing be set up as the last will and testament of the said Sam'l Fielder deceased, and that the same be recorded,

                            R. M. Tarrant Clerk.
Attest

(15)

(P.53)
B. Robertson — Last Will & Testament — Proven and set up at the September Term 1855

In the Name of God Amen.

I Burrell Robertson of the County of Dyer and State of Tennessee being weak in body but of sound mind and memory and considering the uncertainty of this frail and transitory life do therefore make ordain publish and declare this to be my last will and testament, that is to say

First; I lend to my beloved wife during her widowhood one hundred & sixty two acres of Land; and should she marry then, she to have one third of the same during her natural life it being all of my tract of land lying west of the Road, and two acres in the North West corner of the tract lying East of the Road.

Secondy; I give and bequeath to my wife two cows and calves, Four sows and pigs one black Mare, Fifteen Hundred lbs. of Pork Fifty Barrels of corn Forty bushels of wheat. Four stacks of Fodder if saved upon the place all my house hold and kitchen furniture Three Plows and Gear and Twenty five Dollars in cash.

Thirdly, I loan to my wife one sorrel mare colt till my son William Robinson is Twenty one years of age, then I give said mare to him.

Fourthly; I also give my wife Ten Shoats. Fifthly; I leave the Fifty acres of land East of the Road to be sold $250 of the purchase money to be paid; the balance on a credit of one, two, three and four years. I also have all my pork hogs to stay on the place till they are fat and then sold as my Executor may think best and I leave all the residue of my estate both Real & personal to be sold and my debts paid; and the residue to be put at interest and the interest to be expended in schooling my children.

Sixthly; I give to my Daughter Cenelope Swain her portion of said money when collected and my estate settled.

(P.54) Seventhly; At my wifes death I leave the above 16 acres of land to be sold on a credit of one two and three years, and of the proceeds of the same, I give to my son William Robinson $25 and to my son Burwell Robinson $75 and to my daughter Lucintha Robinson $40 and to my daughter Harriet Robinson $100 and to my son Stephen Robinson $100 The residue to be equeally divided among my six children "Viz" Pennelope William Lucintha; Burwell, Harriet; & Stephen likewise I make constitute and appoint Robert Johnson to be Executor of this my last will & testament, hereby revoking all former wills by me made. In witness whereof I have hereunto subscribed my name and affixed my seal this 4th day of June 1855.

Signed and sealed in presence of us
J. L. Farmer
G. F. Perry

Burwell Robinson (Seal)

(16)

(P.54 Cont'd)
State of Tennessee)   September Term 1855
Dyer County   )

This day a paper writing purporting to be the last will and testament of Burwell Robinson deceased was produced here into open Court, and J. L. Farmer and G. F. Perry the subscribing witnesses thereto were called here into open court, and after being duly sworn depose and say that they were personally acquainted with the Testator and that he signed and published said will in their presence on the same day it bears date and that they witnessed the same in his presence at his request and that he was of sound and disposing memory at the time of making said will to the best of their knowledge and belief.

It is therefore ordered by the court that said paper writing be set up as the last will & testament of said Burwell Robinson & to be Recorded

Attest   R. M. Tarrant   Clerk.

(P.55)
Jessee Swanner   )   It is my will in case of death of
   Last Will   (this spell of ~~sickness~~ illness that my
      &   )   beloved wife Louiza Swanner have during
Testament   (her life or widowhood all of my personal
Proven and set at the)   & real estate except four pork hogs she
October Term 1856   (has & is entitled to full & entire pos-
                            session of my farm & houses and all ap-
purtenances there unto with all my stock including horses cattle, & stock hogs except the Four Hogs already described to use for her benefit & the benefit of her youngest Daughter Avenella so long as she remains single & lives with her mother.

Should my beloved wife neglect to keep my property together & seem to be prodigal & wasting the same there & in that case I want my property with personal & real equeally divided between my children, my wife retaining a childs part & in case she should take care of my property confided to her care during her life time at her desease. I want all my property equeally divided among my children to wit: Jesse G. Swanner, James W. Swanner, Louis F. Swanner, Louvenia J. Swanner, Avinella Swanner my lawful heirs &c.

In testimony of all the foregoing I hereunto set my hand & affixed my seal this the 22nd of Jany. 1856.

                                        Jesse Swanner (SL)
Attest
J. B. Powell
T. S. Singleton

State of Tennessee)   August Term 1856.
Dyer County   )

This a paper writing purporting to be the last will & testament of Jesse Swanner deceased was produced

(P.55 Cont'd) here in open Court and duly proven by the oath of T. S. Singleton one of the subscribing witnesses thereto, who testified that he was personally acquainted with the testator, that he signed and published the last will and testament in his presence for the purposes therein contained and requested him specially to bear witness there to, (P.56) that he signed it in his presence and at his request & that he was of sound & disposing memory at the time of executing said will.

           R. M. Tarrant Clerk

State of Tennessee) October Term 1856.
Dyer County   )

  This day J. B. Powell one of the subscribing witnesses to the last will and testament of Jesse Swanner deceased came here into open Court and testified that he was personally acquainted with the Testator that he signed and published the last will and testament in his presence for the purposes there in contained and requested him specially to bear witness there to - that he signed it in his presence and at his request, and that he was of sound and disposing memory at the time of executing said will.

 It is therefore ordered by the Court that the same be set up as the last will and testament of Jesse Swanner deceased T. S. Singleton the other subscribing witness there to having duly proven the will at the August Term of this Court 1856.

Attest   R. M. Tarrant Clerk.

(P.57)
W. P. S. Fielder   ) I W. P. S. Fielder being of sound mind,
Last Will   (mind and memory do make & publish this
  &   ) my last will & testament in manner and
Testament   (form following: i e: to say, I commend
Proven and set up at the) my soul into the hands of a merciful
December Term 1856   (God in Christ I wish my body to be
            buried close to my two infants but
west of them in a plain Christian like manner; no parade. I wish all my lawful debts to be paid & all my property remain as it now is for the use of my wife & children; only such of it as it would be best to sell which I leave to the judgement of my wife S. B. Fielder. The money which is owing to me I wish to be lent out at six per cent with the understanding that the borrower pay the Tax on it bey giving bond & two approved securities. I wish wife in conjunction with my children to have the controle of all my property buying & selling for the family so as to promote its best interest; my lands I except which shall not be sold in any case untill my youngest child that shall be living at the time shall have arrived at the age of eighteen years; at which time I wish all my property to sold & equeally divided between wife and children she retaing her life time estate in that portion of the land that the law allows her; In the mean time if any of the children marry or arrive at the age of Twenty one, they shall be privileged to settle on either tract of land near the lines so as to give all an equel chance & shall not pay any rent, for

(P.57 Cont'd) all they may clear & cultivate for five years there after also I wish all my children to be learned to read write & cypher so far as to be able to attend to their own business matters; but in case my wife shall marry or die; then in either case all my property shall be sold & divided as stated above; by my children if old enough; but if none of them are twenty years old or can not give sufficient security; then by some one when the county court may appoint (P.58) he giving bond & approved security. My Sons shall in case my property is sold be free at the age of Twenty & those under that age shall be put to the Carpenters, or Blacksmith's trade at the age of Eighteen untill they arrive at that age they shal lavor on the farm & go to school wherever they can get the best homes in point of morals and old fashioned religion, as to my daughters I recommend them to the Masonic Fraternity to obtain suitable homes for them. I wish particular care to be taken of their morals and religious education. I pray God however that my wife may be permitted to live & see to the raising & education of all my children in which case they will have a home & mother.

                                            W. P. S. Fielder (seal)

August 18, 1856
Test
A. T. Fielder
S. A. York.

Codicile to the above will.

By my children are meant the following B. T. W. Fielder, A. M. J. Fielder, J. F. Fielder M. E. H. Fielder, S. M. L. Fielder, M. A. F. Fielder and the one now in it's mothers womb to them and theirs bodily heirs.

    As witness my hand and seal this 26th day of December 1856.

                                        W. P. S. Fielder seal

Test
A. T. Fielder
S. A. York

State of Tennessee)   December Term 1856
Dyer County   )

    This day a paper writing purporting to be the last will & testament of W. P. S. Fielder was produced here into open Court and A. T. Fielder and S. A. York subscribing witnesses to the last will & testament of W. P. S. Fielder deceased, came here into open Court and testified that they were personally acquainted with (P.59) the Testator, that he signed and published the said last will & testament in their presence for the purposes there in contained, and requested them specially to bear witness there to that they signed it in his presence and at his request, and that he was of sound and disposing memory at the time of executing said will.

    It is therefore ordered by the Court that the same be set up as the last will & testament of W. P. S. Fielder deceased

(P.59 Cont'd) and T. B. Fielder the wife of the said W. P. S. Fielder deceased came here into open court, and was appointed administrator of said deseased with the will annexed and with A. T. Fielder and A. W. Swift entered into and acknowledged bond in the penal sum of Four Thousand Dollars conditioned and payable as the Law directs and she was then duly qualified.

Attest   R. M. Tarrant Clerk.

(P.60)
Wm. Dearmore) I William Dearmore make this my
  Last Will (last will and testament hereby revok-
    &) ing and making void all other wills
Testament (by me at any time made.
Proven and set up at the)
December Term 1856 (First: I direct that my funeral expenses and all my debts be paid as soon after my death as possible out of any money that I may die possessed of or may first come into the hands of my Executor.

First: I give and bequeath to my dear wife Elizabeth Dearmore all my household and kitchen furniture for her to dispose of such a part among my children as she may think proper. I also give my wife Elizabeth Dearmore my negro woman Chana to her and to hold during her natural life then said negro woman Chana after my wifes death to be sold and the money to be equally divided among my lawful heirs; I like wise give to my wife Elizabeth Dearmore Amanda Lewis and Ned and any other children that Chana may have to have and to hold untill W. James Dearmore comes of lawful age, then said negroes Amand Lewis & Ned and any other children that Chana may have to be equeally divided among all my children and in case that any one of my children should be dead and have a child or children, said child or children to have the part their parent was entitled to, I like wise give to my wife Elizabeth Dearmore one hundred acres of land it being a part of the Tract of Land on which I now live including my present residence Bounded as follows, Begining at a stake the south east corner of said tract of land in the west boundary line of Stephen Chitwood tract of land, thence west one hundred and eighteen poles to a stake & pointers in the east boundary line of Wm. D̶e̶a̶r̶m̶o̶r̶e̶ Cummings tract of land, thence north with said line passing said Cummings North East corner One hundred and thirty six and one half poles to a stake. Thence east one hundred and eighteen poles to a stake in my east boundary line thence south one hundred thirty six (P.61) and one half poles to the beginning, so as to contain just one hundred acres, Secondly; I give to my two daughters Martha Ann Dearmore and Susan Elizabeth Dearmore the tract of land that I got of Thos. H. Fowlkes containg by estimation one hundred and ninety five acres to be equeally divided between them quantity and quality.

Thirdly: I give and bequeath to my daughter Aycenia Dearmore the residue of the tract of land on which I now live supposed to be eighty one and one fourth acres.

Fourthy: I give and bequeath to my Son Wm. James Dearmore at

(P.61 Cont'd) the death of his mother Elizabeth Dearmore the Hundred acres of land that I give my wife Elizabeth Dearmore during her natural life, I also give and bequeath unto my son Wm. James Dearmore the sum of Five Hundred Dollars to be paid to him by my Executor out of any money he may have in his hands after paying all my just debts and the remaininder of money if any to be equeally divided between all my lawful heirs.

I do hereby nominate and appoint Elizabeth Dearmore my wife my Executrix of this my last will and testament. In witness whereof I do to this my will set my hand & seal this the 13th day of February 1856.

        William Dearmore (seal)

Signed sealed and published in our presence and we have subscribed our names hereunto in presence of the Testator.

H. Parks
William Martin

State of Tenness) December Term 1856
Dyer County)

  This day the Last Will and Testament of Wm. Dearmore deceased was produced here in Court and H. Parks and Wm. Martin the subscribing witnesses there to came here into open Court and testified that they were personally acquainted with the Testator that he signed and published said will & Testament in (P.62) their presence for the purpose therein contained and requested them specially to bear witness there to that they signed it in his presence and at his request and that he was of sound and disposing memory at the time of executing said will.

It is therefore ordered by the court that the same be set up as the Last will and testament of the said Wm. Dearmore deceased.

Attest   R. M. Tarrant Clerk.
               By Wm. M. Watkins D. Clerk.

(P.63)

Daniel E. Parker Sr.	) State of Tennessee **Dyer County**
Last Will	(
&	) I Daniel E. Parker Senior of Dyer
Testament	(County State of Tenn. do make the
Proven and set up at the	) following disposition of my prop-
January Term 1857	(erty and it is my last will and
Recorded 6th January 1857.)	Testament.

  I give to my wife Martha Parker one third of my home tract of land including my dwelling house and as much of the Farm as it may be necessary for her to cultivate yearly to make a support during her life time. I give my wife Martha Parker all of my household and kitchen

(P.63 Cont'd) furniture, all of the plantation tools; one third of stock of cattle, Hogs and sheep, one yoke of Oxen Waggon or cart as she may select; one third of my crop that may be on hand at the time of my death; also negro woman Martha and her **two** children Eliza and boy Gran, Man Ellick and his wife Margaret and their three children Bill Pernett and Winney, girl Abbey daughter of Rachel & Man Eramus, the above named Negroes I give my wife during her life time, and at her death to my son Daniel E. Parker Jr. It is my wish that my wife and Son Daniel E. Parker live together there by doing away the necessity of dividing my property, Injoin it and my son Daniel to take especial care of his Mother; though I have no fears on that subject.

I give to my Daughter Mary Ann Harris during her life time the tract of land I purchased of my Brother William Parker containing estimation Eight Hundred and five acres, also one other tract of land adjoining it I purchased of George R. Mulherene, estimated One Hundred and Fifty one acres. I also give my daughter Mary Ann Harris the following named negroes during her life time, to wit; Doldman Harbert, man Nelson, man Lewis, man Nicholas, man Dock or Larkin Boy James, Woman Eliza and her four children, Tom, Mary and William Woman Viney and her five children. Andrew, Tack, Henry Isbell and Martha; and Woman Pricilla and her two children Lutitia and George The above named land and negroes I wish my Daughter to have the use and profits there of during her life time, and at her (P.64) death to be equeally divided between her children.

I also give my Daughter Mary Ann Harris all Horses, Mules, Cattle, Hogs, Oxens, Carts Plantation tools crop on hand at the time of my death.

I give also to my son Daniel E. Parker Jr. all the property I gave my wife Martha Parker during her life time of every description I also give my son Daniel E. Parker my home plantation and my adjoining tracts of land containing Thirty odd Hundred Acres, together with all the negroes on the plantation or that I may be possessed of at the time of my death, Stock of all kinds, cart or wagon crop of all kinds not given to my wife or otherwise disposed of at the time of my death.

I also give to my son Daniel E. Parker Jr. all Notes & accounts which may be due me at the time of my death, together with all the money on hand at the time of my death, and my other property and possessions both real or Mised, and all other interest whatsoever. I direct my son Daniel to pay all my just debts as soon as possible.

I do nominate and appoint my son Daniel E. Parker Jr. my sole Executor to this my last will and testament In witness thereof I have hereunto set my hand and affixed my seal this the 30th day of May one Thousand Eight Hundred and fifty six.

In presence of   Daniel E. Parker   (seal)
A. Benton
R. H. McGaughey
A. G. Ferguson

(22)

(P.64) Cont'd
State of Tennessee) January Term 1857
Dyer County   (
On motion and it appearing to the Court that Daniel E. Parker Senior late citizen of Dyer County has departed this life in this County; a paper writing purporting to be the last will and Testament was produced here in Court and there upon came here into open Court Abner Benton Albert G. Ferguson and Richard H. McGaughey the (P.65) subscribing witnesses there to; who being first duly sworn depose and say that they were personally acquainted with said Testator in his life time that he signed and published the said paper writing as his last Will and Testament - that they signed the same at his request in his presence, and in presence of each other, and that he was at that time of sound mind and disposing memory - it is therefore ordered that said paper writing be set up and recorded as the last will & Testament of the said Daniel E. Parker Senior deceased.

And thereupon came here into open Court Daniel E. Parker Jr. the Executor named in the said Will and brings with him Richard H. McGaughey, Albert G. Ferguson, Samuel Walker, and Pemberton P. Ledsinger, and they entered into and acknowledge Bond in the penal sum of One Hundred and Fifty Thousand Dollars conditioned and payable as the Law directs - and he then duly sworn.

It is there fore ordered that Letters Testamentary issue to him &c -

Attest   Robert M. Tarrant Clerk
                              By   Wm. M. Watkins Deputy Clerk.

(P.66)
Nuncupative Will   )   27th January A. D. 1857
     of   (The undersigned being present at
Thomas J. Connell dec'd   )   House of Hn. Thos. J. Connell on
Set up and established at   (the night of the 26th January 1857
March Term 1857 &   )   during his last sickness were called
Ordered to be Recorded   (on to bear witness in mind the dis-
Recorded 3rd March 1857   )   position he wished made of his estate
                                both Real and personal. The said
Thos. J. Connell then proceeded to State that he wanted his entire property kept together for the space of one year and if in the opinion of competent judges the negroes were making any thing, they were still to be kept together on the farm; but if their farming was not profitable, at the end of the year; then he wished Mrs. Connell to take five or six of the negroes such as she wanted to be kept on farm and the remainder to be hired out. Mrs. Connell to have one third of the negroes. If the farming of the negroes should not be profitable in the opinion of competent judges, Mrs. Connell to have one third of his land, and the remainder to be equally divided between his two Daughters, and at the death of Mrs. Connell all the Land to his two Daughters. He also states that he wished Henry Pursell son of Dr. J. H. Pursell to have two negro Boys about the size of the said Henry Pursell

(P.66 Cont'd) to grow up with him. He also said he intended to give Henry Pursell a tract of Land. He also stated that he wished all the Lands held in partnership by Connell & Ferguson to be sold.

He request that M. R. Hill, A. G. Ferguson and H. L. Fowlkes to settle his estate.

        H. L. Fowlkes,
        H. B. Fowlkes,

State of Tennessee) This day a paper writing signed by H. L.
Dyer County   ) Fowlkes and H. B. Fowlkes was produced in open Court & propounded as, the nuncupative will of Thomas J. Connell; and it appearing that Connell has departed this (P.67) life and was a resident in Dyer County at the time of his death; and it being proved to the satisfaction of the Court by the oaths of said H. B. Fowlkes and H. L. Fowlkes that said paper writing contains the disposition which the said Connell said he desired to make as to his property and affairs & what he wished done with them after his death & that said verbal directions were given by said Connell during his last sickness at his own dwelling house in Dyer County in the presence and hearing of both of said witnesses & that they were specially called upon by said Connell to bear witnesses there to & that he was of sound mind & memory at the time that said verbal will was reduced to writing & signed by them within ten days after the making thereof & it appearing that the widow and next of kin have been duly cited to appear here at this day and take such action as they see proper relative to the probate of said will - - and it further appearing by the oaths of said two witnesses that said paper writing contains the valid nun cupative will of said Connell - and that the same should be established as such.

It is therefore ordered by the Court that said paper writing be established as the last will and testament of said Connell and be recorded.

There fore came into open Court H. G. Ferguson and H. L. Fowlkes two of the Executors named in said will & took upon themselves the execution there of; took the oaths required by Law, and entered into Bond & security as the Law directs.

It is ordered that Letters Testamentary is true to them.

        R. M. Tarrant Clerk
      By Wm. M. Watkins D. Clerk

(P.68)
J. H. Cunningham   (I James H. Cunningham do make and
 Last Will   ) order this my last will and testament
  &   (in manner following.
Testament   )   (Viz)
Proven and set up at (First: I give my soul to God who gave
the May Term 1857   ) it 2nd I wish my body to be decently buried by my Executor and my burial expenses first paid out of any money that may first come into his

(P.68 Cont'd) hands.

 3rd I want all my perishable property sold for the purpose of paying my just debts.

 4th I give and bequeath to James H. Brewer and John M. Brewer 50 acres of land to be equally divided between them said land lies south of and joins the land of John Cunningham and if my perishable property should not be sufficient to pay all of my just debts I want said James H. & J. M. Brewer to pay the balance of my debts after my perishable property is executed.

 5th I want my friend James G. Brewer to execute this my last will and testament.

 Witness my hand and seal this the 2nd day of April 1857.

      his
    James X H. Cunningham (seal)
      mark

Executed & acknowledged in
our presence the day date above written

 Asa Griffin
 Manuel Cox.
    May Term 1857

State of Tennessee) This day a paper writing purporting to
Dyer County) be the last will & Testament of J. H. Cunningham was produced here in open Court and Asa Griffin and Manuel D. Cox subscribing witnesses there to came here into open Court, and being first duly sworn depose and say that they were personally acquainted with the testator and that he signed & acknowledged the execution of said will as having been done by him for the purpose therein contained, and that they signed it in his presence and at his request, and that he was of sound and disposing memory at the time of executing said will. (P.69) It is therefore ordered by the Court that the <u>the</u> same be set up as the last will and Testament <u>of</u> of the said deceased and that the same be recorded.

Attest   Robert M. Tarrant Clerk
             By Wm. M. Watkins Deputy Clerk.

(P.70)
C. W. Curtis   ) I Clement N. Curtis of the County of
 Last Will   (Dyer and State of Tennessee do make and
& Testament   ) publish this my last will and testament
          (in manner and form following.
Proven and set up at)
May Term 1857   ) First: My will and desire is that
Recorded 4th May 1857) after my deceased so much of my property
           as my wife Sarah F. Curtis may think she has not immediate use for shall be taken by my Executor and sold (except my two jennets which I want to remain unsold and the money arising from said sale to be disposed of as here inafter devized.

(24)

(P.70 Cont'd) 2nd I leave to my wife Sarah F. Curtis the use of all my property with in and with out doors to raise and school my children and support herself on so long as she remained a widow, but my will and desire is that she buy a small tract of land with some improvements thereon, and pay for the same to the amount (not exceeding one thousand dollars) out of the money and notes that I may die possessed of, and that she reside on the same and use and enjoy the profits of said tract of land, keep my children together; raise support and school them during her widowhood; but if my wife Sarah F. Curtis shall marry then I give and bequeath to my four children: (viz) Elizabeth Paris Curtis, Sarah Drucilla Curtis, Harriet Curtis and Louisiana Curtis the whole of my estate to be equeally divided amongst them, to them and their heirs forever.

My will and desire is that the money arising from the sale of such property as my wife may think proper to be sold shall be by executor appropriated to the use and benefit of my wife and children in manner and foth above stated; and if my wife select and buy a tract of land as requested above I want my Executor to attent to; that so far as to see that there be a good title made and that the same be and remain for the use of my wife and children in the manner above stated. And I hereby make and ordain John F. Sinclair Executor of this my last will and testament. In witness where-of I said Clement N. Curtis have here unto set my hand and seal this the 21st day of April A. D. 1857.

C. N. Curtis (seal)

Signed sealed published and declared by the said Clement N. Curtis as his last will and Testament in presence of us E. B. Curtis   W. P. Rice   W. B. Ward.

(P.71)
State of Tennessee)   May Term 1857
Dyer County   )
This day a paper writing purporting to be the last will and testament of C. N. Curtis deceased was produced here in open Court and W. P. Rice and E. B. Curtis subscribing witnesses there to came here into open Court and after being duly sworn depose and say that they were personally acquainted with the testator, that he signed said paper writing in their presence for the purposes therein contained and that they signed it in their presence and at his request and that he was of sound and disposing memory at the time of executing said will. It is therefore ordered by the court that said paper writing be set up as the last will and testament of the said deceased; and that the same be recorded.

Attest   Robert M. Tarrant Clerk
                    By Wm. M. Watkins Deputy Clerk.

(P.72)

William Martins	)	In the Name of God; Amen, I

William Martins Last Will & Testament
Set up and established
May Term County Court 1857

In the Name of God; Amen, I William Martin of the State of Tennessee and County of Dyer being sound in mind and memory but not in usual health do make this my last will and testament as to such worldy goods as I may die possessed of. I dispose of the same as follows.

First: I recommend my soul to God who gave it; and my body to the earth to be buried in a Christian like manner.

Secondly; I wish Elizabeth C. and Martha Jane Cribbs each to have a medium horse in value, John J. to have a cow and calf one Bedstead Feather Bed and furniture. I give my two daughters Julia F., and Victora one horse each as above. Bridle & Saddle one cow & calf, one bed stead Feather Bed & furniture each which will make all of my children equeal the remainder of my children having had such property given off to them here to fore, I also give my son Thomas W. Eighty acres of land of the west end of the tract of land he now is living on known as the Lenox tract during his life but it is not to be livable for his debt in no way whatever, neither is he to transfer nor sell it; after his death it is to go to his wife and children, he is to have the land at valuation & what may be lacking to make him equeal in the division to be made up in property or money. I wish an equeal division to be made between all of my children, the children of my Daughter Adaline to have her part equily. Elizabeth C. Cribbs & children to have her part & not to be subject to a division with Cribbs other children the part following to Wm. S. Staritt to go to his present wife Emeline & Children and not to be subject or liable to his debts in any way whatever. I do this because of his much indebtedness & wishing to leave my property to my own children all the rest of my children to have their part and dispose of the same as they may think proper. I wish my land in lots as follows: My home tract of land to be divided in two lots layed off East and west, my seventy three acres occupant tract beginning at the South West of the land corner of the land; that I have set aside to Thomas W. Martin this I wish (P.73) it and my negro woman Abagail to be valued together so as to make sd. land near equeal with the other lots, the remaining ballance of the tract that Thomas W. Martin's living on to be considered as one Lot & valued as the same my Town Lot valued & drawn for my remaining three negroes Henry, Madison & Harrett to be valued separately, and after all being valued to be drawn for by my Eight children namedly Elizabeth C. Cribbs, John I. Ann Miller, Emaline Starett, Martha Cribbs, Julia F. Victoria & the children of my daughter Adaline, Thomas Wm. being previously provided for my chattel property to be sold & money if any to be considered in said valuation & division.

    I do hereby appoint Joseph Miller Executor of this my last will and testament as witness whereoff I have hereunto set my hand and seal this the 14th day of March A. D. 1857

Test   William Martin (L.S.)
Jos Prichard   T. J. Frazier

(P.73 Cont'd)
State of Tennessee) May Term County Court 1857
Dyer, County)

This day a paper writing purporting to be the last will and testament of William Martin deceased was presented here into open Court and T. J. Frazier and Jos Prichard subscribing witnesses there to came here into Open Court and after being duly sworn depose and say that they were personally acquainted with the testator, that he signed said will in their presence to be his act and deed for the purposes there in contained; and that they signed it in his presence and at his request; and that he was of sound and disposing memory at the time of executing said will.

It is there fore ordered that said will be set up as the last will and testament of said deceased and be recorded.

Attest   Robert M. Tarrant Clerk.
                    By Wm. M. Watkins Deputy Clerk.

(P.74)
Sidney Forchee) In the name of God Amen
 Last Will & (I Sidney Forchee of the County of Dyer
Testament) and State of Tennessee being of sound
Set up and established) mind and memory but mindful of the
April Term 1857) certainty of death and the uncertainty
of life do make ordain and constitute this my last will and testament revoking all others here to fore by me made.

Itom 1st I will and bequeath my spirit unto God who gave it; my body to the earth to be decently buried.

Itom 2nd I direct all of my just debts to be paid as soon as possible and after the payment of my debts as before mentioned I will & bequeath to my beloved wife Mary Ann Meldria Fochee during her natural life or widowhood all of my personal and real estate to be disposed of as she pleases.

Itome 3rd At the death of my wife I direct my estate to be equeally divided between my children to wit. William Lya, Thos. Vaughen, Mary Hays, George Washington, Joseph Penyman Jno. Henry; and any others my wife may bear with in nine months from and after my death.

Itom 4th At the marriage of my wife I direct that my estate to be equeally divided between my children and wife.

Itom 5th: I here by nominate and appoint my friend James Powell Executor of this will & testament. In testimony of all which I do here unto set my hand and seal This 15 - May 1857
Test   his
Thos. H. Fowlkes   Sidney X Fochee
James Powell   mark
James Hendrix

(28)

(P.75)
State of Tennessee) April Term 1857
Dyer County)

This day a paper writing purporting to be the last will and testament of Sidney Forchee was presented here into open Court and Thomas H. Fowlkes one of the subscribing witnesses there to came into open Court and after being duly sworn depose and says that he was personally acquainted with the testator, that he signed said will in his presence to be his act and deed for the purposes there in contained; and that he signed it in his presence and at his request; and that he was of sound and disposing memory at the time of executing said will, and T. J. Frazier, Jos Chitwood and A. Wilkins came into open court and being first duly sworn depose and say that they are personally acquainted with the hand writing of James Powell one of the subscribing witnesses there to, and that the signature to said will purporting to be his is genuine. It is therefore ordered by the court that the same be set up as the last will and testament of the said Forchee deceased; and be recorded.

Attest
           R. M. Tarrant Clerk
        By W. M. Watkins D. Clerk

(P.76)
F. L. Sanders) In the Name of Almighty God; Amen; I
Last Will & (Ferdinand L. Sanders of the county of
 &) Dyer and State of Tennessee being of
Testament (sound and disposing mind and memory;
Proven and set up at) but well knowing the shortness and un-
July Term 1857 (certainty of mortal life the certainty
         of death; and remembering the unalterable decree of the Great Judge of all, that dust thou art and unto dust shalt thou return; do make and ordain and publish this my last will and testament hereby revoking and making void all other wills and testaments here to fore made and published be me; that is to say;

First; I direct that all of my just debts shall be paid out of any money that shall first come into the hands of my Executrix.

Secondly; That if I shall die before my beloved wife Elija J. Sanders and with out issue. I give and bequeath to her all of my property both real and personal for and during the term of her natural life, But if she should have any child or children then the said property to go to my wife for life or until her second marriage remainder to said child or children; to be divided among them share and share alike.

Third; That if I shall die without issue and my wife shall marry again; I direct that the negroes and their increases belonging to her at the time of her marriage with me; shall be divided amongst her issue by said second marriage after her death; and if she shall die leaving no child or children then to be divided amongst such of her relations as she shall direct.

Fourthly; At the death of my said wife leaving no sorrowing child

(P.76 Cont'd) or children by me I give and bequeath unto my niece Maratha Hale daughter of my sister Nancy P. Hale and her heirs forever my two negro boys Bob and Jimbo and all of my real estate, and personal property not otherwise appropriated.

Lastly: I do here by nominate constitute and appoint my well beloved wife Eliza J. Sanders, sole executrix of this my last will and testament.

In witness whereof I have here unto set my hand affixed my seal the 4th day of February in the year of Our Lord one Thousand eight hundred fifty four and of the Independence of the United States of America the 78th.

          F. L. Sanders (seal)

(P.77)
Signed sealed and acknowledged in our presence and we have hereunto subscribed our names in the presence of the testator and of each other the 4th day of February A. D. 1854	The words before her second marriage interlined before signing.

  H. L. Fowlkes
  T. E. Richardson

State of Tennessee) July Term 1857
Dyer County   )

  This day a paper writing purporting to be the last will and testament of F. L. Sanders was produced here in open court and T. E. Richardson and H. L. Fowlkes subscribing witnesses there to came here into open court and being first duly sworn depose and say that they were personally acquainted with the testator; and that he signed and acknowledged that he executed said paper writing for the purposes there in contained; and that they signed it in his presence and at his request; and that he was of sound and disposing memory at the time of executing said will. It is therefore ordered by the court that said paper writing be set up as the Last will and testament of the said Sanders deceased, and that the same be recorded.

Attest   Robert M. Tarrant Clerk
          By Wm. M. Watkins D. Clerk.

(P.78)

Richard Henderson
 Last Will
  &
Testament
Proven and set up at
July Term 1857
	Grove Mount Dyer County
	  March 24th 1857
	
	I Richard Henderson do make and ordain this my last will and testament and first I bequeath my soul to God and my body to the grave.

I will and bequeath to my beloved wife Jain Henderson during her natural life my plantation where on I now reside all the house hold and Kithin furniture, my plantation tools including, Thrasher, wagon and two yoke

(P.78 Cont'd) of oxen four cows and caves four mules or mares, the one half of my stock of hogs and one half of the sheep all the poultry and Bee stands my libery of books, her saddle and bridle and one years provition George Robert Mailly Jane and Caroline and two hundred dollars in money.

I will and bequeath to my son Rufus G. Henderson my negro boy Robert at my wifes death and three hundred dollars out of the sales of my lands.

I will and bequeath to my son John O. Henderson Fifty acres of land the place where on he now lives and my negro man George at my wifes death.

I will and bequeath to my son William R. Henderson my negroes Thomas and Philis.

I will and bequeath to my son Ezekiel A. Henderson my negro boy Jerry and my negro girl Caroline at my wifes death.

I will and bequeath to my son Samuel C. Henderson my negroes old Jerry and Mary and Yancey.

I will and bequeath to Samuel C. Henderson my negro girl Milly at my wifes death as Trustee for my daughter Girzah E. Gillespie and his children also Trustee for the money she will be entitled to out of the sales of my property.

I will and bequeath to Rufus G. Henderson my negro girl Jane at my wifes death as Trustee for my daughter Mary J. James and his children.

I will and bequeath to my deceased Daughter Isabela C. Fites four children one hundred dollars each to be paid out of the sails of my lands.

I will and bequeath to my two Grand children James F. Henderson children to Richard Burges - Henderson my negro boy (P.79) Elbert and to Matilda Isabela Henderson my negro Girl Mary Ann.

It is my will that the lands I own in the tenth district be sold when my Executors thinks best. What money is left from Paying debts and expenses, and not willd; and the proceeds of other property be equeally divided amongst my living children: -- after my wifes death the plantation where I now reside be sold with any other property that remains and not willed, -- the proceeds to be equeally divided amongst my then living children.

I nominate and apoint my two sons Rufus G. Henderson and Samuel C. Henderson my Executors signed and sealed.

Elias Dodson Richard Henderson (sealed)
Wm. Maddrey

(P.79 Cont'd)
State of Tennessee) July Term 1857
Dyer County)

    This day a paper writing purporting to be the last will and testament of Richard Henderson was produced here in open Court and Elias Dodson and Wm. Maddrey the subscribing witnesses there to came here into open court; who being first duly sworn depose and say that they were personally acquainted with the testator; and that; he signed and acknowledged that he executed said paper writing for the purposes there in contained; and that they signed it in his presence at his request, and that he was of sound and desposing memory at the time of executing said will. It therefore ordered by the court that said paper writing be set up as the last will and testament of Richard Henderson deceased; and that the same be recorded.

Attest   Robert M. Tarrant Clerk
                                      By Wm. M. Watkins D. clerk.

(P.80)
William B. Gleaves)
    Last Will (
        &)
    Testament (
Proven and set up at)
October Term 1857)

    I William B. Gleaves being fully sensible of the uncertainty of life and the certainty of death do this day make and published this my last will and testament hereby revoking and making void all others (if any) here to fore by me made. It is my will first that all my just debts be paid including burial and funeral expenses.

    It is my will and desire secondly that after the payment of my just debts &c as aforsaid that my beloved wife Louisa P. Gleaves shall have the entire controll of my farm and all the property belonging there to during the time that she remains my widow, and it is my will and desire further that if she and my unmarried children can live together in place during that time then I request that they do so; but if not it is still my desire that she (my widow) shall have the entire controll of my farm and all the property belonging there to during her widowhood but no longer, but if my beloved wife Louisa P. <u>Glaves</u> should marry then it is my will and desire that she have the use of thirty three and one third acres of land including the dwelling house &c we now live in during her natural life and also the use of one horse saddle and bridle, one cow and calf and two beds during her natural life. And if she shall marry it is my will and desire that the balance of my property shall be divided as here in after be provided.

    I have given off of my estate to Susan Miller wife of Franklin Miller and to Sarah Ann Davis wife Nathaniel Davis all the property that I desire them to have in any event. And I have given to Mary Manies wife lately deceased of <u>Seminiel</u> Manies all the property that I intend my Grand children by her to have.

    If my beloved wife should marry then it is my desire that

(P.80 Cont'd) all my property be equeally divided among my children excepting those already who have received their portion and excepting also that (P.81) portion of my property: to wit: thirty three & 1/3 acres of land &c as aforesaid which she is to have the use of during her natural life in the event that she married. I have an interest in a tract of land in Obion County Tennessee which I bought by a swap from John W. Wright; it is my will and desire that as soon as a deed can be obtained for that according to the contract made with said Wright that it be sold by my Executors upon such terms as he may think best; and the proceeds after paying all expenses equeally divided among my children who have not received their portion as afore said. It is my will and desire further that if any negroes do not demean and behave themselves as they should that my Executor sell them all and dispose of the proceeds according to the meaning and intention of this my last will and testament: that it is to say if my wife does not marry I want her to have the use of the proceeds during her natural life and then divided equeally among those of my children who have not received their portion as afore said; but if she does marry then she is only to have the part already designated in that event and the proceeds of said negroes are to be equeally divided among my children that have not received their share of my estate as afore said. I desire that the proceeds of all debts due me after paying my just debts be disposed of according to the foregoing clauses of this my will that is to say, I wish the remainder be put out at interest and divided equeally among my children who have not received their share as afore said severally as they may be come twenty one years of age.

It is my desire further that my female children who are entitled to distributive shares under this my will shall have said shares free from the controll of their husbands if they marry during their natural lives; and then to their issue severally if they leave any, but if they die leaving (P.82) none then said share or shares is or are to revert back and be divided equeally among those of my children who have not received their share or portions as afore said. In the vent that my widow does or does not marry at her death what ever property that may be remaining in her possession coming from my estate. It is my will and desire that the same be equeally divided amongst those of my children who have not received their shares as afore said.

I do here by nominate and appoint my known and tried friend Chas. C. Moss to execute and carry out this my last will and Testament and vest in him the powers here in granted. In the Name of God Amen.

Witness my hand and seal this the 25th day of September 1857.

W. B. Gleaves (seal)

(P.82 Cont'd)
Signed sealed and acknowledged in our presence by the said William B. Gleaves who requested us to attest the same on this the 25th day of September one thousand eight hundred and fifty seven

Witnesses (G. M. Sanders
(F. F. Ferguson

(P.83)

Noah Perry) State of Tennessee Dyer County
Last Will (January 13th 1858
&)
Testament (
Proven and set up) I Noah Perry do make and publish this my Last will and Testament, hereby Revoking and making null all other wills by me at any time made. First I direct that my funeral expenses and all my Debts be paid as soon after my death as possible out of any money that I may die possed of or may first come into the hands of my Executor. Secondly I give and bequeath to my wife Milly Perry three hundred and one half acres of Land including my house and improvements ajorning the same. I also give and bequeath to my wife, the following negro property first a negro,man Jorden woman Marina & Emiling Boys Denis & Tack, during her life and at death of my wife to be sold and equeally divided between my children.
at the March
Term 1858

Thirdly, it is my will that my seven youngest children to wit Simon, Margaret, Marlen, John Adline, Franklin, and Buck hannan be Educated out of any moneys that shall come into Exd. free of charge to them, say So fare as a common English Education

Fourthly, Sons James &c Noah T. Simon S. Jno. A. Franklin P, and Buck hannan the Remainder of my lands Say Seven hundred acres which is worth ten Dollars per acre to be equeally divided between them.

Fifthly the remainder of my ~~property~~ negroes to be hyerd out, during my wifes life time, at which time they shall be divided amongst children Daughters to wit, Louisa, Ann & Milla Jane Stallings Elizabeth Stallings Sarah Francis Margaret Louisa Marcela and Adalad shall have five hundred Dollars each. The said negro property, more then my Sons. The children of my Daughter Mary E. Riddick not included having given her during her life all the property that I designed for her.

(P.84) Sixthly, the remander of my property ~~to to wit~~ Specified when to be sold, and the proseeds after paying my debts to be equeally divided amongst my children. Lastly I do here by nominate & appoint John F. Sinclair and James H. Perry my Executor.
    In witness where of I do to this my will set my hand & seal, date above   Noah Perry (seal)
R. L. Hinton
T. P. Stallings

(34)

(P.84 Cont'd)
State of Tennessee) March Term 1858
Dyer County Court)

    This day a paper writing purporting to be the Last will and testament of Noah Perry dec'd. was produced here into open court and R. L. Hinton & T. P. Stallings subscribing witnesses & after being duly sworn, depose & say that they were personally acquainted with Noah Perry the Testator & that the said Perry Signed Seald published & acknowledged said paper writing in their presence as his Last will & testament and that he was of Sound mind and disposing memory at the time of dowing the same and that the said Perry Requested them to bear witness there to & that they signed it as witnesses in his presence & in the presence of each other. It is there fore ordered by the court that said paper writing be set up & established as the Last will & Testament of the said Noah Perry Dec'd and that the same be recorded. Where upon came J. S. Sinclair & J. H. Perry together with David Bowen & J. P. Davis their Securitis & entered into an acknowledged bond in the penal sum of twenty four thousand dollars payable as the Law directs & they were sworn as Executors of the Last will & testament of the said Noah Perry dec'ed & letter was ordered to be issued to them.

Attest   R. M. Tarrant clerk.

(P.85)
John F. Algia's) I John F. Algea do make and pub-
Last will & Testament (lish this as my last will & Testa-
Proven & Set up July Term) ment, hereby revoking all others
1858) by me at any time made,

    First I direct that all my debts & my funeral expenses be paid as soon after my death as possible out of any money that I may die possessed of or that my first come to the hands of Executor. Secondly I give & bequeath to my son Robert H. Algea my negro boy Elisha and value him at four hundred & fifty Dollars,

    Thirdly I give to my Daughter Margaret J. Franklin a negro girl Mary now in her possession and valued at five hundred dollars.

    Fourthly, I give daughter Eliza P. Williams a negro girl Harriet now in her possession, and valued at Six Hundred Dollars.

    Fifthly, I give to my Son J. S. B. Algea, one negro woman Amanda and her child Barbary now in his possession valued at Six hundred fifty dollars and Sixty acres of land off the South end of the land on which I now live.

    Sixthly, I give to my Son Robt. H. Algea & J. F. Algea that potion my tract of land lying viz. of a line to be run due north from the north east corner of W. H. Franklin tract of land where he now resides, to E. Woods South boundary line

(P.85 Cont'd) Sd. north boundary line to be run to the Sam bomdren of the compass, that the west boundry line of tract of land runs So as to make the tract hereby given the Same width at the north & South ends - Sd. land to be equeally divided between them

Seventhly I give to Son I. F. Algea a negro girl Isabel and value her at three hundred Dollars.

Eightly, I give to my son Abner H. Algea a negro boy Jim and value him at five hundred Dollars and as all my other children have had a horse sadle & bridle & bid & furniture I gave to my Son Abner H. the same articles to be given to him when he is twenty one years (P.86) of age or if he needs them before that time they are to be given to him.

Ninthly - I give to my wife Sarah Algea all my household & kitchen furniture all the Stock grain and farming utensils on the farm, of any and all Kind whatsoever. Also the following Slaves to wit, Frank, Phily Jenny & infant Chila Vend & William to be hers during her natural life, and at her death to be divided between my legal heirs as here in after mentioned, I also give to my wife Sarah during her natural life the ballance of my tract of land not here in before disposed of, and at her death, I give Sd. land to my Son Abner H. Algea.

Ninthly, After the death of my beloved wife I will that my Six grand children the Lawful heirs of my deseased Son James G. Algea, Shall with all my children here in named be first made equeal in the division of my property that is them who have had negroes of best value shall have anything more. And my Sd. Grand children who have not had a negro shall have money or property to make them equeal with all the ballance of my children. Then remainder of my property to be equeally divided among all my lawful heirs my six grand children to be counted as one heir; the land given in this will to my Several Sons, is not to charged to them in the equeal division of my estate, they are to have the land given to them with out accounting for it in the division and one to be made equeal with the other in the division of my personal property and if the negroes given to my wife can not be divided at her death So as to make my heirs equal then I will that Sd. slaves be sold and the proceeds divided as here in directed & I hereby appoint my sons Robt. H. Algea & J. S. B. Algea my Executors in witness whereof I do to this my will set my hand and seal this the first day of July A. D. 1857 Eighteen Hundred and fifty seven.

Signed Sealed & published   John. F. Algea (seal)
in our presence and we
(P.87) Subscribed our names in the presence and at the request of the testator.

Smith Park   )
P. D. McCorkle.)

(P.87 Cont'd)
State of Tennessee) July Term 1858
Dyer County Court)
    This day a paper writing purporting to be the Last Will & Testament of John F. Algea

(Editor's Note: Incomplete)

(P.88)
Charlotte Wilkins) State of Tennessee
  Last Will & (Dyer County Court
Testament)
Proven and Set up (Sept. 3rd 1858
At December Term 1858)
Recorded 6th December 1858(I Charlotte Wilkins do this day make and publish this my last will and testament hereby revoking and making void all other wills by me ever made.

    First, I will and decree that my funeral expenses and all my debts be paid out of any money I may have at my death or that may first come into the hands of my Executor. Secondly: I will and bequeath to my son Newton B. Wilkins One hundred dollars, One cherry Bed stead with Bed and furniture and eight curley maple chairs and one folding table. Thirdly: I will and bequeath to my son John N. Wilkins one clock and one square table and ten head of hogs. Fourthly, I leave the balance of my property to be sold; and after setting apart one hundred dollars for N. B. Wilkinson and paying my debts, I leave the remainder to be equeally divided between all my children. In testimony where of, I have here unto set my hand and affixed my seal this the day and date above written

Test
R. H. Davis
S. A. E. Davis   Charlotte Wilkins (seal)

State of Tennessee) December 6th 1859
Dyer County Court)
    This day a paper writing purporting to be the last will and testament of Charlotte Wilkins was produced here in open court and B. H. Davis and S. A. E. Davis subscribing witnesses there to came here into open court; and being first duly sworn depose and say that they were personally acquainted with Charlotte Wilkins: and that she signed & acknowledged that she executed the same for the purposes there in ¢ø#t∂¡#¢d contained; and that they signed it in her presence & at her request and that she was of sound and disposing memory at the time of executing said will. It is there fore ordered by the court that said paper writing be set up and established as the last will & testament of Charlotte Wilkins deceased and at the same be recorded

Attest
                                          R. M. Tarrant Clerk.
                            By Wm. M. Watkins Deputy Clerk.

(P.89)
Narcissa McCarroll) State of Tennessee
   Last Will & (Dyer County
   Testament)
Proven and set up at (
April Term 1859)
Recorded 4 April 1859)

        I Narcissa McCarroll do make and publish this my last will and testament, here by revoking and making void all former wills by me at any time here to fore made: And first I direct that my body be decently interred in a manner suitable to my condition in life. And as to such worldly estate as it has pleased God to entrust me with, I dispose of the same as follows: First, I direct that all my debts and funeral expenses be paid as soon after my desease as possible, out of any moneys that I may die posessed of, or may first come into the hands of my executors from any portion of my estate real or personal. Secondly, I give and bequeath to my son James McCarroll my tract of land lying in Benton County near Casadon, also to the said James one yearling colt and one mule and one bed and furniture. The remainder of my effects consisting of stock, house hold furniture &c I wish sold and the proceeds after paying all my debts to be applied to educate my son James - I do here by appoint make and ordain my esteemed friend neighbors and relative Robert Campbell executor to this my last will and testament. In witness where of I hereunto set hand and seal this the year of Our Lord Nov. 30th 1958

Signed in the   Narcissa McCarroll (seal)
presence of
I. G. Tucker &
R. W. Tucker

State of Tennessee) This day a paper writing purporting to be
Dyer County Court) the last will and testament of Narcissa
                    McCarroll was produced here into open Court and I. G. Tucker and R. W. Tucker subscribing witnesses there to came here into open court and being first duly sworn depose and say that they were personally acquainted with Narcissa McCarroll (P.90) and that she signed and acknowledged that she executed the same for the purposes there in contained, and that they signed it in her presence and at her request & that she was of sound and disposing memory at the time of executing said will, It is there fore ordered by the court that said paper writing be set up and established as the last will and testament of Narcissa McCarroll deceased and that the same be recorded

Attest   R. M. Tarrant Clerk.
                                By. Wm. M. Watkins D. Clerk.

(P.91) S. R. Sudbury) State of Tennessee
      Last Will & (Dyer County Court
      Testament)
      Proven and set up at(In the Name of God Amen
      June Term 1859) I Shadrach R. Sudbury of the
      Recorded June 1859) County of Dyer and State of

(P.91 Cont'd) Tennessee being sound of mind but frail in body do make this my last will & testament here by revoking and making void all other will or wills by me at any other time made. First, I commit my soul to God who gave it, and my body to its mother Earth, Secondly; I direct that my body be decently intered. Thirdly, I direct that out of my monies or effects that I may die possessed of that my burying & funeral expenses be paid & also all of my just debts as soon as possible: Fourthly; I give and bequeath to my beloved wife Susan Sudbury all of my property both real and personal during her natural life or widowhood and at her death or marriage to be equeally divided between my three children Jeremiah W. Sudbury, John B. Sudbury and Sarah Francis Sudbury, viz: the share or part that may fall to John B. & Sarah Francis Sudbury on a final division is to remain in their possession for their use and benefit, and to raise and support their families and children during their said John B. and Sarah F. Sudbury's life time, and at their death to be equeally divided between their respective children if any they may have living; and also John B. and Sarah F. Sudbury shall be authorized when they come in possession of their shares to sell the same if they believe they can lay out the money to a better advantage and interest for themselves and children, and the land or property purchased with said money to descend to their children as above stated, and also in a final division of my estate I desire my daughter Sarah F. Sudbury to have the two girls Mary & Jane and their children if any there may be as part of her share of my estate but if said Francis should never have children I desire the said two girls Mary & Jane & other children to fall back as other of my property, and be equeally divided between J. W. Sudbury, and John B. Sudbury at sd. said Francis death as also any other portion or part that may descend to her of my estate. I also desired all of my property personal & real to remain in the care & possession of my wife Susan during her widowhood or natural life, but she may loan to my above named children if she thinks (P.92) proper to do so but to be returned at her pleasure or when legally demanded but at her marriage or death a general division to take place immediately. I also desire that the mill and my equeal interest in the gin and Carding Factory may be continued and run as here to fore, and the profits arising from them be equeally divided as my other property, and I here by appoint my two Sons Jeremiah W. & John B. Sudbury my executors with out bing bound to give security to execute and carry out the intentions of this my last will & (<u>intestived</u> before signing) In testimony where of I have here unto set my hand and seal this the day of February A. D. 1857

Test   Shadrack R. Sudbury (seal)
J. J. Davis

G. W. Walker
Elias Parrish

            Codicl to the above Will.

The land on which I live containing two Hundred and seventy five acres with the appurtenances attached I give to my two

(P.92 Cont'd) sons J. W. & John B. Sudbury and I give & bequeath to my daughter Sarah Francis (now Sarah Francis Farwell) one hundred acres where on she now lives, this codicil is not intended to effect the above will in any way, only in the exchange of land my son J. W. Subury made me a deed to the one Hundred acres that I now bequeath to Sarah Francis and in exchange I bequeath to him her interest in the land where on I live which givs to sd. J. W. Subury two hundred of the sd. two hundred and seventy five acres - In witness where of I here unto set my hand and seal this 10 day of May A. D. 1859

Attest   Shadrack R. Sudbury (seal)
J. B. Smith
Americus Sedcock
B. S. Wilcox

(P.93)
William Parker   ) I William Parker of the County of
  Last Will   (Dyer & State of Tennessee being of
      &   ) sound body and mind desire this to
Testament   (be my last will and testament. First:
Proven and set up at   ) After paying all my just debts I desire my estate divided among my nieces
August & September   (sire my estate divided among my nieces
Term 1859   ) & nephews as the Law directs; to wit;
Recorded September 1859) Mary Ann Harris and Daniel E. Parker,
                                  Stephen Wood, Mary Fowlkes, and Pheby Mahan, Isaach Parker, Mary Ann Walker, Francis Parker, Martha Parker, James Dickey, Daniel Dickey, Isaach Dickey, Willis Dickey, Martha Deckey, May Terry and Pheby McGeely. To Samuel Walker I give one dollar; to the heirs of John Dickey dec'd. I give a note of twenty dollars I hold aginst Thomas Dickey, to the heirs of John Parker dec'd of Missourie I give one dollar.

     I nominate and appoint Dr. A. Harris my Executor to wind up and settle my estate as I have directed. In testimony whereof I have here unto affixed my hand an seal, this the 3rd day of January 1859.

A. S. Harris
J. N. Haynes   William Parker (seal)

(P.94)
Elizabeth Hodge   ) In the Name of God Amen.
    Last   (
Will & Testament   ) I Elizabeth Hodge of the County
Proven and set up at   (of Dyer and State of Tennessee being
the September Term 1859) of sound and disposing mind and memory
Recorded September 1859(but calling to recollection the the
                                 mortality of the body do make and constitute and ordain this my last will and testament revoking all others by me at any time made. In the first place I commend my soul to God who gave it; and my body I commit to the earth to be buried in a decent christian like manner, and that my burial expenses together with all my lawful debts (if any) be paid as early after my death as possible. In the next place I give and bequeath unto my nephew Nelson Allen the tract of land on which I now reside containing by estimates one hundred and seventy five

(40)

(P.94 Cont'd) acres to him his heirs and assigns forever. I also give and bequeath unto the said Nelson Allen the following negroes, to wit, one negro man named Harry, one old negro, woman named Rachel, one negro man named William, one negro man named Aron, one negro boy named Matthew, and one other negro woman named Rachel and her child named Tennessee to be hers forever. I further give and bequeath unto the said Nelson Allen my waggon, and six choice head of horses if there be that many further I give and bequeath unto the said Nelson Allen Eight head of the choice of my cattle if there be that many. I further give and bequeath unto the said Nelson Allen thirty five head of the choice of my hogs if there be that many. I further give and bequeath unto the said Nelson Allen two large feather beds and Bedsteads and furniture, and one small bed & Bedstead and furniture, also one Bureau one sugar chest one Dinning Table One side Board, one candle Stand one clock, one dozen chairs and all my cupboard ware and all my cooking utensils and milk vessels and wash tubs and water pails, also two looking glasses In the next place I give unto George Murry the son of my niece Sarah Ann (P.95) Murry dec'd.four hundred acres apart of a League of Land which I am possessed of in the Counties of McClennen and Bell and State of Texas. I also give unto Elizabeth Ann Murry the daughter of my said niece Sarah Ann Murry dec'd four hundred acres of land out of the above named League of land. If either of the above mentioned children should die before arriving to the age of twenty one years or before marrying, I leave it all to the surviving one. In case they should both die before marrying or arriving at the age of twenty one years then and in that case I give & bequeath the above mentioned land to my sister McDanells children to be equeally divided among the living heirs. I give and bequeath to my nephew Austin Stanley Three hundred acres of Land out of the above mentioned League. I give and bequeath unto George A. Stanley son of my nephew Austin Stanley Three hundred acres of land out of the said above mentioned League; to be theirs forever. I give and bequeath six hundred acres of the above mentioned League of Land to living children of my sister McDanell to be equeally divided amongst them forever; the ballance of the above mentioned League of Land I leave to be sold to be applied by my Executors to any incidental expences that may occur. I further give and bequeath unto my nephew Nelson Allen all my farming tools and Barouch. It is further my will and desire that should there be any property or money belonging to or due my estate which I have not above disposed of in this will that it be equeally divided between George Murry and Elizabeth Ann Murry children of my niece Sarah Ann Murry dec'd forever to be paid over to them by my Executor I nominate and appoint, my nephew Nelson Allen and Alfred T. Fields my Executors to this my last will and testament. In witness whereof I have here to set my hand and seal this day of June A. D. 1857

Test
S. Rice
Lovell Coffman.

                        her
Elizabeth X Hodge (seal)
                        mark

(41)

(P.96)

Thomas J. Talley Last Will & Testament Proven and set up at the June Term County Court 1860 Recorded June 8th 1860	In the Name of God Amen. I Thomas J. Talley of Dyer County Tennessee being solemnly surpressed of the uncertainty of life and the certainty of death, do make and publish this

my last will and testament hereby revoking and making void all others by me here to fore made (if any) It is my will and desire first - that all my just debts, burial and funeral expenses be paid.

And secondly it is my will and desire that my beloved wife Permelia C. Talley have the free and unreserved control of all my property, including money, chosen in action, personal and real property of which I may die seized and possessed (unless it be necessary to resort to the same to pay my just debts &c) during her unmarried state with the restrictions and modifications (if any) here in expressed. If she marries before my youngest child becomes twenty one years of age then it is my will and desire that she have one third in value of all the land of which I may die seized and also a childs part of my personal property to be and enure to her use and benefit during her natural life only but at her death it is my will and desire that the remainder in said one third of my real estate and said childs part of my personal property so given to her in case of her marriage be equeally divided amongst my children that may be living at that time or in case some be dead leaving children then the children of those that may be dead are to have the share that the deceased child would be entitled to (if living). If my beloved wife should marry as afore said before my youngest child becomes of age the balance of my estate not already disposed of in that event I wish divided equeally amongst my children then living share and share alike, and in case some be dead leaving children then the children of those that may be dead to have the share that the deceased child would be entitled to if living. If my bloved wife should not marry again it is my will and desire that she have the free and unreserved control (P.97) of all my property until my youngest child becomes twenty one years of age, but then my will and desire is that it be divided in the following manner to wit: She is to have one third in value of my real estate and a child part of my personal estate to be and enure to her use and benefit during her natural life, but at her death the remainder in said share to be equally divided amongst my children, then at her death living and in case some be dead leaving children then the children of the desceased child or children to have the share that the deceased child would be entitled to if living. And the balance of my estate at the time I want equeally divided amongst my children then living share and share alike, and in case some be dead leaving children then the children of the deceased child are to have the share that the deceased child would be entitled to if living. I now own one negro woman named Nancy aged about twenty eight years. It is my desire that if I do not dispose of her before my death and

(P.97 Cont'd) invest the proceeds, that she be sold as soon after my death as possible at private sale by my Executors and Executrix to the best advantage and the proceeds vested in a negro girl which must be held subject to the provisions of this will in the same way that Nancy would if not sold. I now own one half as tenant in common with Lucy Morris of about five hundred and thirty six acres of land which lies near where I now live in Dyer County. If I should not sell my interest in said land and vest the proceeds in land suitable for a home for my wife and children before my death it is my will and desire that as soon as said land can be sold for a good profit that it be done at private sale by my Executrix and Executors or such as may qualify, and the proceeds vested in other land suitable for a home for my wife and children which when purchased shall be subject to the spirit and intention of this my last will and testament as if owned by me at my death or if I should sell the same (P.98) and die, and die before the proceeds are vested then I want the proceeds vested as aforesaid. It is my will and desire that the proceeds be vested in whatever location that mybeloved wife may desire, but where ever located it is to be held and disposed of in different events as directed herein as if I had died seized and possessed of the same. I here by nominate and appoint Sonenzo Watkins George W. Talley and my beloved wife Permelia C. Talley the Executors and Executrix of this my last will and testament and vest them or such of them as may qualify with authority and power to execute and carry into effect the powers here in to them granted.

Witness my hand and seal this the 28th Sept. 1857

Thos. J. Talley (seal)

We the undersigned witness to the foregoing will saw the said Thos. J. Talley sign and acknowledged the foregoing will and testament, for the purposes there in contained, and bear witness to the same at his request in his presence, and in the presence of each other this the date above.

Attest
R. W. Peacock
W. J. Mahan
H. W. Vaughan

State of Tennessee) June Term (1st day of term) 1860
Dyer County Court)

This day a paper writing purporting to be the last will and testament of Thomas J. Talley deceased was produced here in open Court and R. W. Peacock and H. W. Vaughan two of the subscribing witnesses there to came here into open Court, and being first duly sworn, depose & say that they were personally acquainted with the said Thomas J. Talley that he executed signed sealed & published said paper writing in their presence, and for his last will and testament on the day it bears date - that he was of sound mind and disposing memory - that he specially requested them to bear witness there to (P.99) and that they subscribed the same

(43)

(P.99 Cont'd) as witnesses in his presence and in the presence of each other.

It is there fore ordered by the Court that said paper writing be set up and established as the last will and testament of the said Thomas J. Talley deceased and that the said be recorded, by the Clerk.

                                        Will M. Watkins Clerk,
                                        of Dyer County Court.

Thomas H. Williams   ) I Thomas H. Williams of the
   Last Will   (County of Dyer and State of
and Testament   (Tennessee do make and and
Proven and set up at the   ) publish this my last will and
December Term County Court 1860(testament hereby revoking and
Recorded December 6th 1860   ) making void all other wills
                                        by me at any time made. First:
I direct that all my just debts be paid as soon after my death as possible. Secondly: - I give and bequeath to my beloved Mother my interest in a tract of land in Dyer County on which she now lives, and which was purchased and is now owned jointly and equeally by my Brother T. M. Williams and my self during her natural life time or as long as she make it her individuial home. Thirdly: - I direct that after my Mothers death or when she may abandon the land above described as her home, that the land be sold and the proceeds equeally divided between my brother T. M. Williams, my sister Martha A. Westbrook and my Sister Susan L. Williams. Fourthly: After all my just debts are paid, I give and bequeath the remainder of all my effects equeally to my brother Louis M. Williams and my Sisters Martha A. Westbrook and Susan L. Williams Fifthly; I give to my mother the entire present crop on the place, all the stock and farming implements and every thing else which I own on the place to use or dispose of as she may see proper. Lastly: I nominate and appoint my Brother Louis M. Williams as my Executor. In witness where of I do to this my will set my hand and seal this Nov. 19, 1860

                                        Tho. H. Williams (seal)

(P.100) Signed sealed and published in our presence In witness where of we subscribe our names in the presence of the Testator
                        A. G. Harris
                        M. O. B. Gauldin

State of Tennessee)   December Term 1860
Dyer County Court)
                        This day a paper writing purporting to be the last will and testament of Thomas H. Williams deceased, was produced here in open Court and A. G. Harris and M. O. B. Gauldin subscribing witnesses there to came here into open court and being first duly sworn depose and say that they were personally acquainted with the said Thomas A. Williams - that he executed signed sealed and published said paper writing in their presence & for his last will & testament on the day it

(P.100 Cont'd) bears date - that he was of sound mind and disposing memory that he specially requested them to bear witness there to, and that they subscribed their names as witnesses in his presence and in the presence of each other. It is therefore ordered by the court that said paper writing be set up and established as the last will and testament of the said Thomas H. Williams deceased - and that the said be recorded by the clerk.

Attest

Will M. Watkins Clerk,
of Dyer County Court.

(P.101)

James G. Tinsley	)	In the Name of God - Amen.
Last Will and	(	
Testament	)	I James G. Tinsley of the County of
Proven and set up	(	Dyer, State of Tennessee being sound
at Febrary Court 1861	)	in mind but frail in body do here by
Recorded Febry. 7, 1861	)	make this my last will and testament.

First, I give my soul to God who gave it and my body to its Mother Earth. I desire my body to have desent intement and after my funeral and burial expenses and just debts are paid, I constitute and appoint my beloved wife Frances Mason Tinsley my Executrix and Guardian for my children with out giving bond &c and I desire after the payment of my just debts for my said wife to have full possession & right to my land, notes and any other property I may leave for her the benefit and to raise and school my children, I bequeath property & effects to my said wife during her natural life or widowhood also giving her the power to sell my land for her & childrens benefit provided it may be deemed best for their interest, and with the money to purchase other land for a home for my wife and children -

In witness whereof I have hereunto set my hand and affixed my seal this 21st day of September 1860

Test.
Thos. Nash
Thomas Shelton

James G. Tinsley (seal)

State of Tennessee) February Term 1861
Dyer County Court)
This day Thomas Shelton one of the subscribing witnesses to will of J. G. Tinsley dec'd came here in open court.

State of Tennessee) January Term 1861
Dyer County Court)

This day a paper writing purporting to be the last will and testament of James G. Tinsley deceased, was produced here in open Court and proved by the oath of Thomas Shelton, one of the subscribing witnesses there to - who being duly sworn (P.102) in open Court, depose and say: That he was personally acquainted with the deceased Tinsley that he Signed and published said paper writing as and for his last will and Testament in presence of both witnesses, that

(P.102 Cont'd) the witnesses both signed the Same at the testators request, in his presence and in presence of each other - And that the said Jame. G. Tinsley was then of Sound mind and desposing memory -

Attest.   Will M. Watkins Clerk.

State of Tennessee)   February Term 1861
Dyer County Court)
        This day Thomas Nash one of the subscribing witnesses to the will of J. G. Tinsley dec'd came here into open court, and being first duly sworn depose and Says: That he was acquainted with the Testator and that he signed sealed and acknowledged said will in his presence for the purposes there in contained and that he was of Sound mind and memory - And that he signed it as witness in his presence and in the presence of Thomas Shelton, the other subscribing witness there to, and at the request of the testator.

    It is therefore ordered by the court that the Same be set up and established as the last will and Testament of said J. G. Tinsley and recorded.

Attest   Will M. Watkins Clerk.

Last Will and Testament)   I Allen A. Justice being of sound
        of   (mind and disposing memory, believing
Allen A. Justice dec'd) that my Earthly end is fast approach-
                        (ing, do make and publish this my last
Set up April Term 1861) will and testament, hereby revoking
                          all others by me at any time here to
fore made.

    First - My will and desire is that all my just debts, be paid by my Executors out of the first money that comes to their hands. -

Second - I give to my beloved wife the negro girl Manda, which was given her by her father.

(P.103)   Third: I desire my Negro Woman Sarah be sold, and my Executors are fully authorized to sell and convey her without the aid of any court decree & may sell her publicly or privately they may deem best, the proceeds of the sale to be assets in their hands.

    Fourth: I desire that my beloved wife & children shall have a comfortable home: I there fore Authorize & empower my Executors, with my wifes consent, if it is thought best, to sell my land and use such of the proceeds may be necessary in purchasing for her & the children an other home, all of which is to be done with out the aid of a court decree - If it is not thought best to sell, then they will remain on the place - may object being to enable my Executors with the consent of my beloved wife, to do what ever is best, for the interest of my family.

    I hereby appoint Smith Parks and William Parks my Executors

(P.103 Cont'd) to this my last will and both on either of them can carry out its provisions

Witness
M. O. B. Gauldin
T. M. Harrell

A. A. Justice (seal)

State of Tennessee) April Term 1861
Dyer County Court)

    This day a paper writing purporting to be the last will and Testament of Rev. Allen A. Justice, late a citizen of Dyer County deceased, was produced here in open Court, and proved according to law by the oaths of M. O. B. Gauldin and Thos. M. Harrell, Subscribing witnesses thereto, to be as it purports, the Last will and testament of said A. A. Justice –

    It is there fore ordered by the court that the same be set up and established and be recorded –

Attest   Will M. Watkins clerk.

(P.104)
Last will & Testament) State of Tennessee) I do by this my
       of   (Dyer County   (last will & test-
Hiram Wellsberger de'd) July 18th 1861   ) ament give & be-
Sit up August Term 1861)   ) queath to my wife
                                                                           Anna Wellsberger,
after that all of my just & lawful debts, shall have been paid, all the effects personal and real estate, that may belong to me –

    In testimony where of I hereunto Subscribe my name

                                                      Hiram Wellsberger

Witness to same
M. V. Richardson
R. C. Parr

    It is my wish that my wife Anna Wellsberger execute this my will

                                                     Hiram Wellsberger

State of Tennessee) August Term 1861
Dyer County Court)

    This day a paper writing purporting to be the last will and testament of Hiram Wellsberger was produced in open court here and proven according to law by the oaths of M. V. Richardson and R. C. Parr, Subscribing witnesses there to, to be as it purports to be, the last will & testament of Hiram Wellsberger desceased –

    It is there fore ordered by the court that the same be set up and established – and be recorded

Attest   Will M. Watkins clerk.

(P.105)

Last Will & Testament of Joanna B. Williams dec'd Set up and Established January 6th 1862

I Joanna B. Williams of sound mind do make and publish this my Last Will and Testament, hereby revoking and making void all other wills by me made at any time.

First. I direct that all my just debts be paid as soon after my death as possible

Secondly: I will and bequeath to each one of my children, or their representatives, the Sum of Five Dollars.

Thirdly: I will and bequeath to my Daughter Susan L. Williams my negro man Lafayette and two hundred dollars in money -

Fourthly - I will and bequeath to my son George M. Williams My Negro man Richard -

I direct that the balance of my estate be consisting of a house and Lot near Newbern, the same on which I now live, Moneys, household and Kitchen furniture and stock, be sold an other proceeds be given to my son Peter W. Williams after paying all first claims--

In case my son Peter W. Williams should die before he gets his portion of my estate, I direct that it be divided equeally between my Daughter Susan L. Williams and my son George M. Williams.

Sixthly: I nominate and appoint my friend Guy Douglass my executor -

In witness Where of I to this my Last Will and Testament set my hand and seal this Oct. 5th 1861

Signed in the presence of   Joanna B. Williams (seal)
Guy Douglass
Mary A. Bell.

State of Tennessee)   January Term 1862
Dyer County Court)

This day a Paper Writing purporting to be the Last will and Testament of Joanna B. Williams dec'd late a citizen of Dyer county was produced here in open court and proved according to Law, by the oaths of Guy Douglass and Mary A. Bell Subscribing witnesses there to to be as it purports, the Last will and testament of the said Joanna B. Williams dec'd It is therefore ordered by the court that the same be set up and Established as the last will and Testament of the said Joanna B. Williams dec'd and that the same be recorded and filed

Attest   Will M. Watkins clerk,
             By W. C. Doyle Deputy

(P.106)

Last Will and Testament) I James L. Smith do here
       of (by make and publish this
James L. Smith deceased) my last will and testament
Proven and Established at the (disposing of my worldly ef-
January Term 1862 Dyer County Court) fects as follows.

                  TO WIT ---

First: Let all my just debts be paid -

2nd I do hereby give and bequeath to my Sister Mary Ann Smith my entire Estate, real, personal and mixed: in witness whereof I have this day here unto, set my hand and Seal

    This June the 8th 1861

Done in presence of   J. L. Smith (seal)
Hugh T. Hanks
W. J. Mahan

State of Tennessee)   January Term 1862
Dyer County Court)

        This day a paper writing purporting to be the Last will and Testament of J. L. Smith, dec'd was produced here in open court and proved by the oaths of H. T. Hanks and W. J. Mahan, Subscribing witnesses there to, according to Law, to be as it purports, the Last Will and Testament of the said J. S. Smith deceased -

   It is therefore ordered by the court that the same be set up and established - that it be recorded and filed -

   Attest   Will M. Watkins clerk
                                      By W. C. Doyle   Deputy

(P.107

Last Will and Testament) I Lewis Warren being Sound
       of (in mind, do will and desire
Lewis Warren dec'd) that my son William Simon
Proven & Established at the (Warren shall have half of my
February Term County Court 1862) tract of land, that I now
                                                 live on, at my death to have
and to hold forever - the fore said land is situated in the State of Tennessee Dyer County and in civil District No 3 - and bounded as follows: Towit Begining at a Stooping Poplar & Elm, Joseph Shearons W. E. corner in Rutherfords South boundary line: Runs South with said Shearons West boundary 80 poles to a Stake & Birch pointers, by Postons N. E. corner: Thence West Two Hundred poles to an Elm & Hickory pointer: Thence North Eighty poles to a Stake in a Pond, in Rutherfords line Thence East Two Hundred poles, with said Rutherfords line to the be- gining - Containing One Hundred acres, more or less - It is my desire that a line be run North & South through the said

(P.107) tract of land, and my son William Simon have the East portion of it - For him and his heirs, to have and to hold forever - This is all the interest I intend for my son William Simon to have in any of my lands -

This January 20th 1862   his
Test.   Lewis X Warren
Joseph A. Crews   mark
    his
Steven X Howard
    mark

State of Tennessee)   February Term 1862
Dyer County Court)

    This day a Paper Writing purporting to be a Will or Deed, of Lewis Warren, deceased was produced here in open court, and proved by the Oaths of Joseph A. Crews and Steven Howard, to be as it purports, the Last Will and Testament of the said Lewis Warrin deceased - or a Deed from the said deceased to William Simon Warren his son -

It is there fore ordered by the court that the same be set up and established as the Last will and Testament of the said Lewis Warren deceased and that the same be recorded and filed

Attest   Will M. Watkins clk.
           By W. C. Doyle Deputy

(P108)

Last Will & Testament   )   January 12 in the year of
    of   (Our Lord 1862
David Baird dec'd   )
Proven and Set up at the   (State of Tennessee)
February & March Term of the)   Dyer County   ) I David
County Court of Dyer County 1862)   Baird
being sound in mind and of disposing Memory, make this my Last will and Testament, revoking all other wills -

    First : I desire that all my just debts be paid including funeral expenses.

    2nd I will to my wife Mary Baird Fifty & one half acres land, on the North end of my tract of land, including the houses, during her Natural life - also my negro man Joseph and Patsy (a woman) - with all the house hold and Kitchen furniture - to hold the same during her natural life - also all the stock, with every thing belonging to the farm

    I will to my daughter Rebecca a Town lot in Newbern to have for her separate and individual use, Separate and apart from her husband, to hold as her own property and to dispose of as she may sees fit - valued at Five hundred and fifty dollars - Watever else may be coming, if any in a final division, to go

(50)

(P.108 Cont'd)   jointly to my daughter Rebecca and her husband A Jones.

I here to fore have given my daughter Martha Baird a full share of my estate - consequently make no further provision for her in this will -

I will to my son William the parcel of land as his absolutely after the death of my wife Mary what I willed her during her natural life for which is 50½ acres for my son William to hold finally as his, to all intents and purposes - which is his entire interest in my estate, Except the negro boy Joe -

I will to my three daughters, to wit: Rebecca, Mary and Elizabeth the Southern half of my tract of land 50½ acres - (I value this land at $1,500) to be equeally divided among them, as they may see fit to divide the same.

I also will to my daughter Elizabeth my negro girl Elizapeth, valued at $550. -

I further bequeath to my daughter Mary a promisory note I hold against the Estate of her dec'd husband - for about $200 Dollars - also enough of the assets (P.109) of my estate to make her equeal to Rebecca, Elizabeth and my son Andrew R. Baird -

I have already given my son A. B. Baird Eleven Hundred and ten dollars, for which I hold his receipt -

I further desire that my wife have every thing now on the farm, such as corn, meat, hogs, cattle, horses wagon, buggy &c &c - My general bequest is that my son A. R. Baird, Mary W. Rebecca & Elizabeth be made equeal by the sale of my mountain land in Middle Tennessee after after the death of my wife -

After the death of my wife I desire at the death of my wife Mary that Joe and Patsy be sold Privately and the effects be equeally divided among and between my 2 Sons & 3 daughters to wit: Rebeca, Mary, A. R. William and Elizabeth. -

I appoint my Son J. W. Baird my Executor without giving bond or Security

Signed and sealed in our)   David Baird (seal)
presence   )
Attest: Nathaniel Porter
        Richard Heath - This January 12, 1862

State of Tennessee)   February Term 1862
Dyer County Court)
                    This day a Paper Writing purporting to be the Last Will and Testament of David Baird deceased, was produced here in open court and proved by the oath of Richard Heath, one of the subscribing witnesses there to, according to law to be as it purports - the last will and testament of

(P.109 Cont'd)   David Baird deceased -

March Term 1862

This day a paper writing purporting to be the Last will and Testament of David Baird deceased, was produced here in open court, and proved by the oath of Nathaniel Porter, One of the subscribing witnesses there to, to be as it purports the Last will and Testament of the said David Baird deceased - It is therefore ordered by the court that the said Paper Writing be set up and established as the Last Will and testament of the said David Baird deceased - and that the same be recorded by the clerk.

Attest.   Will M. Watkins clerk.
                                                By M. C. Doyle D. Clerk.

(P.110)
Nuncapative Will   )   We Robert Johnson and Reading
    of   (Williams, do state that the
Thomas Ford dec'd   )   Nuncapative will of Thomas Ford
Proven and established at (was made by him on the 15th day
June Term County Court 1862) of April 1862, in our Presence
                            to which we were specially requested to bear witness by the Testator himself in the presence of each other - That it was made in his last, in his own, habitation or dwelling house at Chestnut Bluff when he had been resident about two years, and the same is as follows, Viz:

It was his will and desire that his effects should be disposed of after his death in the following Manner - First he wished his estate to be settled and equeally divided between his mother Amy Ford and his two Sisters Mary Ford and Julia Ford - Saying that the property where the dwelling house was belonged to his mother and that the store house & property belonged to him -

Second - He wished Robert Johnson to Settle his business and divide the proceeds as above stated, as he had rather he would do it than any person he knew of -

Made out by us and signed this 22nd day of April 1862

                                                Robert Johnson
                                                Reading Williams

State of Tennessee)   June Term 1862
Dyer County Court)
                      This day a Paper Writing purporting to be the Nuncupative Will of Thomas Ford deceased, was produced here in Open Court - and it appearing to the Court that the parties have been summoned to contest the same - and no one appeasing to contest or object to the same - and the same being proven by the oaths of Robert Johnson and Reading Williams according to law - It is there fore ordered by the court that the said Paper writing be and the same is hereby set up and

(P.110 Cont'd) established as the Last Will and testament of the said Thomas Tord deceased and that it be recorded

Attest   Will M. Watkins Clerk
                                               By W. C. Doyle Deputy

(P.111)
Last Will and Testament) State of Tennessee
           of   (Dyer County
Samuel C. Henderson Dec'd)
Proven & established at the June (I Samuel C. Henderson
and August Term County Court 1862) do make & ordain this my
                                                last will & Testament.

1st I will & bequeath to my wife Martha Henderson all my Estate, both real & personal, for a period of fourteen years - The property then to be divided equally between her & my then living children I also enpower my wife Martha to sell the place I now reside on, whenever it can be sold for its value - & the title from her shall be valid. Money arising from the Sales of this place to be laid out for other property as she think best.

2nd I do nominate and appoint R. G. Henderson & E. A. Henderson as agents to wind up my estate & pay all amounts collected over to my wife Martha without any Schedule rendered to County Court.

Witness   Samuel C. Henderson
John R. Forks
Wm. R. Prichard

State of Tennessee) June Term 1862
Dyer County Court)
                        This day a paper writing purporting to be the Last will and Testament of Samuel C. Henderson, deceased was produced here in open court, and proven in part to be, as it purports the Last Will and Testament of the said Samuel C. Henderson deceased by the oath of William R. Prichard one of the subscribing witnesses there to

Attest   Will M. Watkins Clerk
                                            By W. C. Doyle Deputy

State of Tennessee) August Term 1862
Dyer County Court)
                        This day a Paper writing purporting to be the last will and Testament of Samuel C. Henderson deceased was produced here in open court and proved by the oath of John R. Foster, one of the subscribing witnesses there to, according to law, to be as it purports, the Last will and Testament of the said Samuel C. Henderson dec'd - It is there fore ordered that the same be set up and Established as the Last Will and Testament of the said Samuel C. Henderson deceased - and that it be recorded by the clerk.

Attest   Will M. Watkins clerk.
                                            By W. C. Doyle Deputy

(53)

(P.112)

Last Will & Testament of Suffield Fumbanks dec'd Proven and set up at the April Term of the County Court for Dyer County 1863

Know all men by these presents that I Suffield Fumbanks of the county of Dyer and State of Tennessee being of sound mind and knowing the uncertainty of life and certainty of death and being desirous of making some disposition of my worldly effects do make and ordain this my last will and Testament To wit

In the first place I will and give unto my wife Mary Ann Fumbanks during her natural life all my Lands, or Real Estate together with the tenements thereon

2nd It is my will that at the death of my said wife my two sons Andrew Lewis Fumbanks and John Calvin Fumbanks have all my lands together with the tenements there on I herein give unto them as aforesaid.

3rd I give unto my two sons above named each one Thousand Dollars to be paid by my Executors here-in-after named to them out of any money belonging to my Estate.

4th I give unto my Grand Daughter (the daughter of my daughter Carolin King) Elmira C. King - Six Hundred Dollars to be paid by my executors to her according to Law.

5th It is my will that the remainder of my Estate at my death be divided equally among my children here-in-after named to wit Magdelane King wife of Jethro King Andrew Lewis Fumbanks, John Calvin Fumbanks and Martha Ann Cobb wife of Jacob Cobb - After paying my Funeral expenses and debts out of the said remainder of my Estate.

6th I do hereby nominate and appoint my two Sons Andrew Lewis Fumbanks and John C. Fumbanks my Executors

In witness whereof I do to this my will set my hand and seal, this the 17th day of March A. D. 1863
                              his
                Suffield   X   Fumbanks (seal)
                              mark.

The foregoing will signed sealed and published in our presence, and we have Subscribed (P.113) our names hereto in the presence, and at the request of the Testator - This 17th day of March 1863.
                Christian S. Cobb
                Edward H. White
                Joseph H. Moore
                    Witnesses

State of Tennessee) April Term 1863
Dyer County Court)
            This day a paper writing purporting to be the last will and testament of Suffield Fumbanks Dec'd

(54)

(P.113 Cont'd) late a citizen of Dyer County was produced here in open court, and proved according to Law by the oaths of Christian S. Cobb and Edward H. White Subscribing witnesses thereto, to be as it purports to be the last Will and Testament of said Suffield Fumbanks Deceased. It is therefore ordered by the court that the same be set up and established as the last will and Testament of the said Suffield Fumbanks Deceased, and that the same be recorded and filed by the clerk.

Attest   Stephen D. Whitten Clerk.

(P.114)

| Last Will & Testament of Alfred P. O'Neil Dec'd Proven & Established at the January & April Term of the of the County Court of Dyer County 1863 | State of Tennessee Dyer County. |

I, Alfred P. O'Neil do make and publish this as my last will and Testament, hereby revoking and making void all other wills by me at any time made

First - I direct that my Funeral expenses and all my debts be paid as soon as possible after my death out of any money that I may die possessed of or may first come into the hands of my Executor.

Secondly - I give and bequeath to my dear wife Margaret O'Neil all of the tract of Land that I now live on consisting of One hundred and Twenty four acres during her natural life to-gether with the appurtenances thereto belonging - and all of the household furniture and the stock and the crop on the place at my death, and Farming utensils, and one wagon, and our Bororeche, and, -

Thirdly - After the death of my wife that the above described Tract of Land I will to be divided equeally between my bodily heirs and -

Fourthly - That all my negro property and notes that I may be possessed of or money at my death I will that to be equally divided between my dear wife and my bodily heirs and -

Lastly - That I do hereby nominate and appoint Henry W. O'Neil my Executor of my last will and Testament and also guardian for my children.

In Witness whereof I do th this my will set my hand and seal this November the 27th 1863

                                          A. P. O Neil (seal)

Signed, sealed and published in our presence and we have subscribed our names hereto in the presence of the Testator - This November the Twnty seventh - One Thousand Eight hundred

(P.114 Cont'd) and Sixty two
Attest.
          John E. Bell
          F. Albritton

State of Tennessee) January Term 1863
Dyer County Court)

  This day a paper writing (P.115) purporting to be the Last Will and Testament of A. P. O'Neil Dec'd was produced here in open Court and proven in part to be as it purports the Last will and Testament of the said A. P. O'Neil Deceased by the oath of John E. Bell one of the subscribing witnesses there to

Attest   S. D. Whitten Clerk

State of Tennessee) April Term 1863.
Dyer County Court)

  On motion and it appearing to the Court that F. Albritton one of the subscribing witnesses to the Last Will and Testament of A. P. O'Neil deceased has removed beyond the limits of the State of Tennessee. Alexander B. Stallcup, William C. Vail and W. C. Doyle, after being first duly sworn deposed and said that they were acquainted with the hand writing of the said F. Albritton from having seen him write and being familiar with his writing and that they are satisfied that the signature to said will purporting to be his is genuine.

  It is there fore ordered by the court that said Paper Writing be set up and established as the Last will and Testament of A. P. O'Neil Deceased and that it be Recorded by the Clerk.

Attest   S. D. Whitton Clerk.

(P.116)
Last Will & Testament) In the Name of God - Amen
   of   (I Mary Edwards do make and
Mary Edwards Dec'd) publish this my last will and
Proven & Established at the(Testament hereby revoking &
June Term County Court 1863) making void all other wills
          by me made at any time.

First - I direct that my funeral expenses and all my just debts be paid as soon after my death as possible out of any monies or effects I may be possessed of or may first come into the hands of my Executor.

Secondly - I give and bequeath to my Son James W. Edwards all my land including the part my son Alva Edwards gave to me, making in all seventy eight acres and some poles over, also I bequeath to my son James aforesaid all of my personal property of every description.

Thirdly - Out of the effects of my estate or property here in bequeathed to my son James as afore said he is to pay as I

(P.116 Cont'd) bequeath to Mary Junina Edwards One Hundred and Ninety Dollars, and to each of my other children William G. Edwards, David K. Edwards, Elizabeth Ann Edwards and Elva Jane Ward to each Five Dollars.

Lastly - I nominate and appoint my son James Edwards my Executor to carry out this my last will and settle up my Estate I witness whereof I do to this my last will set my hand and seal

                her
        Mary X Edwards(seal)
                mark

Signed Sealed and published in our presence and we have subscribed Our names hereto in the presence of the testator - this 20th day of December A. D. 1862

                                          W. F. Nash
                                          T. J. Moore

State of Tennessee)   June Term 1863
Dyer County Court)

This day a paper writing purporting to be the last will and testament of Mary Edwards Dec'd late a citizen of Dyer County was produced in open Court and proved according to law by the oaths of W. F. Nash and S. F. Moore subscribing witnesses thereto, to be as it purports to be the last will and Testament of Mary Edwards Deceased - It is therefore ordered that the same be set up and established (P.117) as the last will and Testament of Mary Edwards Dec'd and that the same be recorded and filed

Attest   Stephen D. Whitten Clerk

Last Will & Testament   ) In the Name of Almighty God
        of   (Amen.
Joseph Ellis Dec'd   )
Proven and Established at the(I Joseph W. Ellis of the
June Term County Court 1863) County of Dyer and State of
                                      Tennessee being of sound body and mind but concious of the uncertainty of life and the certainty of death do make and publish this my last will and testament hereby revoking all others heretofore made by me That is to say.

Item 1st At my death I wish my Body to be decently buried, and all of my debts discharged as soon as possible by my Executor heretofore to be appointed

2nd I give and bequeath unto my beloved wife the one third in value of all my real estate including the House wherein I now live. I also give and bequeath to her an equal share of my personal property to be divided between her and my children hereinafter named. The Real Estate She is to hold for and during her natural life and then the same is to be disposed of as I may hereinafter direct.

(P.117 Cont'd)
Item 2nd I give and bequeath unto, my children Nancy Ellis, Almedia Ellis, Margarett Eveline Ellis, Charlotte Greene Ellis, Richard Ethalary Ellis, Mandy P. Ellis, William W. Ellis, George Washington Ellis, all of my property both real and personal to be divided between them as soon after my death as practiceable my children to whom shall be alloted the land in which my wife has a dower interest shall take possession of the same on her death,

To my children David T. Ellis Martha A. Seals; William H. Ellis and Francis J. Ellis I give and bequeath the sum of One Dollar each, they having failed to discharge the duties of children to a parent.

I hereby nominate and appoint Charles H. Ledsinger Executor of this my last will and Testament.

In Testimony whereof I have hereunto set my hand and affixed my seal the 30th day of November 1861

                    his
Joseph W. X Ellis (seal)
                    mark

Signed sealed and acknowledged in our (P.118) presence and in the presence of the Testator and of eachother Nov. 30th 1861

A. G. Pierce)
D. P. Pierce)

State of Tennessee)   June Term 1863
Dyer County Court)
                    This day a paper writing purporting to be the last will and testament of Joseph W. Ellis Dec'd was produced in open court and duly proven according to Law to be as it purports to be the last will & Testament of Joseph W. Ellis Dec'd by the oaths of David P. Pierce and Albert G. Pierce subscribing witnesses thereto.

It is therefore ordered by the court that the same be set up and established as the last will and Testament of Joseph W. Ellis dec'd and that the same be recorded and filed by the Clerk.

Attest   S. D. Whitton clerk.
                                                 of Dyer County Court.

(P.119)
Last Will & Testament   ) I Henry Cherry have
        of   (this day made and
Henry Cherry Dec'd   ) published this my
Proven and Established at   (Last will and Testa-
the July Term of Dyer County Court 1863) ment - revoking all
                                                                others heretofore by
me made, in manner following viz -

First - I commit my soul to God who gave it, and my Body to be

(P.119 Cont'd) decently buried and my burial expenses, to be paid out of any money that may first come to the hands of my Executor.

Second, I give and bequeath to my beloved wife A. M. F. Cherry our Bay Mare and one Mule Colt and one Black Horse 3 years old this Spring one years provision for herself and family, and all the property she had and possessed at the time she and myself were married - and one Cow & Calf.

Thirdly - I want all the balance of my property to be sold and the proceeds thereof together with all my notes, say one on J. H. Moss & E. G. Stallings for between 6 & $700 - and one on William Singleton for about $11.00 equally divided between my wife A. M. F. Cherry and my Five children say R. A. Cherry, E. S. Cherry A E Cherry, G. W. Cherry & D H Cherry

Fourthly - and Lastly I do hereby nominate and appoint J. S. Fanner to execute this my last will and Testament. This the First day of June 1863.

```
Signed Sealed and published   )              his
in our presence, and we have set(   Henry   X   Cherry (seal)
our names hereunto in presence )            mark
of the Testator               )
W. B. Stallings
Henry Jones
```

State of Tennessee)   July Term 1863
Dyer County Court)
    This day a paper writing purporting to be the last will and Testament of Henry Cherry Dec'd late a Citizen of Dyer County was produced in open Court and proved according to law by the oaths of W. B. Stallings and Henry Jones Subscribing witnesses thereto to be as it purports to be the last will and testament of said Henry Cherry Dec'd It is therefore ordered by the court that the same be set up and established as the last will & Testament of said Henry Cherry Dec'd and that the same be recorded and filed by the clerk

Attest   Stephen D. Whitton clerk.
                                        of Dyer County Court.

(P.120)
Last Will & Testament   ) In the Name of God. Amen.
    of   (
Alexander McCulloch Dec'd)   I Alexander McCulloch of
Proven & established at the(the County of Dyer & state of
Sept. Term 1846 of Dyer   ) Tennessee viewing the uncertain-
County Court -   ) ty of life & the certainty of
                                   death and being of sound mind
and memory do make and ordain this to be my last will & Testament, hereby revoking all other wills heretofore by me made - My will and desire is that my Body shall be buried in a plain & decent manner & my Soul return to God who gave it -

(P.120 Cont'd) With regard to my worldly affairs I hereby will & bequeath unto my beloved wife Francis F. McCulloch my negroes, Lucy a woman aged about Fifty years Kate, a woman aged about Eighteen years & her child 18 months old & Ned a Boy aged about Ten years

It is further my desire that all my Real Estate shall be sold as soon after my death as practicable, and all of my stock of every description, and after the payment of all my just debts, I wish my son James McCulloch & my son-in-law Nathaniel Burton to move me beloved wife to the State of Texas & to purchase a small tract of land out of any money that my property may be sold for, the tract of land to be purchased in Texas to contain Two Hundred acres or there abouts upon which to settle my beloved wife, And at the death of my wife Francis, my will and desire is that my son James shall have the land hereby directed to be purchased in Texas. I further will and bequeath at the death of my beloved wife Francis, my will and desire is that my son James shall have the land hereby directed to be purchased in Texas. I further will and bequeath at the death of my beloved wife that all my property money & Negroes shall be equally divided between my son James McCulloch & my two Grand sons Benjamin Estice Benton & Alexander McCulloch Pierce share and share alike except Five Hundred Dollars which I hereby give & bequeath to my daughter Elizabeth Tarrant wife of Robert Tarrant which is to be paid so soon as my Executors may be able to make sales of property & collect the same after the death of my beloved wife.

I have given to my Daughter Mary Ann (P.121) wife of - William L. Mitchell her portion of my Estate, I therefore give her no more - I have also advanced to my Daughter Sarah M. S. Cribble in her lifetime. I therefore give nothing unto her heirs - Alexander, John A, Benjamin & Henry Estice McCulloch: an all men & able to provide for themselves. I therefore give them no more - than what they have allready received.

Alexander McCulloch Pierce, as provided for above is the oldest son of my Daughter Adelade Pierce wife of Albert G. Pierce.

I hereby nominate & appoint my beloved wife Francis F. McCulloch, James C. McCulloch & Nathaniel Benton my Executors & Executrix, with full power & authority to carry out & execute this my last will & Testament.

In Testimony whereof I have hereunto set my hand & seal this 14th day of July A. D. 1846.

In presence of us   Alex McCulloch (seal)
J. H. Doyle
A. Benton

Recorded in my office Sept. 17th 1846

                                         J. H. Doyle Clerk

(P.121 Cont'd)

The foregoing will was ordered to be again Recorded by the County Court of Dyer County Term at the July term 1863

Attest   S. D. Whitton Clerk.

(P.122)

| Last Will & Testament of William R. Prichard dec'd Proven & Established at the December Term 1863 of Dyer County Court | In the Name of God Amen   I William R. Prichard of the County of Dyer and State of Tennessee being sound in mind and memory |

but in low state of health do make and ordain this my last will and testament, in manner and form as follows. <u>To wit</u> First - I recomend my Soul to God who gave it, and my body to the earth to be intered in a Christian like manner.

Secondly - After all my just debts and burial expenses are paid I give all my Estate both personal & Real to my beloved wife Sarah A. Prichard during her life or so long as she remains in her widowhood - and if she should marry then and in such case, I wish such property above mentioned to be equally divided between her my wife Sarah Ann and my two children, namely Louisa A. Prichard and Mary F. Prichard.

    In witness whereof I have set my hand and seal, I do also nominate and appoint Jas Prichard Executor of this my last will and Testament.

Signed and delivered in the presence of us.

December the 1st day 1863

George W. Prichard)   Wm. R. Prichard (seal)
Thomas J. Finch   )

State of Tennessee)   December Term 1863
Dyer County Court)

    This day a paperwriting purporting to be the last will and Testament of William R. Prichard Dec'd was produced here in open court and duly proven by the oaths of George W. Prichard and Thos. J. Finch Subscribing witnesses thereto to be as it purports the Last will and Testament of William R. Prichard Dec'd

    It is therefore ordered by the Court that said paper writing be set up and established as the last will and Testament of said deceased and that the same be recorded by the Clerk.

Attest   S. D. Whitten Clerk,
                                                               of Dyer County Court.

(P.123)
Last Will & Testament of Redding William Dec'd
Proven and Set up at the Feby & March Terms 1864 of Dyer County

I Redding Williams do make and publish this my last will and Testament hereby revoking and making void all other wills by me at any time made.

First - I direct that my Funeral expenses and all my debts be paid as soon after my death as possible out of any monies I may die possessed of or that may first come into the hands of my executor.

Secondly. I direct that at my death my heirs Maneza Moore Drusilla Bettis, Nancy Leggett, Celia Williams James William Mary Vandergriff Emily Williiams, and my grand Son Joseph T. Reddick Select Five disinterested persons to value my Tract of Land containing Seventy five acres, and that my Son-in-law G. W. Bettis take the land at whatever it may be valued at paying to each of the above mentioned heirs their proportionate part of the money the land may be valued at. At the expiration of two years after my death.

I give and bequeath to Celia Williams Jas Williams Emily Williams, One Bed and furniture, my other heirs all having had the same.

I also give and bequeath to Celia, and Emily Williams our Cow and calf. Two Hundred and fifty pounds of Pork and Five Barrells of Corn each. And my present crop of cotton, I give and bequeath to Amanda Williams wife of Calvin Williams Dec'd Five Dollars her husband Calvin Williams having already had his proportional share of my property. I give and bequeath to Walter Williams Son of Calvin and Amanda Williams Five Dollars

And whatever balance is remaining after paying my debts to be equally divided between Maneza Moore Drusilla Bettes, Nancy Legget, Celia Williams Jas Williams Mary Vandergriff and Emily Williams, and Joseph T. Reddick, Son of Delphia Reddick Dec'd, I do hereby nominate and appoint my son-in-law G. W. Bettis my Executor to this my last will and Testament. In witness whereof I do to this my last will set my hand and seal This Dec 19th 1863

Redding Williams

Signed Sealed and published in our (P.124) presence and we have subscribed our names in the presence of the Testator. This December 19th 1863

J. A. Nunn
J. B. Parker

State of Tennessee) February Term 1864
Dyer County Term)
    This day a paper writing purporting to be

(P.124 Cont'd) the last will and testament of Redding Williams Dec'd was produced in open Court and duly proven in part by the oath of James B. Parker one of the Subscribing witnesses thereto to be as it purports to be the last will and testament of Redding Williams Dec'd

March Term 1864

This day a paper writing purporting to be the last will and testament of Redding Williams Dec'd was produced here in open court and duly proven by the oath of Isaac A. Nunn, One of the Subscribing witnesses thereto It is therefore ordered by the court that said Paper writing be set up and established as the last will and testament of Redding Williams Dec'd and that the same be recorded by the Clerk.

Attest   S. D. Whitten Clerk.

(P.125)

Last Will and Testament of Susannah W. Fielder
Proven and established at the April term of Dyer County Court 1864

In the Name of God, Amen.
I Susannah W. Fielder of the County of Dyer and State of Tennessee being of sound mind and disposing memory but calling to recolection that it is appointed unto man once to die, do therefore make and ordain and publish this to be my last will and testament in manner and form following. That is to say my Body I commit to the Earth to be buried in decent Christian like manner my soul I commit to God who gave it. After paying all my just debts and my funeral expenses it is my will and desire that the remainder of my entire estate real and personal or the effects thereof be divided into seven shares and distributed as follows My Son William P. S. Fielder being dead it is my will and desire that his bodily heirs or his children have set apart one Seventh to them their heirs and assigns. To my Son Alfred F. Fielder his heirs and assigns. I give one seventh to my Daughter Mary E. Coffman being dead it is my will and desire that her bodily heirs or her children have set apart one Seventh to them theirs heirs and assigns.   To my Daughter Sarah A. York her heirs and assigns, I give one seventh My Daughter Francis A. Coop being dead and leaving but one child whose name is William A. H. Coop it is my will that one Seventh be set apart for him and his bodily heirs, and if he should die without any bodily heirs then it is my will and desire that the share set apart for him shall be equally divided into six shares and given to my children or their represenatives as heretofore and hereafter named and set forth To my son John R. Fielder his heirs and assigns I give one Seventh Tom my son Benjamine T. Fielder his heirs and assigns I give One Seventh And I appoint Alfred T. Fielder and Benjamine T. Fielder my Executors to carry out this my last will and Testament

In witness whereof I have hereunto set my hand and seal This 30th day of May 1859   Susannah W. Fielder (seal)
In presence of G. S. Rice   J. B. Powell

(63)

(P.125 Cont'd
State of Tennessee)   April Term 1864
Dyer County Court)

        This day a paper writing (P.126) purporting to be the last will and testament of Susan W. Fielder Dec'd was presented here in open Court and duly proven by the oath of James B. Powell one of the subscribing witnesses thereto to be as it purports the last will and testament of Susannah W. Fielder Dec'd It is therefore ordered by the Court that said Paper writing be set up and established as the last will and testament of Susannah W. Fielder Dec'd

Attest   S. D. Whitten Clerk.

Last Will & Testament) I John W. Rogers being
of (of sound mind and memo-
John W. Rogers Dec'd) ry do make and publish
Proven and established at the (this my last will and
April Term of Dyer County Court 1864) Testament Believing that
                                                          the Laws of the State
of Tennessee make a proper and equitable distribution of property - it is my will that my property real and personal, after the payment of my just debts and funeral expenses Should be distributed in exact accordance with said Laws of said State, exactly as if I had not made this will but reserving to myself the right to say who shall manage my Estate under said Laws, I do hereby nominate and appoint my well beloved wife Sarah Jane Rogers Executrix of this my last will and Testament and that she shall enter upon and discharge the duties of Executrix without giving bond or security as usually required by Law.

        In testimony whereof I have hereunto Set my hand and seal this 10th day of March 1864

                                    John W. Rogers (seal)

State of Tennessee)   April Term 1864
Dyer County Court)

        This day a paper writing purporting to be the last will and Testament of John W. Rogers Dec'd was produced here in open Court and duly proven by the oaths of James N. Todd and Saml R. Latta Subscribing witnesses thereto, to be as it purports the last will and Testament of John W. Rogers Dec'd. It is therefore ordered that said Paper (P.127) writing be set up and established as the last will and testament of said John W. Rogers Dec'd and that the same be recorded.

Attest   S. D. Whitten Clerk.

Last Will & Testament) Know all men by these
of (presents that I, A. M.
A. M. Barnett Dec'd) Barnett in view of the
Proven and established at the (great fact, that it is
June Term 1864 of Dyer County Court) appointed unto man to
                                                          die and in view of the
uncertainty of human events, have on this the 19th day of

(P.127 Cont'd   May A. D. 1864
Made this my last will and Testament - as follows,

First - I will my soul to God who gave it feeling grateful for the many blessings which have followed me all along lifes troubled way.

Secondly - I will that I shall be decently buried and the expenses thereof immediately paid out of the surplus means which I shall have for such and other purposes.

Furthermore - I will to the child of my Deceased son, Three Hundred Dollars which is now due from the Estate of my son to me. I also will to the Estate of child of my son John Barnett Twenty five Dollars to be paid out of my Estate - My reason for leaving no more to my deceased son or his child is that he has been raised up to manhood and that I have heretofore given to him what I thought to be right, with a Knowledge that I leave my wife in delicate health and but little able to labour for support with two children to educate and raise

All the balance of my estate including lands tenements &c &c stock of every kind with my notes and accounts, I will to my beloved wife Caroline and her two Children Finis and Charles.

I will whatever money I may have on hand at my decease shall be left in the hands of my wife Caroline for the benefit of herself & children.

I hereby appoint Albert G. Ferguson to execute this my last will and Testament it being the only valid will which I have and rendering null and void all similar wills which may claim to have eminated from me.

(P.128) I will and direct that my debts be paid out of my notes and accounts & Surplus money, and all my notes and accounts be left in the hands of my wife as her individual property to be collected by her as such. and used according to the direction of her own judgement.

Furthermore - I leave with my wife Caroline the privilege of hereafter selecting and making choice between the place on which I am living at the date of this will and my residence near Dyersburg as her future home

In presence of witnesses I subscribed to all the foregoing will with sound mind fully capable of executing mentally this Indenture for the future disposal of my temporal affairs

Witness
P. C. Walker
J. H. Cooper

A. M. Barnett (seal

State of Tennessee)   June Term 1864.
Dyer County Court)
This day a paper writing purporting to be the last will and testament of A. M. Barnett Dec'd was

(P.128) produced here in open court and duly proven by the oaths of Dr. P. C. Walker and James H. Cooper subscribing witnesses thereto to be as it purpots the last will and testament of A. M. Barnett Dec'd.

It is therefore ordered by the court that said paper writing be set up and established as the last will and testament of A. M. Barnett Dec'd and that the same be recorded by the Clerk.

Attest   S. D. Whitten Clerk

(P.129)
Last Will & Testament)   I Stephen B. Akin do
        of   (make and publish as my
Stephen B. Akin Dec'd   ) last will and Testament
Proven and established at the   (hereby revoking and making void all other wills
July Term 1864 of Dyer County Court) by me at anytime made.

First - I direct that my funeral expenses and all my debts be paid as soon after my death as possible out of any money that I may die possessed or may first come into the hands of my Executor.

Secondly - I give and bequeath to my wife Cathrine A. Akin all my property both personal and real during her natural life or widowhood - then to be equally divided among all my children.

Thirdly - It is my will and wish that each of my sons shall have the privilege of raising and Keeping a horse apiece.

Fourthly - It is my will and wish if my wife Catharine Ann Akin should die before my two youngest sons become large enough to support themselves, that they have a reasonable allowance made to support them and school them.

Fifthly, It is my will and wish that there be no public Sale of any of my property by my executor -

Lastly - I nominate and appoint my son Abner A. Akin my Executor. In witness whereof I do to this my set my hand and seal - this April 11th 1863

S. W. Archibald
T. H. Akin   S. D. Akin (seal)

State of Tennessee)   July Term 1864
Dyer County Court)
                      This day a paper writing purporting to be the last will and Testament of Stephen B. Akin was produced here in Open court and the execution thereof duly proven by the oaths of S. W. Archibald and Thos. H. Akin subscribing witnesses thereto to be as it purports the last will and testament of Stephen B. Akin Dec'd.

It is therefore ordered by the court that the same be

(P.129 Cont'd) set up and established as said last will aforesaid and that the same be recorded and filed by the Clerk.

Attest   S. D. Whitten Clerk.

(P.130)

Last Will & Testament of George W. Cocke dec'd Proven and set up at the August & September Term 1865 of Dyer County Court	July 16th 1859 I George W. Cocke considering the uncertainty of human life and wishing to dispose of all the property that I now have which I do in the following manner.

    I loan to my wife Mary Ann R. Cocke all my part of the tract of land whereon I now live for and during her natural life and the following slaves Jack Teneb Emmily Mary & her child Nanni & Betty and One half of my stock of every description plantation tools household and Kitchen furniture at her death to go to my Son Alonzo Cocke and to his heirs forever I also give to my son A. Cocke one negro man named Charles and the residue of my estate I do constitute and appoint my son Alonzo Cocke as my only executor this Sixteenth day of July 1859 witness my hand and seal

Attest   George W. Cocke
J. E. Bell
F. J. Cocke

State of Tennessee)   August Term 1865
Dyer County Court)

    This day a paper writing purporting to be the last will and testament of George W. Cocke dec'd was presented here in open Court and was duly proven in part by the oath of J. E. Bell one of the subscribing witnesses thereto to be as it purports the last will and Testament of George W. Cocke deceased and it is ordered that it stand over <u>untill proven</u> by the other subscribing witness thereto

State of Tennessee)   September Term 1865
Dyer County Court (

    On motion and it to the Court that F. J. Cocke one of the subscribing witnesses to the last will and testament (P.131) of George W. Cocke dec'd being dead - John Irvin and R. J. Davis after being first <u>duly</u> sworn deposed and said that they were acquainted with the hand writing of the said George W. Cocke from having seen him write and being familiar with his writing and that they are satisfied that the signature to said <u>will</u> purporting to be his is genuine - It is therefore ordered by the Court that said paper writing be set up and established as the Last will and testament of George W. Cocke deceased and that it be recorded by the Clerk

(67)

(P.131 Cont'd)
Last Will and Testament) State of Tennessee
of (Dyer County Court
F. M. Howe dec'd) September Term 1865
Proven and set up at the (
September 1865 Dyer County Court) This day a paper writing
purporting to be the last
will and testament of F. M. Howe was produced here in open
court and Andrew Hart and Allen Finley the Su Subscribing
witnesses thereto came here into open court and being duly
Sworn depose and say that they were personally acquainted
with said testator that he signed and published said paper
writing in their presence as his will and requested them especially to witness the same and that they did subscribe the
same in his presence and in the presence of each other and
that said testator is dead It is therefore Ordered that
said paper writing be set up and established as the last will
and testament of F. M. Howe dec'd and be recorded

(P.132)
Last Will and Testament) Know all men by these
of (
Milly Privitt - dec'd) I Milley Privitt being in
Proven & Set up at the (my Propper mind make this my
October Term County Court) last will and testament and appoint William Marchant to carry
Recorded Oct. 4, 1865)
into effect it's provisions without being required to give Security in the provision

TO WIT
Whereas I am entitled to an amount not
Known by me Father David Baileys estate of __ County, North
Carolina and Judal Goddin his adminstrator and designing to
give all or a part of the said means to my Grand Daughter Mary
Ann Privitt I hereby will and bequeath to her after my death
five hundred dollars ($500) of said legacy which shall by
Wm. Marchant be received and held for her until she married
or becomes of age and on her marriage it shall by said Marchant
be invested for the benefit her and her issue and not to be
subject to the debts of her husband but it remains Solely for
her and her children if any She may have. And to be invested
at the direction of Wm. Marchant given under my hand & seal
this __ day July 1859

Milley Privitt (Seal)

Witnesses)
David M. Craig)
Edwin Ferrell)

State of Tennessee) October Term 1865
Dyer County)
On motion and it appearing __ the Court
that Edwin Ferrell one of the subscribing witnesses to the
last will and testament of Milley (P.133) Privitt deceased
has removed beyond the limits of the State of Tennessee W. G.
Normont & D. M. Craig after first being duly sworn deposed &

(P.133 Cont'd) said that they were acquainted with the hand writing of the said Edwin Ferrell from having seen him write and being familiar with writing and that they are Satisfied that the signature to said will is genuine and that D. M. Craig One of the witnesses to the last will and testament of Milley Privett Dec'd being first duly sworn deposed & said Milley Privitt signed & acknowledged the same in his presence and requested him to witness the same It is therefore ordered by the court that said paper writing be set up and established as the last will and Testament of Milley Privitt Dcd and that it be recorded by the clerk.

Attest   T. H. Benton   Clerk.

Last will and Testament) In the Name of God Amen
of G. R. Gooch dec'd Proven (
and set up November Term 1865)   I G. R. Gooch of the
Dyer County Court   (county of Dyer & State of
Recorded 15 Novmeber 1865   ) Tennessee being of Sound
                                   mind and disposing Memory
and being sensible impressed of the uncertainty of life and the certainty of death do make and publish this my last will and testament hereby revoking all others heretofore made by me (if any) Item 1st - It is my will and desire that as soon after my death as possible all my property both real and personal be sold and my Executor can sell the same either for cash or a credit either privately or publicly as he may think most advantageous to my estate and all my just debts and funeral epenses paid - Item 2nd I give and bequeath to my Daughter Sarah J. Gooch One thousand dollars ($1000.00) including in the amount Three Hundred (P.134) and twenty Six Dollars in gold now on hand and direct that as soon after my death as the Same can be done that my Executor take said money and also my said Daughter Sarah J. Gooch to the State of North Carolina and leave her with my Daughter Eliza Edwards that Edward Edwards my son-in-law be requested to act as her Guardian and after his appoinment and qualification then my said Executor is to leave said money with him as her Guardian for her use and benefit - All the expenses in going to returning from and taking my said daughter to North Carolina or that are necessarily incurred in the premesis are to be deducted out of the balance of the estate it being my intent that she have that amount including Said gold placed in her guardians hands in North Carolina but the Six hundred and Seventy four dollars can be paid in current bank notes Item 3rd - The balance of my estate I desire to be equally divided amongst my beloved wife Nancy Gooch and the balance of my children and grand child of my deceased Son share and share alike excluding the said S. J. Gooch from any part thereof the One Thousand dollars given to her in item 2nd being all that I intend for her to have out of my estate - The Grand child aforesaid is to have equal share that its father would be entitled to if living

Item 4th I do hereby appoint W. C. Gooch my Son my Executor to carry out the powers herein granted. Witness my hand and seal this the 9th day of October A. D. 1865 done in our presence and

(P.134 Cont'd) we in the presence of eachother and we witness
the same at the special)
instance and request of)
the testator   )   his
Jesse Clark   )   G. R.X Gooch   (seal)
J. F. Child   )   mark
C. C. Moss.   )

(P.135)
State of Tennessee)   November Term 1865
County of Dyer   )
   This day a paper writing purporting to
be the last will and testament of G. R. Gooch dec'd late a
citizen of Dyer County was produced here in open Court and
proved according to law by the Oaths of J. F. Childs Jesse
Clark and Charles C. Moss Subscribing witnesses thereto to be
as it purports to be the last will and testament of said G. R.
Gooch deceased It is therefore order by the court that the
same be set up and established as the last will and testament
of the said G. R. Gooch deceased, and that the same be recorded
and filed by the Clerk

Attest   Thos H. Benton clerk.

Last will and testament)   In the Name of God Amen
of Henry Fowlkes dec'd   (I Henry Fowlkes of Dyer County
proven and Set up   )   State of Tennessee being well
November Term 1865   (Stricken in years but of sound
Dyer County Court   )   and of disposing mind and memory –
Recorded 15 November 1865)   Thank God knowing that it is ap-
                             pointed unto all men once to die
do make and publish this my last will and testament hereby
revoking all others in manner and form following that is to
say

 Item first – it is my desire and direction that all my
just debts be paid as soon as practicable after my death Item
2nd I give and bequeath unto my son George A. Fowlkes at my
death and that of my wife the tract of land on which I now live
containing about Three hundred acres the balance of the Hale
tract also another tract of 205 acres Known as part of the
(P.136) Benton tract purchased by me lying west of my home
place and also one other tract of land of two hundred thirteen
and a half acres deeded to me by S. C. Brown by her attorney
James C. Rogers containing in all Seven hundred and eighteen
and a half acres – with the tenements and appurtenances thereunto belonging to have and to hold the same to him and his
heirs forever – Item 3rd I give and bequeath to my two Grand
children Emily A. Pursell and Henry Thomas Pursell lawful children of my daughter Rebecca those two tracts or parcels of
land containing in all 541¾ acres and Known as the Williams
tract and the balance of the tract purchased by me of Benton
it being the balance of my real estate not bequeathed to my
son George A. Fowlkes with the tenements and appurtenences
thereunto belonging to have and to hold the same to them and
their heirs forever – At my death and that of my wife –

(P.136) Item 4 It is my wish that should my wife survive me that all my property both real and personal - remain in her posession during her natural life and at her death all my estate excepting that bequeathed in the foregoing part of this my last will and testament to my Son George A. Fowlkes and 2 grandchildren Emily A. Pursell and Henry Thomas Pursell to be equally divided among all of my heirs share and share alike Lastly I hereby nominate and appoint my two sons H. L. Fowlkes & Asa Fowlkes Executors and my wife Nancy Fowlkes Executrix of this my last will and testament witness my hand seal this the 29 day of July 1857

Signed sealed and published in presence of us who have subscribed the same in the presence of the testator and of each other
(P.157)
July 29 1857   )
D. J. Williamson (Henry Fowlkes (seal)
J. S. McDavid   )

State of Tennessee) This day a paper writing purporting to
County of Dyer   ) be the last will and testament of Henry
                     Fowlkes dec'd late citizen of Dyer
County was produced here in open court and the two Subscribing witness thereto being dead - the hand writing of Said Subscribing witnesses thereto was duly proven by the Oaths of R. H. McGaughey C. C. Moss F. G. Sampson who after being first duly Sworn Say that the signatures of D. J. Williamson and John S. McDavid as witnesses to said will was executed by them - that they have often seen them write and being familiar with their handwriting - and that the signature of Henry Fowlkes to Said Will was proven by the oaths of C. C. Moss & A. G Pierce who after being first duly sworn said that they believéd it to be his signature from having seen him write and being familiar with his handwriting It is therefore ordered by the court that the same be set up and established as the last will and testament of the said Henry Fowlkes deceased and that the same be recorded and filed by the clerk   Attest

                                          T. H. Benton clerk.

Last will and Testament   ) March 26 1862
of Abraham Canada dec'd   (State of Tennessee Dyer County.
proven and set up November) I A. Canada do leave all of my
Term 1865 Dyer County Court(property to Annie Canada the
Recorded 15 November   ) wife of said Canada the property
         1865   ) is as follows One hundred and
                              74½ acres of land horses hogs
and cattle and household Kitchen furniture and all claims in due me which said Annie Canada is to have the privilege doing what she pleases with until her death and then to my heirs Eliza Ann Canada
                                          his
Test W. B. Arnold   A   X   Canada
  his   mark
-I X Canada
   mark

(P.138)

State of Tennessee) This day a paper writing purporting to be
County of Dyer) the last will and testament of Abraham
Canada deceased late a citizen of Dyer
County was produced here in open Court and duly proved by the
oaths of Isaac Canada and William Arnold the two subscribing
witness thereto - to be as it purports to be the last will and
testament of Abraham Canada dec'd It is therefore ordered by
the court that the same be set up and established as the last
will and testament of the said Abraham Canada deceased And
that the same be recorded and filed by the clerk

Attest   F. H. Benton Clerk.

Last will and Testament)   State of Tennessee
of Daniel Hendricks   (Dyer County
proven and Set up   )
December Term 1865   (I Daniel Hendricks of the
Dyer County Court Recorded) county and State aforesaid being
29 December 1865   )   of sound mind & memory do this
                            the 14th day of April One thousand
eight hundred and fifty eight make ordain and publish this my
last will and testament in manner and form following viz:
first - I wish to be decently buried at the expense of my Estate -
2ndly I wish all of my just debts paid - 3rdly I will and bequeath to my son William R. Hendricks my plantations and tract
of land on which I live at the time of my wife Death it containing fifty five acres with all the appurtenances thereunto to
the use of Said William R. Hendricks his heirs and assigns forever - I further will and bequeath that there shall be eight
dollars set apart from the proceeds the sales of my perishable
property to be equally divided between my two daughters Ann
Trout and Elizabeth Fields - And I further will that my Son
William R. Hendricks receive forty Dollars from my estate - and
if there Should be anything (P.139) left that it shall be
equally divided between all of my children except Polly
Temperance Chaffin which I have gave them all I intend to give
them. I hereby make and appoint Unah C. Hendricks my Executor
to this my last will and testament Signed and Sealed the day
and date above written in the presence of

R. H. McNail
C. E. White   Daniel Hendricks (seal)

State of Tennessee) December Court 1865
Dyer County   )
         This day a paper writing purporting to
be the last will and testament of Daniel Hendricks deceased
was produced here in open court and duly proven by the oaths
of R. H. McNail & C. E. White the 2 Subscribing witnesses
thereto to be as it purports to be the last will and testament
of Daniel Hendricks deceased - It is therefore ordered by the
court that the same be set up and established as the last will
testament of the said Daniel Hendricks deceased that the same
be recorded by the clerk
Attest   T. H. Benton clerk
                                    Dyer County Court.

(P.139 Cont'd)

| The Last will and Testament of Archy Wilkins Proven and Set up August Term 1866 Dyer County Court Recorded Sept 8th 1866 | State of Tennessee Dyer County January 16th 1866 - I Archibald Wilkins being in bad health, but in my proper mind do make and publish this my last will and Testament hereby revoking and making void all other former wills |

made by me and after Commending my Soul to God who gave it my body to be decently but not extravagantly buried I dispose of my worldly goods as follows to wit - my land in the State of Ark. Columbia County it being (P.140) One thousand acres - I will and bequeath equally and jointly to the eight following heirs to wit N. P. Tatum William Sawyer Archibald S. Wilkins Malinda Wilkins George Spence Christina C. Wilkins Margaret A. Wilkins and the three children of Daughter Elizabeth Hart to come in as one heir and receive one eigth part as their mothers share

I also hold one note against S. P. Baker my agent in Arkansas given for one hundred and eighteen Dollars and 80 cents which I leave to the above named heirs for the purpose of paying any Tax other charges that may be against said land as to defray the expense of dividing said land - All my land in Tennessee Dyer County with all other property money notes accounts or ____ at Law of which I may die possessed after paying all my debts, I will and bequeath to my four following named children to wit - Josephine, Wm. Penn Emerson Etheridge and Lucy Bell equally and jointly but leave it to my wife during her life for the purpose of enabling her to raise and educate said four children - I furthermore make and nominate my wife Mary Wilkins Executrix to this my last will and testament, In witness whereof I have set up my name and fixed my seal this the day and date above written

Witnesses Joseph Barker &
Edmond Chitwood   Archibald Wilkins (seal)

State of Tennessee) County Court August Term 1866 - This
Dyer County   ) day a paper writing purporting to be
                     the last will and testament of Archibald
Wilkins deceased late a citizen of Dyer County was produced here in open court and proved according to Law by the oaths of Joseph Barker & Edmond Chitwood the two subscribing witnesses thereto to be as it purports to be the last will and testament of said Archibald Wilkins dec'd It is therefore ordered by the court that the same be set up and established as the last will and Testament of the said Archibald Wilkins and that the same be recorded and filed by the Clerk

Attest   F. H. Benton Clerk Dyer
                                              County court.

| (P.141) Last will an Testament of N. A. Whittenton dec'd Proven & set up August Term 1866 Recorded Sept. 10, 1866 | State of Tennessee Dyer County July 6th One thousand eight hundred and |

(P.141 Cont'd) Sixty Six I N. A. Whittenton of Dyer County fifth civil District of the State of Tennessee being of sound mind and memory and considering the uncertainty of this frail and Transitory life do therefore make ordain and publish and declare this to be my last will & Testament - That is to say first after all my lawful debts are paid and discharged the residue of my estate real and personal I give bequeath and dispose of as follows to wit. To my beloved wife the land and appertenances Situated thereon Known and described as the bluff Tract of land now owned by the Sd N. A. Whitten lying in Dyer County 5 civil District of Tennessee together will all of my stock consisting of horses cattle hogs sheep also the household and Kitchen furniture To have and to hold against all demands whatever during her life time or widowhood at the experation of sd time - what may yet remain is to be equally divided between my lawful heirs Share & share alike - Likewise I make constitute and appoint my wife E. M. Whittenton to be executor of this my last will & testament hereby revoking all former wills made by me - In witness whereof I have hereunto Subscribed my name and affixed my Seal the sixth day of July One thousand eight hundred & sixty six

                          N. A. Whittenton (seal)

The above written instrument was Subscribed by the said N. A. Whittenton in our presence and acknowledged by him to each of us and he at the same time published & declared the above instrument So Subscribed to be his last will & testament and we at the Testators request and in his presence have signed our names as witnesses hereto and written opposite our names

                          M. W. Baker (seal)
                          Thos. H. Johnson (seal)

(P.142)
State of Tennessee) County Court August Term 1866
County of Dyer   ) This day a paper writing purporting to be the last will and Testament of N. A. Whittenton dec'd late citizen of sd. county was produced before me and duly proven by the oaths of M. W. Baker & Thos. H. Johnson the two Subscribing witnesses thereto to be as it purports to be the last will & Testament of the said N. A. Whittenton dec'd It is therefore ordered by the court that the same be set up and established as the last will and testament of the said N. A. Whittenton dec'd and that the Same be recorded and filed by the clerk.

Attest   T. H. Benton   Clerk.
                                    Dyer County Court.

Last will and   ) State of Tennessee Dyer County
Testament of James D. Anderson (
dec'd proven & set up August) This the last will & testa-
& Sept. Court 1866 &   (ment of James D. Anderson after
Recorded 10 September 1866) my Death I do give and bequeath
                                             to my brother John E. Anderson

(P.142 Cont'd) all my interest in a certain tract of land the deed of which is drawn jointly to us also all notes & dues that are due to me and all money that I may die possessed of after paying all my just debts and burrying me decently - I also give and bequeath all to my brother John E. Anderson witness my hand and seal this the 16 day of July 1866 James D. Anderson (seal)
Test Andrew Hart & John Hicks

State of Tennessee) County Court August Term 1866
Dyer County)
        This day a paper writing purporting to be the last will and testament of James D. Anderson dec'd was produced in open court and duly proven in part by the oath of John Hicks one of the Subscribing witnesses thereto, to be as it purports to be the last will & testament of the Said James D. Anderson dec'd

(P.143)
September Term 1866
        This day a paper writing purporting to be the last will and testament of James D. Anderson dec'd was produced here in open court and duly proven by the Oath of Andrew Hart one of the Subscribing witnesses thereto. It is therefore ordered by the court that Said paper writing be set up and established as the last will and Testament of James E. Anderson dec'd and that the Same be Recorded & filed by the Clerk.

Attest   T. H. Benton Clerk.
                                                Dyer County Court.

Last will & testament) In the Name of God Amen,
of B. T. Blake dec'd (
Proven & set up September) I, B. T. Blake of Dyer County
Court 1866 & Recorded (& state of Tennessee being of
10th day of September 1866) sound mind & memory and considering the uncertainty of life do then make and declare this to be my last will & Testament That is to Say after all my legal debts are paid and discharged the residue of my estate real and personal I give bequeath & dispose of as follows to wit all letters and papers contained in my valise to burned without examination, my mare and colt Buggy & harness I give to Mrs. Martha Douglas, I give to my niece Miss. A. B. Hallet my Store House in Newbern Tennessee and my Library except my bible which I give to my brother Moses Blake I give to each of my name sakes viz - Benjamin the son of Moses Blake of E. T. Seay of Misses Hassel & of Graham Gillespie One hundred dollars to be held in trust by their respective fathers or guardians until said boys are eighteen years old and then Spent for a watch I give lands except the lots in Newbern to the Children of my deceased Sister Mary my Clothes I leave to Guy Douglas to be used or given away as he may see fit (they are not to be sold.) The remainder of my property I leave & give to my Sister Lucy Hallit & my brother Moses (P.144) Blake to be divided equally between them I also make consitute &

(P.144 Cont'd) appoint Smith Parks to be executor of this my last will & Testament hereby revoking all others by me made In witness whereof I have hereunto Subscribed my name and affixed my seal this the 16 day of July One Thousand eight hundred & Sixty three.

Acknowledged in presence of
G. B. Tinsley
W. H. Hampton

B. T. Blake (seal)

Codicil

I B. T. Blake being of Sound mind and disposing memory do hereby revoke the appointment of Smith Parks as Executor of this my last will & Testament and in his Stead do appoint my true and tried friends Guy Douglas and Will M. Watkins to execute this my will - with full power and authority to carry out and perform all the duties of Executors and to enforce the provisions in the body of this will Set forth I direct that my Dark bay mare and One of my colts to be given to Mrs. Guy Douglas as a Slight Testimonial of my regard of her - I also direct that my Buggy and my other Colt be given to Mrs. A. B. Morris both these last bequest to be free gifts to Mrs. Douglas & Mrs. Morris

In testimony whereof I, have hereunto Set my hand and seal this 25 day of August 1866

Signed sealed and
published in our
presence and we
were personally
requested by
the Testator to witness the same and have hereunto Signed our names in the presence of the Testator and in the presence of eachother   R. H. McGaughey
John S. Keffington
W. C. Doyle
J. F. Child.

(P.145)
State of Tennessee) This day a paper writing purporting to
Dyer County   ) be the last will and testament of B. T. Blake late citizen of Dyer County dec'd was produced here in open court and duly proven by the oaths of R. H. M. Gaughey W. C. Doyle & John S. Keffington to be as it purports to be the last will & testament of the Said B. T. Blake dec'd - It is therefore Ordered by the court that the Same be Set up and established as the last will and Testament of Said Blake and that the Same be recorded and filed by the CClerk

Attest

T. H. Benton   Clerk
Dyer County Court

(P.145 Cont'd)

Last will & Testament) In the Name of God Amen
       of   (I <u>Burrell</u> Robinson of the county of
Burril <u>Robertson</u>   ) Dyer & State of Tennessee being of
Proven and Established(Sound mind and memory, and consider-
at the January Term   ) ing the uncertainty of this frail
1863 Dyer County Court) and Transitory life, do therefore
                                make Ordain and publish and declare
this to be my last will and testament   That is to say

First after all my lawful debts are paid and discharged the
residue of my estate, the interest which I hold in the tract
of land as bequeathed to me by my father Burril Robinson deceased I give bequeath and dispose of as follows, To my beloved
Sister Harriet M. Kinkead and Brother Stephen M. Robinson to
have and to hold and dispose of as they may think proper Likewise I make constitute and appoint James H. Nunn to be my Executor of this my last will and testament   In witness whereof
I have hereunto Subscribed my name and affixed my seal the 24
day of November One thousand eight hundred and Sixty Six

Test Harriet Rouse   his
    Robert <u>Kinked</u>   Burril X Robinson (seal)
                                                mark
            J. F. Perry
            J. W. Hassell

(P.146)
State of Tennessee) January Term 1867 Dyer Cty County
Dyer County   )
                      This day a paper writing purporting to
be the last will and testament of Burril Robinson dec'd was
produced here in open court and duly proven by the oaths of
J. F. Perry & J. W. Hassell the two subscribing witnesses
thereto to be as it purports to be the last will and testament of the said Burril Robinson dec'd. It is therefore
ordered by the court that the same be set up and established
as the last will and testament of said Robinson dec'd and
that the same be recorded by the clerk

Attest   T. H. Benton, Clerk

Last Will and testament) I, John Mills of Dyer County being
of John Mills dec'd   (of sound mind but weak in body health
Proven and established) do make this my last will and testa-
February term 1867   (ment.
Dyersburg Tenn.   )
                            First, I desire my just debts
paid out of my means on hand and coming and if any balance
be due then the remainder out of any of my personal property
my family can best spare.

Secondly: I desire my daughter Eliza Jane and the younger
childrenl live on my land and keep the rest of my property on
the place and till the land so raise and support them during
her life, but if she marries and leaves then my oldest son

(P.146 Cont'd)   will take of my means & children & support them.

Thirdly - When my youngest daughter marries or attains the age of twenty one years I desire my land sold by my Executors and the proceeds equally divided between all my children. I hereby appoint my friend John W. Wright my Executor of this will.

John W. Wright   John J. Mills
R. S. Crow.

State of Tennessee)   February Term 1867,
Dyer County   )   Dyer County Court.

This day a paper purporting to be the last will and testament of John Mills dec'd. was produced here in open Court and proven by the oaths of John W. Wright and R. S. Crow subscribing witnesses thereto to be as it purports to be the last will & testament of said Mills dec'd - it is therefore ordered by the court that the same be set up and established as the last will & testament of said Mills and the same be recorded by the clerk.

Attest   T. H. Benton Clk.

(P.147)
Last Will and Testament   )   In the Name of God Amen
        of   (I, Edward Bradshaw of Dyer
Edward Bradshaw   )   County, Tennessee do hereby
dec'd. Set up and established(make and publish this my last
Febry. Term 1867   )   will and Testament in manner
Dyer County   )   and form following, this is
                                 to say - It is my will and
desire that my mortal remains be decently buried and all my just debts paid as soon as practicable after my death out of the money I may leave at my death or that which shall first come into the hands of my Executors. Then it is my will and desire that my daughter Elizabeth S. Lacks shall have the use of the lease she now lives on (twelve acres) for the years 1867 & 1868 free of charge, Third, I give and bequeath to my youngest son Thomas E. Bradshaw one Sorrel horse already known as his one bed one trunk and one small table out of my estate and the residue of my estate real and personal I give and bequeath to my following named children and Grandchildren to be divided between them thus - to my children James E., John T., Samuel B. Thomas E., Elizabeth S. Lacks, Amanda R. Gauldin, Elvira C. Richmond, Mary F. Walker, Roberta W. Powell, and Clarissa A. Hall each one share, and to my granddaughter Zennyra F. Richmond one share and to my Grandsons Robert B. & Jessie E. Bradshaw one share jointly, - my daughter Lucinda Terry and my grandson William E. Garratt of Virginia have already received as much of my estate as I wish them to have and must have no more. Lastly I nominate and appoint my two sons James E. Bradshaw and John T. Bradshaw Executors of this my last will and testament and it is my will and desire that they execute this will without giving any bond. In testimony of all which I have here unto set my hand and seal hereby

(78)

(P.147 Cont'd) revoking and making void all former wills by me at any time heretofore made, this 24 day of December 1866.

```
Signed Sealed and published      )           his
in our presence who have subscribed (   Edward X Bradshaw
our names hereto at the request of  (           mark.
the Testator in his presence & in   )
the presence of each other Dec. 24th, 1866)
```

Elijah P. Kirk & J. M. Thompson

(P.148)

State of Tennessee) Febry Term county court 1867
Dyer County   )

    This day a paper writing purporting to be the last will and testament of Edward Bradshaw dec'd was produced here in open court and proven by the oath of E. P. Kirk one of the Subscribing witnesses thereto to be as it purports to be the last will and testament of Said Bradshaw dec'd It is therefore ordered by the court that the same be Set up and established as the last will and testament of said Edward Bradshaw dec'd and that the same be recorded by the Clerk.

Attest   T. H. Benton Clerk.

```
Last will and     )  State of Tennessee Dyer County
Testament of      (
Margaret E.       )  S, S, I Margaret E. Griffin in the full
Griffin dec'd     (  belief of the Existence of a God and the
Proven and Set up)  conviction that my illness will prove
March Term 1867   )  fatal desire to dispose of my goods and
Dyer County Court(   effects as follows viz  The one half of
                     the amount of money in the hands of my
```
Guardian I bequeath to my beloved brother Nympheas Reddick and Sisters Nancy Louisa Reddick Mary Etta Reddick and Ella Ora Reddick respectively the Same to be divided equally between the aforesaid persons To my beloved brother Nympheas Reddick I bequeath my new trunk to my Sister Nancy Louisa Reddick I bequeath my Saddle T my beloved mother Sarah E. Reddick I bequeath my rocking chair - To my beloved Grand mother I bequeath the remaining one half of my money in the hands of my Guardian: and also to her I bequeath my mare and colt It is my desire that all of my indebted that has or may hereafter occur Shall be paid out of the amount of money now in the hands of my Guardian before the aforesaid distribution shall have been made, and I further desire that my friend George W. Taylor be appointed Executor of this my last will and Testament In witness whereof I have hereunto affixed my mark and (P.149) placed my private Seal this the neneteenth day of August A. D. One thousand eight hundred and Sixty Six

```
                                              her
Attest W. W. Biggs                  Margaret  X  Griffin (seal)
       Mary Jane Echols                       mark
```

State of Tennessee) March Term County Court 1867
County of Dyer   ) This day a paper writing purporting to be

(P.149 Cont'd) the last will and testament of Margaret E. Griffin deceased was produced here in open court and proven by the oath of Mary Jane Echols one of the 2 Subscribing witnesses thereto (which was not objected to) to be as it purports to be the last will and testament of Said Margaret E. Griffin dec'd It is therefore ordered by the court that the same be Set up and established as the last will and testament of said deceased and that the same be recorded by the Clerk.

Attest   T. H. Benton clerk.

Last will & testament of G. W. Gause
Proven & Set up April Term 1867 Dyer County Court

In the Name of God Amen

I George W. Gause of Dyersburg in Dyer County and State of Tennessee calling to mind the uncertainty of life and being of sound mind and of disposing memory (Blessed be Almighty God for the same) do make and constitute and ordain this my last will and Testament in the following manner to wit Item first - I commit my Soul to Almighty God Trusting in his redemption through my Saviour Jesus Christ. Item 2nd - It is my will and therefore direct and authorize my Executrix or Executors (hereinafter mentioned) not to have a Sale of my effects after my Death, but everything to remain together as though I were living and manage to the best advantage for the interest of my family Item 3rd I have given to my Daughter Mrs. Elizabeth B. Jordan One hundred and thirteen acres of land and have made them a Deed for the Same which I consider their full proportion of my estate and therefore authorize my Executrix and Executors So to consider it

Item 4 My two Daughters Mrs. Martha J. Miller and Mrs. Mary Alice Greaves I have not given them (P.150) anything from the fact of my estate being Shortened So much by the war and as my wife Mary A. Gause has the management of my estate I leave the matter with her and my Executors to dispose of the best way they can at all times having an eye to the Education of my two Sons James Ezra & Thomas Richard Gause the latter I wanted educated for a Lawyer

Item 5th It is my wish that should my wife Mrs. Mary A. Gause in connection with my Executor deem it best at any time to sell the house and lot in Dyersburg and buy elsewhere either a farm or lot I wish them to do so or should my wife feel disposed to have a division of the estate before her death She can do So first taking into consideration the education of my two Sons above Stated in Item 4th

Item 6th Should my wife have no division of my estate during her life time then after her death I wish my Executor to divide my estate between the following children viz Martha J. Miller Mary Alice Suase Frederick B. Gause James Ezra and Thomas Richard Gause first taking into consideration the amount necessary to complete the Education of my two Sons James Ezra and Thomas Richard Gause

(P.150 Cont'd)

    Lastly I nominate and appoint my wife Mary A. Gause and my Son Fredric B. Gause my Executrix and Executor to this my last will and testament Given under my hand and Seal this 1st day of March Anno Domini One thousand Eight hundred and Sixty Seven. Signed Sealed published and declared to be the last will & Testament of the Testator in presence of the Subscribing

E. G. Sugg
W. P. Sugg   Geo. W. Gause

State of Tennessee)   April Term County Court 1867
Dyer County   )

    This day a paper writing purporting to be the last will and testament of George W. Gause was produced here in open Court and proven by the oaths of E. G. Sugg & W. P. Sugg to be as it purports to be the last will & testament of said G. W. Gause dec'd It is therefore ordered by the court that the Same be set up and established as the last will and Testament of Said Gause and that the same be recorded by the Clerk   Attest

            Thos. H. Benton clerk.

(P.151)

Last will and Testament of Miss. Ann Smith dec'd proven and established at the August Term 1867 of Dyer County Court) I Ann Smith being Sound in mind but feeble in body do make and publish this as my last will and testament first I direct that my funeral expenses and all my expenses and all my debts be paid as soon after my death as possible out of any moneys that I may die possessed of; Secondly I give and bequeath to my two sisters Tabitha Caroline and Elizabeth Woodbrige Smith my entire estate both real and personal; Lastly I do hereby nominate and appoint Daniel E. Parker my Executor - In witness whereof - I do to this my will Set my hand and Seal - this the 15 day of July 1867

Test S. C. Barkley
       D. E. Parker   Ann Smith (seal)

State of Tennessee)   August Term Dyer County Court 1867
County of Dyer   )

    This day a paper writing purporting to be the last will and testament of Miss Ann Smith dec'd was produced here in open court and there being no likelehood of contest it was proven by the Oath of D. E. Parker one of the two Subscribing witnesses thereto to be as it purports to be the last will and testament of said Ann Smith dec'd it is therefore ordered by the court that the same be set up and established as the last will and testament of said Ann Smith dec'd and that the same be recorded by the clerk.

       Attest   T. H. Benton   Clerk

(P.151 Cont'd)
Last will & Testament of Stephen D. Whitten dec'd
Set up & Established August Term 1867 of Dyer County Court

I Stephen D. Whitten in feeble health but of Sound mind and memory do hereby make and publish this my last will and testament - 1st I commend my body to decent burial and my Soul to God who gave it

2nd I will and bequeath to my beloved wife Mary Whitten my house and lot in the town of Dyersburg where I now live (P.152) to be hers for and during the term of her natural life at her death to go to my heirs at Law

3rd I give and bequeath to my wife Mary Whitten all my household and Kitchen furniture including herein all my furniture carpets beds bedsteads Bedding Sewing machine tables Sofas table ware cooking stove and utensils - clock - Book case & Books (Excepting such books as were bought for the children and are Known and recognized as their Individual property) Side Saddle & Bridle intending to include herein all the personal property with which my house is furnished.

I also give and bequeath to her my large gray horse named Frank - but I advise her to sell Frank and if She needs a horse to obtain one of less value 4th It is my will that of my personal property not herein before bequeathed and remaining after the payment of my just debts One tenth /1/10/ thereof shall be paid to my Sister Narsissa 5 the ballance of my personal effects are to be divided into two equal shares One of which shares I will and bequeath to my wife Mary Whitten to be hers for and during the term of her natural life at her death to be divided equally between her two children Lucy E. Latta and Samuel Latta or to the Survivors of them or in case of their death before thier mother to go to my heirs at Law but it is my express desire and will that the shares thus given to my wife shall be paid her without requiring her to give any bond or to be any way responsible for it to any one at her death

6 the other of the ten shares mentioned in the (P.153) above 5 clause of my will I give and bequeath to my two Sons Massiller & James Whitten to be expended by their Guardian in their Education as far as it will go.

7 It is my will and desire that my true and tried friend Peter E. Wilson my partner in business in whom Integrity I have the utmost confidence Should wind up our business - either by selling my interest therein or buying it himself or closing it out otherwise; and account to my Executor for my interest in Sd partnership

Lastly I hereby nominate and appoint my friend S. R. Latta Executor of my last will and Testament -
witness my hand and seal 2nd day of July 1867

S. D. Whitten

(P.153 Cont'd)
signed sealed and published
in our presence and in
testimony thereof we
have hereunto Set our
hands in presence of each
other and of the testator July
2nd 1867

    F. G. Sampson
    W. C. Doyle
    P. E. Wilson

State of Tennessee)   August Term Dyer County Court 1867
Dyer County   )

    This day a paper writing purporting to be the last will and testament of Stephen D. Whitten dec'd was produced here in open court and duly proven by the oaths of Peter E. Wilson & W. C. Doyle two of the Subscribing witness thereto to be as it purports to be the last will and testament of said Stephen D. Whitten dec'd. It is therefore ordered by the court that the Same be set up and established as the last will and testament of said S. D. Whitten dec'd and that the Same be recorded by the clerk   Attest

                        T. H. Benton

(P.154)
Last will & Testament   ) I, A. J. Fullerton hereby make and
of A. J. Fullerton dec'd(publish this my last will and tes-
Set up September   ) tament
Term 1867   )

    First let all my just debts be paid -

    Second, I give to my wife Mary Ann Fullerton all my personal property remaining after the payment of my debts - Third - I also give to my wife Mary Ann Fullerton Twenty five acres of my home place (the place where I now reside) including my dwelling together with all the improvements about and the Spring, said Twenty acres is to be hers in fee and is to be laid off as follows - Beginning at the Southwest corner of the tract - running thence east so far as to take in the house spring and improvements - thence north and west so as to include twenty five acres - Fourth I give to the three daughters of my deceased brother Hugh Fullerton the balance of my home place say about thirty (30) acres which will make them about 10 acres apiece - Fifth I give and bequeath to my nephew James A. Fullerton Son of my dec'd Hugh Fullerton the tract of land on the Obion River Known as the ferry place; on the plank road

Sixth the tract of land purchased by me a few days ago at Tax Sale Situated on the Obion river and Known as the Snow tract I give and bequeath to Cathrine Taylor wife of Crawford Taylor and to Cynthia Ann Duncan jointly

    Lastly I, hereby nominate and appoint my wife Executor of

(82)

(P.154 Cont'd) this my last will and testament and hereby expressly waive the necessity of her giving bond as Executrix - Witness my hand and seal this the 6 day of August 1867 before signed

    A. J. Fullerton

(P.155) Signed sealed and delivered in our presence in testimony whereof we have hereunto Set our hands and seals in presence of eachother and the Testator this August 6, 1867

          S. R. Latta &
          E. R. Verner

State of Tennessee) County Court September Term 1867
Dyer County   )

    This day a paper writing purporting to be the last will and testament of A. J. Fullerton dec'd was produced here in open court and dully proven by the oaths of S. R. Latta & E. R. Verner the two Subscribing witnesses thereto, to be as it purports to be the last will and testament of A. J. Fullerton dec'd It is therefore ordered by the court that the same be set up and established as the last will and testament of said Fullerton died and that the same be Recorded by the Clerk and Mary Ann Fullerton was dully sworn
Attest   Thos. H. Benton Clerk.

Last Will & Testament) I, J. W. Echols of the county of
of Joseph W. Echols dec'd(Dyer and State of Tennessee do
Set up September Term) make and constitute the following
1867   ) to be my last will when I shall
            happen to die - that is to say I
had the following named brother and Sisters Some of whom are now dead Benjamin F. Echols Elizabeth Depoyster Nancy ____ Sarah J. Clements and Mary Ann Leeroy- but as Seven of them have not treated me well I am desirous that whatever property and effects that I may leave at my death after my just debts are paid shall be distributed as follow that is I will and bequeath to my Sister Nancy all the land Town lots &c that I own in the State of Illinois Two hundred and twenty acres of land on which B. M. Clanahan now (P.156) now has a lease, and to my niece little Mary Ann Leeroy, I give and bequeath my negroes and all that remains belonging to me both personal and real and I desire that when I shall happen to die that my Mercantile business be at once wound up - that there be no more goods purchased and the whole matter at once settled up

 Witness my hand and seal this 10 day of November A. D. 1860
        J. W. Echols (seal)

State of Tennessee Dyer County April 13th 1865

 I J. W. Echols of said county and state being still living and of disposing mind do on account of certain changes in the disposition of my worldly effects after my Death shall have

(P.156 Cont'd) happened - That is to say I now wish to give and bequeath to my niece Mary Ann Leeroy now Mary Ann Yeargin the House and lot that I lately purchased from Wm. C. Doyle and my negro woman named Eliza and all her children that she now has or may hereafter have - and to my Sister Mary Ann Leeroy I give and bequeath all my land and other negroes and personal effects of all and every Kind that I own or possess in the State of Tennessee except as above stated - and my sister Nancy ___ her heirs and assigns all my property in Illinois as originally Stated in the within Testament

Given under my hand and seal this day above written

Attest
W. M. Watkins
B. T. Harter

J. M. Echols (seal)

"State" of Tennessee Dyer County June 5th 1866 I J. W. Echols do hereby authorise and empower my sister Mary Ann Leeroy to Execute and Administer my whole estate without giving any (P.157) Secuirty Witness my hand and seal the day and year June 5, 1866

Attest
W. M. Watkins
B. T. Harton

J. W. Echols (seal)

I still desire my Sister Mary Ann Leeroy to have all that I have above bequeathed to her and all the land I may Since acquire and all personalties aquired before or Since or that may _____ to me hereafter this 7th day of August 1867

Attest
W. M. Watkins

J. W. Echols

State Tennessee) County Court September term 1867
Dyer County   )
This day a paper writing purporting to be the last will and testament of J. W. Echols dec'd was produced here in open court and duly proven by the oaths of W. M. Watkins & B. T. Harton the two subscribing witnesses to the fore going will to be as it purports to be the last will and Testament of Said J. W. Echols dec'd - It is therefore ordered by the court that the Same be set up and established as the last will and testament of said J. W. Echols dec'd and that the same be recorded by the clerk Mrs Leeroy was then duly qualified as Executrix of said Echols dec'd

Attest
(P.158)

T. H. Benton Clerk.

Last will and testament) In the Name of God Amen
of David Parrish dec'd (I David Parrish of the County of
proven and Set up   ) Dyer and State of Tennessee being
Novbr. County Court 1867(weak in body but sound in mind do
                          make this my last will and testament hereby revoking all others heretofore by me made -

(P.158 Cont'd) 1st I will my Soul to God who gave it, And my body to it's mother Earth - 2nd I desire my body to have a decent Interment; 3rd I wish my funeral and burial expenses together with my Just debts paid by my Executor as soon as practicable 4th having heretofore given to my children Elias Parrish Mary Jane, Walker Martha Bessent Wm. N. Parrish and Sally Ann Hassell I have provided for them and Settled them and 5 I give and bequeath unto my beloved wife Mariel Parrish the One half of all the property including Lands and to my youngest Son James Bonds, Parrish the other half of my land and perishable property and at my Said wifes Death - I will all to my Said son James &c. Including the half I now leave my wife 6th and I will that my beloved wife and son Eliash Parrish be my Executrix and Executor to carry out and execute this my last will and testament

    In witness whereof I hereunto set my hand and affixed my seal this 21st day of September A. D. 1866

Attest Thomas Miller
        J. C. Pate
        W. H. Parrish

           his
David X Parrish (seal)
      mark

State of Tennessee) County court November term 1867
Dyer County   )

    This day a paper writing purporting to be the last will and testament of David Parrish dec'd was produced here in open court and duly proven by the Oaths of Thomas Miller and John C. Pate Subscribing witnesses to the foregoing will - It is therefore ordered by the court that the same be set up and established as the Last will and testament of said David Parrish dec'd and that the same be recorded by the clerk.

        Attest   Thos. H. Benton Clerk.

(P.159)
Last will and testament) I Martha Brockman do make and
of Martha Brockman dec'd(publish this as my last will
Proven and set up Febry) and testament hereby revoking and
Term county court 1868 (making void all other wills by me
                            at any time made first I direct that my funeral expenses and all my debts be paid as soon after my death as possible out of any money that I may die possessed of or may first come into the hands of my Executor Secondly I give and bequeath to Secont Thomas State King I give my bed stead bed 1 quilt and one counterpane I bequeath to Zylpha Alice my saddle one quilt I gave and bequeath to Zylpha King my mother my wardrobe and three quilts I will after this is done to divide equally between Thomas State and Zylpha Alice all the remainder of my estate whatever it may be lastly, I do nominate and appoint my Executor James M. King In witness whereof I do to this my last will Set my hand and seal this the 27 - of Sept 1867

                              Martha Brockman (seal)

(P.159 Cont'd)
Signed Sealed and published in our presents and we have subscribed our names hereto in the presents of the testator this the 27 - day of Sept 1867

      Test Nathan King
          J. A. Olive

State of Tennessee) County Court Febry term 1868
Dyer County   )
   This day a paper writing purporting to be the last will and testament of Martha Brockman dec'd was produced here in open court and duly proven by the oaths of Nathan King and J. A. Olive Subscribing witnesses thereto to be as it purports to be the last will and testament of said Martha Brockman dec'd It is therefore ordered by the court that the same be set up and established as the last will and testament of said Martha Brockman dec'd and that the same be recorded by the clerk -
        T. H. Benton Clerk.
  Attest

(P.160)
Last will and testament   ) State of Tennessee Dyer
of <u>Asbury</u> Freeman dec'd   (County
Set up and established February) In the Name of Almighty <u>God</u>
County court 1868   (I Ashbury Freeman do make
               this as my last will and
Testament - I will that my body, shall be decently buried
2nd And after my just debts shall be paid out of my personal effects I want my beloved wife to hold all in her hands untill her death or marriage Should she marry again both land estate and at her death or marriage the land is to be equally divided between my beloved children, James P. Freeman and Nancy J. Freeman. I mean the houses tract of 90 acres where we now live,
3rd And should I now die I want my beloved daughter Almeda Freeman to have the land I last bought in the place of the one I bought of her last fall -

4 - I hereby appoint P. C. Ledsinger my Executor of this my last will and testament this 27 - day of July 1866

Gilbert Cozart).   Ashbury Freeman (seal)
  his   (
Jasper X Cozart)
  mark   (
R. M. Tarrant)

State of Tennessee) County Court February Term 1868
Dyer County   )
   This day a paper writing purporting to be the last will and Testament of Ashbury Freeman dec'd was produced here in open court and duly proven by the oaths of Gilbert Cozart and Robert M. Tarrant Subscribing witness thereto to be as it purports to be the last will and testament of said Ashbury Freeman dec'd It is therefore ordered by the

(P.160 Cont'd) court that the same be set up and established as the last will and testament of said Ashbury Freeman dec'd and that the same be recorded by the clerk.

Attest   T. H. Benton   Clerk.

(P.161)

| Last Will and testament of J. J. Zimmerman dec'd Set up and established March term county court 1868 | Dyer County Tennessee
Febry 15, 1868

Know all men by these presents that I J. J. Zimmerman of the county and State aforesaid Being at this time |

in my right mind having full control of my Senses in every respect do in the presence of the undersigned witnesses make this my will to wit; that my entire effects both personal and real of any and every description whatever is the property of J. G. Dunnevant at my decease or death except the amount of such property and effects to pay all my liabilities which Sufficient sum the said Dunnevant is to pay prior to his appropriating any part of the same to his own use or benefit the remainder of such effects as stated in the body of this will the Said J. G. Dunnevant his heirs Executors and assigns are to have and to hold forever   Signed in the presence of

Test   C. F. Woodruff
      Daniel G. Tucker
      A. Enochs   J. J. Zimmerman (seal)

State of Tennessee)   County Court March term 1868
Dyer County   )
                     This day a paper writing purporting to be the last will and testament of J. J. Zimmerman dec'd was produced here in open court and duly proven by the oaths of Daniel G. Tucker and Alfred Enochs Subscribing witnesses thereto to be as it purports to be the last will and testament of said J. J. Zimmerman dec'd It is therefore ordered that the same be set up and established as the last will and testament of said Zimmerman and that the same be recorded by the clerk

Attest   T. H. Benton   Clerk.

(P.162)

| Last will and Testament of Wilson Hall dec'd Set up and established December 7th 1868 | I Wilson Hall being of sound mind and disposing memory have this day made this my last will and testament hereby revoking all former will by me at any former time heretofore made |

Item 1st   My will and desire is that as soon after my death as may be all my debts and funeral expenses be paid out of the first money coming into my Executors hands -

Item 2nd   I give to my beloved wife Sarah all my personal property of every kind and description consisting of household and kitchen furniture farming utensils horses cattle mules hogs

(P.162 Cont'd) sheep crop on hand money notes everything of which I may die possessed not otherwise disposed of for and during her natural life. She may sell and dispose of any of said property and have the use of the means in it stead if she with the consent of my Executor deem it best So to do and at the death of my beloved wife Sarah then all the estate on this item of my will mentioned I direct to be sold and the proceeds of the same to be equally divided between my children or their represenatives equally share & share alike. Item third I give to my son James M. Hall the tract of land on which I now live containing One hundred and thirteen and One half acres (having deed on the balance of the Original tract this day to my other two sons this gift is made on the following conditions first my son James M. Hall is to pay my daughter Elizabeth, C. Everette Three hundred dollars, 2ndly my wife is to have a good comfortable house on it during her natural life She is to live in the house with my said son or to have a house of her own as she may desire and to be comfortably supported during her natural life by my said son (P.163) but with her consent he may use such of the property as is given her in this will but not to convert it to his own property but to use it in aiding to support and provide for my beloved wife as that is this object in giving it to her

  Item 4th I hereby appoint Smith Parks as my Executor to this my last will and Testament this 11th day of March 1867

Test W. J. Smith
   D. R. Hendricks   Wilson Hall (seal)

State of Tennessee) Commissioners Court
Dyer County   )   December Term 1868
        This day a paper writing purporting to be the last will and testament of Wilson Hall was produced here in open court and duly proven by the oaths of W, J. Smith & D. R. Hendricks Subscribing witnesses thereto to be as it purports to be the last will and testament of said Hall It is therefore ordered by the court that the same be set up and established as the last will and testament of said Wilson Hall dec'd and that the same be recorded by the Clerk.

 Attest   Thos. H. Benton Clerk

Last will & Testament) I Charles H. Ledsinger do hereby
   of   (make & publish this my last will
C. H. Ledsinger dec'd) and testament Item 1st Let all
Set up and established (my just debts be paid Item 2nd
February Term Cty Ct 1869) I give and bequeath to my beloved
              wife Nancy T. Ledsinger all of my
personal property - money Choses in action &c. except as herein after provided to be hers absolutely Item 3rd I give to my beloved wife Nancy T. Ledsinger for and during the term of her natural life all of the real estate of which I die seized or possessed - and said real estate at the death of my of my wife Nancy T. Ledsinger I will and bequeath to my following named Children to wit Thomas T. Ledsinger Zenobia F. Fowlkes wife of

(P.163 Cont'd) George A. Fowlkes Robert W. Ledsinger John P. Ledsinger James Z. Ledsinger and Margaret E. Ledsinger to be divided between (P.164) them and in case of the death of any of the above named children before their mother without issue - the said property is to go to the survivors or of them but should any of the above named children die before their mother leaving children such children in the division of said property are to stand "in loco parentis" Item 4th To all of my children except Robert W. & James Z. & Margaret E. Ledsinger I have given each a horse cow & calf two sows & two ewes to preserve equally as nearly as possible it is my desire that my wife as soon after my Death as possible out of the property herein given to her provided she can do so without inconvenience to herself should give to each of said children Robert W., Jame Z., & Margaret E. Ledsinger a horse of the value of $150.00 a cow and calf of the value of $2000 2 sows and 2 ewes or to each of them the value of said property in money If my wife cannot do this in her life time (and it is altogether at her option whether she does or not) then upon a division a division of my property as provided for in Item No 3 of this will the said Robert W., James Z. & Margaret E. Ledsinger are to have each Say $200.00 more than the three other children named in said Item No 3

Item No 5 I am the owner of one undivided (1/3) part of a tract of land of about 227 acres - the same on which my brother P. C. Ledsinger now lives - descended to me from my brother Robert Ledsinger. My brother P. C. Ledsinger has been using and occupying said land for many years, without accounting to me for any of the rents and profits, Now therefore to prevent trouble and Litigation in regard to the same if my brother P. C. Ledsinger will within twelve months from my death pay to my Executrix the sum of Two thousand ($2000.) dollars, I hereby authorize and empower my said Executrix to convey said land to the Said P. C. Ledsinger by deed and to execute to him full receipts and acquittances for the rents and profits due to me - but if he fails within said periof to accept of these terms & to pay said Sum of Two thousand Dollars then my Executrix is hereby directed to (P.165) apply for a division of said land and to have an account taken of the rents & profits due and to collect all that acount of Equity will decree and any money that may come into the hands of my Executrix under this Item of my will shall at once be divided among my six children named in Item No 3 of this will or the survivors of them and in the same way as therein provided for the division of my real estate

Item No 6 A suit is now pending against me in the circuit court of Dyer County Instituted by Alexander Williams and Mary E. his wife as Administrators of John W. Norton dec'd in which suit I expect to recover judgment against In the event that I recover said judgment and the same is collected I hereby direct my Executrix after paying the expenses by me incurred in defending said including the fees of my attorneys out of said judgment to pay the balance thereof to the legally appointed Guardian of James Norton and Leonara Norton children of John W. Norton dec'd for the use and benefit of said children The reason why

(P.165 Cont'd) my daughter Mary E. now intermarried with Alexander Williams is left out of the provisions of this will is; that I have already done for her more than I can do for the balance of my children and given her more than I can give to them - Lastly I hereby nominate and appoint my wife Nancy T. Ledsinger Executrix of this my last will and testament and having every confidence in he prudence and not intending that she shall be responsible further than she desires to any one except my condition I hereby expressly waive the necessity of her giving bond as Executrix Interlined before signed Witness my hand Sept 15, 1868

Signed and published in   Charles H. Ledsinger
our presence and we
have signed the same
in presence of each
other and of the testator
Sept 15, 1868 E. R. Vernon
    & S. R. Latta witnesses

State of Tennessee)   Commissioners court February Term 1869
Dyer County   )
                       This day a paper writing purporting to be the last will and testament of Charles H. Ledsinger dec'd was produced here in open court and proven by the oaths of E. R. Vernon & S. R. Latta Subscribing witnesses thereto to be as it purports to be the last will and testament of said C. H. Ledsinger (P.166) It is therefore ordered by the court that the same be set up and established as the last will and testament of the said C. H. Ledsinger dec'd and that the same be recorded by the clerk

Attest   Thomas H. Benton clerk.

Last will and   ) State of Tennessee
Testament of   (Dyer County.
Willis Chamberlain   )
dec'd Set up and estab-(Know all men by these presents that
lished February Term) I Willis Chamberlain being feeble
    1869   ) in body but Sound of mind do make
                                and set up this my last will and testament and do hereby revoke all others that I may have mad previous to this - First I give my wife Wennie 2 cows & calves one horse one sow & five shoats and eight sheep Two beds furnished One safe two tables One trunk One chest One set of chains all of the household and Kitchen furniture Ten Barrells of corn 10 Bushels of wheat and four hundred pounds of pork and one third of my real estate including my dwelling house as her dower for life and at her death to be equally divided between my heirs All other property that I may die possessed of both real and personal shall be equally divided between my heirs Viz Dempsy A. Chamberlain Nancy E. Ferrill and Mary M. Davis - and do hereby nominate and appoint Daniel E. Parker Executor of this my last will and testament done October 21st 1868   his
Test J. M. Ferrill   J. C. Hickman   Willis X Chamberlain
                                                                      mark

(91)

(P.167)
State of Tennessee) Commissioners Court
Dyer County) February 1st 1869

This day a paper writing purporting to be the last will and testament of Willis Chamberlain deceased was produced here in open court and duly proven by the oaths of J. M. Ferrill & J. C. Hickman the two Subscribing witnesses thereto to be as it purports to be the last will and testament of the said Chamberlain It is therefore ordered by the court that the same be set up and established as the last will and testament of said Chamberlain deceased and that the same be recorded by the clerk

Attest   Thos. H. Benton clerk.

Last will and testament) In the Name of God Amen
of Mary E. Wilkins dec'd(I Mary E. Wilkins of the county of
Set up and established) Dyer and State of Tennessee being
March court 1869) sound in mind & memory but in a
feeble State of health do make and ordain this my last will and testament following to wit 1st I recommend my Soul to God who gave it and my body to the earth to be intered in a christian like manner 2nd I wish all of my just ___ to be paid off and discharged 3rd I give and bequeath unto my Daughter Josephine Wilkins one feather bed and covering I also give and bequeath unto my Daughter Angeline Wilkins a feather Bed and covering. 4th I wish the remainder of my personal effects to be sold and all of the money I have on hand to be equally divided between my four youngest children namely Josephine Wilkins Wm. P. Wilkins Emerson Echridge Wilkins and Lucy B. Wilkins I do nominate and appoint Joseph Chitwood Executor of this my last will and testament as witness (P.168) my whereof I have hereunto set my hand and seal this the 12th day of February 1869

                                                her
signed sealed and   )   Mary X E. Wilkins (seal)
delivered in our   (mark
presence Jas Prichard)
    G. Chitwood   (

State of Tennessee) Commissioners court
Dyer County) March term 1869

This day a paper writing purporting to be the last will and testament of Mary E. Wilkins dec'd was produced here in open court and proven by the oaths of Jas Prichard & G. Chitwood Subscribing witness thereto to be as it purports to be the last will and testament of the said Mary E. Wilkins It is therefore ordered by the court that the same be set up and established and Recorded by the clerk and filed
Attest   T. H. Benton   clerk
                                    of Dyer County Court.

(P.168 Cont'd)

Last Will and Testament of Margaret Dickey dec'd
Set up and established November Term 1869

State of Tennessee
Dyer County

I Margaret Dickey being in usual good health of body and of sane mind do this the 20 day of January Eighteen hundred and sixty nine declare this to be my last will and testament, 1st I will my body to the Earth whence it came. And my Soul to God who gave it 2nd It is my will that out of my worldly effects, at my decease that all my just debts shall be paid and a sufficiency used to secure my body a decent burial 3rd I then will that my brother Hiram J. Thomas shall have the use of all means belonging to me that he shall have in his hands at my death for the space of four years by him paying simple interest on same

4th I then will to my nephew D. P. McCorkle Esq. Four hundred dollars in money

5th I then will to my nephew John E. McCorkle Three hundred dollars in money.

(P.169) 6th I then will to my nephew Anderson J. McCorkle the use of my house and lot in the town of Trenton Gibson county Tenn. Twelve months

7th I then will to my nephew Finis A. McCorkle Three hundred Dollars in money 8th I then will to my niece Elizabeth J. Reeves (wife of Wyatt Reeves) Four hundred dollars in money 9th I then will to my niece Latina M. Gregory (wife of John Gregory) four hundred dollars in money - 10th I then will to my nephew W. T. Woods the tract or parcel of land willed to me by my Father said land lies adjoining the said Wm. T. Wood land on which he now lives and contains by estimation Sixty acres more or less I also will to the said nephew W. T. Woods one half of my town lot in the Town of Trenton Gibson county Tenn. (after Anderson J. McCorkle has the use of it twelve months) which I hold by deed to me from J. P. Thomas 11th I then will the other half of the above described house and lot after - after Anderson J. McCorkle has the use of it twelve months) to Cora Alice daughter of the above named nephew, Wm. T. Woods 12th I then will to my niece Martha Ann Doak wife of W. E. Doak four hundred dollars in money - 13th I then will to my niece Sarah Jane Green (wife of A. Green four hundred dollars in money. 14th I then will to my niece Susan A. Trout (wife of Wiley S. Trout) Four hundred dollars in money, and if there be a remainder of my effects after the above distributions are made as therein specified it is my will that such remainder shall be equally distributed to the above named legatees. I hereby appoint my nephew David P. McCorkle Esqr. as my Sole Executor to the within last will and testament made and subscribed to by me and my seal affixed thereto in the presence of the subscribing witnesses this 20th day of January A.D. 1869

Test M. R. Hendricks
    W. H. Franklin

Margaret Dickey (seal)

(93)

(P.170)
State of Tennessee) County Court Novr. term 1869
Dyer County)
                          This day a paper writing purporting to be the last will and testament of Margaret Dickey deceased was produced here in open court and duly proven by the oaths of M. R. Hendricks & W. H. Franklin Subscribing witnesses, to be as it purports to be the last will and testament of said Margaret Dickey dec'd It is therefore ordered by the court that the same be set up and established as the last will & testament Margaret Dickey dec'd and that the same be recorded and filed by the clerk

Attest   T. H. Benton clerk
                                              of Dyer county court.

Last Will & Testament) A <u>written</u> will and testament
        of   (James Dunston do make and publish
James Dunston dec'd   ) this my last will and testament
Set up and established   (hereby revoking and making void
December county court 1869) all other wills by me made at any
                                           time 1st I direct that my funeral expenses and all my debts be paid as soon after my death as possible out of any moneys that I may die possessed of or may first come into the hands of my Executor. Secondly I give and bequeath to my lawful wife Rebecca Dunston One Sorrel mare one bay mule two years old one spotted mule 5 months old one cow four years old one yearling twelve months old past also my present crop both corn and cotton and shot gun Household and Kitchen furniture

Thirdly all the notes and accounts coming to my estate is to be equally divided between Mary Ann Oakley & Caroline Jane Dunston and Rachel Elizabeth Ridens. In witness whereof I do to this my will Set my hand and Seal

                                              James Dunston

Signed sealed and published in our presents and we have Sub-
(P.171) scribed our names hereto in the presence of the testator October 1 day 1869   John Abbott & E. R. Shane

State of Tennessee) County Court Dember Term 1869
Dyer County)
                        This day a paper writing purporting to be the last will and testament of James Dunston deceased was produced here in open court and duly proven by the oaths of John Abbott & E. R. Shane Subscribing witnesses thereto to be as it purports to be the last will and testament of the said James Dunston dec'd It is therefore Ordered by the court that the same be set up and established as the last will and testament of the said Dunston dec'd and that the same be recorded by the clerk

Attest   T. H. Benton clerk
                                          of Dyer County court

(P.172)
Last Will and Testament)   State of Tennessee Dyer County
     of   (
W. C. Hall Dec'd   )   In the Name of God Amen.
Set up June 6, 1810   (

         I William C. Hall being of sound mind and disposing memory but of feeble health and calling to mind the mortality of the body do make constitute and Ordain this my last will and testament in manner and form following (viz) My body I commit to the earth to be buried in a decent Christian like manner. And my soul to God who gave it. It is my will and desire that all my lawful debts together with my burial expences be paid as soon after my death as can conviently be done by my executor whom I shall hereafter appoint It is further my will and desire that Soloman S. Hallowell have the entire remainder of my estate after paying my debts as aforesaid and I hereby will unto him my entire estate as aforesaid, both real and personal Because when I was a stranger comparatively he took me in, and when I was out of a home he took me in and acted the part of a good Samaritan and I hereby appoint Soloman S. Hallowell my Executor to carry out my last will and testament. In witness whereof I have hereunto set my hand and seal

    This the 25th day of May 1870

Signed sealed in the   )   W. C. Hall (seal)
presence of A. T. Fielder (
John I. Craig   )

State of Tennessee) June Term 1870
Dyer County   )

        This day a paper writing purporting to be the last will and testament of W. C. Hall deceased was produced here in open court, and the execution thereof duly proven by the Oaths of A. T. Fielder and J. I. Craig Subscribing witnesses thereto, Who testified that they were personally acquainted with the Testator that he signed and published the said paper as his last will and testament in their presence and for the purposes therein set forth and requested them specially to bear witness thereto, and that they signed it in his presence, and at his request and that he was of sound and disposing memory at the time of the Execution of said will - It is therefore ordered by the court that said paper writing be set up as the last will and testament of the said W. C. Hall dec'd and that the same be recorded &c

Attest   Will M. Watkins clerk
                                        H. P. Doyle D. C.

(P.173)
Robert A. Moore's   )   State of Tennessee Dyer County
Last will and   (
Testament Set up June 6th 1870)   In the Name of God Amen
June Term Dyer County Court   (

        I Robert A. Moore being of

(P.173 Cont'd) sound mind and disposing memory and calling to mind the mortality of the body do make constitute and ordain this to be my last will and Testament in form following (viz) My body I commit to the earth to be buried in a decent Christian like manner. And my soul to God who gave it for Christ Sake As to what worldly goods it hath pleased God to bless me with; I will as follows First I desire that all my lawful debts be paid by my executor whom I shall hereafter named as soon as posible without injury to my estate. It is further my will that my Executor whom I shall designate shall sell the house and lot upon which I now reside containing eleven acres Either publicly or privately as in his judgment he may think best or swap it for some other place suitable for my family to live upon, and any sale or swap made by him shall be valid if he shall sell it. then it is my will that all or so much of the proceeds arising from such shall be laid out in the purchase of a suitable place for a home for my family. My wife to have and hold her Dower in the place so bought or swaped for as though I had been in possession of the same at my death.

It is further my will that my Executor shall sell either publicly or privately as he may think best my interest in one house in the Vilage of Friendship, and three lots which I have an equal interest with my Brother Jo M R Moore and appropriate the proceeds as he may think best to the use and benefit of my wife and children and it is my will that any sale made or any conveyance made by my Executor whom I shall name properly signed by him as such shall be lawful and valid. And I hereby designate and appoint my Brother J S Moore my Executor to settle up my Estate and carry this will into effect.

In witness whereof I have set my hand and affix my seal this the 23rd day of March A. D. 1870

Test
A. T. Fielder
Wyatt <u>Sunsford</u>

R. A. Moore (seal)

"See next Page"

(P.174)
State of Tennessee) June Term Dyer County Court 1870
Dyer County)

This day a paper writing purporting to be the last will and testament of Robert A. Moore deceased was produced here in open court and the Execution thereof duly proven by the oaths of A. T. Fielder and Wyatt Lunsford subscribing witnesses thereto who testified that they were personally acquainted with the testator that he signed and published the said paper as his last will and testament in their presence and for the purposes therein set forth and requested them specially to bear witness thereto and that they signed it in his presence and at his request, and that he was of sound and disposing memory at the time of the execution of said will -

It is therefore ordered by the court that said paper writing be set up as the last will and testament of the said

(96)

(P.174 Cont'd)   Robert A. Moore dec'd and the same be recorded &c

Attest   Will M. Watkins clerk
                                         By H. P. Doyle D. C.

Last will & Testament)   State of Tennessee Dyer County
         of   (
M. B. Carroll dec'd   (I M. B. Carroll being of sound mind
Set up August 1st 1870)   and memory do make and publish this
                          my last will and testament hereby
removing all others if any at any time made. It is my will
first that all of my just debts be paid and then that my estate
go to my beloved wife C. F. Carroll during her life or widowhood
and then at her death I want the Same equally divided between my
children But if she should marry I want her to come in for a
childs share as if there were no will

   I hereby appoint my said beloved wife as my Executrix.

   Witness my hand and seal this 25th June 1869

Witnesses   M. B. Carroll (seal)
W. A. Hudson
H. S. Fowlks

(P.175)
State of Tennessee)   August Term County Court 1870
Dyer County   )
                      This day a paper writing purporting to
be the last will and Testament of M. B. Carroll deceased was
produced here into Open Court and the execution thereof duly
proven by the oaths of W. A. Hudson and H. S. Fowlkes subscribed witnesses thereto, who testified that they were personally acquainted with the Testator that he signed and subscribed the same as his Last will and Testament in their presence and for the purposes therein set forth and requested them
to bear witness thereto and that they signed it in his presence
and at his request and that he was of sound and disposing memory
at the Execution of said will.

   It is therefore ordered by the court that said paper writing be set up as the last will and Testament of the said M. B.
Carroll dec'd and the Same be recorded &c

Attest: Will M. Watkins clerk
                                         H. P. Doyle   D. C.

Last will and Testament)   State of Tennessee Dyer County
         of   (
Nicholas C. Gentry dec'd) I Nicholas C. Gentry being in my
Set up August 1st 1870 (right mind do hereby publish and
                            make known to the world this my
last will and Testament, revoking all and every will heretofore
made by me; as follows to wit: In view of the uncertainty of
life and the certainty of death that justice may be done and

(P.175 Cont'd) had after my desires,

    I do appoint and by these presents request my true and tried friend & neighbor Thomas W. Jones to act as my Executor to carry out these my last desires, after my death.

First: I desire that all of my just debts be paid out of my personal estate Second: that my dear wife Eunice be protected in the proper use of all of my real and personal Estate, so long as she lives or remains a widow, For the purposes of raising and educating all of the minor children borne to me by my said wife Eunice. And after her death that all of my property both real and personal be sold and equally division be made between my son Charles born to me by my first wife Mary (P.176) Ann and my children born to me by my said wife Eunice.

    In witness whereof I hereunto set my hand and seal this the 24th day of May 1870

Attest   N. C. Gentry (seal)
Jno H Moss
Benj. Blackwell
J. W. Hassell

State of Tennessee)   August Term County Court 1870
Dyer County   )
    This day a paper writing purporting to be the last will and testament of Nicholas C. Gentry deceased was produced here in open court and the execution thereof duly proven by the oaths of John H. Moss, Benj. Blackwell and J. W. Hassell subscribing witnesses thereto who testified that they were personally acquainted with the Testator; that he signed and published the said paper as his last will and testament in their presence, and for the purposes therein set forth, And requested them specially to bear witness thereto, and that they signed it in his presence and at his request and that he was of sound mind and disposing memory at the time of the execution of said will -

    It is therefore ordered by the court that said paper writing be set up as the last will and testament of the said Nicholas C. Gentry deceased and the same be recorded &c

Attest   Will M. Watkins   clerk

(P.177)
Last Will and Testament of James Chambers dec'd Set up & established October Court 1870 and ordered recorded W. M. Watkins County Court Clerk	State of Tennessee Dyer County In the Name of God Amen I James Chambers being of sound mind and disposing memory but in feeble health and calling to recollection that it is appointed unto man to die do make consti-

tute and Ordain this my last will and testament in manner and form following that is to say, My body I commit to the earth to

(P.177 Cont'd) be buried in a plain decent Christian like manner and my soul I commit to God who gave it.

It is further my will and desire that all my lawful debts be paid as soon after my death as practicable without injury to my estate. It is further my will and desire that my wife Mary A. Chambers have during her natural life a Dower out of my real estate to be laid off as in such cases the law directs as set forth in the code upon her application to the county court.

It is further my will and desire that my wife Mary A. Chambers have what the law would allow an insolvent debtor so far as the same maybe on hand at my deat and nothing more as she has had the use and benefit of certain moneys in her possession when we were married

It is further my will and desire that my son Josias Chambers his heirs and assigns have forty acres of land off the east end of the tract of land I purchased of Anna A. and Maruna Sims It is further my will and desire that my son Robert T. Chambers his heirs and assigns have the ballance of the tract above named which I have not willed to my son Joisias Chambers together with so much of the tract upon which I now reside as will make him in all forty acres to be run off so as to include the Lease I gave him and upon which he now resides. It is further my will and desire that my Son William S. Chambers his heirs and assigns have all the ballance of my lands not willed to my two sons named above, subject to my wife Mary A. Chambers Dower during her natural life

It is further my will and desire that the bodily heirs of my deceased daughter Cathrine A. Stanfield have five hundred dollars in money. It is further my will and desire that my son William S. Chambers have all the remainder of my estate, ater paying all of my just debts and expences of settling up my estate not heretofore mentioned as the land willed to him is subject to my wifes Dower.

It is further my will and desire that Alfred T. Fielder act as my executor to carry out this my last will and (P.178) testament. In witness whereof I have hereunto set my hand and seal this the 3rd day of August A. D. 1870

Test
J. K. Strayhorn
F. M. Baker

James Chambers (seal)

State of Tennessee) October Term County Court 1870
Dyer County)
    This day a paper writing purporting to be the last will and testament of James Chambers dec'd was produced here into open court for probate

Where upon came J. K. Strayhorn and F. M. Baker subscribing witnesses thereto who being duly sworn Depose that they

(P.178 Cont'd) were personally acquainted with the Testator that he signed and published the said paper as his last will and testament in their presence and for the purposes therein set forth and requested them specially to bear witness thereto and that they signed it in the presence of the Testator and in the presence of eachother and at his request and he was of sound mind and desposing memory at the time of the execution of said will.

It is therefore ordered by the court that the said paper writing be set up and established as the last will and testament of James Chambers dec'd and be recorded by the clerk.

Attest   Wm. M. Watkins Clerk
                                             By Hick P. Doyle D. C.

(P.179)

Last Will and Testament of Thomas C. Mitchell dec'd Set up & established Janry Term 71 Recorded January 14th 1871 Will M. Watkins clerk	State of Tennessee Dyer County

I Thomas C. Mitchell of Dyer County do make this my last will and testament hereby revoking all others by me at any time made. First I give to each of my daughters One hundred Dollars for the purpose of placing monuments over them - Second: I direct that after my death a marble Box tomb be erected over my grave by my Executors - Third the property which I have placed in the possession of my daughter and son-in-law Newton C. Warren and Susan G. his wife - I give unto my said daughter Susan G. for and during her natural life to her own sole and seperate use and at her death to go to her children and their heirs forever Fourth: As to the residue of my estate both real and personal I direct that the same shall remain under the care of my executors, until the youngest child of either of my said daughters now living or hereafter to be born, shall become twenty one years of age, and the said estate with its accumulation shall be equally divided among all my grand children then living, and if any are dead leaving issue, such issue to stand in the place of the parent and receive the parents share. If any one or more of my negroes shall become unmanageble or disobedient, so as in the opinion of my executors to render it proper to sell such slave or slaves, They shall have power to do so and to loan out the proceeds or reinvest it in other negroes and my Executors will keep my slaves together on my farm until the period for a final Division but in case the negroes become too numerous to work the farm proffitably, then my executors are to hire out such as cannot be proffitably imployed on the farm.

The funds which may come into the hands of my Executors Either at my death, or from the proceeds of the labor or sale of the property (as herein provided for) shall by my Executors be kept constantly invested at interest until said period of final division, when the whole estate shall be divided as above directed -

(P.179 Cont'd) Fifth - My Executors may at my death and from time to time thereafter sell off any portion of my (P.180) stock which which they may deem proper at private sale - and the house-hold furniture on hand at my death, I wish my two daughters to have and divide between themselves without a sale.

Sixth - The powers herein confined upon my Executors are to be exercised by any person or persons who may hereafter lawfully have committed to them the Execution of the provisions of this will -

Seventh - My boy "Bob" I wish to remain hired out in the neighbohood of his wife as long as my Executors think it proper -

Eighth - I appoint as the Executors of this will my Son-in-law Thomas W. Jones and my friends John F. Sinclair and Ralph Sinclair, but should they decline serving or any two of them decline then they may nominate two or more persons to act as Executors - and should a vacancy occur at any time in the office of Executor my Son-in-law Thomas W. Jones during his life time may nominate some person or persons to act -

In testimony whereof I have signed & sealed this paper this 27th day of August A. D. 1860.

Signed Sealed and)
published in the (
presence -)   Thomas C. Mitchell (seal)
M. R. Hill. (
John A. Wilkins)

State of Tennessee) In the matter of will of Thomas C.
Dyer County   ) Mitchell dec'd late of Dyer Co. Tenn.

On this day Thomas W. Jones and John F. Sinclair produced in open court, a paper writing, purporting to be the last will and testament of Thomas C. Mitchell dec'd and thereupon said John F. Sinclair declined and refused to qualify as the executor of said will, and thereupon said John F. Sinclair (Ralph Sinclair one of the executors nominated in said will being dead) nominated said Thomas W. Jones as sole executor of said last will and testament, said paper writing purporting to be the last will and testament of said Thomas C. Mitchell dec'd being attested by the signatures of (P.181) M. R. Hill and John A. Wilkins as subscribing witnesses thereto and there upon came into open court Robert P. Caldwell and Smith Parks witnesses who being duly sworn prove that they were well acquainted with M. R. Hill and John A. Wilkins the attesting witnesses to said will - and that the said M. R. Hill and John A. Wilkins are both dead, they further prove that they are well acquainted with the hand-writing of said attesting witnesses, and that said signatures are in the handwriting of said M. R. Hill and J. A. Wilkins and thereupon came also here into open court Jno. F. Sinclair and N. C. Warren witness who being duly sworn prove that they were well acquainted with said Thomas C. Mitchell in his life time - that he is now dead.

(P.181 Cont'd) They also prove that they were well acquainted with the handwriting of said Thomas C. Mitchell dec'd and that the signature of said testator to said paper writing is in the handwriting of said Thomas C. Mitchell.

Said will being duly proven It is ordered by the Court that the said paper writing be and is hereby set up and established as the will of said Thomas C. Mitchell deceased and that the same be recorded as such by the clerk.

Attest

William M. Watkins Clerk
By Hick C. Doyle   D. C.

(P.182)
Last Will and Testament) State of Tennessee
of (Dyer County
George A. Fowlkes dec'd)
Set up and established (I George A. Fowlkes citizen of
Febry Term 1871 Recorded) Dyer County Tennessee make and
Febry 11th 1871 Will M. (publish this my last will and
Watkins Clerk By) Testament.
Hick C. Doyle D. C. (

Item 1. Let all my just debts be paid as soon as possible out of my personal effects - which I hereby direct my Executors to sell to create a fund for that purpose and for distribution as provided in the 2nd Item of my will.

Item 2nd The ballance of the fund arising from the sale of my personal property after payment of my debts I hereby direct to be divided equally between my wife and my three children share and share alike.

Item 3rd I give my wife Zenobia Frances Fowlkes Dower of all the real estate of which I die seized and possessed that is one third part of the same during the term of her natural life, quality and quantitity considered including my present Homestead.

Item 4th I hereby give and bequeath my real estate as follows First to my youngest child and only Son,

I give and bequeath my farm known as the Motherell place containing about 500 acres bought by me of John Motherell

Second, To my two daughters George Anna Fowlkes and Jenny Fowlkes I give and bequeath my home place to be equally divided between them by a line running north and south George Anna to have the eastern end and Jenny to have the western end I also give and bequeath to my two said daughters my bottom farm, situated on the north side of the Obion river containing 300 acres to be equally divided between them.

Item 5th The division and beqest of my real estate, as provided for in the 4th Item of this will is not to be made or take effect until my said youngest child and only Son comes of age or marries but the whole of my real estate outside of the Dower given my

(P.182 Cont'd) wife in Item 3rd of my will - is to remain in remain in common between my three children and the rents and profits arising there from is to remain in common and to be used by their guardian or guardians as far as may be necessary and as nearly equally as may be for their support and Education in the event of the death (P.183) of my son before he comes of age or marries - then the property hereby bequeathed to him shall vest at once in his heirs at law.

Item 6th I hereby advise my wife to rent out her Dower hereby given her, except such portion around the homestead as she may be able to cultivate profitably.

Item 7th In the event of my wife's death before my sons becoming of age or marrying then and in that event my real estate shall at once vest in my children in the proportion and shares provided for in the 4th Item of this my will.

Item 8th I hereby nominate and appoint guardian of my children

Item 9th I hereby nominate and appoint my wife Zenobia Frances Fowlkes my Executrix of this my last will and testament requiring no security of her as Executrix

    In testimony whereof I have hereunto set my hand this the 10th day of November 1870

                                  George A. Fowlkes

Signed and acknowledged)
in our presence, and   (
in testimony thereof   )
we have hereunto set   (
our hands in presence   )
of each other and the   (
Testator this the 10th   )
day of November 1871   (
    Joseph Smith
    William P. Menzies

State of Tennessee) February Term County Court 1871
Dyer County   )
                    This day a paper writing purporting to be the last will and testament of George A. Fowlkes late a citizen of Dyer County dec'd was produced here in open court for Probate -

Where upon came Joseph Smith & W. P. Menzies Subscribing witnesses there to who being first duly sworn depose and say that they were personally acquainted with the testator in his lifetime that he signed and published the said paper writing as his last will and Testament in their presence and for the purposes there in set forth and requested them specially to bear witness there to and that they signed it in the presence of each other and in the presence of the Testator and at his (P.184) request and that he was of sound and disposing memory at the time of executing the same said will. It is therefore ordered by the

(P.184 Cont'd) court that the said paper writing be set up and established as the last will and testament of George A. Fowlkes dec'd and the same recorded by the clerk.

Attest

             W. M. Watkins Clerk.
          By H. P. Doyle D. C.

| Last Will and Testament of James B. Cunningham dec'd Set up and established June 5th 1871 Recorded June 24th 1871 Will M. Watkins Clerk | State of Tennessee Dyer County |

I James B. Cunningham being of sound mind now a resident citizen of the aforesaid State and county do make this and publish this as my last <u>Will</u> and Testament, hereby revoking and making void all others by me at any time made.

<u>Firstly</u> - I bequeath my soul to God - who gave it my wife and all my children to the charge and prayers of the C. P. Church and mercy of God.

<u>Secondly</u> - I bequeath that all of my debts be paid out of the first monies that the executors may receive from sales of real or personal estates or notes or monies which I may die possessed.

<u>Thirdly</u> - I bequeath that my executor either one year from my death sell all of my real estates except my homestead (where I am now living) ½ mile north of Newbern Either privately or publicly on such terms as he may deem best, part only Cash or wholey so.

<u>Fourthly</u> - That as Cora Lee, Mattie Lou and Joe Hanie have secured them ($5000.00) Five Thousand Dollars each in life Policies - as follows $5000.00 in the Southern at Memphis and $10,000.00 in St. Louis Mutual at Saint Louis Mo. at my death - I order will and bequeath that Mr. Andrew S. Parks their uncle be qualified as their Guardian as the law directs by making good and sufficient and approved bond to the court then he said Guardian proceed to draw said amount $15,000.00 and invest it securely to the greatest profit for their the childrens interest and that they have so much of the (P.185) interest only yearly as they in his judgement need.

<u>Fifthly</u> - I bequeath to my beloved wife Mary W. the homestead which I value at $3,000.00 and all the house hold and kitchen furniture except that already claimed by the several children as heir looms from their ancestors also one fourth of proceeds of my real estate when sold.

<u>Sixthly</u> - That if my wife shall have any children living at my death by me, that the same be first made equal out of the proceeds of assets of my estate to the (3) three first children, and that said child have the same for Guardian A. S. Parks and invest said childs means in the best way he may think best

(P.185 Cont'd) for said child, so that the interest on it may support said child.

Seventhly - I bequeath that all my children live with my wife and that the Guardian pay her for board for them on such terms as they may agree. She remaining my widow but if she shall marry then the children may have their choice to board with her or some one else, being advised by their guardian for their Interest.

Eighthly - I nominate and hereby appoint Mr. Andrew S. Parks my executor and also the guardian of children he complying as the law directs in such cases.

In the presence of these witnesses I affix my name this July the 24th 1870 A. D.

James B. Cunningham (seal)

Witnesses
G. B. Tinsley
James M. Sherrod.

Codicil No. 2. After mature reflection I feel satisfied that it may be best for my beloved wife and children to so change the seventh item of this my last will & Testament to which this is added as codicil No. 2. As to allow my children to have such home or homes as my beloved wife & executors may think best, and my will and desire is that they may remain with my beloved wife on the terms mentioned in Item Seven or not as shall be deemed best for their interest by my executors my beloved wife asserting there to, this provision is for Cora Lee, Mattie Lou and Joe (P.186) Hanie. I also think it best for the interest of all the parties that Hamilton Parks Jr. be also appointed as one of my executors and Guardians for my children, and I hereby so nominate and appoint him such executor & Guardian on the same terms and conditions that his brother Andrew S. Parks is appointed my executor and Guardian for my children in this will. I further will and direct that my executors in the sale of my real estates as heretofore directed sell and convey the same without the aid or intervention of any court Decree whatever.

And that my will may be more surely understood and carried out by my executors. I direct that my beloved wife and the four children be made equal in the division of the proceeds of my estate, taking the same share and share alike. My beloved wife taking the homestead at the valuation in Item five of this will, and the household and kitchen furniture there in given her at Two hundred dollars.

April 26th 1871

Witness
Smith Parks
J. N. Wyatt

Jas. B. Cunningham

(105)

(P.186 Cont'd)
State of Tennessee) June Term County Court 1871
Dyer County)

This day a paper writing purporting to be the last will and Testament of James B. Cunningham late of Dyer County deceased was produced here in open court for Probate, whereupon came G. B. Tinsley and J. M. Sherrod subscribing witnesses there to and Smith Parks and J. N. Wyatt subscribing witnesses to codicil No. 2 of said will. Who being first duly sworn, depose and say as follows that they were personally acquainted with J. B. Cunningham in his life time, that he was of sound and disposing memory at the time of the execution of the same. And that he signed and published the said paper writing as his last will and Testament in their presence and for the purposes there in set forth and requested specially to bear witness there to and that they signed it in his presence and in the presence of each other & at his request. It is therefore ordered by the court that the said paper writing be set up and established as the last will and Testament of said J. B. Cunningham Dec'd and the same be recorded by the clerk and placed on file in the county court Clerk office.

    Attest W. M. Watkins Clerk
      By Hick P. Doyle D. C.

(P.187)

Last Will and Testament) State of Tennessee
   of   (Dyer County
Samuel B. Shaw dec'd)
Set up and established (In the Name of Almighty God Amen.
Aug. Term 1871   )
Recorded Aug. 21st 1871 (I Samuel B. Shaw of the County of
Wm. M. Watkins clerk.) Dyer and State of Tennessee being
              in bad health but of sound mind
and knowing the uncertainty of life and the certainty of death do hereby make and constitute this my last will and testament hereby revoking all other wills by me made.

Item 1st - That my body be decently buried when I am dead.

Item 2nd - That all my just debts be paid as soon after my death as my Executors here in after mentioned may find it convenient to do so.

Item 3rd - I will to my beloved brothers Craig N. Shaw and David A. Shaw and my beloved sister Martha E. Shaw all of my property of every description both personal and real to be divided between them equally so that each one will receive one third of my estate.

Item 4 - I will the fine black mare of mine which my brother Thomas J. Shaw rode into the Confederate Army and got captured to be a set off against the note he holds against me for some Sixty or a hundred dollars it being a note I gave Wm. C. Wagster.

(106)

(P.187 Cont'd)
Item 5th - I will that my brothers Craig N. and David A. Shaw be and I hereby appoint them my executors to carry into effect the provisions of this my last will and testament.

    Done at my residence in the Fourth Civil District of Dyer County Tennessee on this the 3rd day of June 1871. In witness whereof I hereunto Subscribe my name.

Attest   )   Sam'l B. Shaw
H. L. W. Turney(
Wm. D. Taylor)

State of Tennessee)
Dyer County   )   August Term County Court 1871

    This day a paper writing purporting to be the last will and Testament of Samuel B. Shaw dec'd was produced here in open Court for probate where upon came (P.188) H. L. W. Turney and Wm. D. Taylor Subscribing witnesses there to who being first duly sworn depose as follows that they were personally acquainted with the testator in his life time. That he was of sound mind and disposing memory at the time of the execution of the same and that he signed and published the said paper writing as his last will and testament in their presence and for the purposes therein contained and requested them specially to bear witness thereto and that they signed the same in the presence of the testator and in the presence of each other.

    It is therefore ordered by the court that said paper writing be set up and established as the last will and testament of said Sam B. Shaw deceased, and the same be recorded by the clerk and placed on file in the county clerks office
Attest
                                      Will M. Watkins   Clerk
                                      By H. P. Doyle   D. C.

Last will and Testament)   State of Tennessee
         of   (Dyer County
Agness Walker dec'd   )   In the Name of God Amen.
Set up and Established   (
Sept. Term 71 Recorded)   I Agness Walker being of
Sept. 9th, 1871   (sound mind do make and cause to
Will M. Watkins Clerk   )   be written the following as my
By Hick P. Doyle D. C.   (will To-wit.

I will and bequeath that after I am dead that all my just indebtedness be paid after which I will and bequeath to my daughter Malissa C. Walker my mare (Pett) Buggy and Buggy harness. I also will and bequeath to my daughter Mallissa C. Walker all of my entire interest in my husbands (Mathew P. Walker deceased) estate consisting of money collected and money that should have been collected - - - This September 1869
Witness
John M. Drane, Louisa P. Drane   Agness Walker

(P.189)
State of Tennessee) September Term County Court 1871
Dyer County)

This day a paper writing purporting to be the last will and testament of Agness Walker dec'd produced here into open court for probate, where upon came John M. Drane and Louisa P. Drane Subscribing witnesses there to, who being first duly sworn deposed as follows To-wit That they were personally acquainted with Agness Walker the Testatrix in her life time that she was of sound and deposing mind at the time of the execution of the same and that she signed and published the said paper writing as her last will and testament in their presence and for the purposes therein contained and requested them specially to bear witness thereto, and that they signed the same in the presence of the Testatrix and in the presence of each other.

It is therefore ordered by the Court that the said paper writing be set up and established as the Last will and testament of said Agness Walker deceased and that same be recorded by the clerk, and placed on file in the county clerks office
Attest

    William M. Watkins   Clerk
    By Hick P. Doyle   D. C.

Last will and Testament) I R. G. Henderson of the County of
    of   (Dyer and State of Tennessee make
R. G. Henderson dec'd) this my last will. I give devise
Set up and established (and bequeath my estate and property
Oct. 4th, 1871 Recorded) real and personal as follows; that
Nov. 27th, 1871   (is to say; I want all my property,
W. M. Watkins Clerk   ) both real and personal to go to my
By Zach Watkins D. C. (wife, during her life time, and
           then should Jane outlive her, I
want her to have Two Hundred Dollars and at the death of my wife, I want the proceeds then the to be divided equally between the children. The monies coming from North Carolina, I want as much as Eight Hundred Dollars to go to my last children, and the ballance to as she chooses, I would appoint or choose B. H. Harmon of Dyer County, State of Tennessee, as my Executor to execute this my will. I want the sale of my lands to go on as I have contracted and that the Executor to have power as myself if living. I want the sale of all my personal property (P.190) to take effect as I have commenced it and the proceeds first to go to the discharge of my indebtedness.

In witness whereof I have signed and sealed and published and declared this instrument at home near Friendship, Tennessee This Sept. 28th, 1871.

        R. G. Henderson (seal)

The said R. G. Henderson at said place and said date signed and sealed this instrument and published and declared the same as and for his last will and we at his request and in

(P.190 Cont'd) his presence & of each other have hereunto written our names as subscribing witnesses.

       F. M. Boling, witness
       N. T. Perry - witness

State of Tennessee)
Dyer County) October Term of County Court 1871

This day a paper writing purporting to be the last will and testament of R. G. Henderson, deceased was produced here into open court for probate; Whereupon came F. M. Boling and N. T. Perry subscribing witnesses thereto, who being first duly sworn, deposed and said as follows to-wit; that they were personally acquainted with the Testator in his life time; that he was of sound and disposing memory at the time of the execution of the same, and that he signed and published said paper writing as his last will and testament in their presence, and for the purposes there in contained and requested them specially to bear witness there to and that they signed it in the presence of the Testator and in the presence of each other. It is therefore ordered that said Paper writing be and the same is hereby set up and established as the last will and Testament of the said R. G. Henderson, deceased and be recorded by the clerk, &c.

   Attest W. M. Watkins Clerk.
      By Zach Watkins D. C.

(P.191)
| Last Will and Testament of W. K. Waddie deceased Set up and established at the February Term A. D. 1872 Recorded Febry 15th 1872, Will M. Watkins Clerk By Zach Watkins D. C. | State of Tennessee Dyer County I William K. Waddie being in feeble health but sound of mind hereby make this as my last will and testament, revoking at the same time all former wills heretofore at any time made by me. |

Item 1st First my Executor first pay all my debts and burial expenses out of any money coming to his hands -

Item 2nd My children by my first wife having all had the portion of my estate I intended for them, I give them nothing more except to confirm them in the gifts and allotments heretofore made them.

Item 3rd My will and desire is that my beloved wife Ann have entire control and possession of my two children- the children of my second wife - That she take their mothers place in every particular, have the same charge and control of them in possession, morals and education that their natural mother would have if living - and I give to my beloved wife Ann and to my little son John William about Ten years old last September and to my little son Joseph Kimbo Waddie, about four years old the present January all my property whether real

(P.191 Cont'd) personal or mixed to be divided between them as though my beloved wife was their natural mother, to be divided as the law divides it between them - this includes my Life Policy and all the estate, possessions or property of every kind and description it may be of which I am possessed -

I hereby nominate and appoint my beloved wife Ann my Executrix to this my last will and Testament and make her Testamentary Guardian for my children John W. and Joseph K. Waddie -
January 5th 1872   W. K. Waddie
Witnesses
Smith Parks
J. R. Westbrook

State of Tennessee)   February Term of the County Court 1872
Dyer County   )   Monday Febry 5th 1872,

This day a paper writing purporting to be the last will and testament of W. K. Waddie dec'd was produced here into open court for probate Whereupon came Smith Parks and J. R. Westbrook subscribing witnesses thereto, who being first duly sworn deposed (P.192) and said as follows: That they were personally acquainted with the Testator in his life time, that he was of sound and disposing memory at the time of the execution of the same and that he signed and published said paper writing as his last will and testament in their presence and for the purposes therein contained and requested them specially to bear witness thereto; and that they signed it in the presence of the Testator and in the presence of each other.

It is therefore ordered that said Paper Writing be and the same is hereby set up and established as the last will and testament of the said William K. Waddie, deceased and be recorded by the clerk &c.

            Attest   William M. Watkins   clerk.
               By   Zach Watkins   D. C.

Last will and Testament) State of Tennessee Dyer County
       of   (
Sarah Ann Stallings   ) I Sarah Ann Stallings of the
Set up and established   (County of Dyer and State of
Febry 5th /72 Recorded Febry) Tennessee make this my last
16th 1872   W. M. Watkins clerk(will and testament -
By Zach Watkins D. C.   )

        I give, devise and bequeath my estate real and personal property as follows: that is to say, a tract of land containing by estimation Fifty four acres (54) the land that my husband Cannah Stallings give me by conveyance in the year 1859 and also from John P. Davis in the year 1863 Said land is situated and being in the first civil district of Dyer county State of Tennessee,

(110)

(P.192 Cont'd) bounded as follows: North by Ben Howell and A. Rogers; East by N. T. Perry South by B. H. Harmon and west by T. M. Boling, To Cannah Stallings and his heirs at my death, should I die first -

In witness whereof I have signed and sealed and published and declared this instrument as my last will at home on the 28th day of March A. D. 1871

            her
         Sarah Ann X Stallings (seal)
            mark

The said Sarah Ann Stallings at home on said date above signed and sealed this instrument and published and declared the same as and for her last will. And we at her request and in her presence and in the presence of each other have hereunto written our names as subscribing witnesses.

Attest: B. H. Harmon
              W. J. Hall

(P.193)
State of Tennessee) February Term of the County Court
Dyer County   ) Tennessee 1872,
          Monday the fifth of Febry 1872

This day a Paper writing purporting to be the last will and testament of Sarah Ann Stallings was produced here into open court for Probate. Where upon came B. H. Harmon and W. J. Hall subscribing witness thereto, who being duly sworn deposed and said that they are personally acquainted with the Testatrix that she was of sound and deposing memory at the time of the execution of the same and that she signed and published said paper writing as her last will and testament in their presence and for the purposes therein contained and requested them specially to bear witness thereto; and that they signed it in the presence of the Testator and in the presence of each other.

  It is therefore ordered that said Paper writing be and the same is hereby set up and established as the Last will and Testament of the said Sarah Ann Stallings and that the same be recorded by the Clerk &c.

         Attest Will M. Watkins, Clerk
           By Zack Watkins D. Clerk.

Last Will and Testament   ) State of Tennessee
    of   (Dyer County
Cannah Stallings   )
Set up & Established Feb. 5th 1872 (I, Cannah Stallings of
W. M. Watkins Clerk   ) the County of Dyer,
By Zack Watkins D. C.   (State of Tennessee, make
                   this my Last Will and
Testament, - I give, devise, and bequeath my real estate and Personal property as follows, that is to say all my personal-

(P.193 Cont'd) ties as monies, stocks, household and kitchen furniture and all interests, notes &c, after all just creditors have been satisfied at my death to Sarah Ann Stallings, my wife, should she be so fortunate as to live the longest In testimony whereof I have signed and sealed and published and declared this instrument as my last will at home, on the 28th day of March A. D. 1871

           Cannah Stallings (seal)

The said Cannah Stallings at home on the date above, signed and sealed this instrument and published and declared the same as and for his last will and we at his request (P.194) and in his presence and in the presence of each other have hereunto written our names as subscribing witnesses

   Attestation of witnesses, B. H. Harmon
              W. J. Hall.

State of Tennessee) February Term of the Dyer County Court,
Dyer County   ) 1872
          Monday Feby. 5th 1872

This day a Paper writing purporting to be the Last Will and Testament of Cannah Stallings was produced here in open court for probate; Whereupon came B. H. Harmon and W. J. Hall subscribing witnesses thereto who being duly sworn deposed and said as follows to wit, That they are personally acquainted with the Testator and that he was of sound and disposing memory at the time of the execution of the same & that he signed and published said Paper writing as his Last will and testament in their presence, and for the purposes therein contained and requested them specially to bear witness thereto and that they signed it in the presence of the Testator and in the presence of each other.

  It is therefore ordained that said Paper writing be and the same is hereby set up and established as the last Will & Testament of the said Cannah Stallings and that the same be recorded by the Clerk &c.

    Attest - W. M. Watkins Clerk
       By Zack Watkins, D. Clerk.

(P/195)
State of Tennessee) September term of Dyer County Court
Dyer County   (Monday, Sept. 2, 1872

This day a paper writing purporting to be the last will and testament of Mary Caldwell was produced here in open court for probate. Where upon came Thomas Miller and George Miller subscribing witnesses thereto who being duly sworn deposed and said as follows to wit: that they were personally acquainted with the testatrix and that she was of sound and disposing memory at the time of the execution of the same, and that she signed and published said paper writing as her

(P.195 Cont'd) last will and testament in their presence and for the purposes therein contained and requested them specially to bear witness thereto and that they signed it in the presence of the Testatrix and in the presence of each other

It is therefore ordered that said paper writing be and the same is hereby set up and established as the last Will and testament of the said Mary Caldwell and that the same be recorded by the Clerk &c.

    Attest   W. M. Watkins   Clerk
  By Zack Watkins D. C.

(P.196)
Last Will and Testament (State of Tennessee
      of) Dyer County
Mary Caldwell Dec'd.)
Set up & established 24th Oct. 1867 (I, Mary Caldwell of the
Probated Sept. 2, 1872) County & State above
Recorded Sept. 5, 1872 (mentioned being in sound
William Watkins Clerk.) mind, but frail in body, knowing the uncertainty of live, but certainty of death do make this my will and testament, first I will my soul to God who gave it and my body to its Mother earth. I will that my burial and funeral expenses together with my just debts be first paid, out of any means I may die possessed of. I will that my Son James P. have eighty acres out of one hundred fifty acres including the house, the houses I live in is on it being (the one hundred & fifty acres) paid for out of my own money, and the balance seventy acres to be equally divided between my two sons William & Robert M. Caldwell and I will that said William, Robert M., & James P. Caldwell pay to Mary B. Dunevant five hundred dollars each to pay an equal part as she may need the means to assist in educating her, the other one hundred and fifty acres I will to Catherine B. Mabry, Mary I. Craig Martha Ann Powell, William Caldwell, and Robert M. Caldwell to be equally divided and all my personal property which I may be possessed of at my death I will to be equally divided between my six children above named, and I hereby nominate and appoint my three sons, William, Robert M. & James P. Caldwell my executors to carry out this my last will and testament. In whereof I have hereunto set my hand and affixed my seal in the year of our Lord one thousand eight hundred (P.197) and sixty seven this 24th day of October & year above written.

    Test. Thomas Miller   Mary Caldwell
          George Miller   (seal)

                    For Probate See 199 or 195

(113)

(P.197 Cont'd)

Last Will and Testament) This my last will and Testament
       of   (made this March the 12 in the
John M. Hart dec'd   ) year of Our Lord one thousand
set up and established (eight hundred and Seventy - It
March 12th 1870   ) is my will and desire that after
Probated Oct. 7th 1872 (my debts and funeral expenses are
Recorded Oct. 26th 1872) paid that all my effects be con-
William M. Watkins Clk.(verted into money and that equal-
By Zach Watkins D. C.) ly divided between my four brothers
                                         D. J. Hart, W. P. Hart, and M. J.
Hart and my two sisters H. F. Patterson & R. T. Parker. It
is my will and wish that each of these Legatees as named a-
bove give equally each year an amount sufficient to board our
mother with some one of said Legatees and clothe her comfortably during her natural life. It is my will and wish that my
executors have power to sell and make deeds to my lands and
other real estate, without getting an order from court for
said purposes. It is my will and wish that my brother R. S.
Hart & B. T. Hillsman take possession of and execute this my
last will.

                                                              John M. Hart (seal)

Witnesses   R. B. Moore)
               J. B. Moore(

                -- "Nuncupative codicil" --

I wish to alter my will previously made so as to give to the
Cumberland Presbyterian church the sum of five hundred dollars in gold now deposited in my safe with my will and other
valuables, and I appoint Milton J. Hart and Dan'l E. Parker,
_____ who shall dispose of it as they may deem best for general interest of the church, September 3rd 1872

(P.198)   Monday Oct. 7, 1872
This day a paper writing purporting to be the last will and
testament of John M. Hart deceased was produced here into
open court for probate. Where upon came R. B. Moore, one of
the subscribing witnesses thereto here into open court, who
having first been duly sworn deposed and said that he was
personally acquainted with the testator in his life time; that
he was of sound and disposing memory at the time of the execution of said paper writing, and that he signed and published
said paper writing as his last will and testament in his presence and for the purposes therein contained and requested him
specially to bear witness thereto and that he signed the same
in the presence of the testator, where upon also came Dan'l E.
Parker and M. J. Hart here into open court, who being duly
sworn deposed and said that they were personally acquainted
with the Testator John M. Hart in his life time; that he was
of sound and disposing memory at the time he made a declaration (which they, said Parker and Hart have reduced to writing and is attached to said will) to them that it was his wish
that his will be so altered "as to give to the Cumberland

(114)

(P.198 Cont'd) Presbyterian church the sum of five Hundred dollars in gold, and appointing D. E. Parker and M. J. Hart " to dispose of it as they may deem best for the general interest of the church that he made said declaration in their presence, and requested them to be witnesses to the same - that the paper writing annexed to his will is substantially the declaration made by said Testator in their presence: that they reduced the same to writing: It is therefore ordered by the court that said paper writings, be and the same are hereby set up and established as the last will and Testament of the said John M. Hart, and that the same be recorded by the clerk & filed

    Attest:

                    Zach Watkins   D. C.

(P.199)   "Monday September 2, 1872

This day a paper writing purporting to be the last will and Testament of Mary Caldwell dec'd was produced here into open court for probate where upon came Thos. Miller and George Miller subscribing witnesses thereto who being first duly sworn deposed and said that they were personally acquainted with the Testatrix in her life time. That she was of sound and disposing memory at the time of the execution of the same and that she signed and published the said paper writing as her last will and testament in their presence, and for the purposes therein contained and requested them specially to bear witness thereto, and that they signed the same in the presence of each other. It is therefore ordered by the court that said paper writing be and the same is hereby set up and established as the last will and testament of the said Mary Caldwell deceased and that the same be recorded by the clerk and placed on file."

    Will recorded on Pages 196 - 7

(P.200) Last Will of John Huguely
        State of Tennessee) November Term
        County of Dyer   ) County Court
                           Monday Nov. 4, 1872

        This day a paper writing purporting to be the nun-cupative will of John Huguely dec'd was produced here in open court for probate; where upon came G. W. Blankenship and W. Y. Huguely, subscribing witnesses thereto who after being first duly sworn deposed as follows; that they were personally acquainted with the Testator in his life time; that he was of sound and disposing memory at the time of making the said will; that he requested them specially to bear witness to the disposition he desired should be made of his estate; that his desire was made known to them shortly before his death, and that the said paper writing is a true record of said Testators declaration to them, having had the same reduced to writing as they understood it. It is therefore ordered by the court that said paper writing be set up and

(P.200 Cont'd) established as the last will and Testament of the said John Huguely dec'd, and be recorded by the Clerk and filed -

In the Name of God Amen.

    I John Huguely of Dyer County Tennessee, being mindful of my mortality do this 24 day of October, in the year of Our Lord 1872 make & publish this my last will & testament, in manner following.

    1st I bequeath all my real estate and personal property, after my just debts are paid, to my Mother Sister Martha, they having helped me to acquire said property & waiting upon me during my illness, also I do constitute & appoint my brother S. E. Huguely to be executor of this my last will & testament
witness,   G. W. Blankenship
witness,   W. Y. Huguely,
Recorded Nov. 9, 1872"

Attest   Zach Watkins D. C.
      witness   G. W. Blankenship
      witness   W. Y. Huguely

(P.201)
Last Will &c of Ephraum Powers Sr. dec'sd

| Last Will & Testament of) Ephraum Powers dec'd Set up & established Dec /73 Recorded Jan. 31st 73 Zach Watkins D. C. | In the Name of God: Amen -

    In the year of our Lord one thousand Eight Hundred and Sixty nine I Ephraum Powers being feeble in body but sound in mind do make this my last |

will and testament:

    After my just debts are paid I will and bequeath to my wife Wealthy Powers all of my property consisting of land, Stock, household and kitchen furniture, during her natural life and after death my estate shall be equally divided between my two sons, John and Ephraum Powers, dividing the land east and west -

    I leave my two sons, John Powers and Ephraum Powers, Executors to my Estate and hereby exempt my Executors from giving security - August the 11th 1869

                                     his
Witness -   Ephraum X Powers
Thomas D. Harwell,   mark
T. Griffin
W. R. King

State of Tenn.)   December Term of County Court of Said
Dyer County   )   County. Monday December 2nd 1873

(P.201 Cont'd)

This day a paper writing to be the last will and testament of Ephraum Powers Sr. dec'd was presented here into open court for probate. Where upon came Thomas D. Harwell, Timothy Griffin subscribing witnesses thereto, who being duly sworn deposed and said that they were personally acquainted with the Testator in his life time that he was of sound and disposing memory at the time of the execution of said paper writing and that he signed and published said paper writing as his last will and testament in their presence and for the purposes there in contained and requested them specially to bear witness thereto and that they signed the same in the presence of the Testator and in the presence of each other. It is therefore ordered by the court that said Paper writing be and the same is hereby set up and established as the last will and testament of said Ephraum Powers Sr. dec'd and that the same be recorded by the clerk & filed.

Attest   Zach Watkins D. C.

(P.202)

Last will & Testament of Crawford E. White dec'd
Probated July term 1873
Recorded July 15th 1873
W. M. Watkins Clerk

I, Crawford E. White being in usual bodily health and sound in mind, do make this my last will and testament

Item 1st: I desire that all my just debts be paid and then I give all the remainder of the remainder of the effects that I may own at my death of every sort and kind real, personal and mixed and choses in action to my beloved wife Francis J. White and her heirs and assigns forever, having heretofore done all for my children that I intend doing for them -

Item 2   I hereby appoint Smith Parks Executor of this my last will and Testament

Executed in our presence this the 24th day of April 1869
    J. N. Wyatt
    R. P. McCracken

C. E. White

State of Tennessee)   July Term of the County Court 1873
Dyer County   (Monday July 7 /73

This day a paper writing purporting to be the last will and testament of C. E. White deceased was produced here into open court for probate: There upon came J. N. Wyatt and R. P. McCraken, subscribing witnesses thereto here into open court who being first duly sworn deposed and said that they were personally acquainted with the Testator in his life time; that he was of sound and disposing memory at the time of the execution of the same and that he signed and published the said paper writing

(P.202 Cont'd) as his last will and testament in their presence and for the purposes therein contained, and requested them specially to bear witness thereto; and that they signed the same in the presence of the testator and in the presence of each other; It is therefore ordered by the court that said paper writing be and the same is hereby set up and established as the last will and testament of the said C. E. White deceased and that the same be recorded by the clerk and filed

Attest
    Zach Watkins D. C.

(P.203)

Last will & Testament of Jackson Pace deceased
Probated at Aug. Term 1873
Recorded August 20th 1873
W. M. Watkins clerk.

I, Jackson Pace of the State of Tennessee and the county of Dyer do this the 23rd day of June in the year of our Lord one Thousand Eight hundred and Seventy three make my last will and testament

    I Jackson Pace do appoint J. R. Herrin, as my Executor of this my last will and Testament to execute and settle all of my just debts and claims, and I do further more give the said Lera Heath untill December the twenty-fifth, Eighteen Hundred and Seventy five to make the last payment on a tract of land sold by me to him - And I, Jackson Pace do request J. R. Herrin make an equal division of my affects to my children after all of my just debts are settled and paid - I do further more give and bequeath to Rainey Hallum the sum of fifty Dollars - I also give and bequeath to Ellen Herrin, the sum of fifty-dollars - The above two sisters are to have the above amount and then an equal division then amongst my children -

    Given under my hand and seal, day and date above written

Test: signed Jackson Pace (seal)
W. J. Farris
J. T. Stockton

State of Tennessee) August Term of the County Court 1873
Dyer County   (Monday August 4, 1873

    This day a paper writing purporting to be the last will and testament of Jackson Pace deceased was produced here into open court for probate, Thereupon came W. J. Farris and J. T. Stockton, subscribing witnesses thereto, here into open court, who being duly sworn deposed and said that they were personally acquainted with the testator in his life time - that he was of sound and disposing memory at the time of the execution of the same and that he signed and published said paper writing as his last will and testament in their presence and for the purposes therein contained and requested them specially to bear witness thereto That they signed the same in the presence of the Testator and in the presence of each other. It is therefore ordered by the court that said

(118)

(P.203 Cont'd) paper writing be and the same is hereby set up and established as the last will and testament of Jackson Pace deceased and the same be recorded by the clerk and filed.

Attest
    Zach Watkins D. C.

(P.204)

Last Will and Testament of Edward Haskins dec'd Probated Oct. & Nov. term 1873 Recorded November 1873 W. M. Watkins clerk	I, Edward Haskins being of sound mind and disposing memory have this day made and published this my last will and testament, hereby revoking all former wills by me at any time heretofore made, -

Item 1st - I desire and direct all of my debts and my personal expenses to be paid out of the first money coming into the hands of my Executrix.

Item 2nd - I give and bequeath to my beloved wife Harriet J. Haskins all my household property farming utensils, stock of every description crop and provisions on hand, money, notes, accounts and everything belonging to me at my death, not otherwise herein disposed of, to be used by her at her discretion, in raising and educating our minor children, and to be used at her discretion. She may dispose of any of said estate, as she deems best in advancing the interest of our children - May give them such parts of it as she may judge proper or may sell and dispose of it as she may think right and prudent for her to do. -

Item 3rd I have already given to my two sons ____ and John C. what I desire to give them.

Item 4 - I give and bequeath to my daughter Lucy M. Haskins one hundred and thirty acres of land off the west end of the tract of my land known as the home tract of land and purchased by me of McLemore & Valux

Item 5 - The balance of said tract of land mentioned in item 4 and known as my home tract of land be the same more or less I give to my son Aron Haskins subject to the following restrictions and limitations that is as this tract of land includes the homestead, I give it first to my beloved wife Harrit J. for and during her natural life, including all the necessary out buildings as well as the mansion house, and after the death of my beloved wife, then said tract of land goes to my son Aron.

Item 6 - I give to my two younger daughters Eliza Carter and Harriet Jane Haskins my tract of land purchased from Calvin Ferrill and containing about two hundred and twenty one acres more or less to be divided between them equally agreeable to quality and quantity - And I refer to my deed which is

(119)

(P.204 Cont'd) of record for particulars as to notes and bounds of said land it joins my home tract on the north.

Item 7 - My house and lot in Newbern Tennessee known as the Westbrook Lauderdale lot, I hereby authorize my Executor and Executrix to sell at their discretion, on such terms as they may think proper and convey the same by general warranty titles or otherwise, without the aid or intervention of any court whatever and the proceeds belong to my beloved wife as directed in item second of said will.

(P.205) Item 8 - I hereby nominate and appoint my beloved wife Harriet Jane and my son Creed Haskins Executrix and Executor of this my last will and testament This 13th of August 1867

Witnesses -   Ed. Haskins (seal)
R. P. McCraken
J. A. C. Manley

Codicil No. 1 -

Owing to changes in my family occasioned by the death of my beloved daughter Harrit I hereby change item six of my will to which this is a codicil so as to give to my daughter Eliza Carter Haskins one hundred and Twenty one acres of the land mentioned and described in said item six off the south of said tract - and I give to my beloved wife Harriet J. Haskins absolutely and in fee simple one hundred acres of said tract of land mentioned and described in item six of my will of the North end or side of said tract - And in the event of my selling said one hundred acres during my life then I give to my beloved wife Harrit J. all of the proceeds of such sale as may be undisposed of, absolutely and without qualification or reserve to be hers to use and dispose of as she may deem best - Feb. 13, 1873

Witness   Ed. Haskins
G. B. Tinsley
J. K. P. Harrwell

State of Tennessee)   October Term of the County Court 1873
Dyer County   )   Monday Oct. 6, 1873

This day a paper writing purporting to be the last will and Testament of Edward Haskins deceased, was produced here before the court for probate: Thereupon came into open court Smith Parks and L. M. Williams and G. B. Tinsley who being first duly sworn deposed and said that they are acquainted with the handwriting of J. A. C. Manley one of the subscribing witnesses to said will: that the said J. A. C. Manley is dead and that the handwriting purporting to be the handwriting of the said J. A. C. Manley is his own genuine signature - There upon also J. K. C. Harrell and G. B. Tinsley subscribing witnesses to the Codicil to said will, who being duly sworn deposed and said that they were personally acquainted with

(P.205 Cont'd) Edward Haskins in his life time; that he was of sound and disposing memory at the time of the execution of said Codicil and that he signed and published the same as the Codicil to his said will in their presence and for the purposes therein contained and requested them to specially to bear witness thereto and that they attested the same in the presence of the testator and of each other.

OVER

(P.206)
State of Tennessee(November Term of the County Court 1873
Dyer County   (Monday Nov. 3, 1873

     This day a paper writing purporting to be the last will and testament of Edward Haskins deceased was presented to the court for further Probate, the execution for the same having been proven by _____ one of the subscribing witnesses thereto at the Oct. term of this court 1873; There upon came R. P. McCrakin, a subscribing witness thereto here into open court, who being first duly sworn, deposed and said that he was personally acquainted with Edward Haskins, in his life time; That he was of sound and disposing memory at the time of the execution of said paper writing and that he acknowledged the execution of the same as his last will and testament in his presence and for the purposes therein contained and requested him specially to bear witness thereto that he signed the same in the presence of the testator and in the presence of J. A. C. Manly the other subscribing witness thereto; It is therefore ordered by the court that said paper writing be and the same is hereby set up and established as the last will and testament of the said Edward Haskins and be recorded by the clerk and filed

Attest
          Zach Watkins   D. C.

(P.207)
Last will and Testament)	I, David C. Weakly being in feeble
of (	health, but of sound mind do make
David C. Weakly dec'd)	and publish this as my last will
Probated Nov. term 1873(	and testament hereby revoking all
Recorded Nov. 25,.1873)	former wills by me heretofore at
W. M. Watkins clerk (	any time made -

     Item 1st - I desire that all of my just debts and funeral expenses be paid out of the first money coming to the hands of my Executor.

     Item 2nd - I give to my beloved wife Elizabeth S. Weakly all my property and effects real and personal or mixed of which I may die seized or possessed including stock of every description, farming utensils, provisions, crop on hand, household and kitchen furniture money choses in action every species of property or estate for and during her natural life.

(121)

(P.207 Cont'd) Item 3rd - If my beloved wife should desire it she may at any time sell any of the personal property and use the proceeds in such way as she may deem necessary and proper for her comfort and convenience. And if she should become dissatisfied with our home and desire to change it for any other place or home my Executor is authorized upon her requesting him so to do in writing to see the tract of land on which I now reside and make to the purchase a good title to the same without the aid or decree of any court and use the proceeds to procure her such comfortable home as she may desire.

Item 4th - Having already given my son William S. Weakly all I am able heretofore, I do not include him in the benefit of this will.

Item 5th - At the death of my beloved wife, I desire that the land on which I live or if that be sold and exchanged for another home for my beloved wife then that real estate be sold by my executor without the aid of any court decree and convey the same to the to the purchaser by a paper conveyance for cash or on time as he may deem best for the parties interested, together with all the property and effects herein given to my beloved wife that may be remaining on hand at her death and the proceeds thereof be equally divided between my daughter Martha A. Fryar, my daughter Ella Doyle my daughter Issabella S. ____ my daughter Elizabeth Weakly and my son M. H. P. Weakly & my son David R. Weakly

Item 6 - I hereby appoint Smith Parks Executor of this my last will and testament - This 19th day May 1870

Witness   D. C. Weakley
H. Parks
R. P. McCracken

(P.208)
State of Tennessee)   November Term of County Court 1873
Dyer County   (Monday Nov. 3/73

This day a paper writing purporting to be the last will and testament of D. C. Weakly deceased was produced before the court for Probate. Thereupon came Hamilton Parks and R. P. McCraken the subscribing witnesses to the same here into open court who being first duly sworn, deposed and said that they were personally acquainted with the said D. C. Weakly in his life time: that he was of sound and disposing memory at the time of the execution of the same and that he acknowledged the execution of said paper writing in their presence as his last will and testament for the purposes therein contained and requested them to specially bear witness thereto: That they signed the same in the presence of the Testator and in the presence of each other: It is therefore ordered by the court that said paper writing be and the same is hereby set up and established as the last will and testament of the said D. C. Weakly deceased and the same be recorded by

(P.208 Cont'd)   the clerk and filed

  Attest
    Zach Watkins D. C.

(P.209)

Last Will and Testament of Elizabeth B. Jordan dec'd Probated November Term 1873 Recorded November 20/73 W. M. Watkins clerk.	In the Name of God Amen! I, Elizabeth B. Jordan of Dyersburg, Tennessee being of sound mind and disposing memory, do hereby make and publish this my last will and testament, hereby

revoking and making void all former wills by me at any time made in manner and form following, That is to say: Item - I give and bequeath all my property, real and personal of every description to my beloved husband Thomas A. Jordan, to have and to hold the same to him, and his heirs and assigns forever.

  And I hereby nominate and appoint my husband Thomas A. Jordan sole executor of this my last will and testament -

  In witness whereof I have hereunto set my hand and seal this 22nd day of September in the year of our Lord 1870

           Elizabeth B. Jordan (seal)

Signed sealed & published
in presence of us who
have subscribed our names
in presence of Testatrix
on her request September 22,
1870

M. J. Miller
Ella Watson
Tennie Rook

State of Tennessee(November Term of the County Court 1873
Dyer County   ) Tuesday Nov. 4, 1873

  This day a paper writing purporting to be the last will & Testament of Elizabeth B. Jordan deceased, was produced before the court for probate: Thereupon came here into open Court M. J. Miller, Ella Watson and Tennie Rook, subscribing witnesses to the same, who being duly sworn deposed and said that they were personally acquainted with the Testatrix in her life time: that she was of sound mind and disposing memory at the time of the execution of said paper writing and that she signed and published said paper writing in their presence as her last will and testament and for the purposes therein contained and requested them to specially bear witness thereto: that they signed the same in the presence of the Testatrix and in the presence of each other: It is therefore ordered by the court that said paper writing be and the same is hereby set up and established as the last will and testament of said Elizabeth B. Jordan dec'd and that the same be recorded and filed
Attest   Zach Watkins D. C.

(P.210)
Last Will & Testament (In the Name of God Amen!
       of   ) I, Virginia L. Smith wife of J. W.
Virginia L. Smither dec'd(Smith being of sound mind and dis-
Probated December 15/73) posing memory do make and publish
W. M. Watkins clerk.   (this my last will and testament
                                        hereby revoking and making void
all others by me made. I will and desire that all my just
debts be paid I will and desire that J. W. Smith, my husband
have in fee simple the house and lot on which we now reside
and any other real estate that I may be the owner of at the
time of my death: To have and to hold and dispose of it as
he may desire; and I do hereby nominate - and appoint my husband, J. W. Smith my sole Executor - witness my hand and seal
this the 5 Nov. 1873
Done in our presence and we bear witness)   V. L. Smither
to the execution of the above will at   (
the request of the testator and in the)
presence of each other   (

R. H. McGaughey) witnesses
Maggie Sampson (

State of Tennessee) December Term of the County Court 1873
Dyer County   (Tuesday December 2, 1873

     This day a paper writing purporting to be the last will
and testament of Virginia L. Smither deceased was produced
before the court for probate. There upon came here into
open court Dr. R. H. McGaughey and Maggie Sampson, subscribing witnesses to said paper writing who being first duly
sworn deposed and said that they were personally acquainted
with Mrs. Virginia Smither the Testatrix in her lifetime:
that she was of sound and disposing memory at the time of the
execution of the same: and that she signed published and acknowledged the execution of said paper writing as her last
will and testament in their presence and for the purposes
therein contained and requested them to bear witness thereto:
that they signed the same in the presence of the testatrix
and in the presence of each other. It is therefore ordered
by the court that said paper writing be and the same is hereby set up and established as the last will and testament of
the said Virginia L. Smither dec'd and that the same be recorded by the clerk & filed

(P.211)
Last will and testament (In the Name of God, Amen:
      of   ) I, D. S. Wait do hereby make,
Deloss S. Waits deceased(ordain and publish this my last
Probated Dec. Term 1873) will and testament in manner and
Recorded Dec. 15, 1873 (form following to wit:
W. M. Watkins Clerk.   )
                               I desire that my body be
decently buried - Second - I give and bequeath to my son
Charles I. Wait one half the lot on which I now live in
Dyersburg, Tennessee, to him and his heirs forever. I

(P.211 Cont'd) give and bequeath the other half of the same lot in Dyersburg, to my wife - In witness whereof I have hereunto set my name this 30th day of November 1873

Witness.
John M. McGinnis
W. B. Sampson

         his
        D. X S. Wait
        mark

State of Tennessee) December Term of County Court 1873
Dyer County   (Tuesday December 2/73

  This day a paper writing purporting to be the last will and testament of D. S. Wait deceased was produced before the court for probate: There upon came John M. McGinnis and W. B. Sampson, subscribing witnesses the said paper writing here into open court who being first duly sworn deposed and said that they were personally acquainted with the Testator in his life time; that he was of sound and disposing memory at the time of the execution of the same and that he signed published and acknowledged the execution of said paper writing as his last will and testament in their presence and for the purposes therein contained and request them specially to bear witness thereto; that the signed the same in the presence of the Testator and in the presence of each other: It is therefore ordered that said paper writing be and the same is hereby set up and established as the last will and testament of the said D. S. Waits deceased and that the same be recorded by the clerk and filed

  Attest Zach Watkins D. C.

(P.212)

Last will & Testament of Joshua Sawyer dec'd
Probated Febry. Circuit Court 1874
Recorded Febry 24th 1874
W. M. Watkins clerk.

In the Name of God Amen I, Joshua Sawyer of Dyersburg, Tennessee being of sound and disposing mind and memory, though old and frail in body and health do make and publish this my last will and testament, hereby revoking and making void all former wills by me at any time heretofore made in manner and form following, that is to say; First, I command my soul to God who gave it and desire that my body be decently interred in the earth - Second: I give and bequeath unto my son Quinton T. Sawyer one dollar. Third: I give and bequeath unto my daughter Narcissa Gooch one dollar. Fourth: I have already given unto my son Monroe Sawyer, as much of my estate as I wish him to have in his own individual right; Fifth: I give and bequeath all the property; of which I die seized and possessed, of every discription (excepting of course that I have directed to my son Monroe) unto my son Monroe Sawyer, in however for the support and maintainance of his mother as long as she shall live my widow and the remainder at her death or marriage to go to my son Dennis F. Sawyer, his heirs and assigns forever - Lastly: I hereby nominate and appoint my son Monroe Sawyer to be sole Executor of this my last will and testament. In witness

(P.212 Cont'd) whereof I have hereunto set my hand and seal this 8 day of August in the year of Our Lord 1873

                                                    his

Signed sealed)   Joshua   X   Sawyer
and published (mark
in presence of us)
who have hereunto (
subscribed our)
names in presence (
of the testator)
and at his request(
August Eighth 1873)
W. C. Doyle
Wat. Sampson
I. G. Sampson.

State of Tennessee

    Be it remembered that a Circuit Court was begun and held for the County of Dyer at the Court House in the town of Dyersburg on the First Monday in February (being the second day of said month) in the year of Our Lord 1874 and the 98 year of American Independence.

    Present and presiding the Honorable Sid B. Black Judge of the thirteenth Judicial Circuit &c

    Thursday February 5th 1874 Court met this morning pursuant to adjournment, present and presiding the (P.213) Honorable Sid B. Black Judge &c.

                                        "devi Savit vel Non"

Monroe Sawyer Ex &c (
       vs.   )   Came the parties and came also a jury
W. H. Gooch & wife (of good and lawful men to wit: John E.
                            Roberts, W. G. Trout, S. A. McKnight,
W. C. Hassell, G. W. McDearman, G. B. Miller, Sam. B. McClanahan, W. B. Fields, J. M. Thompson, Jo. S. Wallace, L. C. Thompson and J. A. Hall who being elected tried and sworn the truth in the issue joined upon their oaths do say that the writing mentioned in the issue is the last will and testament of Joshua Sawyer deceased.

    It is therefore ordered & adjudged by the court that said writing is the last will and testament of said Joshua Sawyer dec'd and that the plaintiff recover of the defendants and on motion of H. L. W. Turney, their security in the prosecution bond all the costs herein accrued. For which let execution issue - It is further ordered that the clerk of this court certify a copy of the record in this cause to the county court of Dyer County together with the original will to be there recorded

State of Tennessee)   I, Wat B. Sampson clerk of the Circuit
Dyer County   (Court of Dyer County; do hereby certify
                            that the foregoing Transcript is a full,

(126)

(P.213 Cont'd) true and perfect copy of all the records in the cause indicated, as appears of record in my office in Book "B" Page 276

(seal) Given under hand at office in Dyersburg this February 20th 1874

           Wat B. Sampson
             Clerk.

(P.214)
Last Will and Testament   (I, Malissa C. Walker give
of Malissa C. Walker dec'd   ) all the interest that I am
Probated Febry County Court 1874(entitled to in my Fathers
Recorded March 10th 1874   ) estate, to my sister Adaline
Zach Watkins D. C.   (S. Wynne, This the thirteenth
                 day of March Eighteen hundred
                 and seventy three,

Attest: Malissa C. Walker
  William Taylor
  Mollie Taylor

State of Tennessee) Febry, Term of County Court 1874
Dyer County   ) Mon. Febry. 2/74

  This day an instrument of writing purporting to be a nuncupative will of Malissa C. Walker deceased was produced before the court for probate; There upon came into court William Taylor and Mollie Taylor subscribing witnesses to the same, who being duly sworn, deposed and said that they were personally acquainted with the Testatrix in her life time; that she was of sound and disposing memory at the time she stated to them the disposition she wished to be made of her effects; that the paper writing here presented to the court shows the disposition that she said she wanted to be made of her property: It is therefore ordered by the court that said writing be set up and established as the nuncupatibe last will and Testament of the said Malissa C. Walker deceased and that the same be recorded by the clerk and filed

A True copy from minutes of the court:

       Attest: Zach Watkins D. C.

(P.215)
Last Will and Testament   ) Notice to all whom it
of Anna Canada dec'd   (may concern - That I
Probated at Febry & March Terms 1874) being in my right mind,
Recorded March 10, 1874   (do this day in the pres-
Zach Watkins D. C.   ) ence of two witnesses
                   make my last and only
will and testament to wit: For the kindness shown me by my brother Robert Prichard give and bequeath to him all of the property and notes named in this obligation on opposite page at and after my death, he paying out of it all my lawful debts and burial expenses the balance I want said Robert

(127)

(P.215 Cont'd) Prichard to have & act. to get & keep the same as I would if I was here and alive in person - and to my brother Benjaman Prichard I give and bequeath his notes that I hold on him - for his kindness to me - also our chest, our safe and falling leaf table, two chairs and dinnerpot, to said Banjaman Prichard my brother - This the 13th day of October 1873

```
                                                her
Test                                    Anna    X    Canada
Jno. C. Hale                                   mark
John R. Prichard
```

State of Tennessee) Febry. Term of the County Court 1874
Dyer County   (February 2nd 1874

This day a paper writing purporting to be the last will and testament of Anna Canada deceased was produced before the court for Probate: Thereupon came into court J. R. Prichard one of the subscribing witnesses thereto, who having been duly sworn deposed and said that he was personally acquainted with the Testatrix in her lifetime, that she was of sound and disposing memory at the time of the execution of said paper writing; that she signed and published said writing as her last will and testament in his presence and for the purposes therein contained and requested him specially to bear witness thereto - That he signed the same in the presence of the Testatrix and in the presence of J. C. Hale the other subscribing witness thereto -

State of Tenn.(March Term of the County Court 1874
Dyer County   ) March 2nd 1874

This day a paper writing purporting to be the last will and testament of Anna Canada dec'd was produced before the court for probate: Thereupon came into court Jno. C. Hale one of the subscribing witnesses to the same, who being duly sworn deposed and said that he was personally acquainted with the Testatrix in her lifetime; that she was of sound and disposing (P.216) memory at the time of the execution of the same; that she signed published and acknowledged the execution of the same in his presence as her last will and testament and for the purposes therein contained and requested him specially to bear witness thereto: that he signed the same in his presence and in the presence of the other subscribing witness thereto: It is therefore ordered that said Paper writing be and the same is hereby set up and established as the last will and testament of Anna Canada dec'd and that the same be recorded and filed

   Attest:
          Zach Watkins   D. C.

```
Last Will and Testament                     ) I, Stephen Duncan
of Stephen Duncan dec'd                     ( being of sound and
Probated Sept. Term 1873 June Term 1874)      disposing memory do
Recorded June 30th 1874                     ( make and publish
William M. Watkins clerk                    ) this as my last will
```

(P.216 Cont'd) and testament, hereby revoking any former will by me at any time heretofore made.

Item first: My will and desire is that all my debts be paid by my Executors as soon after my death as may be, he using the first money that comes to his hands for that purpose.

Second.
    I give to my daughter Margaret C. my daughter Mary I. L____ my daughter Elizabeth C. Hall, my daughter Cynthianna, & my daughter Louisa, and to my son John A. my son William C. and my son James S. each, the sum of Five dollars; and if any of them be dead, then to their legal representatives this amount with what I have already given them is all of my estate which I desire any of them to have

Third
    I give to my beloved wife Tyrsa A. Duncan and the lawful heirs of her body all the ballance of my estate not herein otherwise disposed of: of whatsoever kind or description it may be, whether the same be real personal or mixed.

Fourth:
    I hereby appoint William Parks my executor to this my last will and testament (P.217) and in case of his death or failure to qualify as such executor, then I appoint Smith Parks to be my Executor, This the 11th day of October 1859.

```
                                                his
Witnessed by us      )          Stephen X Duncan
at the request of    (                   mark
the testator who     )
acknowledged to      (
us the execution     )
of the same          (
    James T. Bone    )
William Patton       (
```

State of Tennessee)   September Term of County Court 1873
Dyer County   (Monday Sept. 1st 1873

This day a paper writing purporting to be the last will and testament of Stephen Duncan deceased was produced before the court for Probate. Whereupon came here into open court James T. Bone one of the subscribing witnesses to the said Paper writing who being first duly sworn, deposed and said that he was personally acquainted with the said Stephen Duncan in his lifetime - that he was of sound and disposing memory at the time of the execution of said paper writing and that he signed and published said paper writing as his last will and Testament in his presence and for the purposes therein contained and requested him specially to bear witness thereto - that he signed the same in the presence of the Testator and of the other subscribing witness William Patton

State of Tennessee)   June Term of County Court
Dyer County   (Monday June 1st 1874

(P.217 Cont'd)

This day a paper writing purporting to be the last will and testament of Stephen Duncan deceased was produced before the court for further Probate: Thereupon came into open court William Patton a subscribing witness thereto who being duly sworn deposed and said that he was personally acquainted with the Testator in his life, that he was of sound and disposing memory at the time of the execution of said writing that he signed and published said writing as his last will and testament in his presence and for the purpose therein contained and requested him to witness the same - that he signed the same in the presence of the Testator and in the presence of James T. Bone the other witness thereto. It is therefore ordered by the court that said paper writing be and the same is hereby set up and established as the last will and testament of said Stephen Duncan dec'd and that the same be recorded by the clerk and filed

(P.218)

Last Will & Testament of C. J. Coker dec'd Probated Febry Term 1875 Zach Watkins Clerk	I, C. J. Coker hereby make and publish this as my last will and testament, hereby revoking all others by me made at any time heretofore -

First - I wish all my debts paid out of any moneys I may have or the first moneys that may be collected -

Secondly - I will all my entire estate both real and personal to my son Napoleon Coker -

Thirdly - I hereby appoint my son Napoleon Cocker, my Executor to this my last will and testament - My will is that he be qualified and enter fully on all the duties of his Executorship without being required to give bond and security as is usual in such cases.

In testimony whereof I have hereunto set my hand and seal - this the 30th day of December 1872

          C. J. Coker (seal)

State of Tennessee) February Term of the county court of
Dyer County (the said county 1875
          Monday February 1st 1875

This day a paper writing purporting to be the last will and testament of C. J. Coker dec'd was presented to the court for Probate; Thereupon came into court W. C. Doyle, L. C. McClerkin and H. L. W. Turney, who being duly sworn deposed and said that they were personally acquainted with the said C. J. Coker dec'd in his life time and was also acquainted with the handwriting said Coker and that said paper writing and the signature thereto is the genuine handwriting of the said deceased. It is therefore ordered that said paper

(P.218 Cont'd) writing be set up and the same be recorded by the clerk & filed

Attest   Zach Watkins D. C.

(P.219)
Last Will & Testament   ) I, Faustina B. Parks, of Dyer
of Faustina B. Parks dec'd   (County, Tennessee, being of sound
Probated March term 1875   ) mind, make this my last will and
Recorded March 3/75   (testament. I will and bequeath
Zach Watkins clerk   ) to my beloved husband, Hamilton
                               Parks Jr. all my property, real,
personal and mixed including my undivided half interest in the
Clay Sick tract of land in Dickson County, Tennessee being the
same that my father, Joab Hardin gave me in his last will and
testament.

Signed and acknowledged, in the presence of these witnesses this January the 25th 1875 -

Witness.   F. B. Parks
J. S. Smith Parks
Benj. H. Eatherby

State of Tennessee) March term of the County Court 1875
Dyer County   (Monday March 1st 1875

This day a paper writing purporting to be the last will and testament of Faustina B. Parks dec'd was produced before the court for Probate: Thereupon came here into open court J. S. Smith Parks and Benj. H. Eatherby subscribing witness to the same who being duly sworn deposed and said that they were personally acquainted with the said Testatrix in her lifetime - that she signed and published said Paper writing as her last will and testament in their presence and for the purposes therein contained and requested them to bear witness thereto and that they signed the same as witnesses in the presence of the testatrix and in the presence of eachother: It is therefore ordered by the court that said paper writing be and the same is hereby set up and established as the last will and testament of the said Faustina B. Parks dec'd and that the same be recorded by the clerk and filed

A true copy from the minutes,

Attest   Zach Watkins Clerk.

(P.220)
Last Will and Testament   (Know all men by these
of Cullen G. Cribbs dec'd   ) presents that I, C. G.
probated at April & March terms/75(Cribbs of Dyer County and
Recorded April 22, /75   ) state of Tennessee being
Zach Watkins Clerk   (in good health and of
                                    sound and disposing mind
and memory, do make and publish this my last will and testament, hereby revoking all wills by me at any time heretofore

(P.220 Cont'd) made - and as to my worldly estate, and all the personal property I shall die seized and possessed of or to which I shall be entitled at the time of my deceased also the following tracts of land lying and situated in the 7th civil District of Dyer County, Tennessee, bounded as follows: Beginning at John B. Fays southwest corner running thence east along said Fays line one hundred and eighteen poles to a stake; thence north one hundred and thirty five and one half poles to a stake: thence west one hundred and eighteen poles to a stake on said Fays' west boundary; thence south with said line to the Beginning, containing by estimation one hundred acres more or less. 2nd tract bounded as follows; Beginning at a poplar with two gum pointers James Walkers beginning corner, running thence north fifty six poles and 17 links to an elm with white oak and ash pointers; thence west one hundred and ninety nine poles to a stake with sweet gum, dogwood and Iron wood pointers; thence south fifty-eight poles and 17 links to a white oak with gum pointers Walkers southwest corner; thence east one hundred and ninety seven & 3/5 poles to the beginning containing by estimation seventy-one acres and one quarter more or less. I devise bequeath and dispose hereof in the manner following to wit;

First, my will is that all my just debts and funeral expenses shall by my Executors hereinafter named be paid out of my estate as soon after my decease as shall by them be found convenient -

I give, devise and bequeath to my beloved wife Elizabeth C. Cribbs all my personal property of all kinds in possession or in action whatsoever and also the above described lands to have and use during her natural life and at her death to go to my four daughters by my beloved wife Elizabeth C. Cribbs equally - That is to say: I wish after the death of my wife Elizabeth C. that the property (or so much of the personal property as is not disposed of by my wife during her life and the lands) be divided equally between my four daughters H. E. C. Cribbs, J. Cribbs, Parchina J. E. Cribbs and Sarah H. Cribbs and should either of them die without issue before my wife I wish such share or shares to go to the others and to the issues of the others then alive.

I have given to my children by my first wife, all the property I intend for them to have out of my estate, except an interest in a tract of about Three (P.221) hundred acres of land which I have in Carroll County Tennessee - My will is that the above mentioned 300 acres of land, situated in the County of Carroll and State of Tennessee be sold at my death and the money equally divided between all my children by both my first and last wife.

And lastly I do nominate and appoint my wife Elizabeth C. Cribbs and _____ to be the Executors of this my last will and testament -

In testimony whereof I the said C. G. Cribbs have to this

(P.221 Cont'd) my last will and testament subscribed my hand and affixed my seal this 10th day of January in the year of our Lord one thousand eight hundred and sixty eight.

        Cullen G. Cribbs (seal)

Signed sealed and published and declared by the said C. G. Cribbs as and for his last will and testament in the presence of us who at his request and in his presence and in the presence of each other have subscribed our names as witnesses thereto
    E. S. Palmer
    H. L. W. Turney

State of Tennessee) March Term of County Court 1875
Dyer County   (Monday March 1st 1875

  This day a paper writing purporting to be the last will and testament of Cullen G. Cribbs dec'd was produced before the court for Probate; thereupon came H. L. W. Turney one of the subscribing witnesses here into open court, and having been duly sworn deposed and said, that he was personally acquainted with the said Cullen G. Cribbs in his lifetime, that he was of sound and disposing memory at the time of the execution of said paper writing that he signed and published the said paper writing in his presence and in the presence of E. S. Palmer another witness thereto, to be his last will and testament and for the purposes therein contained, that he signed the same at the request of the Testator and in the presence of both the Testator and the other witness thereto

State of Tennessee(April Term of County Court 1875
Dyer County   ) Monday April 5th 1875

  This day a paper writing purporting to be the last will and testament of Cullen G. Cribbs dec'd was produced before the court for further Probate: Thereupon came into court E. S. (P.222) Palmer, a subscribing witness thereto who being duly sworn, deposed and said that he was personally acquainted with the Testator in his lifetime - that he was of sound and disposing memory at the time of the execution of said paper writing and that he signed and published said paper writing as his last will and testament in his presence and in his presence of H. L. W. Turney the other witness thereto - and for the purposes therein contained and requested them the said witnesses, to specially bear witness thereto - that he signed the same in the presence of the Testator and H. L. W. Turney; It is therefore ordered by the court that said paper writing be and the same is hereby set up and established as the last will and testament of the said Cullen G. Cribbs dec'd and that the same be recorded by the clerk & filed

True copy from the minutes of the March and April Courts 1875

    Attest Zach Watkins, Clerk.

(P.223)

Last will & Testament of Eliazor Wood dec'd Probated May term /75 Recorded May 7th 1875 Zach Watkins Clk.	In the Name of God Amen - I, Eliazor Woods of the County of Dyer and State of Tennessee being of sound mind and memory and considering the uncertainty of life,

do therefore make, ordain, publish and declare this to be my last will and testament, that is to say; First - After my just debts are paid out of the notes and accounts on hand, the balance, if any, of said notes are to be equally divided between my children, viz: W. T. Woods, John Quincy Woods, Martha A. Doak, Sarah J. Greer and Susan A. Trout -

Second - I will to my wife Lucinda and my son John Quincy all my land on the north side of the road, leading from Yorkville to Dyersburg being my homestead - also all the land between said road and the fifty seven acres, deeded by me to my daughter Susan A. Trout said land and for the maintenance of my said wife and son and at her death or marriage said lands shall become the absolute property of my said son John Quincy - and in case of the death of my said son without bodily heirs, said lands are to be equally divided between my children I will all my household and Kitchen furniture to my wife and son John Quincy also all of the perishable property.

I hereby make constitute and appoint William Killough the Executor of this my last will and testament revoking all former ones by me made -

Witness my hand and seal this the 1st day of August A. D. 1874 -

Witness:
   John E. McCorkle
   Wm. H. Franklin

State of Tennessee)   May Term of the County Court 1875
Dyer County   )   Monday May 3/75

This day a paper writing purporting to be the last will and testament of E. Woods, dec'd was produced before the court for probate; Thereupon, came here into open court John E. McCorkle and William H. Franklin, subscribing witness to the same, who being duly sworn deposed and said that they were personally acquainted with said E. Woods in his life time; that he was of sound disposing memory at the time of the execution of said Paper writing and that he signed and published said writing as his last will and testament in their presence and for the purposes therein contained and requested them to bear witness thereto - and that they signed the same in the presence of the Testator; It is therefore, ordered by the court that said paper writing be and the same is hereby set up and established as the last will and testament of said E. Woods dec'd and that the same be recorded & filed -

A true copy from the minutes: Attest: Zach Watkins clerk.

(134)

(P.224)

| Last Will & Testament of William P. Menzies dec'd Probated January Term 1876 Recorded January 25/76 Zach Watkins Clerk | In the Name of God Amen; I, W. P. Menzies of Dyer County Tennessee being of sound and disposing mind and memory but conscious of the certainty of Death, do make ordain, publish |

and declare my last will and testament, hereby revoking all other wills by me at any time heretofore made - in manner and form following, that is to say;

Item First: I desire that all my just debts be paid as soon as practicable, after my decease and also my burial expenses out of any moneys that I may leave on hand or which may first come into the hands of my Executrix from the sales of perishable property -

Item 2nd: I will and bequeath all my land and tenements and _____ and perishable property, with all other property that I may be possessed of and also all moneys and notes that I may have in my possession to my wife, Sarah E. Menzies as long as she shall live and then to be equally divided between the heirs of my body.

And I hereby appoint my wife Sarah E. Menzies my Executrix of this my last will and testament.

In testimony of all which I have hereunto set my hand and seal this Feb. 22nd 1870

W. P. Menzies (seal)

Attest:
Eugene B. Pendleton

State of Tenn.)   January Term of the County Court 1876
Dyer County   )   Wednesday January 5/76

In the matter of) This day a paper writing purporting to be the last will and testament of William P. Menzies, late a resident of Dyer County dec'd was produced here in open court and the execution thereof duly proved by the oath of E. B. Pendleton, one of the subscribing witness thereto, to have been executed by said William P. Menzies with whom the witnesses were well acquainted as his last will and testament on the day of its date - and that said William P. Menzies, was then of sound and disposing mind and memory - and it appearing to the court that J. G. Rainey the other subscribing witness to said will is not now in the state of Tennessee and cannot be had here as a witness - The signature of said Jesse G. Rainey, to (P.225) said will was duly proved by the oaths of F. G. Sampson & W. B. Sampson, who both depose that they are acquainted with the handwriting of said Rainey, having often seen him write and verily believe said signature is the proper handwriting of said Jesse G. Rainey - and said E. B. Pendleton deposed that said W. P. Menzies, executed said will in presence

(135)

(P.225 Cont'd) of both himself and said Rainey and requested them both to subscribe it as witnesses, which they both did in his presence.

It is therefore ordered by the court that said will be set up & established as the last will and testament of said William P. Menzies and that the same be recorded -

And thereupon, Sallie E. Menzies the Executrix named in said will, came into open court together with Robert G. Menzies and Eugene B. Pendleton, her securities and they entered into and acknowledged bond in the sum of Three Thousand Dollars conditioned that she discharge faithfully all the duties that on her, as such Executrix - and she was duly sworn - Seb leitus testamentary issue to her

Attest: Zach Watkins Clerk.

(P.226)

| Last will and Testament of Tabitha Caroline Smith dec'd Probated Oct. Term 1876 Recorded Oct. 6th 1876 Zach Watkins clerk | I, Tabitha Caroline Smith of the County of Dyer State of Tennessee being sound of mind but am feebled by age recognizing extreme certainty of death do make and set up this |

as my last will and testament and hereby revoking and annulling all wills that I may have made previous to this.

First: I will and bequeath to my sister Elizabeth W. Smith my entire estate both real and personal (which we are now holding in common) should she survive me, at her death, or at my own if I should be survivor I wish it distributed in the following manner - First the sum of Twelve hundred and fifty dollars with interest from the date - be paid to my Nephew Daniel E. Parker and the ballance of my estate be equally divided between my Brother James M. Smith of Martenville Virginia and the heirs of my sister Martha Parker deceased Mary A. Harris and Daniel E. Parker and that one sixth part of Mary A. Harris portion be paid direct to her eldest son J. K. Polk Harris - and I do nominate and appoint Daniel E. Parker to execute this my last will and testament and no bond or security shall be required of him.

In testimony whereof I have hereunto affixed my name and seal - This February the eighth eighteen and seventy three

T. C. Smith (seal)

Test   (N. Coker
     witness (M. J. Hart

State of Tennessee) October Term of the County Court 1876
Dyer County   ) Monday Oct. 2nd 1876

This day a paper writing purporting to be the last will and testament of Tabitha Caroline Smith dec'd was produced before

(136)

(P.226 Cont'd) the court for probate; Thereupon came into open court N. Coker and M. J. Hart subscribing witnesses thereto who being first duly sworn deposed and said as follows to wit: That they were personally acquainted with the Testatrix in her life time that she was of sound and disposing memory at the time of the execution of the same and that she signed and published said paper writing as her last will and testament in their presence and for (P.227) the purposes therein contained and requested them specially to bear witness thereto, and that they signed it in the presence of the Testatrix and each other.

It is therefore ordered that said paper writing be and the same is hereby set up and established as the last will and Testament of the said Tabith Caroline Smith deceased and be recorded by the clerk & filed

    Attest   Zach Watkins clerk

(P.228)
Last Will and Testament) I, Thos. H. Johnson do make and
of Thos. H. Johnson dec'd(Publish this my last will and
Probated Nov. Term 1876) testament, hereby revoking all
Recorded Nov. 24th 1876 (other wills and making void all
Zach Watkins Clk.) others, made by me at any time
made, - First; I want my funeral expenses paid and all of my debts - as soon after my death as possible out of any moneys that I may die possessed of, or may first come into the hand of my Executrix, secondly and lastly, I give and bequeath unto my beloved wife, Minerva W. Johnson, all of my property both personal and real, to be used by her during her natural life, or widowhood. If she marries again she is to have a lifetime Estate in the real Estate, and after her death, the property to descend to each of my children living or their heirs, in equal portions. I hereby nominate and appoint my wife Minerva W. Johnson to be my sole Executrix and she is not required to give or Execute bond to carry out the provisions of this will.

In witness whereof I do, to this my will Set my hand this, the 18th day of October, One thousand, eight hundred and seventy six.

Signed and published in our presence and we have subscribed our names in the presence of the Testator the 18th day of October A. D. 1876

Subscribing witnesses   Thos. H. Johnson (seal)
Jesse Clark)
Thos. H. Benton)

State of Tennessee) November Term of the Dyer County Court
Dyer County   ) 1876 Monday Nov. 6th 1876

This day a paper writing purporting to be the last will and testament of Thos. H. Johnson deceased was produced before

(P.228 Cont'd) the open court for Probate; There upon Jesse Clark Clark & Thomas H. Benton, subscribing witnesses to the same, came into open court, who being first duly sworn deposed and said that they were personally acquainted with the said Thos. H. Johnson in his life time and that he signed and published said paper writing as his last will and testament in their presence and for the purposes therein contained (P.229) and requested them specially to bear witness thereto - That they signed the same as witnesses in the presence of the testator and of each other, that the said Testator was of sound and disposing mind & memory at the time of the execution of said writing; It is therefore ordered by the court that said paper writing be set up and established as the last will and testament of Thos. H. Johnson deceased

A true copy from the minutes of the court

    Attest   Zach Watkins, Clerk

(P.230)
The Last Will & Testament)   In the Name of God, Amen:
of James McCoy dec'd   (
Probated Mch Term 1877   )   I, James McCoy of Dyer County
Recorded Mch. 5th 1877   (Tennessee being weak in body but
    Zach Watkins clk.   )   thank God of sound and disposing
                                            memory do hereby make ordain and
publish this my last will and testament, hereby revoking all former wills by me made in manner and form following to wit: that is to say I commend my soul to God, and desire that my body be decently buried and that all my just debts be paid as soon as may be out of any money I may have on hand at the time of my death.

    Item First: I give and bequeath unto my granddaughter Sallie V. Fitzhugh wife of John L. Fitzhugh all that tract of land I bought from Moses P. Hurley & wife, by deed duly registered in Dyer County Tennessee in conveyance Book R. page 328 containing about ninety acres, to have and to hold the same with the tenements and appurtenances unto the said Sallie V. Fitzhugh during her natural life with remainder in fee to the heirs born of her body, but in the event she dies without issue then said land shall revert to my heirs and their heirs forever.

    Item second: I give and bequeath unto my granddaughter Lugenie McCoy all that tract or body of land, known as my home place to wit: Beginning at the north east corner of the $158\frac{1}{4}$ acre tract on which I now live running west with the north line of that tract and my 110 acre tract to the line of the Paducah & Memphis Rail Road, thence southwardly along the line of the said railroad to the south boundary line of my 108 acre tract thence east to the southeast corner of said $158\frac{1}{4}$ acre tract and north with its east line to the beginning containing about Three hundred and Twenty acres to have and to hold said land with the tenements and appurtenances unto the said Lugenie McCoy during her natural life, with remainder in fee, to the heirs born of her body: but in the event she dies without issue then said land shall revert to my heirs and their heirs forever.

(138)

(P.230 Cont'd)   And I give her my saddle horse "Bob".

   Item Third: I give and bequeath all the balance of my real estate to my son James Henry McCoy to have and to hold the same with the tenements (P.231) and appurtenances to him and his heirs forever.

   Item fourth: I give and bequeath unto my grand-son-in-law John L. Fitzhugh, the two horse wagon and harness and all the hogs (about twenty head) he now has.

   Item fifth: I give and bequeath all the rest residue and remainder of my Estate consisting of stock bonds, clover money &c. to be divided among my said Legatees so so that my said son Henry shall have one half and my said two granddaughters one fourth each of all my estate: And I equalize that division, I hereby value the ninety acres of land given to Sallie V. Fitzhugh at Three thousand Dollars - The Three hundred and twenty acres given to Lugenie McCoy at Three Thousand Five Hundred dollars - And the lands in all given to Henry McCoy at Five Thousand two hundred dollars - including the 37 acres of Luke Kirbys land recently bought at Sherriffs sale, valued at Four Hundred Dollars.

   Lastly: I nominate and appoint my son James Henry McCoy to be Executor of this my last will and testament, and desire him to sell all my stock, farming utensils, household furniture &c. at public sale to the highest bidder for the benefit of my Estate. The bequeath of the wagon, harness & hogs to John L. Fitzhugh and the saddle horse to Lugenie McCoy, are all free gifts. Witness my hand and seal this 16th day of February A. D. 1877

                           James McCoy   (seal)

Signed sealed &
published by James
McCoy in presence
of us who have
hereto, subscribed
our names as witnesses
in presence of the testator
and at his request
     February 16th 1877

William W. McCoy
F. G. Sampson
L. J. Clements

State of Tennessee)   March Term of the County Court 1877
Dyer County   )   Monday March 5th 1877

(P.232) This day a paper writing purporting to be the last will and testament of James McCoy deceased was produced in open court for probate, thereupon came into open court L. J. Clements, W. W. McCoy & F. G. Sampson, subscribing witnesses to the same who being duly sworn deposed and said as follows, that they were personally acquainted with the said James McCoy

(P.252 Cont'd) in his lifetime, that he was of sound and disposing memory at the time of the execution of the said paper writing & that he signed sealed and published the same as his last will and testament in their presence and for the purposes therein contained and requested them to bear witness thereto, that they signed the same as witnesses thereto in the presence of the said James McCoy and of each other. It is therefore ordered by the court, that the said paper writing be and the same is hereby set up and established as the last will and testament of the said James McCoy deceased and that the same be recorded by clerk and filed -

A true copy from the minutes

   Attest Zach Watkins Clk.

(P.233)
The Last Will & Testament of) Know all men by these presents,
Elizabeth T. Hainbrick (that I Elizabeth T. Hainbrick
Probated Sept. Term 1877) of the county of Dyer and State
Recorded November 15/77 (of Tennessee knowing the un-
 Zach Watkins Clerk) certainty of life and the cer-
          tainty of death, do make and
publish this my last will and testament, hereby revoking all other wills by me made before - -

 Item 1st My will is first that my funeral expenses and all just debts owed by me be paid by my executor hereafter named as soon as may be found practicable after my death out of my personal estate. -

 Item 2nd I give and bequeath my land situated in the 6th civil district of Dyer County Tennessee and bounded as follows: Beginning at a stake with sweet gum white oak, hackberry and ash pointers in Asa Fowelks East boundary line; runs thence east 122 poles to a stake with Poplar, hickory, Red bud, Horsebeaur pointers thence north 140 poles to a stake with two Elm, White Oak, and Hickory pointers - Thence west with the A. D. land 122 poles to a stake and pointers - Thence south 140 poles to the Beginning, containing $106\frac{3}{4}$ acres - to the heirs of Francis M. Hainbrick*his wife - encumbered, however, with a life estate and said life estate I will to said Francis M. Hainbrick and Tabitha Hainbrick during their separate lives - Said life estate to be theirs jointly and to be free from the debts, contracts and liabilities of said Francis M. Hainbrick forever.

 Item 3rd - I give and bequeath all of my personal property of every description to my said son Francis M. Hainbrick to be used and enjoyed as he may see proper.

 Item 4th - I hereby (nominate and appoint Joseph Smith Executor of this my last will and testament -

 In witness whereof I have hereunto subscribed my name on
—* and Tabitha Hainbrick

(P.233 Cont'd) this the 9th day of February Eighteen Hundred and seventy seven (1877)

Witness	her
Asa Fowlkes	Elizabeth T. X Hainbrick
Joseph Smith	mark

State of Tennessee) September Term of County Court 1877
Dyer County) Monday September 3rd 1877 –

    This day a paper writing purporting to be the last will and testament of Elizabeth T. Hainbrick, dec'd was produced before the court for probate – Thereupon, came into open court Asa Fowlkes and Joseph Smith subscribing witnesses thereunto who being duly sworn, deposed and said as follows; that they were personally acquainted with Elizabeth T. Hainbrick in her life time – that she was of sound and disposing memory at the date of the execution of said paper writing and that she signed and published the same as her last will and testament in their presence and for (P.234) the purposes therein contained – and requested them to witness the same and that they signed the same as witnesses thereto in the presence of Elizabeth T. Hainbrick and of each other – It is therefore ordered by the court that said paper writing be set up and established as the last will and testament of the said Elizabeth T. Hainbrick dec'd and that it be recorded by the clerk & filed.

A true copy from the minutes

    Attest Zach Watkins Clk.

(P.235)

The Last Will & Testament	In the Name of God – Amen –
A. B. Stallcup dec'd	I, Alexander B. Stallcup do
Probated Oct. & Nov. Term 1877	make and publish this my last
Recorded Nov. 13/77	will and testament – hereby
Zach Watkins Clk.	revoking and making void all others by me at any time made –

First – I direct that my funeral expenses and all of my debts be paid as soon as possible out of any moneys I may die possessed of, or may first come into the hands of my administrator or Executor –

Secondly – I give and bequeath to my beloved wife Adelaid Stallcup a dower interest in all of my real estate as long as she may live, the remaining two thirds to be divided equally between my two sons to wit; Beauford, and Richard Johnson Stallcup

Thirdly – To Margaret Rebecca Anders, I wish and desire to have the sum of "forty" Dollars yearly for as long as she may live, out of any moneys that may be left by me – further, should the money or personal property be exhausted before the death of the said Margaret Rebecca – then the two sons of name above referred to shall be required to furnish her the sum of "forty" dollars yearly as heretofore required by me, and that the real estate of

(P.235 Cont'd) both the boys be liable for said amounts to her yearly.

Fourthly - to the 2 children of Mary Ann Bailey, who is dead, I give nothing, because I have heretofore given to their mother all that I felt able to do & further that I consider that she was fairly dealt, by me -

Fifthly; To the 2 children of my daughter Elizabeth Francis I give nothing - Because I have already given to their mother what I consider her share of my property to wit; the sum of ($1400.00)

Sixthly: to my son Wm. J. Stallcup I give and bequeath the sum of five dollars - having already given him the sum of ($1442.00) which I consider his full share of my property - He is to have nothing more -

Seventhly - To my daughter Harriet Amandy Ballentine the sum of five dollars - and nothing more - I have heretofore given her something and further, her conduct toward me and her life has been so bad and disgraceful that I do not intend for her to have anything whatever that I may leave.

Eighthly - The one third interest of my real estate at the death of my wife to decend to the 2 boys above referred to, to wit; Beauford Stallcup and Richard Johnson Stallcup

Ninthly - If any personal property be left by me - all of it is to be equally divided between my wife Adelaid and Beauford Stallcup and Richard Johnson Stallcup - and if either of them or both should be under the age of twenty one years I desire and request that the County Court appoint a guardian for them to take charge of their portion and manage for (P.236) them untill they shall arrive at their majority - whatever my wife may leave at her death I desire to go to my two children above referred to, to wit; Beauford Stallcup and Richard Johnson Stallcup.

   In witness whereof I do to this my last will set my hand and seal on this the 10th day of February A. D. 1874 -

William Scobey   )   A. B. Stallcup (seal)
L. C. Thompson   .(
Subscribing witnesses)

        Codicil to the Will above named

Should either of the 2 boys to wit; Beauford Stallcup or Richard Johnson Stallcup die before they arrive at the age of Twenty one years then his part of the real estate shall decend equally to Wm. J. Stallcup and Harriet Amandy Ballentine

L. C. Thompson   ) In testimony whereof I have hereunto sub-
William J. Scobey) scribed this my will and testament on this
                               11th day of February A. D. 1874

                                      A. B. Stallcup

(142)

(236 Cont'd)
State of Tennessee) Monday October 1st 1877
Dyer County   ) Oct. County Court 1877

This day a paper writing purporting to be the last will and testament of A. B. Stallcup deceased, was produced before the court for probate. Thereupon came into open court William J. Scobey, one of the subscribing witnesses thereto who being duly sworn deposed and said that he was personally acquainted with A. B. Stallcup the Testator in his lifetime - that he was of sound and disposing memory at the execution of said paper writing and that he signed and published said paper writing as his last will and testament in his presence and presence of L. C. Thompson also a witness thereto - and requested them to bear witness thereto - That he signed same as a witness thereto in the presence of the Testator and the other witness thereto

A true copy from minutes of Oct. Term 1877

      Attest Zach Watkins Clk.

State of Tennessee) November Term County Court 1877.
Dyer County   ) Monday Nov. 5/77

State of Tennessee) November Term County Court 1877
Dyer County   ) Monday Nov. 5/1877

This day a paper writing purporting to be the last will and Testament of A. B. Stallcup dec'd was produced to the court for further Probate - Thereupon came into open court L. C. Thompson subscribing witness to the same who having been first duly sworn, deposed and said that he was personally acquainted with said A. B. Stallcup dec'd in his lifetime - that (P.237) he was of sound and disposing memory at the time of the execution of said paper writing - and that he signed & acknowledged said paper writing in his presence and presence of W. J. Scobey the other subscribing witness and requested them to bear witness thereto - that they (witnesses) signed said instrument as witnesses thereto in the presence of the Testator and of each other - It, is therefore ordered by the court that said paper writing be and the same is hereby set up and established as the last will and testament of said A. B. Stallcup, dec'd - and that the same be recorded by the clerk and filed

A true copy from minutes of Nov. Term of County Court 1877

      Attest Zach Watkins Clerk.

(P.238)
Richard Critchfield dec'd) I, Richard Critchfield do make
Last will & Testament   (and publish this as my last will
Probated January Term 1878) and testament hereby revoking and
Recorded May 22/78   (making void all others by me at
    Zach Watkins clk.) any time made -

(P.238 Cont'd)

First; I direct that my funeral expenses and all of my debts be paid as soon after my death as possible out of any money that I may be possessed of or that may first come into the hands of my executor.

Secondly; I direct that my son by my first wife, R. C. Critchfield have five dollars and no more out of my estate from the fact that he has been disobedient and undutiful to me as his father -

Thirdly; I will and bequeath the remainder of my property of every description both real personal to my wife and all of my children (excepting R. C. Critchfield as above named) to be distributed according to laws of Tennessee

Fourth; I direct that the rents paid of D. W. Brown & Co. for the lease they occupy be applied first to payment of tax - Second to payment of my debts - and that the remainder go to my wife.

Fifth & Last; I direct that my land shall not be sold untill my youngest child arrives at lawful age - Whereof I do to this my will set my hand and seal this 11th day day of February 1876

Attest   R. Critchfield (seal)
B. T. Harton
John Love.

State of Tennessee)   Jan'ry Term of County Court 1878
Dyer County   )   Monday Jan. 9/78

This day a paper writing purporting to be the last will and testament of Richard Critchfield dec'd was produced here in open court for Probate - Thereupon, came into open court, B. T. Harton & John Love the subscribing witnesses to said will, who being first duly sworn, deposed and said that they were personally acquainted with Richard Critchfield in his lifetime - and that he signed and published said paper writing as his last will and testament in their presence and requested them specially to bear witness thereto - and that they signed the said Paper writing in the presence of the Testator and of each other and that said Testator was of sound mind and disposing (P.239) memory at the time of the execution of said will - It is therefore ordered by the court that said paper writing be set up and established as the last will and testament of said Richard Critchfield dec'd

A true copy from the minutes -

                Attest; Zach Watkins Clerk.

(P.240)
Last Will and Testament of   ) I, Samuel Telford
Samuel Telford dec'd Probated Aug. Term 1876(being*sound mind
and Feby. Term 1878 Recorded May 22/78) and disposing
    Zach Watkins Clk.   (memory do hereby
                                                *of

(P.240 Cont'd) make and publish this as my last will and testament, hereby revoking all former wills by me heretofore at any time made; Item First; I direct my Executor to pay all my just debts out of the first money coming to his hands including funeral expenses -

Item Second; I give to my beloved wife Cathrine F. Telford all my property real personal and mixed, including crop, stock, provisions on hand farming utensils. Household and kitchen furniture - the tract of land on which I now reside, conveyed to me by Hiram R. A. McCorkle, and every Species of property and effects of which I may die possessed, for and during her natural life - all of which (except the real estate) she may dispose of if necessary to do so to secure for herself a comfortable and reasonable support & maintenance.

Item 3rd - at the death of my beloved wife I will and direct that all the property set forth & mentioned in item two of this will be handed over to my daughter Martha, S. Hood, excepting of course such items as may have been used up or disposed of by my beloved wife in her support to be hers absolutely - and not to be subject to the control, in any way of her husband or any future husband she may marry.

Item 4th - I hereby appoint Smith Parks Executor of this my last will and testament - This 15th August 1870

                                        Samuel Telford

Witness
T. S. Hamilton
Geo. Parks

State of Tennessee) August Term of County Court
Dyer County   )
                        This day a paper writing purporting to be the last will and testament of Samuel Telford, dec'd was produced before the court for Probate. There upon came into open court T. S. Hamilton one of the subscribing witnesses thereto and being duly sworn deposed and said that he was personally acquainted with Samuel Telford the Testator in his life time - that he was of sound & disposing memory at the time of the execution of said writing - that he signed and published said paper writing as his last will and testament in his presence and for the purposes therein contained - and requested him specially to bear witness thereto - That he signed the same as (P.241) witness in the presence of the Testator and of Geo. Parks, also a witness thereto -

A true copy from the minutes

        Attest; Zach Watkins Clk.

State of Tenn.) February Term of County Court 1878
Dyer County   ) Monday Febry, 4th 1878

    This day a paper writing purporting to be the last will

(P.241 Cont'd) and testament of Samuel Telford, dec'd was produced before the court for further probate. Thereupon came into open court Geo. Parks, a subscribing witness thereto who being duly sworn deposed and said that he was personall acquainted with the said Samuel Telford in his lifetime - That he was of sound and disposing memory at the time of the execution of said Paper writing- and he signed and acknowledged the execution of the same as his last will and testament in his presence and presence of T. S. Hamilton also a subscribing witness - and requested them to bear witness thereto - That they witnessed the same in the presence of the Testator &c.

It is therefore ordered that the said Paper writing be and the same is hereby set up and established as the last will and testament of the said Samuel Telford, dec'd and that the same be recorded by the clerk & filed

A true copy from the minutes;

       Attest Zach Watkins, Clk.

(P.242)
Last Will & Testament of Thomas Olds dec'd
Probated Oct. Term 1878
Recorded Dec. 12/78
   Zach Watkins Clk.

I Thomas Olds do make and publish this as my last will and testament hereby revoking and making void all others by me at any time made.

Item first: I direct that my funeral expenses and all my debts be paid as soon after my death as possible.

Item second: I give and bequeath to my wife Elizabeth Olds all of my personal property of any and every kind after she using a sufficient amount as she thinks best to pay the debts above specified in item first -

Item third; I also give and bequeath to my wife Elizabeth Olds all of the real estate that I may die seized and possessed of, to have for her own use and benefit during her lifetime, my object is to have no sale.

    Given under my hand and seal this 15 day of Sept. 1877

                                      Thomas Olds (seal)

Signed and
acknowledged
in our presence
J. H. Nunn
J. F. Perry

State of Tenn.)   October Term of County Court 1878
Dyer County   )   Monday Oct. 7/78

This day a paper writing purporting to be the last will and testament of Thomas Olds, was produced in open court. Thereupon came J. H. Nunn and J. F. Perry subscribing witnesses thereto,

(P.242 Cont'd) who being first duly sworn deposed and said that they were personally acquainted with the said Thomas Olds - that he signed and published the same in their presence as his last will and testament, and requested them to bear witness to the same - And that they subscribed the same in his presence at his request on the day it bears date and that he was then of sound and disposing mind and memory.

It is therefore ordered that the same be set up & established as the last will and Testament of said Thomas Olds and recorded.

A true copy of the will probate

Attest Zach Watkins Clerk.

(P.243)
Last Will and testament of J. H. Yancey dec'd
Probated December Term /78
Recorded December 12/78
Zach Watkins Clk.

I, James H. Yancey do make and publish this as my last will and testament hereby revoking and making void all other wills by me at any other time made.

First - I direct that my funeral expenses and all my debts be paid as soon after my death as possible out of any moneys I may die possessed of or may first come into the hands of my Executrix.

Secondly; I give and bequeath to my three children Elvy Green Howell, wife of A. W. Howell, John Hartwell Yancey and Thomas Joshua Yancey five dollars each.

Thirdly; I give and bequeath to Sarah Ann Elizabeth Yancey, my wife, all the remainder of my effects, moneys, notes, accounts, judgments, goods and chattles, lands and tenements and if there be at my death any other effects of which I might be the rightful owner I give and bequeath it as above to my wife Sarah Ann Elizabeth Yancey.

Lastly I nominate and appoint Sarah Ann Elizabeth Yancey, my Executrix.

In witness whereof I do to this my last will set my hand and seal this the 18th day of October 1878

James Hartwell Yancey (seal)

Attest: J. H. Davis (seal)
        E. T. Smith (seal)

State of Tenn.) December Term of County Court 1878
Dyer County) Monday Dec. 2/78

This day a paper writing purporting to be the last will and testament of James Hartwell Yancey, was produced before the court for Probate. There upon came into open court E. T. Smith, a subscribing witness thereto who being duly sworn deposed and said as follows that he was personally acquainted with the said James H. Yancey in his lifetime, that he was of sound and disposing memory at the time of the execution of said paper writing, that he acknowl-

(147)

(P.243 Cont'd) edged the execution of the said paper writing in his presence as his last will and testament for the purpose therein contained, and requested them to witness the same - which he did in the presence of the Testator.

A true copy of will Probate

        Attest Zach Watkins Clk.

(P.244)
State of Tenn.) December Term of County Court
Dyer County)   December 3/78

    This day a paper writing purporting to be the last will and testament of James H. Yancey was produced before the court for further probate. Thereupon came into open court J. H. Davis, subscribing witness to the same, who being duly sworn, deposed and said that he was personally acquainted with said Testator in his lifetime, that he was of sound and disposing memory at the time of the execution of said Paper writing, and that he signed and published the same as his last will and testament in his presence and for the purposes therein contained and requested him to witness the same.

    It is therefore ordered by the court that the said Paper writing be and the same is hereby set up and established as the last will and testament of said James H. Yancey dec'd and that the same be recorded and filed.

A true copy
        Attest: Zach Watkins Clerk.

(P.245)
Last Will and testament) State of Tennessee
of F. A. Slater deceased (County of Dyer -
Probated Nov. & Dec. Term /78)
Recorded December 28/78 (Now all men by theas presents
  Zach Watkins Clerk   ) nowing the uncertainty of life and
                                  bein Rashional and in my rite mind
doe this day make my Last will and Testament, revokin all will made by me heretofore. First; I want my boddy buread deacently, but not costly - and all of my just debts paid - and I will to Josephine X Slater, my Dear wife, lifetime Dowry or her widowhood it to be laid of by competent Judge - at hear death or marriage the property to fall back to my children - I will to her one horse or mare to dispose of as she seas fit - I want all the ballance of my property in whatever it may subsist eaquell divided between my children it to bee to theame and their boddy hiars - I want thame edicated the best that can be don with whatever means that may be and I allso resirve all my rite, tital and claim to my dear brother T. L. Slater and his hiars the Barn in frcnt of him beginning at my southwest corner and running west to the river and all so from his southwest corner, running to the River and that I appoint J. W. Parr my administrator to wind up my estate - I also appoint my Brother T. L. Slater to assist him in any way he can this the twelth day of January Eighteen hundred and seventy eight.
Witness, T. L. Slater, C. B. Tanner   F. A. Slater

(148)

(P.245 Cont'd)
State of Tennessee) November Term of Dyer County Court 1878
Dyer County (November 4/78

    This day a paper writing purporting to be the last will and testament of F. A. Slater dec'd was produced before the court for probate; Thereupon came into open court Thomas L. Slater one of the subscribing witnesses thereto, who being duly sworn deposed and said that he was personally acquainted with the said F. A. Slater in his lifetime that he was of sound and disposing mind and memory at the time of the execution of said paper writing and that he made and published said paper writing as his last will and testament in his presence and the presence of the other witness thereto C. B. Tanner and requested them specially to bear witness thereto - and that they, the said witnesses signed the same in the presence of the testator and of each other.

A True copy from the minutes

                    Attest. Zach Watkins Clerk.

(P.246)
State of Tennessee) December Term of Dyer County Court 1878
Dyer County) December 4th 1878

    This day a Paper writing purporting to be the last will & testament of F. A. Slater dec'd was produced before the court for further Probate; Thereupon came into court C. B. Tanner, a subscribing witness thereto; who being duly sworn, deposed & said that he was personally acquainted with F. A. Slater, the Testator in his lifetime - that he was of sound and disposing memory at the execution of said Paper writing - and that he signed and published said Paper writing as her last will and testament in his presence and for the purposes therein contained.

    It is therefore ordered that said Paper writing be and the same is hereby set up and established and that the same be recorded and filed.

A true copy.
           Attest Zack Watkins Clk.

(P.247)   BLANK

(P.248)
Last Will & Testament) I, Peter E. Wilson hereby make and
of P. E. Wilson, dec'd (publish this my last will and tes-
Probated Febry. Term /79) tament -
Recorded Feby. 10/79 (
    Zach Watkins Clk.) Item 1st: Let my debts I owe be paid.

Item 2nd: I give and bequeath to my brother, John W. Wilson everything he owes me in any shape or upon any account, and this includes the indebtedness to me of John W. Wilson & Co. -

(P.248 Cont'd) I also give and bequeath to my said brother my brick store house and lot in the town of Dyersburg Tennessee the same erected by me and in which my said brother Jno. W. Wilson is now doing business, also my watch, buggy, safe, wardrobe, bed & bedding.

Item 3rd: I give and bequeath unto my nephew James G. Algea Five Hundred Dollars, this amount to be in consideration of services by him to be rendered in assisting my Executor in making out lists of my estate real and personal.

Item 4th: I hold a note on R. H. McGaughey, T. E. Richardson and W. M. Watkins for one thousand dollars, dated December 29th 1877, due twelve months after date and drawing interest at 10% per annum - I received by a mortgage on the residence of R. H. McGaughey this said note I give and bequeath to R. H. McGaughey in trust however, for his grand child Mary Walker, daughter of William W. & Myra Walker and the said R. H. McGaughey, as said Trustee, is not to be required to give bond or take oath as Trustee.

This, Item 4th of my will is to be operative and of force only in the event that the said R. H. McGaughey give to my executor a full receipt and acquittance of all claims and accounts he may have against me at the time of my death - Otherwise this item to be in operative and void.

Item 5th: All the money and bonds I may have on hand at my death, and all that may come into the hands of my executor before the final division of my estate, is by my executor to be equally divided between my brother John W. Wilson and my three sisters, Sarah E. Algea, Mary O'Conner, and Susan W. E. Wilson.

Item 6th: All the residue of my estate, real and personal of every kind and character - notes, accounts, judgements, choses in action &c to be divided as near as possible into four equal shares by persons to be selected as hereinafter designated and directed and then to be allotted by lot or by drawing as follows: One share to my brother John W. Wilson and one to each of my said sisters - The division is to be made by two discreet persons; One to be selected by my executor John W. Wilson and one to be selected by my said sisters; and if the two so chosen cannot agree (P.249) or desire to do so, they may select a third person, and then the said three may make the division herein directed; and the division made by them whether by two or three persons shall be final and conclusive, and the title to the property so allotted shall vest thereby to the one to whom allotted, and he or she shall have the right in his or her own name or in the name of my executor named in this will or in the name of my administrator Cum testamento annexo to sue for and recover any of the property or assets so allotted to them; and I further direct that the expenses of said division be borne equally by my said brother and sisters.

I hereby nominate and appoint my brother John W. Wilson, executor of this my last will and testament, and having full confidence in his integrity I direct that he be allowed to execute this

(P.249 Cont'd) will, without being required to give or execute any bond as Executor -

Witness my hand this the 27th day of December 1878

                      P. E. Wilson

Signed, acknowledged and published in our presence and in testimony thereof we have hereunto set our names in the presence of each other and the testator this the 27th day of December 1878

                S. R. Latta, W. Coker
                H. Clark

State of Tennessee) Febry Term of County Court 1879
Dyer County   ) Monday Febry 3rd 1879

In the matter of the   )
Last Will & Testament   (This day a Paper writing purporting
of Peter E. Wilson, dec'd) to be the last will and testament
                            of Peter E. Wilson late of Dyer
County Tennessee deceased, was produced before the court for probate; There upon came into open court H. Clark, W. Coker and S. G. Latta, the subscribing witnesses thereto, who being first duly sworn deposed and said that they were personally acquainted with the said Wilson in his life time, that he was of sound and disposing memory at the date of the execution of said Paper writing; That he signed and published said Paper writing as his last will and testament in their presence and for the purposes there in contained - and that they signed their names as witnesses thereto in the presence of each other and the Testator and at his request; It is therefore ordered by the court that the said Paper writing be and the same is hereby set up and established as the last will and testament of said P. E. Wilson deceased and that the same be recorded by the clerk and filed as required by law.

A true copy from minutes

            Attest; Zach Watkins Clerk.

(P.250)
Last Will and Testament) I, P. M. Watkins being of sound mind
of P. M. Watkins dec'd(and disposing memory and being in
Probated June Term 1879) feeble health and knowing the uncer-
Recorded July 18/79   (tainty of human life, do make, consti-
  Zach Watkins Clk.   ) tute and publish this my last will and
                           testament hereby revoking all others
by me at any time heretofore made.

First I will that all of my just debts be paid, including all sums I may owe for medicine and medical attention.

Second: I will and bequeath to Ann E. Moss wife of Chas. C. Moss, Zach Watkins, B. B. Watkins & the children of W. M. Watkins, to wit: Willie Frances, Lorenzo & Lucinda Watkins the following

(P.250 Cont'd) tract of land of about 234½ acres, lying in the 12th Civil District of Dyer County Tenn. (it being all the property I now own) bounded and described as follows to wit; Beginning at the N. E. corner of the 400 acre tract running thence south 89 poles to a sweet gum 18 inches in diameter, from which a white oak 18 inches in diameter, bear north, distance 43 links, and an oak 2 feet in diameter, bear south 76 degrees East distance 45 links; thence west 190 poles to a sweet gum 2 feet in diameter from which a hickory, 4 inches in diameter bear south 6 links, and a sweet gum, 2 feet in diameter, bear south 64 degrees east; thence south about 118½ poles to the middle of the channel of the south fork of Forked deer River; thence down the same with the meander, about 420 poles to the N. W. corner of said 400 acre tract; thence east 220 poles to the beginning, containing 314½ acres more or less, including & excluding the eighty acre tract sold off by R. Elkin, Lucy M. Elkin & M. A. Morrison to me see Book "R" page 115 of the registers office of Dyer County Tenn.

That is to say; I desire that said Ann E. Moss shall have one fourth of said land, Zach Watkins one fourth, B. B. Watkins one fourth & the said children of W. M. Watkins one fourth or the proceeds of one fourth of the said land.

Third; I hereby appoint and nominate the said Zach Watkins executor of this my last will and testament and hereby authorize and empower him to sell said land, without the aid or intervention of any court, on such terms & conditions, as he may think best, for the the interest of all parties and to execute deed or deeds purchaser - and I direct when the money is paid that said executor pay one fourth to said Ann E. Moss one fourth to Zach Watkins, one fourth to B. B. Watkins as above mentioned, & the remaining one fourth be in by said (P.251) Executor or Trustee, as he may think best, for the use and benefit of said children of W. M. Watkins; and he may use the interest & principal in their education without giving any bond as Trustee; or said Executor is authorized to pay said one fourth to W. M. Watkins in trust, without requiring bond of him, and said W. M. Watkins shall have power to use said money for the benefit & education of said children, said Executor is not required to execute bond for the performance of his duties under this will.

Witness my hand on this the 22 day of April /79

Signed and acknowledged   Permely M. Watkins
in our presence & we
bear witness thereto,
at the request of Testa-
trix -
  R. H. McGaughey
  Addison Henshaw

State of Tenn.)   June Term of County Court 1879
Dyer County   )   Tuesday June 3/79

This day a paper writing purporting to be the last will and

(P.251 Cont'd) testament of Mr. P. Watkins was produced before the court for probate; Thereupon came the witnesses subscribed thereto vz. R. H. McGaughey and Addison Henshaw, who being first duly sworn deposed and said that they were personally acquainted with the said P. M. Watkins in his life time; that she signed and published said paper writing as his last will and testament in their presence and for the purpose therein contained - and asked them to bear witness thereto, That they signed the same as witnesses in the presence of Testatrix and of each other - That said P. M. Watkins was of sound and disposing mind and memory at the time of the execution of said paper writing.

It is therefore ordered by the court that said paper writing be and the same is hereby set up and established as the last will and testament of said P. M. Watkins, deceased and that the same be recorded and filed - Thereupon, Zach Watkins, who's nominated and named in said will as Executor &c, was duly qualified as such - the necessity of his giving bond being expressly waived in said will.

A true copy of probate from minutes of the court

   Attest: Zach Watkins Clerk.

(P.252)
Last Will & Testament of Charles Clay dec'd
Probated June term /79
Recorded July 22/79
 Zach Watkins Clk.

I Charles Clay of Dyer County Tennessee being of sound mind make and publish this my last will and testament hereby revoking all former wills made by me.

Item 1st I direct that my Executor pay all just debts against my estate out of the first money that may come into his hands as Executor.

Item 2nd I hereby give and dedicate as a neighborhood grave yard one half acre of my home tract of land and direct my executor to lay off the same - commencing at my northeast corner in the Dyersburg and Friendship road near the five mile post from Dyersburg.

Item 3rd I direct that my dwelling house, out houses and all the cleared land on my home farm (except the John Moore place) be set up as a home stead for my wife Minerva and my two minor children, Charley and Henry - and as I think they are incompetent to use and cultivate the same to the best advantage I hereby appoint my friend Esquire John H. York, Trustee for my wife and guardian for my said children and direct that he permit them to occupy the family dwelling and to have the use of the out houses, the yard and the lot, the orchard and as much cleared lands as my said wife may be able to cultivate herself - and that he rent out the rest of the land and after paying the Taxes and retaining pay for his services as Trustee annually to pay one third of the remainder or net proceeds to my wife and apply the other two thirds to pay for the clothing, school-

(P.252 Cont'd) ing and medical attendance &c of my two sons Henry and Charley untill my youngest son Henry arrives at the age of Twenty one year; Provided my said wife remains upon said land, but should she remove from said land then and in that event I direct that the net proceeds of said homestead be used by said Trustee for the benefit of my two minor children, to pay for the clothing, schooling, medical attendance &c.

Item 4th I direct that the John Moore house and clearing adjoining and directly south of the above mentioned homestead and dower and known as the "John Moore Place" be rented out "yearly" by my Executor until my son Henry is Twenty one years old - and that said Executor apply the the net proceeds of rent annually, equally between my three children Mrs. Mary Moore, Charles Clay, and Henry Clay - and that the one third going to my daughter be paid to her free from the control or debts of her husband.

Item 5th I give to my son Charley one third of my land - to my (P.253) son Henry one third of my land - and to the children of my daughter Mary Moore one third of my land - all subject to the homestead and dower encumbrance as provided for in item 3rd of this will.

Item 6th I direct that my sons Henry and Charley be sent to school and given a common school education that they be taught to work - and raised properly - That their guardian have the control of them as to where they shall live where they shall attend school &c - but I prefer that their guardian permit them to remain with their mother, provided she in his opinion conducts herself so that it is best for them to stay with her - otherwise he may remove them -

Item 7 Should my wife remove from my home place I direct that her interest in the place be paid to Henry and Charley - and that she ____ the net income of one third of my land, after selling at cash a homestead of $1000.00 in value to my two minor children.

Item 8 I direct that guardian for my children and Trustee for my wife and daughter Mary in renting my lands, rent them to be sown in wheat, oats, or clover, or cultivated in corn, cotton, tobacco &c and have said land so cultivated and kept in repair that the land may not be injured or worn out by continual renting.

Item 9 I give to my wife and the two children Charley and Henry - all my household and kitchen furniture.

Item 10 I hereby appoint my friend Esquire John H. York, my Executor and I appoint him guardian for my children Charley and Henry - And Trustee for my wife and daughter Mary Moore - And direct that he need not be required to give any bond to act as Executor, Trustee or Guardian, In Testimony whereof I subscribe my name on this the 15th day of March 1879 in the presence of

(P.253 Cont'd)
these witnesses

Interlined before signed
Signed and acknowledged in
our presence this
March 15, 1879
Witnesses J. S. Webb
         H. Parks Jr.
         J. H. Nixon

              his
Charles X Clay
             mark

State of Tenn.) June Term of County Court
Dyer County) of Dyer County Tenn.
              Monday June 2/79

    This day a paper writing purporting to be the last will and testament of Charles Clay dec'd was produced before the court for Probate; Thereupon came into open court the following persons, witnesses thereto, to wit; (P.254) J. S. Webb, H. Parks Jr. and J. H. Nixon subscribing witnesses thereto, who being duly sworn deposed and said that they were personally acquainted with said Charley Clay deceased, in his lifetime; that he was of sound and disposing memory at the time of the execution of said Paper writing - That he signed and published said Paper writing in their presence as his last will and testament and requested them to specially witness the same - that they signed the same in his presence and presence of each other; It is therefore ordered by the court that said paper writing be and the same is hereby set up and established as the last will and testament of said Charles Clay dec'd - and that it be recorded by the clerk and filed; Thereupon John H. York who is nominated and named in said will as Executor came into open court and was duly sworn - The necessity of his giving bond and security being expressly waived -

A true copy
        Attest Zach Watkins Clerk

(P.255)
Last will and Testament) I, Andrew S. Parks, being of sound
of Andrew S. Parks dec'd (mind and disposing memory do hereby
Probated August Term 1879) make and publish this as my last
Recorded Aug 12 /79   (will and testament hereby revoking
   Zach Watkins Clk.   ) all former <u>all former</u> wills by me,
                                 at any time heretofore made.

Item 1st I desire and direct that all my just debts and my personal expenses be paid by my Executor out of the first money coming to his hands.

Item 2nd In addition to all the items of property except from execution, I give to my beloved wife, Martha E. Parks all the household and kitchen furniture, plows, gear, farming utensils, and one Buggy which I now have on hand, including the harness,

(P.255 Cont'd) one additional mule or horse as she may prefer, all the cattle of which I am possessed, all the money she may have in her possession at my death as well as any notes and accounts that she may have in her possession at my death belonging to me, as well as my library books & pictures of which I may die possessed - I also give to my beloved wife, Martha E. Parks and her heir my home tract of land in the 9th civil district of Dyer County Bounded as follows; Begin at the Northwest corner of my Jas. M. Atkins purchase in south line of H. Parks old tract; run south to the south west corner of the Atkins purchase, run thence east to Pollus Holland line; then north to his N. W. corner; thence east so far, that by running north; will include the west wing of fence of my southern grass lot, and continue north at the same degree to the north line of my tract of land; thence west with its north line to the beginning, and contains about one hundred and fifty-five acres.

Item 3rd: I hereby appoint my father, Hamilton Parks, my Executor of this my last will and testament, and direct that the court will not require any bond of him as such Executor; and in the event of the death of Hamilton Parks or his inability to discharge the duties imposed by this will, then I appoint my uncle, Smith Parks my executor, of this will with all the power and privileges given to H. Parks & on the same terms and I further direct that my Executor have the same power to sell and dispose of my personal property not herein disposed of that I would have myself were I living - may sell it for cash or on a credit, publicly or privately or dispose of it as his judgement may approve of fully or as I could were I living

        June 19/79   Andrew S. Parks

Witness:
H. Parks Jr.
B. H. Eatherly
J. B. Harris
B. R. Parks

(P.256)
State of Tenn.) Monday August 4, 1879
Dyer County) August Term County Court 1879

In the matter of) This day a paper writing, purporting to be
A. S. Parks will) the last will and testament of A. S. Parks, dec'd was produced the court for probate;
Thereupon came here into open court J. P. Harris and B. R. Parks subscribing witnesses thereto, who being duly sworn, deposed and said that they were personally acquainted with the said A. S. Parks in his lifetime; that he was of sound and disposing mind and memory at the time of the execution of said writing - That he signed and published said Paper writing, as his last will and testament in their presence and for the purposes therein contained and requested them to bear witness thereto - That they signed said Paper writing as witnesses thereto in the presence of the said A. S. Parks and in the

(P.256 Cont'd) presence of each other - It is therefore ordered by the court that the said Paper writing be and the same is hereby set up & established as the last will and testament of the said A. S. Parks, deceased and that the same be recorded by the clerk and filed

Thereupon, H. Parks, who is named as Executor of said last will and Testament came into open court and was duly sworn - the necessity of his giving bond and security being waived in said will -

A true copy, attest
                Zach Watkins   Clerk

(P.257)
Last Will and Testament) Know all men by these presents that
of G. E. Spence, dec'd (I, George E. Spence of district
Probated Aug. term 1879) no. 10 in the County of Dyer and
Recorded Aug. 12/79 (state of Tennessee, farmer being in
    Zach Watkins Clk.) ill health and of sound and disposing mind and memory do make & publish this my last will and testament, hereby revoking all former wills, by me at any time heretofore made - and as to worldly estate and all the property real personal or mixed of which I shall die seized and possessed or to which I shall be entitled at the time of my death - I devise bequeath, and dispose in the manner following to wit: First: My will is that all my just debts and funeral expenses be paid out of my estate as soon after my decease as shall be found convenient.

(Item) I, give, devise, and bequeath to my beloved wife Lucinda Spence all my household furniture, my horses, mules, cattle, poltry, hogs, waggon and farming tools - also all moneys, notes, Book and acts. to be given by my administrator (or executor) to have & to hold the same to her & her and heir by me - I also give her the use, improvements and income of my dwelling house and fifty acres of land and its appurtenances, that I now live on, and one half of the tract of land known as the Horton tract in the bottom for which I have paid for and hold a deed, in the Dist. County and state aforesaid. To have and to hold the same to her for and during the term of her natural life - I give and bequeath to my eldest daughter Rebecca Smith the Book account that I have kept against her, for land horses, crop, hoggs, moneys, good, provision &c &c amounting to some Two Thousand, five hundred and fifty two dollars to have and to hold the same to her the said Rebecca Smith, her heirs and assigns to her & their use and benefit forever -

I give and bequeath to my second daughter, Allie Tansil, the Book Account that I have kept against her for land, a mule, cow & calf, Bed, chairs, table ware, money paid out to Finly, Simpson and Jackson, amounting to some one thousand nine hundred and Eighty one 33 1/3/100 dollars - To have and to hold the same to her the said <u>Allis</u> Tansil her heir and assigns forever.

I give devise and bequeath to my youngest daughter Adar Spence

(P.257 Cont'd) all of my home tract of land lying north of the road leading to Dyersburg & known as the north half of the tract of one hundred acres that I now live on containing fifty acres (minus a few small town lots that I have heretofore executed a deed to various parties for) and one half of the tract of land, known as the Horton tract in the bottom, adjoining B. F. Prichard home tract, containing one hundred acres - and I furthermore give, devise, and bequeath to my youngest daughter Adar Spence, after the decease of my beloved wife Lucinda Spence all the remainder of my lands known as the homestead tract of fifty acres, that I now live on and the other half or fifty acres known as the Horton tract - and all their appurtenances and all the profits income and advantages that may (P.258) result there from, after the decease of my beloved wife Lucinda Spence - and all the personal property to have and to hold the same to the said Adar Spence for her heirs and assigns forever and after the decease of my said wife to her and their use and behoof forever.

In testimony whereof the said Geo. E. Spence have to this my last will and testament contained one one sheet of paper and to this sheet I have subscribed my name and affixed my seal this 14 day of July in the year of our Lord one thousand Eight hundred and seventy nine.

Signed sealed published) G. E. Spence (seal)
and declared by the   (
said Geo. E. Spence   )
as and for his last will (
and testament in the pres-)
ence of and who at his   (
request, and in his pres-)
ence*of each other have   (
subscribed our names as   )
witnesses thereto   (
   Andrew Heart   )
   W. T. Wheeler,   (
John Gardener   )

                Apc VS Rebecca Smith

       Rebecca Smith in Apc with G. E. Spence (Dr)

1878	To	tract of land $1600.00 one clay bank mare $100.00	$1700.00
"	"	cow and calf $30.00 1 sow & pigs $10.00 one Bureau 20.00	60.00
"	"	one bed and clothing 25.00 one set of chain 6.00 bedstead 5.00	36.00
"	"	" folding table and accompaiments 30.00	30.00
"	"	cash at sundry times $300.00 cash paid Dr. Walker 30.00	330.00
1879	"	Provisions 150.00 dry goods 150.00 cash paid Dr. Gardener 75.00	375.00
"	"	cash paid Dr. Hughey	27.00
			2,558.00

*and in the presence

(158)

(P.258 Cont'd)   Alice Tansil

1878   In Apc with G. E. Spence   (Dr)

"	To one tract of land $1600.00 (1869) one mule 150.00	$1750.00
"	" one cow & calf 30.00 one Bed and furnishings 30.00	60.00
"	" " set of chain 5.00 Table ware 8.00 one sow & pigs 10.00	23.00
"	" cash paid to Tinley for Alice $33.33 1/3 cash paid Simpson & others 45.00	78.33 1/3
"	" Sundry debts as securities 70.00	70.00
		$1981.33 1/3

State of Tennessee) August Term of County Court
Dyer County   ) Monday August 4/79

(P.259)   In Matter of G. E. Spence)   This day a paper writ-
                 Will   )   ing purporting to be
                                                 the last will and tes-
tament of G. E. Spence dec'd was produced in open for probate;
There upon, came into open court Andrew Hart, W. T. Wheeler
and John Gardener, subscribing witnesses to the said paper writing, who being duly sworn, deposed and said that they are personally acquainted with G. E. Spence, the Testator in his life
time; that he was of sound and disposing mind and memory at the
time of the execution of said Paper writing that he signed and
published said Paper writing as his last will and testament in
their presence and for the purposes therein contained and requested them to bear witness thereto - That they signed said
paper writing as witnesses thereto in the presence of G. E.
Spence and in the presence of each other - It is therefore, ordered by the court that the said Paper writing be and the same
is hereby set up and established as the last will and testament
of the said G. E. Spence deceased and that the same be recorded
and filed

A true copy
        Attest: Zach Watkins   Clerk.

(P.260)
Last Will & Testament)   I Lucinthy Frost of the county of
of Lucinthy Frost   (Dyer and state of Tennessee do make
Probated Oct. Term /79)   and publish this my last will and
Recorded Dec. 12/79   )   testament in manner following - I
   Zach Watkins Clk.   (nominate and appoint Thomas Miller
                                 Executor and I hereby confer upon
him full power to carry out the provisions of this will - I
give devise and bequeath unto my son Wilson Frost my tract of
land on which I Live consisting of one hundred and twenty two
and one half acres - and I will that Wilson Frost pay to
Emily Turnage ten dollars each year for ten years I also will
my daughter Emily Turnage two Beds, two Bedsteds, and all the
bedclothing belonging to me, also my spinning wheel, two chairs,
also I will that Wilson Frost pay to Emily Turnage one hundred
dollars in consideration of her part of the horse stock - I

(P.260) also will that Missouri B. Stallings, my granddaughter one counterpin and two quilts.

Witness my hand and seal this March 1st 1879

John A. Shelton
W. M. Dean

Lucinthy Frost

State of Tennessee) October Term County Court Oct. 6/79
Dyer County) Monday Oct. 6/79

In the matter of) This day a paper writing, purporting to
Lucinthy Frost will) be the last will and testament of Lucinthy Frost dec'd was produced before the court for probate, There upon came into open court John A. Shelton and W. M. Dean subscribing witnesses to the said Paper writing, who being duly sworn deposed and said that they are personally acquainted with the Testatrix in her life time: that she was of sound and disposing mind and memory at the time of the execution of said Paper writing - that she signed and published said Paper writing as her last will and testament in their presence and for the purposes therein contained - That they witnessed the same in her presence and in the presence of each other; It is therefore, ordered by the court that said Paper writing be and the same is hereby set up and established as the last will and testament of said Lucinthy Frost deceased and that the same be recorded and filed.

A true copy
    Attest; Zach Watkins Clerk.

(P.261)
Ruth B. Tipton) In the Name of God - Amen -
Last Will & testament (
Probated Oct. Term /79)   I, Ruth B. Tipton of the county
Recorded Dec. 17/79 (of Dyer and state of Tennessee, here
  Zach Watkins Clk.) make my last will and testament -
                              First; I will my soul to God who gave it - I having six children which lived to be of lawful age, to wit: Lucretia B. Brewer, Pleasant Wear, Septema Olivia Hull Fowlkes, Willie Blount, Jonathan Caswell, and Lavina Ruth Atkins and I will W. B. Tipton, deceased, him by Rebecca A. Three Hundred dollars. J. C. Tipton Two hundred dollars, S. R. Atkins five Hundred dollars. Whereas J. H. Fowlkes borrowed from S. R. Atkins by W. B. Tipton one hundred dollars & promised to pay lawful interest thereon in the year 1866, I will he pays the same to S. O. H. Fowlkes, his wife, in place of Lavina R. Atkins - and I give Pleast W. Two hundred Dollars - I also will Septema Olivia Hull Fowlkes two hundred dollars I consider we have given Lucinda B. Brown more than any of my children, notwithstanding I will her heirs come in for an equal share of the remainder - I will that Lavina R. Atkins repurchase real estate with her money. Which she is to have and to hold as long as she lives then it is to go to her children, tho I give her power to sell and convey if she sess proper, but she must lay it out in real estate again.

(P.261 Cont'd) I wish my husband W. B. Tipton to have all my property during his lifetime for his support and maintenance - at his death it is to be divided amongst my children above named in the order mentioned above - If there is not enough property to give each the amounts named it is to be divided in that proportion as near as possible - This 23rd 1879

                          her
                     Ruth B. x Tipton
                        mark

Codicil -
    I also wish my husband W. B. Tipton to have the right to sell and reinvest the real estate in other real estate, if he should think best for his interests and comfort

                        her
                     Ruth B. X Tipton
                        mark

Witness - J. W. Lauderdale
         L. C. McClerkin

State of Tennessee) Oct. Term County Court 1879
Dyer County   ) Thursday Oct. 9.79

    This day a paper writing purporting to be the last will and testament of Ruth B. Tipton dec'd was produced before the court for probate - There upon came (F. G. Sampson chairman _____ J. W. Lauderdale (   ) and L. C. McClerkin subscribing witnesses being present (P.262) in open court and having been first duly sworn deposed and said that they are personally acquainted with the said Ruth B. Tipton, Testatrix, in her lifetime That she was of sound and disposing memory at the time of the execution of said Paper writing - and that she signed acknowledged and published said Paper writing as her last will and testament in their presence and for the purposes therein contained - and requested them to bear witness thereto - That they signed the same in her presence and of each other - ordered that said paper writing be set up and established as the last will and testament of said Ruth B. Tipton, dec'd and that the same be recorded and filed.

A true copy.
        Attest Zach Watkins Clerk

(P.263)
Last Will and Testament   ) Know all men by these presents
of Alfred Enochs dec'd   ) that I Alfred Enochs, of the
Probated December Term /79(county of Dyer and state of Tenne-
Recorded December 17/79   ) ssee, farmer, being in feeble
    Zach Watkins Clerk   (health but of sound mind and memo-
                                        ry do make this and publish it as my last will and testament, hereby revoking all former wills at any time made by me - and as to my worldly estate and all the property real and personal or mixed of which I shall die seized and possessed of or to which I may be entitled at the

(161)

(P.263 Cont'd) time of my decease I devise bequeath and dispose thereof in the manner following to wit:

First; my will is that all my just debts and funeral expenses shall by my executors hereafter named out of my estate paid as soon after my decease as shall by them be found convenient.

Second; I give devise and bequeath to my beloved wife Mary F. Enochs all my household furniture, two good work mules, one good buggy horse one buggy and one two horse wagon and suitable harness for the same two good milk cows with a suficing of hogs for herself and family with a sufficiency of provisions and food for herself and stock for one year - and all the poultry that may be on the farm at the time with a sufficiency of farming tools and harness for cultivation of the farm hereafter mentioned - also the interest on all money and notes that I shall have on hand or that may be due me at the time of my decease, together with my present home now including the outhouses with one hundred acres of land about the center of the present home tract, running from north to south - said home tract described as follows; Beginning at a stake and pointers, the northeast corner of lot no (4) Thomas J. Harris tract of (507) acres: thence east ($297\frac{1}{2}$) two hundred ninety seven and one half poles to a dogwood and pointers, the south east corner of the original survey thence north ($295\frac{1}{2}$) two hundred ninety five and one half poles to a stake; thence west to a hickory and Elm the north east corner of said lot no (4) and the south east corner of lot no (3) Henry Cutchin tract of (507 acres) thence south (305) Three hundred and five poles to the beginning, containing (552) acres, more or less, together with all the rents, profits and incomes with the use of the above mentioned properties, means and incomes during her natural life - she having the right to give to or either one of her two youngest daughters any household furniture of the above amounts, being set apart by me for my beloved wife expressly in lieu of her dower right and authorize my Executors hereafter to be appointed as soon as convenient after my decease to carry out the above provisions, -

Third I give and bequeath to my son Joseph W. Enochs the sum of Two Hundred Dollars together with the interest accumulated (P.264) on one certain Promissory note, made by John Enochs to said Joseph - said Joseph having heretofore received from me of my estate in land and other property to the amount of Twenty six hundred and seventy five dollars, they making $2,875.00 the above being the amount in full of my estate intended by me for my said son Joseph, except hereafter provided - Whereas there is an agreement between us and with said said Joseph that he is to remain on my home farm and live with my beloved wife, Mary F. and well to care for and provide for her and family and stock out of the property and effects bequeathed her for that purpose, during her natural life in the manner above mentioned, and in that case I give and bequeath to said Joseph at the death of my said wife, Mary F. the reversion of the mansion house, with the one hundred acres of land set apart to my said wife, Mary F. with all the privileges and appertances thereto belonging to him

(P.264 Cont'd) his heirs and assigns forever in full compensation for the above mentioned services and all claims not mentioned against my estate

Fourth, I bequeath to my son Alfred Enochs the use, benefits, rents and profits of the farm and tract of land now occupied by him during his natural life - and at his death if he shall leave a widow surviving him she shall be entitled to a lifetime dower right in the premises - and in case he shall leave any child or children or descendants of child or children surviving him they shall be entitled to the following described land in their absolute right, according to the rules of descent and partition, subject to dower as above - said land situated in (6th) civil district, Dyer County and state of Tennessee ninety six and one half acres bounded on the south by Alfred Enochs W. by Ben Hicks on the east by V. McKing, on the north, Johnson and Ingram on the west. My said son Alfred having heretofore received of me the sum of Four hundred dollars as a part of my estate together with the use and benefit of said land valued by me at the sum of Twenty four hundred dollars, altogether - that being the amount of my estate intended by me in full except what may be provided for in the final distribution.

Fifth, I bequeath to my son Matthew P. Enochs the use and occupancy, rents, income and benefits of the farm as above described, Beginning at my north west corner, running thence south, one half the length of my west boundary line; thence west to the place of beginning as as to embrace one hundred acres to have the use of said land during his natural life - and if said Matthew P. shall leave surviving him a widow she shall be entitled to a life dower in said land - and in case said Matthew P. shall leave any child or children or descendants of such surviving him they shall be entitled to the reversion with all right, title, and benefit to them forever, according to the rule of descent and partition, subject to the provision of dower as above and further my said son Matthew P. having received of me of my estate divers property and moneys together with the use of said lands of the value Twenty nine hundred and thirty five dollars that being the part of my estate in full intended by me for said Matthew P. except what may be provided for him in the final distribution of my estate.

Sixth, I devise and bequeath to my daughter Adaline S. Enochs One hundred acres of land it being apart of my home tract lying due south of the tract set apart to my son Matthew P. situated in the south west corner of my home tract of land, district, county, and state as above, to have and to hold and to her and her heirs and assigns forever, valued at Twenty five hundred dollars.

Seventh, I devise and bequeath to my daughter Malisa T. Enochs one hundred acres of land situated in the south East corner of my said home tract, bounded as follows - Beginning at my south east corner known as the Peter R. Beveraly corner, thence running west on my south line to mine and Frank Browns corner; thence north thence east, thence south on my east line to the place of

(P.265 Cont'd) Beginning so as to embrace one hundred acres, district, county and state as above set forth to her use benefit and behoof and to her, her heirs and assigns forever valued at Twenty five hundred dollars -

Eighth, I bequeath to my daughter Harriet E. Segraves, formally Enochs, the use, benefits, rents, profits and incomes during her natural life, the reversion and remainder at her decease I will and bequeath to the heir of said Harriet E. body with all the rights privileges and appertenances forever the following described tract of land to wit; Beginning at a stake with two dogwood and white oak pointers, being the south east corner of John Crows land in the west line of G. W. Smiths land, running thence south with said Smiths west line ninety seven and one fifth poles to a stake with hickory, ash and small black pointers, William Taylors North East corner; thence west one hundred and sixty four and seventeen twenty fifth poles to a stake with poplar, Elm and sweet gum pointers to said Taylor's north west corner; thence north ninety seven and one fifth poles to the south west corner of John Crow's land; thence east one hundred and sixty (P.266) four and seventeen twenty fifth poles to the Beginning corner containing one hundred acres, more or less, The said Harriet E. having heretofore received of me of my estate divers properties together with the use and benefits of the above described land, amounting to twenty four hundred and seventy dollars - The said land situated in (6) civil district of Dyer County state of Tenn.

Ninth, I give and bequeath to George A. and Eliza R. Enochs grandchildren and children of my son Robert H. Enochs dec'd the following described tracts of land Beginning at the north east corner of my tract and southeast corner of William Hamptons land; thence west with said Hamptons line to a stake and pointers James W. Enochs south east corner; thence south with James W. Enochs line to a stake and pointers in William Jacksons line; thence east with said Jacksons line to a dogwood in John Wynnis line; thence north to the place of beginning, one hundred and thirty four acres more or less - said land and divers amounts of money and property advanced by me of my estate to my said son Robert H. during his life time, amount to thirty two hundred seventeen dollars and sixty six cents - that being the full amount of my estate intended by me for my said son Robert H. and his heirs unless they may be entitled to an additional amount in the final distribution of my personal estate - the last mentioned tract of land situated in Dyer County and state of Tennessee -

Tenth - I have heretofore advanced to my son William S. Enochs in property and money the sum of in value thirty two hundred and ninety dollars of my estate and to my son James W. Enochs the sum of thirty one hundred and twenty two dollars of my estate and to my daughter Francis E. Taylor, formerly Enochs the sum of twenty seven hundred and sixty nine dollars of my estate and to my daughter Mary Ann Taylor, formerly Enochs the sum of twenty four hundred and sixty five dollars of my estate and to my son John Enochs the sum of Twenty two hundred dollars of my estate and in addition to said amount he is to be charged with the amounts

(P.266 Cont'd) with interest of two certain promissory notes, one made payable to me for one hundred and fifty dollars, the other made payable to Joseph W. Enochs for two hundred dollars - said notes executed by said John Enochs for borrowed money and to be accounted for by him to my estate - It is my intention and will that all and each of my said children be equal heirs, legatees and divisions, to and of my estate, according to my arrangements and amounts already heretofore ordained by me and now set apart (P.267) for each of them and according to the estimates and figures, charging each of them respectively as set forth in this my last will, my said grand children George and Eliza are only to represent the one interest that their father Robert would have been entitled to had he yet survived all the rest and residue of my estate real, personal or mixed of which I shall die seized and possessed of or to which I shall be entitled to at my decease I desire my Executors hereafter to be mentioned by me and I hereby request, direct and empower them to proceed and take charge of said residue above mentioned and as soon as practicable for the best interests of of my estate to convert it into money and to divide the proceeds of all such money among my several children or their decendants according to the amounts in this my will charged to each of them beginning with those that have received the smallest amounts and pay them all the disbursement respectively untill they have all received amounts equal with those that have heretofore received the largest amounts - and I further request and direct my Executors at the decease of my beloved wife, Mary F. Enochs that they proceed and take possession of the reversion and remainder of all the personal property and moneys, notes, accounts and interest of every character pertaining to personally; which was set apart by me and bequeathed to her during her natural life and as soon as practicable for the best interest of my estate to convert it into money and after pay her funeral expenses all other expenses incurred by her and administratuib expenses together with all other reasonable expenses, then as soon as practicable said Executors to proceed and make dividends and disbursment to my several children or decendants according to my desire and the plan above indicated for disbursment - and when all of those that have only received the smaller amounts shall be brought up even with those that have received of my estate the largest amounts then and that case the disbursement shall be equal of the balance of my estate with all my children or their decendants to which I devise and bequeath as above set forth, but in no event any of them shall be required to pay back any that they have received.

And lastly I do nominate and appoint my said son Joseph W. Enochs and my son-in-law William Taylor to be the Executors of this my last will and testament

In testimony whereof I the said Alfred Enochs Sr. have to this my last will and testament contained on ten sheets of paper and to every sheet thereof subscribed my name on the left hand margin thereof and to this the last sheet thereof I have subscribed my name and affixed my seal this the tenth of May in the

(P.268) year of our Lord one thousand eight hundred and seventy seven

         Alfred Enochs (seal)

signed sealed
and declared by
the said
Alfred Enochs Sr.
as and for his
last will and
testament in the
presence of us who
at his request and
in his presence and
in the presence of
each other have
subscribed our
names as witnesses
thereto
 H. C. Porter, witness
 G. W. Gregory

No. 1

The state of Tennessee) I Alfred Enochs Sr. of the above
Dyer County   ) named state and county, being desirous of modefying, changing and explaining some portions of my will heretofore made by me do make and publish these following codicils to my said last will and testament, to wit;

 Codicil 1st In order to provide for the changed condition of my family and property I hereby make the following change and no _____ in the devise of the lands therein described to George Alfred Enochs and Eliza R. Enochs and who are children of my deceased son Robert H. Enochs, dec'd said former devise being contained in the nineth clause of my said last will, viz: It is my desire in order to provide lands for my two said grand children better suited to being divided into two good settlements or farms, during my life to sell said devised lands and purchase other lands for my said grand children but if I fail to sell said lands and purchase other lands in lieu of them while I live then I will and devise that said lands devised in said (9th) nineth item or section of my said will shall go to and vest in said George A. and Eliza R. Enochs share and share alike or in equal parts during their natural lives and at their death to them, the heirs of their bodies, but if either of my said grand children should die leaving no issue then I will and devise that the share or portion of such one of such grandchildren as shall die shall go to the survivor of them under the same limitations as above written in this codicil.

 I further will and direct that said described land if I die without selling it shall be divided between said George A. and Eliza R. into two Parts equal in quantity and value (P.269) and that said division be made north and south and further that the eastern portion of said land after said division shall

(166)

(P.269 Cont'd) be the portion of said George A. but in any event the parts or portions of each of said grand children shall be subject to above written limitations and conditions.

July 21, 1879 A. Enochs
Witness;
G. W. Gregory
W. C. Dickey

No. 2

State of Tennessee) I, Alfred Enochs Sr. of the state and
Dyer County   ) county mentioned being desirous of
changing some portions of my will heretofore made by me, do make this the following codicil to my said last will and testament to wit; In order to provide for the changed conditions of my family and property, I hereby make the following change in the devise of the lands therein described in item or section 6th to Adaline S. Enochs I devise and bequeath that the said land described in item or section (6) be sold by my Executors and the proceeds of the same made use of by them as the residue of my estate is devised to be used by them - and I devise and bequeath to my daughter Adaline S. Enochs a certain tract of land containing 138¼ acres bought by me of my son Joseph W. Enochs known as the John Howard tract of land, provided the said Joseph W. Enochs builds or finishes the buildings now in contemplation upon said tract of land upon the tract of land devised to said Adaline S. Enochs my daughter (said buildings to be paid for out of my own money) and provided the said Joseph W. Enochs acknowledges and has said deed to A. Enochs sign Registered, but in the event said Joseph Enochs does not acknowledge and have said deed registered then and in that event said Adaline S. Enochs is to have the one hundred and fifty acres not transferred by me heretofore by will or deed

Guy Douglass   A. Enochs
H. V. C. Wynne

State of Tennessee) December Term County Court 1879
Dyer County   ) Monday December 1st/79

In the matter of of   ) This day a paper writing
probate of last will &   (purporting to be the last
Testament of Alfred Enochs dec'd) will & Testament of Alfred
                                Enochs, (P.270) dec'd together with codicil was ____ accompanying the same was produced here into open court for probate - Thereupon came here into open court G. W. Gregory and W. C. Dickey, subscribing witnesses to said will and Codicil No. 1 who being first duly sworn, deposed and said that they were personally acquainted with the said Alfred Enochs in his lifetime; that he was of sound and disposing mind and memory at the time of the execution of the same and that he published and declared said paper writings as his last will and testament to them and called them to bear witness thereto-That they witnessed the same at

(P.270 Cont'd) his request and in his presence - Thereupon, also came into open court Guy Douglas and H. V. C. Wynne subscribing witnesses to Codicil No. 2 who being duly sworn deposed & said that they were personally acquainted with the said Alfred Enochs in his lifetime - that he was of sound and disposing mind and memory at the time of the execution of said Codicil No. 2 That he signed and published the same as said codicil No. 2 in their presence and for the purposes therein contained and requested them to witness the same - That they witnessed the same at his request and in his presence, It is therefore ordered by the court that the said Paper writing be and the same are hereby set up and established as the last will and testament of the said Alfred Enochs deceased and that it be recorded by the clerk and filed.

A true copy from the minutes

   Attest Zach Watkins Clk.

(P.271)
State of Tennessee) March Term County Court 1880
Dyer County   ) Monday March 1st 1880

In the Matter of   ) This day a paper writing purporting
H. L. W. Turney's Will) to be the last will and Testament
          of H. L. W. Turney deceased was produced before the court for probate; Thereupon, came here into open court B. B. Watkins, one of the subscribing witnesses thereto; who first being duly sworn disposed and said That he was well and personally acquainted with the said H. L. W. Turney in his lifetime; that he was of sound and disposing mind and memory at the time of the executing of said paper writing. That he signed and published the said paper writing as his last will and testament in his presence and in the presence of F. D. Roberts, also a subscribing thereto and requested them to specially bear witness thereto - That they signed said paper writing as witnesses thereto in the presence of the Testator and in the presence of each other. It is therefore ordered by the court that said paper writing be and the same is hereby set up and established as the last will and testament of said H.L.W. Turney deceased & that the same be recorded by the clerk & filed.

A true copy from minutes

   Attest Zach Watkins Clerk.

State of Tennessee) March Term County Court 1880
Dyer County   )
         Monday March 1st 1880
In the matter of H. L. W.)
Turney's Will   ) This day a paper writing purport-
          ing to be the last will and testament of H. L. W. Turney deceased was produced before the court for probate: Thereupon, came here into open court B. B. Watkins, one of the subscribing witnesses thereto, who first

(P.271 Cont'd) being duly sworn deposed and said, That he was well and personally acquainted with the said H. L. W. Turney in his lifetime; that he was of sound and disposing mind and memory at the time of the execution of said paper writing - That he signed and published the said paper writing as his last will and testament in his presence and in the presence of F. D. Roberts, also a subscribing thereto and requested them to specially bear witness thereto - That they signed said paper writing as witnesses thereto in the presence of the Testator and in the presence of each other. It is therefore ordered by the court that said paper writing be and the same is hereby set up and established as the last will and testament of said H. L. W. Turney deceased & that the same be recorded by the clerk & filed.

A true copy from minutes

   Attest Zach Watkins

(P.272)
H. L. W. Turney's) In the Name of God Amen -
Last Will & Testament (
Probated March Term /80)   I, H. L. W. Turney of Dyer Co.
Recorded March 11/80 (Tennessee do make and constitute
 Zach Watkins Clerk.) this my last will and testament
           hereby revoking all others by me
at any other time -

1 Item - I will that all my just debts and funeral expenses, including a monument for my grave to be selected by my Executor, be paid by my Executor hereafter to be named out of the first moneys derived from my estate which comes into his hands -

2nd Item - I will that all of my personal property except my law Books be sold by my Executor on a twelve months credit taking notes with approved security for the same within sixty days after my death -

3rd Item - I will all of my law Books to the Barr at Dyersburg, Tennessee and desire that they be kept in the clerk & Master's office for the benefit of the Dyersburg Lawyers and those practicing at the Dyersburg Barr -

4th Item - I will that the land I own at the time of my death be sold by my Executor on the first Monday in January or April next after my death - and that it be advertised as long as two months before sale and sold for one third cash, one third due in 12 months and one third due in two years.

5th Item - I will all of the money derived from the sale of my personal and real property and from all other sources which may come into the hands of my Executor or Executor to my beloved mother Mary Turney of De Kalb County, Tennessee after first paying my Executor liberally for executing this my last will.

(P.272 Cont'd) 6th Item - I will that should I die between the 1st day of January and the 1st day of October and W. G. Welch is living in my dwelling house at the time of my death then and in that event that said Welch have the use of said dwelling house and twenty five acres of land free of rents or charges for said year.

7th Item - I hereby nominate and appoint Daniel E. Parker Executor of this my last will and testament.

In testimony whereof I have hereunto set my hand and subscribed my name on this the 20th day of October 1879

H. L. W. Turney

We the undersigned
witnesses to the
above will have
witnessed the same
at the request of
H. L. W. Turney, in
his presence and
in the presence of each
other - October 22, 1879
  B. B. Watkins
  F. D. Roberts

       See page 271 for Probate

(P.273)
D. A. Chamberlain) I, D. A. Chamberlain of Dyer County
Last Will & Testament (and state of Tennessee being of
Probated Aug. Term /80) sound mind but in feeble health and
Recorded Aug. 19th/80 (in view of the uncertainty of life
                            and the certainty of death do make
this my last will and testament -

1st I desire that all of my just debts shall be paid and I further desire that said debts shall be paid by my four children Mary Elisa Boatright, John S. Chamberlain, Carrel C. Chamberlain and Sarah Francis Chamberlain, each paying an equal share; but if any of said children should fail to pay such share or any part of such share I desire that the remaining one or ones should pay all the debts or such amount of such debts as remain unpaid and I further desire that if any one or any of my children should fail to pay said share or any part of said share of the above described debts that my executor to be herein after named by me shall Sell enough of each childs part who has failed to pay their share of my estate which shares I will hereafter designate and pay such debts or pay such children as have paid such debts the amount that they have paid more than their share and I further desire that my executor sell such property and pay such debts at the end of the time prescribed by law to settle estates.

2nd I will & bequeath to my beloved wife Kisih E. Chamberlain

(P.273 Cont'd) all of my property real personal or mixed and all the apertanences thereto together with their rents profits and incomes to have and to hold during her natural life and at her death such property to be divided as hereinafter prescribed by me.

(P.274) 3rd At the death of my wife Kissih E. Chamberlain I will and bequeath to my daughter Mary Eliza Boatright during her natural life and at her death to her bodily heirs the following described tract or parcel of land lying and being in the 5th civil district of Dyer County and State of Tennessee and bounded as follows on the north by P. C. Ledsinger on the South by N. C. White, on the east N. C. White, on the west the George Lane land, containing, (100) One hundred acres more or less such land to be subject to paying her share of my above described debts as arranged by me.

4th At the death of my wife Kissih E. Chamberlain I will and bequeath to my three children John S. Chamberlain Carrell C. Chamberlain and Sarah F. Chamberlain my homestead with all the appertainences thereto and described as follows it lying and being in the 5th civil district of Dyer County and State of Tennessee and bounded as follows, On the North by David Burnim on the south by Elijah Wright on the east by Taylor Troy on the west Burnim land to be divided among them as near equal as possible and each of their shares to be subject to their shares of my above described debts as arranged by me.

5th All of my personal property is to be disposed of by wife Kissih E. Chamberlain as she likes.

6th I nominate and appoint M. H. Davis as executor of this my last will and testament signed sealed and delivered in the presence of following ---

                        D. A. Chamberlain

This the 8th day of July 1880
Witness
    Attest: S. M. Jones
            Wm. Taylor

(P.275)
State of Tennessee) Owing to changes in my mind since making
Dyer County   ) my last will and testament I desire to
                        make the following change or codicil
thereto I desire that the 3rd Section of my will be changed so as to will and bequeath the land therein described to my d̶a̶u̶g̶h̶t̶e̶r̶ daughter Mary Eliza Boatright instead of to Mary Eliza Boatright during her natural life and then to the heirs of her body.

    I hereby set my hand and seal this the 12th day of July 1880
test, Wm. Taylor, J. H. Davis   D. A. Chamberlain

(171)

(P.275 Cont'd)
State of Tennessee) Aug. Term of the county court 1880
Dyer County) Tuesday Aug. 3rd 1880

In Matter of Probate)
of D. A. Chamberlain (This day a paper writing purporting
last will and Testa-) to be the last will and testament
ment (of D. A. Chamberlain deceased was
produced before the court for probate;
Thereupon came here into open court S. M. Jones, one of the
subscribing witnesses to the main body of said instrument and
J. H. Davis, one of the subscribing witnesses to the codicil
of said will, who being duly sworn, deposed and said that they
were personally acquainted with said D. A. Chamberlain, in
his lifetime - that he was of sound and disposing mind and memory at the time of the execution of said will and codicil that
he signed and acknowledge the same as his last will and testament in their presence and for the purpose therein contained -
and requested them to witness same.

State of Tennessee) Aug. Term of county court 1880
Dyer County) Tuesday Aug. 3rd 1880

In matter of Probate)
of last will & Testament (:
of D. A. Chamberlain)
Over

(P.276)
This day a paper writing purporting to be the last will and
testament of D. A. Chamberlain deceased was presented to the
court for further Probate; Thereupon, came into open court
Wm. Taylor, a subscribing witness thereto, who being duly
sworn deposed and said that he was personally acquainted with
the Testator in his lifetime; that he was of sound and disposing mind and memory at the time of the execution of said
paper writing and that he signed and published said paper writing in his presence, as his last will and testament and for
the purposes therein contained and requested him to witness
the same; that he signed the same as witness in the presence
of Testator and of the other witnesses thereto; It is, therefore ordered by the court that said paper writing be and the
same is hereby set up and established as the last will and testament of said D. A. Chamberlain deceased and that it be recorded by the clerk and filed.

A true copy of will and probate from minutes of the county
court.

Attest, Zach Watkins, Clerk.

(P.277)
J. A. Light's) In the Name of God Amen;
Last will & Testament (
Probated Sept. Term /80) I, J. A. Light of the county
Recorded Nov. 12th /80 (of and Dyer and State of Tennessee
Z Watkins Clk.) being of sound mind and memory and

(P.277 Cont'd) considering the uncertainty of this frail transitory life do therefore make, ordain, publish and declare this to be my last will and Testament -

That is to say, first, after all my lawful debts are paid and discharged the residue of my Estate real and personal I give bequeath and dispose of as follows; to wit;

To my daughter Mary, wife of Preston Tipton, my tract of land in Gibson county, on the road between Trenton and Mackleymoresville known as the Tom Yancy farm; I have deeded to my daughter Sarah A. Wife of P. L. Tipton a tract of land situated on the South Side and adjoining the Mitchell Point road about three miles west of Dyersburg which I intend for her division of my real Estate.

To my Son Charlie One hundred and twenty five acres of my home farm, situated on the west side of my land and north of the Mitchell Point road fronting Dr. T. J. Walker.

To my daughter Susan Adie the tract of land that I bought of David McLanahan lying in front of my residence and being a part of my home farm consisting of about 118 acres of land.

To my daughter Martha W. the tract of land lying between the David McLanahan tract and the tract of land deeded by me to Sarah A. wife of P. L. Tipton containing about 116 acres of land.

To my beloved wife the residue of my home farm embracing the residence together with the appurtenances situated thereon, also the personal property that I may leave.

My tract of 141 acres of land situated on Lewis Creek west of Willis Davis, I wish to be sold and the proceeds equally divided between my heirs Mary, Charlie, Susan Adie, & Martha and my wife (P.278) Susan.

In witness whereof I have hereunto subscribed my name and affixed my seal on this the 22nd day of December in the year of Our Lord One Thousand Eight Hundred and Seventy nine.

Joel A. Light (seal)

Joel E. Light Executor

The above written instrument was subscribed by the said J. A. Light in our presence and acknowledged by him to each of us, and he at the same time published and declared the above instrument so subscribed to be his last will and Testament, and we at the testators request and in his presence have signed our names as witnesses hereto and written opposite our names our respective places of residence.

N. Coker Dyersburg, Tenn.
Jos. Smith, Dyer County Tenn.
Jas. T. Hassell Dyersburg, Tenn.

(P.278 Cont'd)

Whereas I Joel A. Light of the County of Dyer and State of Tennessee have made my last will and Testament in writing bearing date of 22 day of December 1879 in and by which I have given to my daughter Mary P. wife of P. M. Tipton a tract of land in Gibson County Tenn. on the road between McLemoresville and Trenton also an equal division of the proceeds of the sale of my tract of land on Lewis Creek with Charlie, Adie, Martha and my wife I also gave in my said will and testament to my daughter Mattie a tract of land lying between the David McLanahan and the tract of land that I gave by deed to my daughter Sarah also an equal division of the proceeds of the sale of my tract of land on Lewis Creek with Charlie Addie Mary and my wife.

Now therefore I do by this writing which I hereby declare to be a codicil to my last will and testament and to be taken as a part thereof order and declare that my will is, that I give to Mary P. the tract of land lying between the tract of land I purchased of David McLanahan and (P.279) the tract that I deeded to my daughter Sarah which contains about 116 acres.

And to my daughter Mattie I give the tract of land in Gibson County known as the Thos. Yancy land.

I further direct my executor to sell my land on Lewis Creek and give half the proceeds to my daughter Mattie and the remainder divided equally between my wife Susan my son Charlie and my daughter Addie,

And lastly it is my desire that this Codicil be made a part of my last will and Testament as aforesaid to all intents and purposes.

In witness whereof I have unto subscribed my name and affixed my seal the 3rd day of August 1880.

Joel A. Light (seal)

The above instrument was subscribed in our presence and declared to be his last will and testament and we at his request hereto sign our names as witnesses

S. B. McLanahan   Residence Dyer County
S. D. Light   "   Dyer County

In the matter of   ) This day a paper writing purporting to be
J. A. Light's Last(the last will and testament of Joel A.
Will & Testament   ) Light dec'd was produced before the court
                      for probate, Thereupon came in open court
N. Coker, and Jas. T. Hassell subscribing witnesses to the main body of said will and S. D. Light and S. B. McLanahan subscribing witnesses to the Codicil thereto who being duly sworn disposed & said that they were personally acquainted with the said

(P.279 Cont'd) J. A. Light in his lifetime that he was of sound and disposing mind and memory at the time of the Execution of the said papers and that he signed and published the same as his last will and Testament in their presence and for the purposes therein contained - and requested them to witness the same. That they signed said paper writing as witnesses (P.280) thereto in the presence of the Testator and of each other.

It is therefore ordered by the court that said paper writing be and the same is hereby set up and established as the last will will and Testament of said J. A. Light, deceased and that the same be recorded and filed.

A true copy from minutes -

        Attest: Zach Watkins, Clerk.

(P.281)
Charity Manning) I, Charity Manning hereby make and
Last Will & Testament (publish this my last will and Tes-
Probated Nov. Term /80) tament -
Recorded Nov. 12th/80 (
  Z. Watkins Clk.)

        I give and bequeath to my daughter Mary Adilaide Brown wife of James L. Brown all the property and effects of which I may die seized and possessed to be hers for and during the term of her natural life - remainder to her heirs at law.

I hereby nominate and appoint my said daughter Mary Adilaide Brown Executrix of this my will - and waive the necessity of her giving bond as Executrix -

    Whereas my hand this the 26th day of August 1874
                    her
        Charity   X   Manning
                mark

Signed Sealed and published in our presence and we have hereunto signed our names in witness thereof at the request of the Testator and in his presence and in the presence of each other,

August 26th 1874

Test - S. R. Latta
      T. H. Benton

                            State of Tenn. Dyer Co.
In the Matter of Charity Manning) Nov. term Co. Court 1880
Last Will and Testament)

This day a paper writing purporting to be the last will and testament of Charity Manning dec'd was produced before the court for probate. Thereupon came here into open Court S. R. Latta and T. H. Benton Subscribing witnesses who being duly sworn deposed and said that they were personally acquainted with the said Charity

(174)

(P.281 Cont'd) Manning in her lifetime that she was of sound and disposing mind and memory at the time of the execution of said writing that she signed and published said paper writing as her last will and testament in their presence & for the purposes therein contained and requested them to witness the same - that they signed the same in her presence and in presence of each other, It is therefore ordered by the court that (P.282) said paper writing be and the same is hereby set up and established as the last will and testament of Charity Manning dec'd and that the same be recorded and filed.

A true copy from minutes

       Attest: Z. Watkins Clk.

(P.283)
Adaline Parks   ) I, Adaline Parks being of
Last Will & Testament   (sound mind and memory but in
Probated November Term 1880) very feeble health do make
Recorded Apl. 11/81   (and publish this as my last
 Z. Watkins Clk.   ) will and testament.

 Item 1st I give to my beloved Husband Smith Parks, all my interest in the property & estate of my deceased father, W. H. H. Miller deceased of every kind & description it may be whether the same has been reduced to possession at or in the hands of the administrators or any other person and this includes the town lot or parcel of land in Yorkville Gibson county Tennessee known as my fathers residence & store which was assigned to me by the Circuit Court of Gibson County in division of the real Estate of my father Wm. N. H. Miller among his heirs and in bounded on the north by the lands of William Zaracor East by Dr. <u>Lulls</u> & Dr. I. T. Burns, land or lots south by the main street and west by Robt. Colines Heotell, lot.

 Item 2nd - I hereby appoint my beloved husband Smith Parks, my executor to this my last will & testament October 2nd 1875 not signed until the 25th of January 1876

Witness as request   Adaline Parks
of Testatrix

   Geo. Parks (Nov. 1/80
   Edward Parks)

State of Tenn.) November Term of the County Court 1880
Dyer County   )

In the Matter of Probate of) This day a paper writing pur-
Last Will & Testament of (porting to be the last will
Adaline Parks   ) and testament of Adaline Parks
           deceased was produced before
the court for probate. Thereupon came here into open court Geo. Parks a subscribing witness thereto who being duly sworn

(176)

(P.283 Cont'd) deposed and said that he was personally acquainted with Adaline Parks the Testatrix in her lifetime that she was of sound and disposing mind and memory at the time of the execution of said paper writing and that she signed and acknowledged the execution of said paper writing in his presence and in presence of Edward Parks, the other subscribing witness thereto and requested them to specially bear witness thereto - That they signed the same in her presence and in the presence of each other that Edward Parks the other witness thereto is now dead that the name Edward Parks is in the own proper handwriting of said Edward Parks - Ordered that said paper writing be and the same is hereby set up and established as the last will and Testament of the said Adaline Parks and that same be recorded and filed -

(P.284)
Last Will & Testament
of P. C. Ledsinger dec'd
Probated Janry Term 1881
Recorded February 15/81
   Zach Watkins Clerk

November 26th 1880
It is my wish and request that my land and other property shall be divided as follows; Commencing at my north East corner, it being mine and Kings and Wrights corner, running thence south to the south east corner, commencing in the center, running west untill it strikes the cleared land on the Dickerson farm; thence north so far untill it becomes strate with the north boundary line of the Dunkin land this land is to belong to Otho and Glen Fowlkes, my grand children -

   Now begin at the south west corner of the ocupant, a portion of the Dickerson land and George Hurts south east corner, running south to the south boundary of my land, now, fall back to where you run the first fence off, say beginning on the Dickerson south boundary line thirty or forty poles west of the south east corner of the Dickerson place, thence west untill you strike the line running through my whole tract, this portion of land to belong to my daughter Nellie

   South of Nellie, Otho, & Glen's land that belongs to my son Gilbert

   Now beginning on the line between me and Segraves in the center of the Troy road; Running north so far by running east on the lowest ground near the ridge through the field, running on the east one hundred poles; thence north fifty poles, thence east to the division line, thence south to the south boundary line of the original tract thence west to the beginning, this land also is to belong to Otho and Glen Fowlkes, they having previously received fifteen hundred dollars more than my other children.

   Now the balance of the home place and all of the timbered land outside of the lines that have been run, to belong to this tract this belongs to my son Jeff -

(P.284 Cont'd)

Now I give my interest in the beach flat tract of land to Gilbert it being one half of the whole tract

I want all my cattle that is fit for market fattened and sold, that can possibly be gotten up, my horses and mules besides those two that Pritchard is to have put in proper fix and sold in the spring except the colts in the bottom, I want them kept untill fall and sold - there is a bay horse a sorrell mare and a gray mare, I also want sold in the spring - the pacing mare at home (P.285) is for Nellie - I want all of my individual cattle stock in the Missippi bottom sold to the best advantage possible and the partnership stock of mine and Buck Wards sold which is from seventy five to a hundred head -

I will all of my means arising from the sale of my stock and other things after my debts are paid deposited with the County Court Clerk for distribution between my children Gibert, Jeff and Nellie as soon as my estate is wound up - Nellie is to have Two hundred and fifty dollars more than Gilbert and Jeff - Nellie is also to have the Piano - there is to be nothing sold inside of my house - all my household furniture, bedding and bed clothes to be divided between Gilbert, Jeff, and Nellie -

I want pork enough put up to do the entire family and allso corn enough kept for them to run the place - the money that is coming to me from Pritchard at the end of the year 1881 belongs to my son Jeff - After killing all the pork hogs - Jeff is to have all of my stock hogs on the home place and Gilbert is to have all of them running at the Beach Flat

It is my wish that my sons Gilbert & Jeff divide my farming tools between them, such as they want & sell the ballance - they paying a fare price for them they may take

It is my wish & desire that my son Jeff have possession and full control of this place that I have given him at my death - The above was signed & witness the 27th day of December 1880

P. C. Ledsinger

Witnessed by;
Jo Smith
& H. L. Fowlkes

In the matter of P. C. Ledsinger) Jan. Term of County Court
Last Will and Testament) 1881
Wednesday Jan. 5/81

This day a paper writing purporting to be the last will and testament of P. C. Ledsinger deceased was produced before the court for Probate - Thereupon came into open court Jo Smith and Henry L. Fowlkes Subscribing witnesses thereto who 'ing first duly sworn deposes and said as follows -

Over

(P.286)
That they were personally acquainted with the said P. C. Ledsinger in his lifetime; that he was of sound and disposing mind and memory at the time of the Execution of the said paper writing; That he signed and published the said paper writing as his last will and Testament and for the purpose therein contained in their presence that they witnessed the same at his request in his presence and in the presence of each other.

It is therefore ordered by the court that the said paper writing be and the same is hereby established, as the last will and testament of the said P. C. Ledsinger Dec'd and that the same be recorded in the will book and filed.

A true copy from minutes

                Attest   Zach Watkins Clerk

(P.287)

John G. Archibald) I, John G. Archibald being of sound
Last will and Testament(mind and disposing memory do hereby
Probated Apl. 4/81) make and publish this as my last
Recorded Apl. 11/81 (will and testament at the same time
   Zach Watkins Clerk) revoking all former wills by me at
                           any time heretofore made.

Item 1st I direct that my funeral expenses and all my just debts be paid by my executor out of the first money coming to his hands and as soon after my decease as may be

Item 2nd I give to my beloved niece Ellen Viola Archibald daughter of my Bro. William P. Archibald all of my estate property and effects whether the same be real personal or mixed of which I may die seized on in any way possessed and including Three fourths of my policy or certificate which entitles my heirs as representatives to two thousand Dollars at my death from the order of the "golden Cross" the other one fourth to be disposed of as in the following item of my will.

Item 3, I give to my beloved nephew, Thomas C. Archibald and my beloved niece Sarah F. Archibald Daughter of my Bro. Samuel W. Archibald and my nephew is the son of Thomas A. Archibald each Two Hundred and fifty Dollars of the policy or certificate of membership in the order of the "Golden Cross", which certificate entitles my heirs or represenatives to two thousand dollars as set forth in Item 2nd of my will - fifteen hundred dollars of which is given in Item two of this will to Ellen V. Archibald and the balance of Five Hundred Dollars of S'd amt., is given in equal shares to my nephew Thos. C. and my niece Sarah F. Archibald.

I hereby appoint Jon. F. Dickey Executor of this my last will and testament this the 12th day of May 1880
Witnesses(Smith Parks
      (J. R. Westbrook   John G. Archibald

(179)

(P.288)
In the Matter of John G. Archibald) April Term of the County
Last Will and Testament) Court
Monday Apl. 4th 1881

      On this day a paper writing purporting to be the last will and testament of John G. Archibald deceased was produced before the court for probate. Thereupon came the subscribing witnesses thereto viz. Smith Parks and J. R. Westbrooks who being first duly sworn deposed and said that they were personally acquainted with the said John G. Archibald in his lifetime that he was of sound and disposing mind and memory at the time of the Execution of said paper writing as his last will and testament in their presence and for the purposes therein contained and requested them to witness the same that they signed the same in his presence and in the presence of each other - _____ Ordered that said paper writing be and the same is hereby set up & established as the last will and testament of J. G. Archibald deceased and that same be recorded and filed.
A true copy from minutes

                Attest Zach Watkins Clerk.

(P.289)
Charles A. Howard's) I, Charles A. Howard of the county of
Last Will & Testament (Dyer and state of Tennessee, being
Probated May Term 1881) desirous of making a disposition of my
Recorded July 19, 1881(property while I am in good health and
  Zach Watkins Clerk.) in my proper mind do make this my last
                               will -

     1st I will that after my death my burial expenses be paid first and then any and all my debts be paid if any -

     2nd I will that one hund hundred and fifty dollars be set apart for grave stones and iron railing around the same - and that Guy Douglass be empowered to have the same put into execution that is; that he have the grave enclosed and suitable stones erected.

     3rd I will that all my effects of any and every description be given to my brother W. J. F. Howard

     4th I will that Clarence Grimms be qualified and act as my Executor to this my last will and testament without being required to give bond or Security for his Executorship - and I request said Clarence Grimms not to make any charge for his services as executor this the fifteenth day of November 1880

Witness   Chas. H. Howard
Guy Douglass
H. V. C. Wynne

(180)

(P.289 Cont'd)
State of Tenn.) May Term of County Court 1881
Dyer County) Monday May 2nd 1881

In the Matter of C. A. Howard's) This day a paper writing
Last Will & Testament (purporting to be the last
will and testament of
Charles A. Howard dec'd late a citizen of Dyer County, was
produced before the court for probate; Thereupon, came into
open court H. V. C. Wynne and Guy Douglass; suscribing witnesses to the same, who being duly sworn deposed and said
that they were personally acquainted with Charles A. Howard,
the Testator - and that he was of sound and desposing memory
at the execution of the same and that he signed and acknowledged the execution of the said paper writing in their presence, as his last will & testament and they signed the same
in his presence and in the presence of each other. It is therefore ordered that said paper writing be set up and established
as the last will and testament of the said Charles A. Howard deceased - and that the same be recorded and filed - Thereupon
Clarence Grimms who is named as Executor of said Will came into
court and was duly qualified, giving bond and security being
waived in said will.

A true copy attest: Z. Watkins Clk.

(P.290)
Will of Miles White

I, Miles White of the City of Baltimore and State of Maryland,
being of sound and disposing mind and memory and remembering
the certainty of death and the uncertainty of the time thereof,
do make publish and declare this my last will and Testament -

In the first place I give and bequeath to my beloved wife
Margaret H. White all my household and kitchen furniture and
my horses, carriages and harness to her and her Executors and
Administrators forever, and I give to her for the term of her
natural life the house and lot which we now occupy as a residence known as 36 South Sharp Street and I also give to her
for the term of her natural life and no longer ground rents
producing three Thousand dollars per annum to be selected by
her and my Executor hereinafter named -

Second - I give and devise to Mary Berry and Martha Chappel to
each one of them, Two hundred dollars per annum during their
natural lives, to be paid to them by my Executor in person, or
to their written orders -

Third - I give and devise unto the children of my nephew, Jason
Trueblood, deseased, One Hundred and sixty acres of land and
Five Hundred dollars to be equally divided between them - and
to my Nephew Miles W. Trueblood if living at the time of my
death, one hundred and sixty acres of land said lands are to be
selected and designated by my Executor within one year after my
decease from my lands belonging to me, lying in the state of

(P.290 Cont'd) Iowa in any county in said state where my Executor and the aforesaid Legatees may agree - and I give and devise unto each of my nieces; Mary Trueblood and Miriam Trueblood and their heirs Three Thousand dollars of the second mortgage Bonds of the Marietta and Cincinnati Railroad said bonds to be held by my Executor hereinafter named, during her natural life, who will pay to them the interest as received -

Fourth - I give and devise unto my grandson, Miles White, son of my son, Francis White, all the land I own, lying between Airguith Street and the wall of the Government Cemetery and Hoffman Street and Parish Lane, except that part now leased and that I may lease during my lifetime - I also give and devise unto my said Grandson all that part that remains not leased at my death of one hundred and forty five feet of ground, fronting on the north east side of Linden Avenue formerly called Gorden Street and running back (P.291) one hundred and fifty feet more or less, to Mason Alley and extending from one hundred feet north west of Musher street to the lot leased by Louisa A. Hoffman to Joseph Hampson - and I also give and devise unto my said Grandson sixteen quarter sections of land containing seventy five hundred and sixty acres, more or less, from any lands I have in the state of Iowa not otherwise disposed of, to be selected and set aside by him and my Executor within two years after my death to him and his heirs. -

Fifth - I give and devise to my Grand-daughter, Sarah Elizabeth White, daughter of my son Francis White, all that part not leased at the time of my death, of a tract of land on the Belair Avenue, adjoining "Clifton" and the lands belonging to the estate of Thomas Hines deceased Two Thousand acres of land lying in the state of Iowa, not otherwise disposed of to be selected and set apart by my Executor within two years after my death and I also give and devise unto my said Grand-daughter all that part that I own, at the time of my death of a lot of ground on the west side of Ensor street, extending from John street to Hoffman street -

Sixth - I give and devise unto my Grandson, Francis A. White, son of my son, Francis White, all the land belonging to to me, which is comprised in a tract of land in the city of Baltimore, known as the "Pierce" tract which said tract of land belonging to me, consists of several lots bounding respectively on Dorceys Lane, Mowrel street, Grayson street, Pulaski street, Laurale street and the former Alms house property, the said lots being estimated to contain all together ten acres, more or less, I also give and devise unto my said Grandson all that part, not leased or sold at the time of my death, of a lot of ground fronting one hundred and fifty five feet on the south west side of Linden Avenue formerly called Gorden street, and commencing at the intersection of the south west side of Linden Avenue with the north west side of Robert Street, to him and his heirs -

Seventh - I give and ~~bequeath~~ devise unto my grandson, Richard J. White, son of my son, Francis White, the lot of ground on

(P.291 Cont'd) the north east side of Mason Ally, extending from Mosher street to McMacker street - and running back to Bolton street excepting one lot of Twenty two feet owned by George P. Frick and forty feet, owned by Joseph Hampson, also one lot of ground on the east side of Johnson street south of Fort Avenue, containing two acres, more or less - and I also give and devise to my said Grandson Two Thousand acres of land lying in the state of Iowa, not otherwise disposed of to be selected (P.292) and set aside by my Executor within two years after my decease to him and his heirs -

Eighth - I authorize and empower my said son Francis White during the minority of either of my said Grandchildren to sell any or all of the land herein before devised to said Grandchildren and to receive the purchase money and to release the purchaser from all legal and equitable obligations of seeing to the application thereof and to convey and unencumbered title to purchasers, or to make leases of said lands or any portion of them for any term or terms of years whatever - and that such sales and leases shall be binding on the said Grandchild and his or her heirs, administrator or assigns to whom I have devised the said land so leased or sold - and in case either of my said Grandchildren shall not arrive at lawful age before the death of my said son Francis, I give the same power and authority to those persons who may then be charged with the execution or administration of this will; provided in the latter case that such sales and leases shall be subject to the ratification of the Orphan's Court as other sales of real estate property are when made by Executors - and I direct and order that the proceeds of such sales shall be invested in ground rents and I give and devise the ground rents so purchased in place of and in the same manner as share given and devised that which was sold and produced the money with which the purchase was made -

Ninth - In addition to the foregoing devise to my said Grandchildren, I also give and devise to each of them, Miles White, Sarah Elizabeth White, Francis A. White and Richard J. White Two Hundred dollars shares of the stock of the Baltimore and Ohio Railroad and Five Thousand - dollars - and I also give to my said Grandchildren Thirty Two Thousand dollars of the second Mortgage Bonds of the Marietta and Cincinati Railroad to be equally divided between them -

Tenth - I give and devise unto Miles White sone of my niece Martha Newby one hundred and Sixty acres of land lying and being in the State of Iowa to be set apart by my Executor within one year after my death to him and his heirs -

Eleventh - I give and devise unto my sister Rebecca White of Raysville in the State of Indiana the interest of ten of the seven per cent second mortgage Bonds of the Marietta and Cincinati Railroad for one thousand dollars each, to be paid to her by my Executor hereinafter named, as the coupon of said Bonds mature during her natural life and at her decease it is my will and desire that my Executor shall (P.293) deliver one of said Bonds to each of her grandchildren as may have arrived at twenty one years of age and to the guardian duly appointed to those

(P.293 Cont'd) of said grandchildren that may be under twenty one years of age, one of said bonds for each of said Grandchildren - and the balance to be delivered to to the mother of said grandchildren.

Twelfth - I do hereby give and bequeath to "Miles White Beneficial Society" of Baltimore City, a corporation created under the provisions of the Maryland Code of Public Laws by a certificate dated the 20th day of June A. D. 1874 and duly recorded in the office of the clerk of the Superior Court of Baltimore City the sum of one hundred thousand dollars to be used for the purposes of said Corporation -

Thirteenth - In case of the death of any one of my aforesaid Grandchildren under age, and unmarried and without issue I give and devise to my surviving grandchildren or grandchild the property and of my estate hereby devised and bequeathed to the Grandchild who may so die, as aforesaid, and in case all of my aforesaid Grandchildren shall die, under age and unmarried and without issue, then I give and devise all the property and shares of my estate hereby devised and bequeathed to my said Grandchildren to their Father, my son Francis White, if he be then living - and if he be not then living to my heirs at law as to the realty and to my next of kin as to the personalty

Fourteenth - I give and devise and bequeath all the rest and residue of my Real Estate, real, personal and mixed of every kind and description to my son, Francis White, his heirs, Executors and administrators forever -

And lastly - I appoint my said son Francis White Sole Executor of this my last will and testament, hereby revoking all former wills and testaments made by me - In testimony whereof I hereunto set my hand and affix my seal this Seventh (7) day of July Anno Domini Eighteen hundred and seventy four -

        Miles White (seal)

Signed, sealed, published and declared by Miles White the above named Testator, as and for his last will and testament in the presence of us who at his request and in his presence and in the presence of each other have subscribed our names as witnesses thereto

        W. Tazewell Fox
        James McNeal Jr.
        J. Swan Frick

Baltimore City S. S.

  On the 16th day of March 1876 came Francis White and solemly declared and affirmed that he doth not know of any will or Codicil of Miles White, late of said city, deceased, other than the above Instrument of writing and that he found the same after the death of the Testator in his secretary where he

(184)

(P.293 Cont'd) usually kept his private papers and that that the Testator (P.294) departed this life on the 12th day of March 1876 -

Affirmed in Open court
    Test;

J. Harmon Brown
Register of Wills, Baltimore City -

Baltimore City, S. S.

    On the 16th day of March 1876 came W. Tazewell Fox, James McNeal and J. Swan Frick the subscribing witnesses to the aforegoing last will and testament of Miles White, late of said city deceased made oath on the holy _____ of Almighty God that they did see the Testator sign and seal this will - That they heard him publish pronounce and declare the same to be his last will and testament - That at the time of his so doing he was to the best of their apprehension, of sound and disposing mind, memory and understanding; and that they subscribed their names as witnesses to this will in his presence, at his request and in the presence of each other -

Sworn to in open court

    Test:

J. Harmon Brown,
Register of Wills for
Baltimore, City.

In Baltimore City Orphan Court:

    The Court after having carefully examined examined the above Last will and testament of Miles White late of Baltimore City, and also the evidence adduced as to its validity, order and decree this 16th day of March 1876, that the same be admitted in the court as the true and genuine last will and testament of the said Miles White, deceased.

        John A. Ingles
        G. W. Lindsay
        John K. Carroll

In testimony that the aforegoing is a true copy taken from the original file and remaining in the office of the Register of Wills for Baltimore City I hereunto subscribe my name and affix the seal of my said office on this 31st day of March in the year of Our Lord One Thousand Eight hundred & seventy six

Test
(seal)

J. Harmon Brown
Register of Wills for
Baltimore City -

Maryland, S. C.
    The State of Maryland
        To all persons to whom these presents shall come greeting; Know ye, that the Last will and testament of Miles White of

(185)

(P.294 Cont'd) Baltimore City deceased, hath in due form of Law been exhibited proved and recorded in the office of the Register of (P.295) Wills Baltimore city, a copy of which is to these presents annexed - and administration of all the goods, chattles and credits hereby granted and Committed unto Francis White the Executor by said will appointed -

    Witness - John A. Ingles Esq. Chief Judge of the Orphans Court of Baltimore city this 18 day of March in the year of Our Lord Eighteen Hundred and seventy six

Test;   J. Harmon Brown
                                Register of Wills for
(seal)   Baltimore City

State of Maryland) I, J. Harmon, clerk of said court and
Orphans Court of) Register of wills of said Baltimore City
Baltimore City   (certify that the foregoing is a true and
                        perfect copy from the records and office books of said court and office of said Register of the Last will of Miles White, deceased and of the probate thereof and grant of letters &c in said court and of the letters testamentary issued thereon and by said Register and said court to Francis White the Executor of said will and that said court is a court of record and that I am the clerk thereof and Register as aforesaid and the keeper of the Books of said court and Registers office

    Witness my hand and seal of office this 12th day of April A. D. 1876   J. Harmon Brown

(seal)

State of Tennessee) I, John A. Ingles, presiding judge of
Orphan Court of (said courts certify that J. Harmon Brown
Baltimore City   ) who signed the foregoing certificate is
                      now and was at the time of signing the same clerk of said court and Register of wills of said Baltimore City and that said court is a court of record and that said certificate and attestation is in due form and by the proper officer.

    Witness my hand at office this 12th day of April A. D. 1876

                                    John A. Ingles

State of Maryland) I, J. Harmon Brown, clerk of said court
Orphan Court of (certify that John A. Ingles who signed
Baltimore City   ) the foregoing certificate is now and was
                     at the time of signing the same the presiding Judge of said court duly commend and qualified - Witness my hand and seal of office this 12th day of April A. D. 1876

                                    J. Harmon Brown
(seal)   Clerk

(186)

(P.296)

State of Tennessee) I, Owen Dwyer, clerk of the County and
Shelby County   (probate court of said county do hereby
                   certify the foregoing (18) Eighteen
pages contain a full true and perfect copy of the last will
and testament of Miles White and the order probating the same
as the same appears of record in Will Record No. "D" Pages 80
to 89 and minute Book 27 page 408 now on file my office -

    In testimony whereof I have hereunto set my hand and affixed the seal of said court at office in the city of Memphis this 3rd day of Jany 1881

                                Owen Dwyer, Clerk
                          By Louis Kittimus, D. C.

(Owen Dwyer)
(Clerk.)
(seal   )

    The proceedings in the Shelby County Court as per record from said court is as follows;

Probate Court of Shelby County

State of Tennessee)
Shelby County   ) S. S.

                    Please before the Honorable J. E. R. Ray Judge of the Probate court of Shelby County, held in the city of Memphis and state and county aforesaid at the April term thereof 1876.

    Be it remembered that heretofore, to wit; On Tuesday April 18th 1876, it being one of the days of said April 1876 term the following of record in the words and figures following, viz; Francis White, by his Attorney Henry G. Smith produces in court a copy of the last will and testament of Miles White deceased and asks that the same be admitted to probate and registration of prescribed in the Code of Tennessee Sections 2182, 2183, 2184, 2185, 2186 &c - and it appearing that said will has been and is probated according to the laws of Tennessee in the Orphans Court of Baltimore City in Maryland, and that the copy now here produced is authenticated and certified as prescribed by the laws of Tennessee to wit: as contained in the section of Code aforesaid & that lands personally devised & bequeathed by said will are situated in this county to wit; Shelby it is ordered that said copy be filed & recorded & also registered in the Registers office of this County and have the same force and effect as if the original had been executed in this state & proved or allowed in the courts of this state -

State of Tennessee) September Term County Court 1881
Dyer County   ) Tuesday Sept. 6/1881

In Matter of Last Will   ) Francis White by his atty's
& Testament of Miles White dec'd) S. W. Cochrane and C.C. Moss

(187)

(P.296 Cont'd) produces in court a copy of the last will of
Miles White deceased and asks that the same be admitted to
probate and registration according to the Laws of Tennessee
as prescribed in the Code of Tennessee sections (P.297)
2182, 2183, 2184, 2185, 2186, 2187, 2188 - and it appearing
that said will has been and is probated according to the law
of Tennessee, in the Orphan Court of Baltimore City in the
State of Maryland and that the copy now here produced is
authenticated and certified as prescribed by the Laws of
Tennessee to wit; as contained in the sections of the Code
as aforesaid and that lands personally devised and bequeathed
by said will are situated in Shelby County, Tennessee, and
that lands bequeathed by said will are situated in this county
to wit; Dyer County, Tennessee he moved that it be recorded
on the will book of this county and court. It is therefore
ordered by the court that said copy be recorded on the will
book of this court and be certified by the Clerk of this court
that the same shall be evidence as here prescribed by Law

A true copy of the record from Memphis and of the action of
the County Court at its September Term 1881

      Attest Z. Watkins, Clerk.

)P.298)
Fannie P. Webb's   ) Dyer County Term, June 2nd 1881
Last Will & Testament (
Proven at July & Oct. Term) I, Fannie Peyton Webb being
County Court /81   (sound in mind make this my last
Recorded Dec. 9th, /81) will & testament. I give to my
 Zach Watkins   (husband W. J. Webb in trust for
           my children all my property real
and personal whatever that - I now own or may die seized and
possessed of. He to sell and convey or exchange, or dispose
of in any manner he may deem best as follows to wit;

The (112½) one hundred and twelve acres and a half, on which
I now live, The (262½) two hundred and sixty two and a half
acres south of C. I. Loves home tract and East of Wm. Pates
home and the (300) three hundred acres in Lake County a part
of C. I. Love 5000 acre tract the same lands allotted to me
by the commissioners out of C. I. Love dec'd estate and all
other lands and property whatever that I may now have or receive as heir of Elizabeth D. Love or any other property
whatever W. J. to use the money or property so attained for the
education and support of my children Julia Elizabeth Webb,
Sue Green Webb. Fannie Love Webb, Wm. Burton Webb, Robt. Wilson
Webb, and John McKanny Webb, and ballance left to be equally
divided between my children, or in case of the death of either
of them to be equally divided among balance, surviving children.

 It is my wish that my husband W. J. Webb as trustee for
my children should keep at least one fourth proceeds of the
above real estate - say ($1,000) One thousand dollars inves-
ted in a home for my children
Chas. I. Love, Oct. 4/81) Witness Fannie P. Webb (seal)
Richard Love, July 5/81)

(P.298 Cont'd)

Love's Landing Dyer Co. Tenn.
July 1st 1881,

Personally appeared before me, T. C. Buchannan Justice of the Peace for Dyer County, Tennessee, Charles I. Love and Richard Love who being duly sworn acknowledged this to be their signatures as witnesses to the will of Fannie P. Webb and the same to be signed by her in her right mind and free will and choice

    T. C. Buchanan J. P. Dyer County Tenn.

State of Tenn.) July Term of the county court /81,
Dyer County)

(P.299) This day a paper writing purporting to be the last will and testament of Fannie P. Webb deceased, was produced before the court for probate. Thereupon came into open court Richard Love, one of the subscribing witnesses thereto, who being duly sworn deposed and said that he was personally acquainted with the said Testatrix in her life time that she was of sound and disposing mind and memory at the time of the execution of said paper writing and that she signed and published said paper writing as her last will and testament in his presence and in the presence of the other subscribing witness thereto - and that said witnesses attested the same at her request in her presence and in the presence of each other -

State of Tenn.) October Term of the County Court 1881, On
Dyer County) this day a paper writing purporting to be
the last will and testament of Fannie P. Webb deceased, was produced before the court for further probate - Thereupon came the said witness, Chas. I. Love, whose name is subscribed as such, here into open court being first duly sworn deposed as follows; That he was personally acquainted with said Fannie P. Webb, (who was his daughter) the testatrix, in her lifetime, that she was of sound and disposing mind and memory at the time of the execution of said paper writing - That she signed and published said paper writing in his presence and of Richard Love witness, as her last will and testament and for the purposes therein contained and requested them to bear witness to the same; That they signed the same in her presence and in the presence of each other. It is therefore ordered by the court that the said paper writing be and the same is hereby set up and established as the last will and testament of said Fannie P. Webb, deceased and that the same be recorded and filed.

A true copy from the minutes

    Attest, Z. Watkins Clerk.

(P.300)
E. L. Palmer	(I, Edward L. Palmer, weak and in
Last will and Testament,)	feeble health, but of sound mind
Probated Dec. Term /81 (	and disposing memory, make and
Recorded Dec. 5/81)	publish this as my last will and
Zach Watkins Clk.	(

(P.300 Cont'd) testament, hereby revoking all others by me heretofore made.

First, I desire my executor to pay all my just debts, including burial expenses, as soon after my death as practicable.

Second, After the payment of any debts I direct that my executor keep so much of my property on hand as may be necessary, (and include in this item all property exempt from execution, as I desire and will that all such property be under the control of my executor) to enable my children to keep house and live together on my farm and run the farm to enable them to make a support for themselves until my youngest son arrives at the age of twenty one years, any surplus property on the farm may be sold by my Executor at any time and in such way as he deems best.

Third - When my youngest son arrives at the age of twenty one years, I direct that my executor sell all the personal property on a twelve months credit and divide the proceeds equally between my four sons Henry A. Edward J. Reuben L. and Charles D. Palmer and my two tracts of land, my home tract of one hundred acres, and the Fifty acres purchased off the south east of E. P. Kirks home tract. I also direct to be divided equally between my four sons or the representative of my four sons share & share alike, according to quality & quantity.

Fourth - I greatly desire that my children should all have at least a good English Education and as the two older boys have already received a fair educa- (P.301) tion and nearly arrived at Mans estate, It is my will that the two older boys, who are substantially already raised, labor on the farm with younger ones, and provide means to secure to the two younger brothers a good English Education - but if the family either cannot or will not provide the necessary means to give to my two younger Sons, such Education as is herein described; then I direct that my executor use such funds as may be in his hands for such purposes, or that out of the personal property or proceeds of the farm he provide means and use it to secure a good English Education to each one of my two younger Sons.

Fifth - I hereby appoint Elias Hall my executor of this my last will and testament.

E. L. Palmer

October 19th 1878
Witness
Smith Parks
P. H. Warren

State of Tenn.) December Term of the County Court/81
Dyer Co.) This day a paper writing purporting to be the last will and testament of Edward L. Palmer dec'd was produced before the Court for probate, Thereupon came into open court Smith Parks and P. H. Warren

(P.301 Cont'd) subscribing witnesses thereto, who being first duly sworn deposed and said as follows; That they were well and personally acquainted with the said E. L. Palmer in his lifetime: That he was of sound and disposing mind and memory at the time of execution of said paper writing; That he signed and published said paper writing as his last will and testament in their presence and for the purposes therein contained; That they witnessed said paper writing at the request of the testator in his presence and in the presence of each other.

It is therefore ordered by the court that the said paper writing be and the same is hereby set up and established as the last will and testament of the said E. L. Palmer dec'd and that the same be recorded by the clerk and filed -

A true copy from the minutes

        Attest: Zach Watkins   Clerk.

(P.302)
John M. Carroll's) State of Tenn., Dyer County,
Last Will & Testament (
Probated May Term /82) I, John M. Carroll do make and publish this, as my last will and testament hereby revoking and making void all others by me at any time made.
Recorded May 2nd /82 (
  Z. Watkins clk.)

First - I direct that fifty acres of land lying & being in the north east corner of my land be set apart for the purposes of paying my debts should it become necessary - should it not become necessary for the above named land to be sold then I desire that John Pope and Julia Carroll remain on the above named land for three more years. First; I direct that all my debts be paid as soon after my death as possible out of any moneys that I may die possessed of, or may first come into the hands of my executrix -

Secondly - I give and bequeath unto my wife, Susannah Margaret Elizabeth Carrell, during her lifetime, the use of my farm, all the household and kitchen furniture also all the stock that may be necessary to carry on the farm; after her death the lands together with all the stock, household and kitchen furniture to be sold and the proceeds to be equally divided between my surviving children after allowing Saban, Franklin and Albert Carrell children of John D. Carrell and his wife Julia Carrell, ten dollars each.

4th I give and bequeath unto my son Asbner Cooper Carrell a yellow suckling colt.

Lastly, I do hereby nominate & appoint my wife Susannah Margaret Elizabeth Carrell my executrix. In witness whereof I do to this my will, set my hand, this the the twenty second day of December one Thousand eight hundred and seventy six.
                                                    J. M. Carrell

(191)

(P.302 Cont'd)
Signed & published in our presence and we have subscribed our names hereto in the presence of the testator this 22nd of December 1876

      Asa Fowlkes
      H. L. Fowlkes

(P.303)
State of Tenn.) May Term of County Court 1882
Dyer County)

    This day a paper writing purporting to be the last will and testament of John M. Carroll, deceased, late a citizen of Dyer County Tenn. was produced before the court for probate - Thereupon came into open court Asa Fowlkes and H. L. Fowlkes subscribing witnesses to the same, who being first - duly sworn deposed and said that they were personally acquainted with John M. Carrell, the Testator, and that he was of sound and disposing mind and memory at the execution of the same and that he signed and acknowledged the execution of the said paper writing in their presence, as his last will and testament - and that they signed the same in his presence and in the presence of each.

  It is therefore ordered that the said paper writing be set up and established as the last will & testament of John M. Carrell deceased and that the same be recorded & filed. Thereupon came Susannah Margaret Elizabeth Carrell who is named as Executrix of said will, into open court and was duly qualified - giving bond & security being waived in said will.

A True copy from the minutes

    Attest; Zach Watkins Clerk.

(P.304)
Last will and Testament) December 20 - 1880
of Jesse Harris, deceased.(
Probated May Term 1882) I, Jesse Harris it is my will
Recorded June 21 - 1882 (that my wyfe Martha Harris my
 Z. Watkins Clk.) pressent wyfe shall have this
          tract of land that I now live on
Seventy Seven acres and a half during her lief and if she dies before her youngest child by mee comes of age I want her children by mee to have the benefits of it till the youngest child is twenty one years old after which they can divide or sell as they see proper there shall bee no sale no further than my wyfe sees proper to sell and dispose of such as she don't want.

The other tract of land beeing eighty acres.

I want my children by me present wyfe Martha Harris to have the profits and benefits of it from my decease and when her oldest child by me comes of age they can divide it as they see proper
Witnesses   Jesse Harris
James Saulsberry, W. R. Stephenson

(192)

(P.304 Cont'd)
State of Tennessee) In County Court May term /82
Dyer County)

    This day a paper writing purporting to be the last will and testament of Jesse Harris, deceased, late a citizen of Dyer County, Tennessee, was produced before the court for probate. Thereupon came into open court James Saulsberry and W. R. Stephenson subscribing witnesses to the same; who being duly sworn deposed and said that they were personally acquainted with Jesse Harris, the Testator, and that he was of sound and disposing mind and memory at the execution of the same and that he signed and acknowledged the execution of the said paper writing in their presence and that he asked them to bare witness to the same.

    It is therefore ordered that the said paper writing be set up and established as the last will & Testament of the said Jesse Harris, deceased, and that the same be recorded and filed.

    Attest; Z. Watkins Clk.

(P.305)
Last Will and Testament of Mary A. Roberts, deceased,
Probated June Term /82
Recorded June 21 - 1882
    Zach Watkins clk.

I, Mary A. Roberts of Dyersburg Tennessee, being of sound mind and memory do hereby make publish and declare this to be my last will and Testament hereby revoking and making void all former wills by me at any time heretofore made.

    I give and bequeath to my Son Frank D. Roberts an acre lot in my orchard, fronting the street and running back length wise the orchard, including the vacant lot between my home place and the lot - conveyed by me to J. F. Roberts.

    I give and bequeath to my son Robt. S. Roberts the balance of my home place consisting of fourteen acres more or less.

    I hereby nominate and appoint my son W. D. Roberts Executor of this my will and having confidence in his integrity I hereby waive the necessity of his giving bond -

    In testimony whereof I have hereunto set my hand this the 8th day of November 1881

    Mary A. Roberts

We, S. R. Latta and Wm. P. Fowlkes have seen the above testator sign the above and declare the same to be her last will and testament; In testimony whereof we have hereunto set our hands in presence of eachother and the Testatrix
This November 8th 1881

Test

    S. R. Latta
    W. P. Fowlkes

(193)

(P.305 Cont'd)
State of Tennessee) In county court June Term 1882
Dyer County   )

This day a paper writing purporting to be the last will and Testament of Mary A. Roberts, deceased, bearing date the 8th day of Nov. /81 was produced before the court for Probate. There upon came into open court S. R. Latta and W. P. Fowlkes subscribing witness thereto who having been first duly sworn deposed and said that they were personally acquainted with the said Testatrix in her lifetime, that she was of sound and deposing mind and memory at the time of the execution of said paper writing, that she signed and (P.306) published said paper writing as her last will and testament in their presence and for the purposes therein contained and requested them to bare witness thereto; That they signed the same as witness in the presence of the testatrix and in the presence of each other. It is therefore ordered by the court that the said paper writing be set up and established as the last will and testament of the said Mary A. Roberts, deceased, and that the same be recorded in will "Book" and filed - Thereupon came W. D. Roberts who is named as Exr. of said last will and testament into open court and was duly qualified - giving bond and security being waived in said will -

A true copy
    Attest -
          Z. Watkins Clk.

(P.307)
Last Will and Testament) I, R. C. Parr of Dyersburg in the
of R. C. Parr deceased, (State of Tennessee hereby make
Probated August Term /82) this my last will and testament.
Recorded August 7/82   (I, direct that my just debts be
  Z. Watkins clk.   ) paid by my executor hereinafter
named as soon after my death as may by him be found convenient. I give to my brother James Wesley all the property real and personal of every description I own or have any right in for him to keep such part as he may wish for his own use or bequest and the remainder to use to dispose of and distribute at such time in such way and with such restrictions as may seem best in his judgement - He making my relatives legal heirs and benefactors the beneficiarys of this distribution in such amounts to each one as he may think right - I hereby appoint James Wesley Parr to be executor of this will and wave the necessity of him giving bond and security.

In testimony whereof I hereunto set my hand this 20th day of September A. D. 1876
                                    R. C. Parr

Witnesses signed in
our presence and the
presence of each other
R. H. Campbell
S. A. Wood
C. C. Jones
G. W. Lavender

(P.307 Cont'd)
State of Tennessee) County Court August Term 1882
Dyer County)

This day a paper writing purporting to be the last will and testament of R. C. Parr dec'd, was produced before the court for Probate; Thereupon came into open court R. H. Campbell and S. A. Wood, subscribing witnesses to the same, who being first, duly sworn deposed and said that they were personally acquainted with the testator in his lifetime; that he was of sound and disposing mind & memory at the execution of said paper writing; that he signed and published said (P.308) paper writing as his last will and testament in their presence and requested them to bare witness to the same; that they signed the same as witnesses in the presence of the testator and in the presence of each other. It is therefore ordered by the court that the said paper writing be set up and established as the last will and testament of the said R. C. Parr dec'd and that the same be recorded in will "Book" and filed. Let Letters Testamentary issue to J. W. Parr who is named as executor in said will the necessity of his making oath & giving bond being waived in said will.

A true copy from the minutes

Attest; Zach Watkins, Clerk.

(P.309)
Last Will and Testament) I, Isaac Harris of the County of
of Isaac A. Harris dec'd (Dyer and State of Tennessee be-
Probated September 4 - 1882) ing of sound mind but feeble in
Recorded September 9th 1882(health desire this to be my last
   Z. Watkins, Clk.) will and testament.

First - After paying all my honest debts I give and bequeath the remainder of my property to my wife and my three living children and I nominate and appoint my father A. G. Harris and my father-in-law J. G. Tucker my executors and clothe them with full power and authority to sell and convey a part of my real estate to wit my tract of land known as the Blake place also my Gin property at Newbern and reinvest the proceeds of sale of said property in other real estate or Bonds if they think it best to make sale of said property above mentioned also to sell and dispose of all personal property as they may think best. This the 9th day of August - 1882

Signed in)
presence of (I. A. Harris
witnesses)
G. Douglass (
A. Harris)

State of Tennessee) In County Court Sept. Term 1882
Dyer County) This day a paper writing purporting to
be the last will and Testament of I. A. Harris deceased was produced before the court for Probate.

(195)

(P.309 Cont'd)   Thereupon came into open court G. Douglass and A. Harris subscribing witnesses to the same, who being duly sworn deposed and said that they were personally acquainted with the said testator in his lifetime: that he was of sound and disposing mind and memory at the execution of said paper writing; that he signed and published said paper writing as his last will and testament in their presence and requested them to bear witness to the same. That they signed the same in the presence of the Testator and in the presence of each other. It is therefore ordered by the court that the said paper writing be set up and established as the last will and testament of the said I. A. Harris deceased and that same be recorded in Will Book & filed and that letters testamentary issue to said name Executors.

A true copy from the minutes

   Attest - Z. Watkins clk.

(P.310)
Last will & Testament) I, William C. Doyle hereby make
of William C. Doyle dec'd (and publish this my last will
Probated Decr. Term 1882) and Testament;
Recorded December 9 / 1882(
 Zach Watkins clk.) 1st   It is my will that all the
By L. D. Hamilton D. C.   property of which I may die
         seized & possessed be divided
among my heirs at law, as provided for under the laws of Tennessee - Except as hereinafter provided.

2nd   I am the owner in my own right; and as tenant in common with other parties of lands in the States of Tennessee and Florida - which lands it may be to the interest of my estate and my heirs at law to dispose of - And desiring that, in such a case - that said lands may be sold without the intervention of courts or legal proceedings, I hereby authorize and empower, my Executrix, or any executor cum-tes tamento annexo - That may hereafter be appointed - to sell any or all of said lands, and execute deed or deeds to purchasers thereof - as fully as I could do if I were living, provided however that such deeds be witnessed and approved by one or more of the following named parties, to wit; John W. Lauderdale Hick P. Doyle, E. R. Vernon or M. M. Marshall.

3rd   My oldest daughter Jennie has been educated - and desiring that my younger children should have like advantages of education it is my will and I so direct that my executrix - or any executor cum testamento annexo that may hereafter be appointed, expend out of the body of my estate an amount sufficient, judiciously applied to give to each of my younger daughters a like education - That is that they be graduated at a respectable College - and that my son John Carroll Doyle be also graduated at some respectable literary school - and then if he so selects - that he be also graduated at a Law, Medical or Theological School; and the sum so expended for the education

(P.310 Cont'd) of my said younger children are not to be charged to them in the distribution of my estate.

4th I hereby nominate and appoint my beloved wife Jennie Doyle executrix of this my will and testament, (P.311) and having full confidence in her judgement fidelity and capability I hereby expressly waive the necessity of her executing bond as executrix.

Witness my hand this the 5th day of October 1882

W. C. Doyle

Signed sealed and published in our presence, in testimony whereof we have hereunto set ourhands in presence of each other and of the Testator.

Oct. 5th /82

S. R. Latta
J. W. Lauderdale
Hick P. Doyle
Belle W. Doyle
M. A. Skeffington

State of Tennessee) In county court
Dyer County   ) December Term 1882

This day a paper writing purporting to be the last will and Testament of W. C. Doyle, late a citizen of Dyer County Tennessee, deceased, was presented to the court for probate, Thereupon came into open court S. R. Latta, J. W. Lauderdale and Hick P. Doyle subscribing witnesses to the same, who being first, duly sworn deposed and said that they were personally acquainted with the Testator, W. C. Doyle, on his lifetime and that he was of sound and disposing mind and memory at the execution of the same and that he signed and acknowledged the execution of said paper writing in their presence, as his last will and testament; and that they signed the same in his presence and in the presence of each other. It is therefore ordered by the court that the said paper writing be set up and established as the last will & Testament of the said W. C. Doyle deceased and that same be recorded and filed - Thereupn came Jennie Doyle who is named as Executrix of said Last will & testament into open court and was duly qualified. The necessity of giving bond being waived in said will. Let letters testamentary issue

A true copy from the minutes

Attest Zach Watkins clerk.

(P.312)
Last Will & Testament   ) I, Willis Sawyer, being sound in
of Willis Sawyer dec'd   (mind, feeble in body, make this,
Probated January Term /83) my last will and testimony setting
Recorded Jany. 9, 1883   (aside all I have heretofore made,
   Zach Watkins clk.   ) First, I will all my just debts to

(P.312 Cont'd) be paid, I will and bequeath to my son Stephen Sawyer the place known as my home place, with the exception of the land lying South of the cross-fence the amounts hereafter to be established, by them, For and in consideration of this bequeath, the said Stephen Sawyer is to care for my afflicted son John Sawyer as long as he may live. In case of the said Stephen Sawyers death, the said bequeath is to go to the support and maintenance of the said John Sawyer. I will and bequeath to my daughter Mrs. Harriet Dunevant and her bodily heirs the remainder of the farm heretofore mentioned - I will and bequeath to my three grand-children, William Avery Cole, Willis Daniel and Louella Cribbs, Two hundred Dollars to be divided as follows: To William A. Cole one hundred dollars, to Willis D. and Louella Cribbs, fifty dollars each, The above amount to be paid by Stephen Sawyer when legally applied for at the expiration of two years from the date of my death.

The reason that I have not mentioned in this will my son William Sawyer and my daughter Mrs. Cathrine Foust, is that I have already deeded to the said William Sawyer Sixty Six acres of land, the said William Sawyer having paid the said Mrs. Cathrine Foust, two hundred and fifty dollars for her interest in the above deeded land I will that my son Stephen Sawyer pay all the debts mentioned for and in consideration of all the perishible property in my possession at the date of my death This Oct. 30, 1882

Attest;
John D. Swift
P. H. Warren

Willis Sawyer

(P.313)
State of Tennessee(In County Court Dyer County Tenn.
Dyer County   ) January Term 1883
This day a paper writing purporting to be the last will and testament of Willis Sawyer dec'd was produced before the court for probate. Thereupon John D. Swift and P. H. Warren subscribing witnesses thereto came into open court and having been duly sworn deposed and said as follows, That they were personally acquainted with the s'd Willis Sawyer in his lifetime; that he was of sound and disposing mind and memory at the time of the execution of the said paper writing, that he published & declared the said paper writing as his last will & testament in their presence and for the purposes therein contained and requested them to bear witness thereto, that they signed the same in the presence of the testator and in the presence of each other. It is therefore ordered that said paper writing be set up and established as the last will & testament of the s'd Willis Sawyer dec'd and that the same be recorded in "Will Book" & filed.

A true copy from the minutes

Attest, Zach Watkins   Clerk.

(P.314)
Last Will & Testament) In the Name of God Amen I
of Henderson Clark dec'd (Henderson Clark, hereby make
Probated February Term 1883) and publish this my last will
Recorded February 6th 1883 (and Testament
   Zach Watkins clk.)

                                       Item 1st: Let my debts be paid.

     Item 2nd: I give and bequeath to my son Charles P. Clark the following tracts of land to wit; One tract of 700 acres lying in Gibson County Tenn. about 3 miles west of Eaton (in the forks of the river valued at $2300.00) one other tract of 190 acres lying in Crocket County in and near Friendship known as the Dr. Smith land valued at $3000.00 One other tract of 375 acres of land in Civil District No. 10 of Dyer County Tenn. known as the Giles Norment tract valued at $3100.00 One tract of 85 acres of land in Civil District No. 2 of Dyer County Tenn. known as the A. B. Jones & wife tract valued at $1000.00 One other tract of 97¾ acres land known as the J. B. Morris land Civil District No. 2. Dyer County Tenn. valued at $1000.00 One other tract of 78¾ acres in Civil District No. 10 of Dyer Cty. Tenn. known as the I. G. Petts tract valued at $650.00 One other tract - of 50 acres land - Known as the A. Quick land - One tract of 60 acres in Dyer County known as the Polly Bradley tract - Also one other tract of land supposed to contain 300 acres - known as the Matthew Jones tract these 3 tracts all ly in the 8th civil District of Dyer Cty Tenn. and all valued at $450.00 total value of the real estate $11,500.00.

Item 3, I give and bequeath to my Daughter Amanda C. Dawson the following the following described tracts of land to wit - One tract of 152 acres of land in civil district No. 5 Dyer Cty, Tenn. known as the V. G. Wynne tract valued at $2736.00 One other tract of 211 acres in District No. 11, of Dyer County Tenn. known as the Giles Norment Mill tract valued at $500.00 One other tract of 110 acres of land in Civil District No. 5, of Dyer Cty, Tenn. known as part of the Bloomingdale land valued at $1650.00 One other tract of 122 acres lying in civil District No. 5, of Dyer Cty. Tenn known as J. R. Neal tract valued at $1300.00 One other One other tract of 200 acres & one tract of 24 acres known as the Gardner land lying in Civil District No. 5, Dyer Cty. Tenn. the 2 valued at $1800.00

(P.315) One other tract of 135 acres lying in District No. 12 Dyer Cty. Tenn., One other tract of 105 acres known as the Hassell land in District No. 3, of Dyer Cty. Tenn. and one other tract of 132 acres lying in Civil District No. 3 Dyer Cty., Tenn. known as the Latta tract these 3 last tracts valued at $3382.00 the whole real estate being valued at $11,368.00

Item 4 - I give and bequeath to the 3 children of Tom Cotton by his first wife (Emily) Daniel, Harry H., & Amanda Cotton the following described lands to wit. One tract of 300 acres of land the Old home tract - known as the H. Clark farm where Tom Cotton

(198)

(P.315 Cont'd)   now lives - lying in Civil District No. 4 Dyer Cty. Tenn. - Valued at $4500.00 One other tract of 160 acres lying in the State of Missouri, Mississippi Cty. known as the Henry Hough land formerly owned by McElmurry valued at $5025.00 One tract of 85½ acres lying in civil district No. 2 of Dyer Cty Tenn. known as the Marshall King land - valued at $1000.00 one other tract - of 39 acres lying in civil district No. 5 - Dyer Cty. Tenn - known as the Capell tract - One other tract of 10 acres in civil District No. 4 lying between S. R. Latta & Wm. M. Watkins valued at $300.00 One other tract of 100 acres lying in civil District No. __ Obion Cty. Tenn. known as the John Wright tract - valued at $200.00 (P. E. Wilson hrs.) are to have $50.00 out of said 100 acres One other tract of 43 acres lying near Fay & Hunters civil District No. 16 Dyer Cty Tenn. - valued at $175.00 the whole real estate valued at $11,500.00.

Item 5 - I give and bequeath to my great Grandchild Charley Vernon a tract of land supposed to be 700 or 800 acres north of the Obion river in Civil District No. 16 Dyer Cty. Tenn. part of the A. Murphy Grant.

Item 6 - In the division of the real estate it appears that my Son C. P. Clark and the heirs (or children) of Tom Cottons first wife (Emily) to wit; Daniel Harry H. & Amanda Cotton have the advantage of Mrs. A. C. Dawson in the real estate in the sum of $132.00 It is my request - & desire that my Executors make up to her the said deficit out of any real estate that may be undivided at the time of my death or in money if not convenient to settle in real estate.

Item 7 - It is my desire and request, that any all real estate coming into my possession after this date by foreclosure of Trustee Deeds or mortgage or otherwise (P.316) and also any and all other real estate and personal property that may be coming to me at my death that my said Executors shall take charge of and make division of the money and lands sd coming in and may sell real estate for division and divide the proceeds equally between my heirs as above mentioned and in case of division of lands by them (Executors) it shall be final.

Item 8 - It is my request & desire that all of the personal property - money notes judgements - choses in action that I may die possessed of be taken possession of by my Executors and controlled by them and paid out by them equally among my heirs - to wit, C. P. Clark - Amanda C. Dawson & the children of Tom Cotton's first wife (Emily) at their discretion and when they chose to do so - (to be paid out however according to the laws of the state) now in Existence.

Item - Any of the real estate allotted by me in the different divisions - If I should sell or dispose of after this date my executors are to pay over to said party or parties to whom said allottment was made the money arising from sale or disposal of said real estate at the figures so fixed by me upon said Item of real estate.

(P.316 Cont'd) Item 10, whatever species of property either of real or personal property that I have prior to this date given off to any or either of my children to wit; C. P. Clark Amanda C. Dawson (or her husband W. A. Dawson) in his lifetime or to my daughter Emily Cotton first wife of Tom Cotton no charge is made for or to be allowed whatever by my Executors - whatever I have given off has been done without any intention of being so charged up.

I hereby nominate and appoint my son Charles P. Clark & Jesse Clark my brother Executors of this my last will and testament and having full confidence in their integrity - I direct that they are not to give any Bond as Executors.

Witness my hand this the 10th day of December 1880

H. Clark

Signed acknowledged and published in our presence (P.317) and in Testimony whereof we have hereunto set our names in the presence of each other and the testator this 10th day of December 1880

James W. Baker
Thos. H. Benton

Codicil

Since the above will having been signed & published by me - I have advanced to my daughter Mrs. Amanda C. Dawson - the sum of Twenty Seven hundred Dollars for the use and benefits of H. L. Baker & wife Betty Baker, Ed Baker & wife Pauline Baker - and my said Executors are to have her charged up with that amount - whenever a division of the Personal property shall take place without interest -

Witness my hand this 28th day January 1881

H. Clark

Signed acknowledged and published in our presence and in Testimony whereof we have hereunto set our names in the presence of each other and the Testator

This 28th day of January 1881.

James W. Baker
Thos. H. Benton

State of Tennessee) In County Court, Dyer County Tennessee
Dyer County   ) February Term 1883

This day a paper writing purporting to be the last will & testament and Codicil thereto, of Henderson Clark, deceased, was produced before the court for probate. Thereupon came into open court James W. Baker and Thos. H. Benton subscribing witnesses to said will & Codicil thereto, who being first duly

(201)

(P.317 Cont'd) sworn deposed and said that they were personally acquainted with the testator in his lifetime That he was of sound and disposing mind and memory at the time of the Execution of said paper writing; that he published and declared the same to be his last will & testament in their presence and for the purposes therein contained and requested them to bear witness thereto, that they signed the body of said will and codicil thereto in the presence of the Testator and of each other. It is therefore ordered that said paper writing be & the same is hereby set up and established as the last will & testament of the said Henderson Clark deceased, and that same be recorded in "Will Book" (P.318) & filed, where upon Charles P. Clark and Jesse Clark who are named as Executors of said last will & Testament came into open court and were duly qualified the necessity of giving bond being waived in said last will & Testament - Let Letters Testamentary issue to them.
A true copy from the minutes

      Attest Zach Watkins Clerk.

(P.319)
Last Will & Testament -) I, Jolly Olds being of sound mind
of Jolly Olds, deceased, (but in bad health declare this to
Probated March Term /83) be my last will and testament that
Recorded March 8th /83 (is to say.
 Zach Watkins clk.)

   First - I give to my son William my young horse named Bob - and to my Daughter Amanda my bay horse named Telden and to David Albritton my clay bank mare - All my other personal property I give to my children Amanda and William -

I give and bequeath to my Son William Olds thirty three 1/3 acres of land of the south end of the one hundred acre tract of land upon which I reside.

I give and bequeath to my Daughter Amanda thirty three 1/3 acre land adjoining and lying north of the tract devised to my son William including my residence -

I give and bequeath to my Grandchildren Arbella, Edwin, Eugine & Wm. Hodge Albritton thirty three 1/3 acres of land north of and adjoining the tract of land devised by me to my Daughter Amanda I direct the thirty acres of land upon which Mr. Tarply now lives, bounded on the South by the lands of Thos. Olds heirs on the East by David Bell North by Mrs. Stalcup and west by the tract of land upon which I reside it ___ the tract of land deeded to me by Thos. Olds to be sold by my Executor for one third cash and the balance on a credit of one and two years note with good security to be given for the purchase money and that my debts be paid with the proceeds of the sale, and if there is a balance left I direct that it be divided between my children Amanda and William Olds.

 Witness my hand this Jany 24th 1883
Attest: J. F. Perry   Jolly Olds
   J. P. Tarply

(P.319 Cont'd)
State of Tennessee) In County Court Dyer County Tenn.
Dyer County   ) March Term 1883.

This day a paper writing purporting to be the last will and testament of (P.320) Jolly Olds deceased was produced before the court (F. G. Sampson chairman Protem presiding) for Probate, Thereupon came into open court J. F. Perry and J. P. Tarply subscribing witnesses to the same who being first duly sworn deposed and said that they were personally acquainted with the said Jolly Olds in his lifetime, That he was of sound and disposing mind and memory at the time of the Execution of said paper writing, That he published and declared said paper writing to be his last will & Testament in their presence and for the purposes therein contained and requested them to bear witness thereto, that they signed the same in the presence of the Testator and in the presence of each other. It is therefore ordered that the said paper writing be and the same is hereby set up and established as the last will & Testament of the said Jolly Olds deceased and that same be recorded in Will Book & filed.

A true copy from the minutes

        Attest Zach Watkins, Clerk.

(P.321)
Last Will & Testament of) In the Name of God, Amen.
Mary McKnight dec'd   (I, Mary McKnight, of Dyersburg
Probated April Term 1883) Tennessee, being old and in firm
Recorded April 12th 1883 (in body, although, thank God, of
  Zach Watkins clk.   ) sound and disposing mind and memory,
do hereby make, ordain and publish this my last will and Testament in manner and form following, that is to say;

First - I commend my soul to God who gave, and desire that my body be decently buried.

Second - I give and bequeath that lot of ground situate on the east side of St. John Steet - opposite the Baptist Church in Dyersburg, Tennessee, sold to me by W. C. Doyle, on which my daughter used to live, with all the tenements and appurtenances to my three little grand children, to wit. B. D. Matthews, Mary Freer Matthews, and Lucy Matthews - children of my late daughter Lizzie Matthews - share and share alike as tenants in common - and their heirs forever.

Third - All the residue of my estate, of every possible character, I will and bequeath to my four grand children, to wit; Samanna McKnight and Ida McKnight (daughters of my son Samuel A. McKnight) Samuel McKnight and Lizzie McKnight (youngest children of my late son Andrew Reed McKnight) to be equally divided between the four.

Last - I nominate and appoint my friend Luther C. McClerkin Sole

(P.321 Cont'd) Executor of this my last will and Testament. In witness whereof I have hereunto affixed my hand and seal December 4, 1878

                                        Mary McKnight (seal)

Signed Sealed and)
Published in the (
presence of us, who)
have subscribed the (
same in her presence)
at her request (
December 4, 1878)
   Sam'l G. Parker (
   B. M. Williams)

State of Tennessee)   Monday April 2, 1883
Dyer County   )   April Term of County Court 1883

This day a paper writing (P.322) purporting to be the last Will & Testament of Mary McKnight dec'd was produced before the Court for Probate. Thereupon came into Open Court Sam'l G. Parker and B. M. Williams subscribing witnesses to the same, who being first duly sworn deposed and said that they were personally acquainted with the said McKnight in her lifetime; that she was of sound and disposing mind and memory at the time of the execution of said paper writing; That she signed and published said paper writing to be her last will & Testament in their presence and for the purposes therein contained and requested them to bear witness thereto, that they signed the same in the presence of the Testatrix and in the presence of each other. It is therefore ordered by the court that the said paper writing be and the same is hereby set up and established as the last will and Testament of the said Mary McKnight and that same be recorded in "Will Book" & filed.

A true Copy from the Minutes

                Attest - L. D. Hamilton D. C.

(P.323)
Last Will & Testament) I, Mary J. Light hereby make and pub-
of Mary J. Light dec'd (lish this my last will and testament.
Probated May Term 1883)
Recorded May 9 - 1883 (I will and bequeath to my daughter,
   Zach Watkins Clerk) Scrapie Fowlkes, wife of Parsha Fowlkes,
                                   one half of my entire real estate and
one half of my entire personal property of every kind whatsoever and that, she, the said Scrapie Fowlkes, is to have and to hold the same, both the said half interest in said real and personal estate, for her sole and separate use and controll free from the liabilities debts or contracts of her present husband, the said Parsha Fowlkes, or any future husband - the said Scrapie Fowlkes taking both said realty and personally to do as she may please with it, having full right to dispose of and sell said half interest in said realty, but in the event the said Scrapie Fowlkes

(204)

(P.323 Cont'd) should die leaving no children and not having sold said real estate then said real estate above willed to her shall go to her sister Pettie Johnston, and if the said Pettie be not then living, then to any children of the said Pettie that may be living - I also will and bequeath to my daughter Pettie Johnston, wife of J. F. Johnston, the other half of my entire real estate and the other half of my entire personal property of every kind whatsoever and she the said Pettie is to have and to hold the same (both said half interest in the real and personal estate) for her sole and separate use and control free from the debts, liabilities and contracts of her present husband, the said J. F. Johnston or any future husband, the said Pettie Johnston taking both said realty and personally to do as she may please with it, having full right and power to sell and dispose of said realty, but in the event the said Pettie should die leaving no children and not having sold said real estate, then the above real estate above willed to her shall go to her Sister Scrapie Fowlkes, and if the said Scrapie be not then living then to any children of the said Scrapie that may be then living.

Before closing this my last will and testament, prompted by the great love and affection I bear my said children, I most earnestly advise and counsel each of them that out of the personalty turned over (P.324) to them by my Executor, that each one take and set aside as much as Four Thousand Dollars to be kept by them, and never encrouch upon said sum - only permitting themselves to spend the interest - I hereby nominate and appoint Wm. E. Johnston executor of this my last will and testament.

Witness my hand this January 1 - 1883

                        Mary J. Light

Signed acknowledged and published in our presence and in testimony thereof, we have hereunto set our names in the presence of each other and in the presence of the Testator, This January 1 - 1883

                        M. M. Marshall
                        P. N. Edwards
                        T. P. Townsend
                        Sol D. Rice

State of Tennessee) Monday May 7 - 1883
Dyer County   ) May Term County Court Dyer County Tenn.
                     1883
This day a paper writing purporting to be the last will and testament of Mary J. Light deceased, was produced before the court for Probate, There upon came into open court M. M. Marshall and Sol D. Rice subscribing witnesses thereto who being first duly sworn deposed and said that they were personally acquainted with the said Mary J. Light in her lifetime that she was of sound and disposing mind & memory at the time of

(P.324 Cont'd) the execution of said paper writing, That she signed and published said paper writing as her last in their presence and requested that they bear witness thereto, That they signed the same in the presence of the Testatrix and in the presence of each other. It is therefore ordered by the court that said paper writing be and the same is hereby set up and established as the last will and testament of the said Mary J. Light and that same be recorded in will Book & filed and that Letters Testamentary issue to executor named therein.

A true copy from the minutes

    Attest L. D. Hamilton D. C.

(P.325)

| Last will and Testament of Mary H. Tarkington dec'd Probated June Term 1883 Recorded June 5th 1883 Zach Watkins clk. | In the Name of God, Amen. I, Mary H. Tarkington, of Dyer County, Tennessee being ripe in years and feeble in health, |

although, thank God of sound and disposing mind and memory do hereby make and publish this my last will and Testament, hereby revoking all former wills by me at any time heretofore made, in manner and form following, to wit;

Item 1 - It is my will and desire that all my just debts be paid as soon as may be by my Executrix out of any personal estate I may leave at my death.

Item 2- I will and bequeath to my son A. W. Tarkington ten acres of my land in the North East Corner. Beginning at my North east corner and running west two-thirds of the distance across my north line; thence South so far that by running East to my line and back north to the beginning will include ten acres. To have and to hold the same to the said A. W. Tarkington his heirs and assigns forever.

Item 3 - I will and bequeath to my son Wm. D. Tarkington five acres of my land, in the North west corner, beginning at my North west corner and running East to the North west corner of the 10 acres herein bequeath to A. W. Tarkington; thence South with his line to his South west corner thence west to my west boundary line, thence North to the beginning - To have and to hold the same to the said W. D. Tarkington his heirs and assigns forever.

Item 4 - I give and bequeath to my daughter Helen Isabella Tarkington all the rest, residue and remainder of my estate real and personal, including the balance of my land and all the improvements: all my household and kitchen furniture, all my stock, my buggy and wagon, my poultry and everything I have, for her and her heirs forever - But if she die without issue born of her body without selling or disposing of said property, the same shall revert to my heirs at law, but she is to pay all my debts, if any, out of said property.

(206)

(P.325 Cont'd)
Item 5 - Lastly I nominate and appoint my daughter Helen I. Tarkington sole Executrix of this my last will and Testament and desire that she be required to give no bond and security for the execution of this will.

In witness whereof I have hereunto set my hand and seal this day of December A. D. 1881.

| Signed, sealed and published in presence of us who have signed our names as subscribing witnesses in presence of Testatrix and at her request Dec. 23rd 1881 | M. H. Tarkington   seal
C. B. R. White
T. P. Martin
Magie F. Martin |

(P.326)
State of Tennessee) In Dyer County Court,
Dyer County) June Term 1883

This day a paper writing purporting to be the last will and testament of Mary H. Tarkington deceased was produced before the court for probate. There upon came into open court C. B. R. White, F. B. Martin and Magie F. Martin subscribing witnesses thereto who being first duly sworn deposed and said that they were personally acquainted with M. H. Tarkington, the testatrix, in her lifetime, that she was of sound and disposing mind & memory at the execution of said paper writing, That she signed and acknowledged said paper writing in their presence as her last will and testament and requested them to bear witness thereto, That they signed the same in the presence of the Testatrix and of each other. It is therefore ordered by the court that the said paper writing be and the same is hereby set up and established as the last will and testament of the said M. H. Tarkington deceased and that same be recorded in will Book & filed.

A true copy from the minutes

Attest Zach Watkins   clerk.

(P.327)
Last will and Testament of Emma S. Willis dec'd
Probated August Term /83
Recorded August 7 - 1883
   Zach Watkins clk.

I, Emma S. Willis do make this my will and Testament.

First, I give to my uncle M. S. Anderson all the money I have now in the hands of my Guardian Moses Will of Evansville, Ind.

Second, I also give to M. S. Anderson all of the household furniture left me by my parents, or the proceeds of the sales of same.

Third; I appoint as the Executor of this will W. A. Jetton of

(P.327 Cont'd) Dyer County Tenn.

In testimony whereof I have set my hand and sealed this paper, This the 8th day of July 1883

Signed and)
sealed in the (
presence of)
E. T. Smith (
W. B. Nash)

          Emma S. Willis (seal)

State of Tennessee) August Term 1883
Dyer County)

  This day a paper writing purporting to be the last will and testament of Emma S. Willis late a citizen of Dyer County Tennessee, was produced before the court for probate. There upon came into open court E. T. Smith & W. B. Nash subscribing witnesses thereto who being first duly sworn deposed and said that they were personally acquainted with the Testatrix in her lifetime; that she was of sound and disposing mind and memory at the execution of said paper writing that she signed and acknowledged said paper writing in their presence to be her last will & Testament and requested them to bear witness thereto, that they signed the same in the presence of the Testatrix and of each of other. It is therefore ordered that the said paper writing be and the same is hereby set up and established as the last will & Testament of the said Emma S. Willis, dec'd, and that the same be recorded in "Will Book" & filed.

A true copy from the minutes

    Attest Zach Watkins clk.
    By - S. D. Hamilton D. C.

(P.328)
Last Will and Testament) I, Susan G. White hereby make and
of Susan G. White dec'd (publish this my last will and Tes-
Probated Sept. Term 1883) tament
Recorded Sept. 4th 1883 (
 Zach Watkins clk.) Item 1st Let all my just debts and funeral expenses be paid.

Item 2nd Being the owner of Twelve (12) shares of the stock of the Boston & Main Rail-Road and Thirty-Two (32) shares of the Stock of the Pennsylvania Central Rail-road, I give and bequeath to my daughter Emma Burbank wife of P. M. Burbank - Seven (7) shares of the Stock of the Boston & Main Rail-road and Seventeen shares of the stock of the Pennsylvania Central Rail Road.

Item 3rd I give and bequeath to my daughter Mira P. Parr wife of Dr. R. C. Parr Five (5) shares of the Stock of the Boston and Maine Rail-road, and Fifteen (15) shares of the stock of the Pennsylvania Central Rail-road. The above rail road stock is to vest absolutely in my said daughters and is not to be

(P.328 Cont'd) subject to the control of or liable for the debts of their present or any future husband, they or either of them may have; and while I do not hereby intend to positively control the stock thus bequeathed, I solemnly advise them as the is a safe and profitable investment the same remain using only the income, unless in case of necessity for the Education or well fare of their children, and I specially deprecate its sale for the purpose of speculation or mercantile ventures.

Item 4th - All the rest and residue of my estate I give and bequeath to my said daughter, the said Emma Burbank, to be hers absolutely.

The only reason why I make a difference in the distribution of my estate, is the fact; that my daughter Mira P. had better and more expensive educational advantages than my daughter Emma.

I hereby nominate and appoint my daughter Mira P. Parr Executrix of this my last will and Testament. Apr. 11th 1882

Mrs. Susan G. White

Signed sealed and published in our presence in testimony whereof we have hereunto set our hands, in presence of each other and the testatrix, April 11th 1882

Test: S. R. Latta
L. C. McClerkin

(P.329)
State of Tennessee) September Term 1883.
Dyer County)

This day a paper writing purporting to be the last will and testament of Susan G. White, deceased, was produced before the court for probate, Where upon came into open court S. R. Latta & L. C. McClerkin subscribing witnesses thereto, who being first duly sworn deposed and said that they were personally acquainted with the Testatrix in her lifetime, that she was of sound and disposing mind and memory at the execution of said paper writing; That she signed and acknowledged the same to be her last will and Testament and requested them to bear witness thereto, That they signed the same in the presence of the Testatrix and of each other. It is therefore ordered that said paper writing be and the same is hereby set up and established as the last will & Testament of the said Susan G. White deceased and that the same be recorded & filed.

A true copy from the minutes

Attest: Zach Watkins Clerk

By S. D. Hamilton D. C.

(P.330)
Last Will and Testament)   WILL
of Joseph Michell, dec'd,(
Probated Oct. Term 1883)   I, Joseph Michell, do make and
Recorded Oct. 5th 1883   (publish this my last will and
   Zach Watkins clk.   )   Testament hereby revoking and
                                making void all others by me at
any time made.

1st First, I direct that my funeral expenses and all my debts be paid as soon after my death as possible out of any moneys I may die possessed of, or that may come into the hands my executors

2nd Secondly: I bequeath to Stephen C. Michell's heirs Six hundred (600) acres of land, entered in the name of Wm. B. Jones, the same land that I bought of the Planters Bank of Tennessee.

3rd Thirdly, I give and bequeath to Heloise V. Michell, during her natural life and to her heirs at her death, But should she (Heloise V. Michell) die without issue, then the land to revert to the heirs of my grand son Joseph Michell, four hundred and sixteen (416) acres of land entered in the name of Joseph Michell, and generally known as the Cane Point tract.

4th Fourthly - I give and bequeath to my old servant Crawford Michell (colored) (100) one hundred acres of land described as follows Beginning at the north west corner of this Jack lot on the river bank then running with the fence east, then running South, then running west and following meanderings of the Mississippi river to beginning of corner, to contain one hundred (100) acres in as near a square as possible and to include all of his improvements, to have and to hold during his natural life, then to revert to my heirs.

5th Fifthly - I reserve two (2) acres of land on my home place, never to be sold or put to any other use except for a grave yard or church - The same land that is now a grave yard on my home place -

6th Sixthly - I direct that all my personal property be sold, all of my debts to be paid to the last cent and whatever balance there may be left, together with all of my real estate, not otherwise disposed of (P.331) to be equally divided between Joseph Olive Michell, Stephen C. Michell or his heirs and Lois Morean Michell.

7th Seventhly - I appoint Joseph O. Michell and Louis M. Michell, my sole Executors not to give any bonds nor security in any way for I have such confidence in their honesty that I do not want them bound in any way, and after my death, I want the heirs of Stephen C. Michell to select and appointed an agent to attend to their business for them.

    I, especially request and desire that any and all contro-

(P.331 Cont'd) versy that may arise from the settlement of my estate - be settled by arbitration if possible, Furthermore - I positively desire that one Dr. J. D. Tinsley - nor none of his heirs - I shall have nothing whatever to do with my estate neither as agent nor in any other way.

This was clearly and distinctly understood before signed

Jos. Michell

Signed and published in our presence and have subscribed our names hereunto in the presence of the testator - this the nineteenth (19th) day of August A. D. 1879

B. O. Michell
M. M. Taylor
Thad L. Powell

Codicil

I give to Joseph O. Michell and Louis M. Michell all my personal property such as cattle, horses, notes and cash that I may be possessed at my death after all my debts are paid. Further I give to Jos. O. Michell children that is Napoleon, Philix, Hugo and Susan my grand children each a filly, one or two year old, two two year old heffier, and I want their father or his administrator to take care of them - cattle & horses and to sell their increase when fit to sell take the money and put it out on interest until they become of age. I give my bed and bedding to Call Morean wife, my watch to Napoleon my rifle to Philix if any of children should die to any of the four remaining I give my amnour to Susan, I give to Crawford all my clothing

Jos. Michell

(P.332)
Signed and published in our presence and have subscribed our names hereunto in the presence of the testator this the sixth (6) day of May 1879

D. Nicholas
M. M. Taylor

No. 2 Codicil

Having in my will (above) a four hundred and sixteen acres as she Heloise has married against my will I only give her two hundred acres on the same condition as above, beginning at the North west corner of the said tract running east to the east corner thence south thence west thence north to the corner -

Jos. Michell

Signed and published in our presence and have subscribed our names hereunto in the presence of the testator.

M. M. Taylor
P. W. Duncan

(P.332 Cont'd)
State of Tennessee) Oct. Term Dyer County Court 1883
Dyer County)

In the matter of the) This day a paper writing purporting
Last Will and Testament (to be the last will and testament
of Joseph Michell dec'd) of Joseph Michell dec'd was presented
by Louis M. Michell one of the Executors named therein in open court to be admitted to probate and set up and established as the last will and testament of said Joseph Michell dec'd and moved that the same be done, and be appointed as the sole Executor the other executor named declining to act. And thereupon comes B. B. Michell and M. M. Taylor, two of the subscribing witnesses to the original will and after being duly sworn testify and say that they knew said Joseph Michell in his lifetime; that he is dead and had his usual place of residence in Dyer County, Tenn. at the time of his death; that said Joseph Michell was of sound and disposing mind and memory at the time of the execution of said original will; (P.333) That said paper writing is his last will and testament; That said testator signed the same in their presence as his last will and testament and that they signed and witnessed the same in the presence of the testator at his request as his last will and testament; and C. Nicholas and M. M. Taylor subscribing witnesses to the first Codicil of said will came into open court and being duly sworn testify and say that they were personally acquainted with said Joseph Michell in his lifetime; that he signed said Codicil as the first codicil of his said last will and testament and that they signed and witnessed the same in his presence and at his request as the first codicil of his said last will and testament; That he was of sound & disposing mind & memory at the time of the execution of said codicil, and M. M. Taylor, one of the subscribing witnesses to the second or codicil no. two of said last will and testament came into open court and after being duly sworn testifies and says that he was personally acquainted with said Joseph Michell, dec'd in his lifetime- and that he signed said codicil no. two as codicil no. two to said last will and testament in witness presence and in presence of P. W. Duncan another subscribing witness thereto, and that witness and said P. W. Duncan signed and witnessed the execution of said codicil no. two in the presence of the Testator, at his request as codicil no. two of his said last will and testament. That said Testator was of sound & disposing mind & memory at the execution of said codicil No. 2 and said Taylor further testifies that said P. W. Duncan whose name is signed as a witness to said codicil is now in an a resident of the State of Mississippi and that he knows his (Duncan handwriting and that the signature to said codicil is in his handwriting and also came B. O. Michell and C. Nicholas in open court and after being duly sworn testify and say that they know the handwriting of said Joseph Michell, dec'd and that the signature of his name to said codicil No. two is in his said Michells proper handwriting. It is therefore ordered by the court that said last will and (P.334) testament be and the same is hereby admitted to probate and set up and established as the last will and testament of said Joseph Michell dec'd, and ordered to be recorded by the clerk and filed, and on motion of Louis M. Michell one of the executors

(P.334 Cont'd) named in the said last will and Testament and it appearing that he is entitled to be sole Executor thereof, it is ordered that he be and is hereby appointed sole Executor of said last will and testament and thereupon comes said Louis M. Michell into open court and qualifies as required by law - the execution of bond being waived by the will.

A true copy from the minutes

     Attest: Zach Watkins Clerk.

(P.335)
Last Will and Testament) Last Will and Testament
of William J. Hughes dec'd(of
Probated Nov. Term 1883) W. J. Hughes
Recorded November 6th 1883(
 Zach Watkins clk.   ) I, W. J. Hughes do make and publish this as my last will and testament hereby revoking and making void all others by me at any time made.

First, I direct that my funeral expenses and all my debts be paid as soon after my death as possible out of any money that I may die possessed of, or that may first come into the hands of my Executors.

Secondly, I give and bequeath to my son Jas. S. Hughes my family Bible.

Thirdly, I direct that my paid up policy in the New York Life Insurance Company be divided among my seven children giving to each an equal share.

Fourthly, the remainder of my property, consisting of the farm upon which I now reside stock farming implements wagon and buggy household and kitchen furniture crop corn in crib and all money that may be left after paying funeral expenses and debts as above directed, I give and bequeath to my wife Permelia J. Hughes during her lifetime upon condition that she keep with her my unmarried children Emma L. Hughes, Bettie C. Hughes and James S. Hughes.

Fifthly, should my wife the said Permelia J. Hughes refuse to carry out the restriction herein imposed or if she should at any time marry again then this will is void so far as she is concerned and my property will be divided as if there were no will, But should she the said Permelia J. Hughes perform her part and the children above mentioned or any of them refuse to live with her or if they should marry then her duty to such child or children is discharged.

Sixthly, upon the death of my wife the said Permelia J. Hughes, I direct that her funeral expenses be first paid and then whatever may be left shall be equally divided between my surviving children or their heirs deducting however from the part of Mrs. Fanny McGaughey and Mrs. Florence Williams the value of

(P.335 Cont'd) one good milch cow each (P.336) Lastly, I
do hereby nominate and appoint my wife Permelia J. Hughes
my executor, In witness whereof I do to this my will, set my
hand, this April 30th 1883.

W. J. Hughes

Signed and published in our presence and we subscribed our
names in the presence of the testator, this the 30th day of
April A. D. 1883

J. H. Pursell
Arch Dickerson

State of Tennessee) In Dyer County Court
Dyer County   )   Nov. Term 1883

In the Matter of the Last   (This day a paper
Will & Testament of W. J. Hughes dec'd) writing purporting
to to be the last
will and testament of W. J. Hughes dec'd was produced before
the court for probate. Thereupon came into open court J. H.
Pursell and Arch Dickerson subscribing witnesses thereto who
being first duly sworn deposed and said that they were personally acquainted with the said W. J. Hughes in his lifetime, that
he was of sound and disposing mind and memory at the execution
of said paper writing, that he signed and acknowledged the same
as his last will & Testament in their presence and requested
them to bear witness thereto, That they signed the same in the
presence of the Testator and of each other. It is therefore
ordered by the court that the said paper writing be and the
same is hereby set up and established as the last will and Testament of the said W. J. Hughes dec'd and that the same be recorded in Will Book and filed.

A true copy from minutes

Attest Zach Watkins Clerk.

(P.337)
Last Will and Testament) In the Name of God Amen.
of Luke Cearley dec'd   (
Probated Dec. Term /83) I, Luke Cearley being of sound mind
Recorded Dec. 6th 1883 (do make and declare this to be my
    Zach Watkins clk.   ) last will and testament
    By L. Hamilton D. C.
                        First, after a decent burial I, want
all of my just debts paid.

Secondly, I feel that I have given to all of my children by my
first wife their full portion and desire them to have nothing
more.

Thirdly, I give and bequeath to my three children by my last
wife that is William B. Cearley, Rebecca Blakemore and George W.
Cearley the homestead or tract of fifty one acres of land on

(214)

(P.337 Cont'd) which I now live provided that my daughter Rebecca Blackemore's interest shall exist only during her natural life and at her death shall revert to my two sons above named.

I also give and bequeath to my two sons William B. and George W. Cearley that portion of land (thirty eight acres) now trusted to Jethro King when the same is redeemed.

In witness whereof I have set my hand and seal on this the fourth day of Nov. 1882 In presence of

E. M. Hall,
J. R. Palmore

Luke X Cearley
(his mark)

State of Tennessee) In Dyer County Court Dec. Term 1883
Dyer County)

In the matter of Last) This day a paper writing purporting
Will and Testament (to be the last will and Testament
of Luke Cearley dec'd) of Luke Cearley dec'd was produced before the court for probate. Thereupon came into open court E. M. Hall and J. R. Palmore subscribing witnesses thereto who being first duly sworn deposed and said that they were personally acquainted with the Testator in his lifetime that he was of sound and disposing mind & memory at the Execution of the said paper writing and that he acknowledged the same in their presence to be his last will and testament and requested them to bear witness thereto. That they signed the same in the presence of the (P.338) Testator and of each other. It is therefore ordered by the court that the said paper writing be and the same is hereby set up and established as the last will and testament of the said Luke Cearley dec'd and that same be recorded in Will Book and filed.

A true copy from the minutes

Attest Zach Watkins clk.
By Loms Hamilton D. C.

(P.339)
Last Will & Testament of) I, Allen Harris of sound mind do
A. Harris, deceased (make this my last will and testa-
Probated Febry Term 1884) ment to wit;
Recorded Feby 22 / 84 (
  Z. G. Watkins Clk.) First; I will that all my just debts be paid -

Second; I do give to my beloved daughter Mary A. Waldran a certain portion of my home tract of land, Beginning at the N. W. Corner running East with the north boundary line 248 poles to a stake, the South East corner of the land bought by H. Fuller of Wm. H. Applewhite, administrator thence south with Bright Harris line to the Center of the rail-road thence with the Rail-road south so many poles as will make 125 acres, thence west to the west boundary line; thence North to the beginning

(215)

(P.339 Cont'd) to be run hereafter -

Third - To my beloved wife I give and bequeath the balance of my home tract lying west of the Rail-road together with my household and kitchen furniture, buggy and buggy mare, two mules and wagon, mower, hay rake and all farming implements -

Fourth - I give and bequeath to my son Stonewall J. Harris the remainder of my home farm together with 105 acres, adjoining the home farm on the south, also two choice mules to be selected by himself.

Fifth - I give and bequeath to my beloved wife and S. J. Harris, my entire crop twenty five head of stock hogs, three sows and my entire stock of cattle.

Sixth - If any of my children are indebted to me it hereby cancelled.

Seventh - It is my will that my entire estate both real and personal not herein bequeathed be given to my beloved wife.

Eighth - I do hereby appoint as my Executor Guy Douglass and my son J. P. Harris.

Witness   A. Harris
M. O. B. Gaulden
M. Dennis Gaulden

State of Tennessee)   February Term of County Court 1884
Dyer County   )   Tuesday Feby 5th /84

    This day a paper writing purporting to be the last will and testament of Dr. Allen Harris, late a citizen of Dyer County Tennessee was produced before the court for probate. Thereupon came here into open court M. O. B. Gauldin and M. Dennis Gauldin subscribing witnesses to said paper writing who being first duly sworn deposed and said that they were personally acquainted with the said Dr. Allen Harris in his lifetime that he was of sound and disposing mind and memory at the time of the execution of the said paper writing - that he signed and published said paper writing as his last will and testament in their presence and for the purposes therein contained and required them to witness the same that they signed their names as witnesses thereto in the presence of the Testator (P.340) and in the presence of each other and at his request. It is therefore ordered by the court that the said paper writing be and the same is hereby set up and established as the last will and testament of the said Allen Harris, deceased and be recorded and filed.

A true copy of original will & probate of same.

                                Attest: Zach Watkins   clerk.

(P.340 Cont'd)

Last Will & Testament of) In the Name of God, Amen.
William N. Shelton dec'd)
Probated March term of (I William W. Shelton of Dyer County,
Dyer Co. Court 1884) Tennessee being; Thank God, in good
Recorded April 28 /84 (health of sound mind and disposing
    Z. Watkins Clk. (memory do make and publish; This my
                              last will and Testament.

    I, do hereby will and bequeath to my beloved Mother Elizabeth Moore Pate, all of that tract of land in civil District No. 2, of Dyer County, on which she now lives. The same land that I inherited from my Father Nelson Shelton, together with all my earthly possessions of any and every description, whatever, to have and to hold the same to her and her bodily heirs forever.

Signed sealed)   W. W. Shelton
and acknowledged (
in the presence)
of G. W. Walker (
W. B. Sampson)
May 14th 1883 (

State of Tennessee) March Term of County Court 1884
Dyer County) Tuesday March 4th 1884

In the Matter of William N. Shelton) This day a paper writing
Last will & Testament) purporting to be the
                                                 last will and testament
of William N. Shelton deceased late a citizen of Dyer Co. Tennessee, was produced before the court for probate. Thereupon came the subscribing witness W. B. Sampson into open court, and being first duly sworn deposed and said that he was personally acquainted (P.341) with the said W. N. Shelton in his lifetime - that he was was of sound and disposing mind and memory at the time of the execution of said Paper writing - that he the said W. B. Sampson wrote the said paper writing for said testator at his request that the said Shelton signed and published the said paper writing as his last will and testament in his presence & in presence of G. W. Walker the other subscribing witness and requested them to witness the same - That they the said witnesses, signed the same as witnesses in presence of Testator and of each other - The said W. B. Sampson further deposed that the said G. W. Walker is now a non resident of the State of Tennessee and a resident of the state of Texas. Ordered that said paper writing be and same is hereby set up & established as the last will and Testament of the said W. N. Shelton deceased and that the same be recorded and filed.

A true copy of Original Will & probate of same

                                                          Attest Zach Watkins Clerk

(P.341 Cont'd)
Last Will & Testament) I, Enos McKnight being at my own
of Enos. McKnight dec'd(residence and of a sound and dis-
Probated April Term of) posing memory but feeble in body
Dyer Co. Court 1884 (and desirous of setting my worldly
Recorded April 28 /84) affairs and disposing of my proper-
  Z. Watkins clk. (ty before my death do make and pub-
                           lish this my last will and testament
hereby revoking all other wills testaments codicils heretofore made.

First - I direct that my body be decently intered and that all my just debts be paid.

Second - I give to my beloved wife Rosanna McKnight one years support from my death to be set apart to her by my executors, I also give to my said wife Rosanna one horse, one cow & calf to be selected by her from my stock at my death also one third of all my household and kitchen furniture to be selected by her.

Third - I give to my son A. A. McKnight as trustee for my wife Rosanna McKnight one thousand dollars (P.342) in cash, to be loaned out at interest by said trustee and the interest thereon to be collected annually and appropriated by said trustee to the support and maintanance of my said wife, Rosanna, and in case the interest on said $1000.00 should prove to be insufficient to support and maintain my said wife in a suitable and proper manner according to her previous station in life, the said Trustee is to take and use enough of the principle of said fund after exhausting the interest aforesaid to provide such support and maintanance each year during the lifetime of my said wife and until the said fund is exhausted if it should become necessary to use the principle thereof as aforesaid and after the death of my said wife Rosanna I direct that my said son A. A. McKnight is to have two thirds of same fund, if any there should remain and I give to my daughter Nancy E. Shelton the other one third of said fund, that may so remain at the death of my said wife.

Fourth - I give to my son A. A. McKnight his heirs & assigns forever the following portion of the land whereon I now reside, situated in Dyer County Tennessee, & District No. 15, all of my said land lying east of the following described line. Beginning at a poplar & mulberry, the south east corner of a 100 acre tract conveyed by Wm. M. King to me & running thence in a North Easterly direction in a straight line to the mouth of the lane, East of my house thence with said lane in a north Easterly direction to my North boundary line.

Fifth - I give to my daughter Nancy E. Shelton all my land whereon I now reside lying west of the said line described in the fourth clause of this will to her and her heirs & assigns forever to be held and disposed of by her in any manner she may please.

(P.342 Cont'd)
Sixth - I direct that all my personal property not herein otherwise bequeathed be by my executors sold & converted into money and it be equally divided between my said son A. A. McKnight and my said daughter Nancy E. Shelton.

    I hereby nominate and appoint my son A. A. McKnight and J. N. McDanell as my executors to execute and carry this will into effect.

                                    Enos. McKnight

(P.343) Witness:)
       E. Jones   (
       J. C. Hendricks)

State of Tennessee) April Term of County Court
Dyer County   ) Monday April 7th 1884

In matter of Last will & Testament) This day a paper writ-
of Enos. McKnight deceased   ) ing purporting to be
                                           the last will and tes-
tament of Enos McKnight dec'd was produced before the court for probate - Thereupon came into court J. C. Hendricks a subscribing witness thereto who being duly sworn deposed & said that he was personally acquainted with the said Enos. McKnight in his lifetime, that he was of sound and disposing mind and memory at the time of the execution of said writing and that he signed and acknowledged the execution of said paper writing as his last will & testament in his presence and for the purposes therein contained and also in presence of the other witness thereto, Viz: E. Jones - that said E. Jones is dead - that he witnessed said Jones sign his name as a witness thereto; also W. G. Dyer & A. L. Pitts citizens of Dyer Co. Tenn. came into court & were sworn and said, that they were personally acquainted with Testator in his lifetime & acquainted with the handwrite of said E. McKnight and that the signature to said writing is in the genuine and proper handwriting of said McKnight - It is ordered by the court that said writing be set up and established as the last will & testament of said E. McKnight dec'd and be recorded and filed - Thereupon A. A. McKnight one of the executors named came into court with J. C. Mitchell, W. G. Dyer, A. L. Pitts and J. C. Hendricks securities and they entered into and acknowledged bond in penal sum of ten thousand dollars conditioned as required &c and A. A. McKnight was also duly sworn. Let letters issue.

    A true copy of original will & probate of same

                              Attest Zach Watkins Clerk.
(P.344)
Last Will & Testament) In the Name of God Almighty;
of F. G. Sampson dec'd(
Probated Nov. Term /84)   I Frank G. Sampson, of Dyersburg,
Recorded Nov. 19, 1884(Dyer County, Tennessee being of sound
 -Zach Watkins Clk.) health and disposing mind and memory

(P.344 Cont'd) thank God and uncertain of the length of my days or duration of my life, I do hereby make this my holographic last will and testament in manner and form following, that is to say;

Item 1st It is my will and desire that my mortal remains be decently buried and that all my just debts be paid by my Executrix as soon as practicable after my decease.

Item 2nd I give and bequeath all my property both real and personal of every kind and character to my beloved wife Rebecca W. Sampson and her heirs forever.

Item 3rd I nominate and appoint my said wife sole Executrix of this my last will and testament.

In testimony of all which I have hereto set my hand this 14th Febry 1868.

       F. G. Sampson

In the Matter of) In County Court Nov. Term 1884
Holographic will of(
F. G. Sampson dec'd) On this the 3rd day of Nov. 1884 came here into open court S. R. Latta Atty. for Mrs. R. W. Sampson widow of F. G. Sampson dec'd and presents to the court a paper writing - purporting to be the Holographic last will and Testament of said F. G. Sampson dec'd and the said S. R. Latta being duly sworn testifies and says, that for over thirty three years he was intimately acquainted with said F. G. Sampson and with his handwriting, That in the year 1868 - as witness recollects - the said F. G. Sampson deposit/ed in deponents safe the accompanying official sized envelope - sealed and on the sealed side written all in the handwriting of said F. G. Sampson, the following words "The last Will and Testament of F. G. Sampson deposited for safe keeping in the safe of S. R. Latta" and on the reverse side of said Envelope his name "F. G. Sampson" also in the proper handwriting of said "F. G. Sampson", deponent further testifies that said envelope from the time of its said deposite has remained in deponents safe - in an inner drawer unopened and unbroken until about a month ago. (P.345) When affiant found the same, and cut open at the end said envelope and found therein the paper writing now offered to the court for probate as the last will and testament of said F. G. Sampson, affiant states as a reason why the same has not been produced and before now offered for probate - the fact that the fact that the deposit thereof had been forgotten by affiant and the circumstances were recalled to his memory by the finding of the same in his safe as above stated about a month ago. Affiant swears to his intimacy with the handwriting of said F. G. Sampson from having seen him write and seen his writing for many years and that he verily believes and has no doubt at all - but that every word of the paper writing here offered as aforesaid including the signature of said Sampson, and every word written on said envelope is in the proper handwriting of said F. G.

(P.345 Cont'd) Sampson

Sworn to before)   S. R. Latta
me, in open (
court Nov. 3 /84)
Jno. E. McCorkle J. P. & chm.)

State of Tennessee)   In County Court Nov. Term /84
Dyer County   )   And thereupon came here into open Court
C. C. Moss and Z. G. Watkins who being first duly sworn by the chairman testify that for many years they were acquainted with F. G. Sampson and with his handwriting, that they have carefully examined the paper writing here now presented for probate as the Holographic will and testament of said F. G. Sampson and the envelope accompanying the same mentioned and described in the foregoing affidavit of S. R. Latta, and they testify that every word of said paper writing as well as the writing on said envelope is in the proper handwriting of said F. G. Sampson as they verily believe, It is thereford ordered by the court that said paper writing be and is hereby set up and established as the last will and testament of F. G. Sampson dec'd and the same is ordered to be recorded as such -

A true copy from minutes

              Zach Watkins   Clerk.

(P.346)
Last Will & Testament)   I, Mary Thompson being of sound
       of   (mind and disposing memory do make
Mary Thompson dec'd)   and publish this my last will and
Probated Jan. Term 1885(testament hereby revoking and an-
Recorded Jan. 23, 1885) nulling all other wills by me here-
     Zach Watkins clerk (tofore at any time made -

Item 1st, I direct that all my just debts and my burial expenses be paid by my Executor as soon after my death as may be out of the first money coming into his hands as such Executor -

Item 2nd, I give to my brother Moses Thompson on the terms and conditions following all the real estate I own or of which I am seized and possessed consisting of two parcels or tracts of land in the 22nd civil district of Rutherford County Tennessee the first tract being the homestead where my Father Robert Thompson resided at his death the whole tract contained three hundred acres and the part of it here given to Moses Thompson was willed to me by my father, and I refer to the s'd will of my father and the records of Rutherford County for the particulars as to metes & bounds and no. of acres of said land, the other tract or parcel is cedar land and does not adjoin the homestead here given, the cedar land is bounded on the North & west by Moses Thompson's land, East by Robert Thompson's land & South by James McCullough the two tracts contain about seventy seven acres, But my Brother Moses Thompson is to pay

(220)

(P.346 Cont'd)   to my Executor one thousand dollars for said land.

Item 3rd As soon after my death as may be desired my Executor to sell all my personal property, and I give all my personal property proceeds, with all the personal estate and effects of every kind and description that I die possessed share and share alike to my Brother Robert Thompson, my Brother Moses Thompson, to my sister Anna Jones, and the three children of my deceased sister to wit, Polly Mayberry Thompson Brown and Nancy Moore they taking the share their deceased mother would have taken were she living.

Item 4 - I hereby appoint Robert F. Jones my Executor of this my last will and testament this 16th day of June 1884

Interlined in 3rd Item before signed

Witness   Mary Thompson
Smith Parks
W. H. Watson

(P.347)
State of Tennessee)   January Term County Court 1885
Dyer County   )

In the matter of Last)
will & Testament of (This day a paper writing purporting
Mary Thompson dec'd)   to be the last will & Testament of
                         Mary Thompson dec'd late of Dyer
County Tennessee, was produced before the court for probate. Thereupon came into open court Smith Parks and W. H. Watson subscribing witnesses thereto who being first duly sworn deposed & said that they were personally acquainted with the said Mary Thompson Testatrix in her lifetime, that she was of sound & disposing mind and memory at the time of the execution of said paper writing. That she signed and acknowledged the same in their presence to be her last will & Testament for the purposes expressed therein, that they signed the same in the presence of each other and of the testatrix as subscribing witnesses thereto - It is therefore ordered by the court that the said paper writing be and the same is hereby set up and established as the last will and testament of the said Mary Thompson dec'd & be recorded & filed -

A true copy from the minutes

                                Attest Z. Watkins clk.
                                By L. D. Hamilton D. C.

(P.348)   Oct. 15th, 1883
Last Will and Testament)
of Thomas Miller dec'd   (State of Tennessee)
Probated Feby Term 1885)   Dyer County   (The last
Recorded February 4, 1885(District No. 2   )   will and
   Zach Watkins Clk.   )   Testament
                             of Thos. Miller,

(P.348 Cont'd)

First, I will to John Nunn seventy five acres in the South East corner of my tract of land bounded as follows; Beginning at the South East corner of my tract and south west corner of J. B. Yorks Dunlap tract, North eighty eight poles to a stake, thence west one hundred and forty eight poles to a stake thence South eighty eight poles to a stake in the south boundary line of my land thence east one hundred and forty eight poles to the beginning I also will that John Nunn have the horse which I have given him and one bed and bed clothes.

Second, I bequeath to Buck Nunn seventy five acres in the North west corner of my tract bounded as follows, Beginning at the N. W. corner of my tract and South west corner of T. J. Miller tract thence south to John A. Sheltons South East corner thence east, north and west so as to include the seventy five acres, provided that said Buck Nunn remains with my family faithfully until he is twenty one years of age if not the land is to go to my wife Louisa Miller, I also want Buck Nunn to have and keep the horse I have given him and have one bed and bed clothes.

Third, I bequeath to my wife Louisa Miller all the remainder of my land included in my deeds containing about two hundred and sixty three acres as long as she lives and at her death I want Betty Nunn to have seventy five acres lying East of the part given to Buck Nunn to be the same width North and south and running East with my North Boundary line far enough to contain the seventy five, the remaining one hundred and eighty eight acres my wife Louisa Miller can dispose of at her death as she pleases. I also bequeath to my wife all the farming implements on the place one reaper one third interest in Thresher my wagon and buggyand my three mules and two mares and about thirty five head of stock hogs and twelve sheep and all the cattle I own, also (P.349) all the household and kitchen furniture of every description all of which is to be hers to use and dispose of as she pleases I also want my wife Louisa to have all the rents and income from the whole farm for the year 1884. I hereby nominate and appointed my wife Louisa Miller as executrix without bond or security - This Oct. 15 - 1883.

Witnesses   Thomas Miller
W. M. Dean
J. B. York

    After signing the above I have thought of my notes, I bequeath to my wife Louisa all the notes and accounts money on hand at my death Oct. 15, 1883

Witnesses   Thomas Miller
W. M. Dean
J. B. York

State of Tennessee)   In County Court
Dyer County   )   February Term 1885,

(P.349 Cont'd)   This day a paper writing purporting to be the last will & Testament & codicil thereto of Thomas Miller, deceased, late of Dyer County Tennessee, was produced before the court for probate, whereupon came into open court W. M. Dean and J. B. York subscribing witnesses to said will and codicil thereto, who being first duly sworn deposed and said that they were personally acquainted with the said Thomas Miller deceased in his lifetime. That he signed said paper writing and acknowledged the Execution of same to be his last will & Testament in their presence, that he was of sound and disposing mind & memory at the Execution of said paper writing, that they signed the body of said will & codicil thereto in the presence of each other and of the Testator. It is therefore ordered by the court that said paper writing with the codicil thereto be and the same is hereby set up and established as the last will and testament of the said Thomas Miller deceased that the same be recorded in will Book & filed - Mrs. Louisa Miller who is named as Executrix of said will came into court and was duly sworn - Bond & security being waived by said will - Let letters testamentary issue

A true copy from minutes

        Attest; Zach Watkins clerk
          By L. D. Hamilton D. C.

(P.350)
Last will and Testament) Dyer County Tenn. Sept. 16th
of Thomas H. Benton dec'd(1884
Probated April Term 1885) In the Name of God Amen.
Recorded April 17 - 1885 (
Zach Watkins clk.   )   I, Thomas H. Benton being
                             of sound mind, do make and publish this my last will and testament hereby revoking all other wills heretofore made by me -

Item 1st I want and direct <u>and direct</u> that all of my just debts be paid out of the <u>first moneys</u> coming into the hands of my executors -

Item 2nd, I direct that my beloved wife Mary E. Benton, shall have all of my personal property - not otherwise provided for -

Item 3rd, I have a Life Insurance Policy in the Hartford Life and Anuity Insurance Co. of Hartford, Cont., for two thousand dollars - payable to me or my heirs - said policy is now held by H. Parks Jr. as collateral security for my personal note of two hundred thirty one & 45/100 dollars, I direct that after paying and discharging said debt or debts - that one thousand dollars of said Insurance policy be paid to my beloved wife Mary E. Benton, and after paying all expenses including expenses of Executorship that one hundred and fifty dollars be paid to my sister - Susan Boggors, and that the remainder be divided equally between my two daughters - Dollie and Fanny May Benton - I hereby nominate and appoint C. S. Nolen,

(P.350 Cont'd) Marcenus E. Benton and Mary E. Benton as Executors and Executrix of this my last will and testament and I hereby waive the necessity of their giving bond and security -

In testimony whereof I have hereunto set my hand and seal - the day and date above written -

                Thos. H. Benton (SS)

Signed sealed and published in our presence and in the presence of each other on this the 16th day of Sept. 1884,

                C. S. Nolen
                I. W. Parr
                G. Chitwood

Codicil

I give and bequeath to my son M. E. Benton, - my policy for two thousand dollars in the Presbyterian Mutual Assurance fund of Louisville Ky. -- Dated Dec. 10th 1884

                Thos. H. Benton

Signed sealed and published in our presence & in the presence of each other - On this the 10th Dec. /84 -

                R. H. Campbell
                C. L. Nolen

(P.351)
State of Tennessee)   In County Court April Term 1885
Dyer County   )   Monday April 6 - 1885

In the Matter of T. H.)   This day a paper writing purporting
Benton's last will &   (to be the last will & Testament of
Testament   )   Thos. H. Benton dec'd was produced
                                    before the court for probate as to the body of same. Thereupon came into open court J. W. Parr and G. Chitwood subscribing witnesses to the body of said last will & testament who being first duly sworn deposed and said that they were personally acquainted with the said T. H. Benton testator in his lifetime. That he was of sound & disposing mind & memory at the time of the execution of said paper writing. That he signed & acknowledged same in their presence to be his last will & testament and requested that they bear witness thereto. That they signed the same in the presence of each other and of the testator. It is therefore ordered by the court that the said paper writing as to the body of same be & it is hereby set up & established as the last will & testament of the said Thos. H. Benton dec'd. Whereupon M. E. Benton who is named as one execution in said will came into court & was qualified, the necessity of giving bond & security as required by law being waived in said will. Let letters testamentary issue - It appears to the court that

(225)

(P.351 Cont'd) Mary E. Benton named as Executrix of said will died intestate before the death of the testator

A true copy from minutes

    Attest Zach Watkins clk.
     By L. D. Hamilton D. C.

                Friday April 17th 1885

State of Tennessee)
Dyer County   ) In County Court April Term 1885,

  This day the codicil to the last will & testament of Thomas H. Benton deceased, was produced before the court for probate - Thereupon came into open court R. H. Campbell & C. L. Nolen subscribing witnesses thereto who being first duly sworn deposed and said that they were personally acquainted with Thos. H. Benton in his lifetime, that he was of sound & disposing mind and memory at the execution of said codicil, that he signed the same in their presence & acknowledged same to be the codicil to his last will & testament and requested them to bear witness thereto, that they signed the same (P.352) as witnesses thereto in the presence of each other & of the said T. H. Benton. It is therefore ordered by the court that said codicil be and the same is hereby set up & established as the codicil to the last will and testament of Thos. H. Benton deceased, that same be recorded in will Book & filed -

A true copy from minutes

     Attest; Zach Watkins clk.
      By; L. D. Hamilton D. C.

(P.353)
Last Will & Testament) In the Name of God Amen.
of Francis Stokes (
Probated May Term /85) I, Francis Stokes of Dyer County Tenn.
Recorded May 7 - 1885(while in the full possession of all
 Zach Watkins clk.) my faculties both mental and physical
          but in view of the uncertainties of
life I do make publish and proclaim this as my last will and testament -

First after paying all of my debts and the expenses of a decent burial of my body I give to my daughter ____ Robinson and son S. H. Stokes the sum of one dollar each - next I give all the balance of my property of any and all kinds of which I may die possessed to my son Clinton Stokes - I hereby name and appoint my said son Clinton Stokes as my Executor and release him from executing any bond as Executor under this will - This April 22nd 1876.
               Francis Stokes
Witnesses:
E. M. Hall
J. W. Hassell

(226)

(P.353 Cont'd)

State of Tennessee) In County Court May Term 1885
Dyer County)

In the matter of Probate) This day a paper writing purport-
of Francis Stokes last (ing to be the last will and tes-
will & Testament) tament of Francis Stokes dec'd -
was produced before the court for
probate. Thereupon came into open court E. M. Hall subscribing witnesses to the same who being first duly sworn deposed
and said that he was personally acquainted with the testatrix
in her lifetime; that she was of sound & disposing mind &
memory at the execution of said paper writing, that she signed
& acknowledged same in his presence to be her last will & testament and ask that he bear witness thereto. That he signed
said paper writing as witness thereto in the presence of said
Testatrix ~~and of J. W. Hassell dec'd another witness thereto~~.
Whereupon C. C. Moss came into open court and being first
duly sworn deposed - said that he was personally acquainted
with J. W. Hassell the other witness in his lifetime. That
he is deceased and that he is well acquainted*with said Hassells handwrite and verily believes said Hassells signature as
witness to said paper writing to be in his Hassells own proper
handwrite - It is therefore ordered by the court that said
paper writing be and the same is hereby set up and established
as the last will and testament of the said Francis Stokes dec'd
and that same be recorded in will book & filed.

A true copy from minutes

    Attest; Zach Watkins clk.
(*P.354)   By; L. D. Hamilton D. C.

(P.355)
Last will & Testament) I, Chas. C. Stevens of Dyersburg,
of C. C. Stevens dec'd(Tenn. being of sound mind and dis-
probated July Term /85) posing memory do hereby make and
Recorded July 20th /85(publish this my last will and tes-
Z. G. Watkins clk.) tament, hereby revoking any others
heretofore made by me at any time -

       To wit

First, I will that all my just debts be paid.

Second - I will, devise and bequeath to my sister Mary L.
Marshall, wife of M. M. Masrshall, all of my property of
every kind real personal and mixed, except as provided hereafter in regard to my life policy in the Abe Lincoln Mutual
Life and Accident Society, Cain Illinois - and I will and
devise to her said property because she is a woman and might
at some time be left alone and would need said property worse
than my brother A. R. Stevens.

  Third - I have a life policy in the Abe Lincoln Mutual

(P.355 Cont'd) Life and Accident Society, Cairo, Illinois, the proceeds from which are made payable to M. M. Marshall and J. R. Watkins in trust to be paid by them on a debt my brother A. R. Stevens owes the estate of Alf. Stevens, with myself and said Marshall and Watkins as securities for said A. R. Stevens of said debt. Now my will and devise is that said M. M. Marshall and Z. G. Watkins shall collect the proceeds of said policy as soon after my death as practicable and apply the same or so much as may be necessary to pay said debt or any balance thereof, and in this event whatever is paid out of said proceeds on said debt shall not be a charge against said A. R. Stevens, but I will, devise and bequeath it to him absolutely. But if said A. R. Stevens should pay off and discharge said debt before the proceeds of said policy are collected or if the proceeds should not be used to pay said debt then I will and devise that the said proceeds of said policy or any surplus thereof not applied to said debt shall be paid to Z. G. Watkins Trustee to be held by him in trust (P.356) for the following purposes, to wit - If my said brother A. R. Stevens keeps sober and does not use intoxicating drink at all of any kind for two years from my death, then I will and devise the proceeds of said policy to him and hereby direct said Watkins Trustee to pay the same to him at the expiration of said two years if the above conditions are complied with; But if said A. R. Stevens does use intoxicating liquors of any kind at all during said two years, then I will and devise the same proceeds of said policy to my sister Mary L. Marshall and hereby direct that said Watkins Trustee to pay it to her at once, that is at any time during the said two years whenever my said brother commences the use of intoxicating liquors - it being my will and intention that my said brother A. R. Stevens shall have absolutely all the said proceeds that shall be used to pay said debt or any part thereof without any conditions, but any surplus of said policy proceeds not necessary to be so used shall be paid to said Watkins, Trustee, for the purposes and subject to the conditions and limitations above mentioned. My Life Policy in the "Knights of Honor I have already had the proceeds made payable to my said sister Mary L. Marshall.

Fourth - I hereby nominate and appoint M. M. Marshall executor of this my last will and testament and waive the necessity of his executing the usual bond required of Executors -

             C. C. Stevens

Signed and acknowledged by the testator in our presence and in the presence of each other on this the 23rd day of May 1885 and we hereby sign our names in his presence and in the presence of each other

    T. L. Wells
    L. D. Hamilton
    B. B. Watkins

(228)

(P.357)

State of Tennessee) In County Court July Term 1885,
Dyer County) Monday July 6th 1885

In the matter of Last) This day a paper writing purporting
Will and Testament (to be the last will and testament
of C. C. Stevens dec'd) of C. C. Stevens dec'd was produced
before the court for Probate. Thereupon came into open court T. L. Wells B. B. Watkins & L. D. Hamilton subscribing witnesses thereto who being first duly sworn deposed and said that they were personally acquainted with C. C. Stevens the testator in his lifetime; that he was of sound and disposing mind & memory at the execution of said Last will & Testament. That he signed and acknowledged the execution of the same as his last will & Testament in their presence and that he requested them to bear witness thereto, that they signed the same as witnesses in the presence of the Testator & in the presence of each other - It is therefore ordered by the court that the said paper writing be and the same is hereby set up and established as the last will & Testament of the said Chas. C. Stevens & that same be recorded in will Book & filed. Thereupon M. M. Marshall named as Execution of said will came into court & was duly sworn the necessity of giving bond being waived by said will -

A true copy from minutes

Attest Zach Watkins clk.
By L. D. Hamilton D. C.

(P.358)

Last will & Testament) In the Name of God, Amen.
of L. W. Sorrell dec'd (
Probated September Term /85) I, L. W. Sorrell of the
Recorded Sept. 20 /85 (county of Dyer and State of
Z. G. Watkins clk.) Tennessee being of sound mind
& memory, blessed be Almighty
God, for the same, do make and publish this my last will and testament - I give and bequeath to my beloved wife Sarah L. Sorrell and daughter Elvica T. Sorrell all of my household furniture and all the rest of my personal property after paying from the same the Medical bill and funeral expenses, to be theirs forever - I also give devise and bequeath to my beloved wife Sarah L. Sorrell and Elvica T. Sorrell, daughter, all the rest and residue of my personal property. I further give and bequeath to my beloved wife Sarah L. Sorrell and Elvica T. Sorrell, daughter, fifty acres of land of the north side of tract beginning at North East corner at the grave-yard, running thence South, thence west clear the tract to the west boundary line making fifty acres including houses and orchard to my beloved wife Sarah L. Sorrell during during her life, after her death to go to my daughter Elrica T. Sorrell, the remainder of the tract to be divided North and South in equal No. of acres amongst the rest of my lawful heirs - and after divided then each lot to be valued then those getting the lots worth the most they are to pay to the others so as to make them

(P.358 Cont'd) equal in valuation giving A. C. Sorrell and C. L. Kee chois lots on account of timber, the remaining heirs to draw for theirs - I do nominate and appoint my beloved wife Sarah L. Sorrell to be the sole Executrix of this my last will and testament. In testimony thereof I set my hand and seal and publish and decree this to be my last will and testament in presence of the witnesses named below - This April 14 in the year of Our Lord one thousand eight hundred and eighty-five -

            L. W. Sorrell

Signed and sealed, declared and published by the said L. W. Sorrell as and for his last will and testament in presence of us who at his request and in his presence and in presence of each other have signed our names as witnesses hereto

            D. L. Walker
            N. C. Sorrell
            J. B. Gardner

State of Tennessee) September Term of Dyer Co. Court 1885
Dyer County   ) Thursday Sept. 10/85

In the matter of probate of) This day a paper writing purport-
L. W. Sorrell, Last will & (ing to be the last will and tes-
Testament.   ) tament of L. W. Sorrell dec'd
              was produced before (P.359) the court for probate - Thereupon came into open court D. L. Walker and N. C. Sorrell subscribing witnesses thereto, who being first duly sworn deposed & said that they were personally acquainted with the said L. W. Sorrell dec'd. That he was of sound & disposing mind and memory at the execution of the said paper writing - That he signed & acknowledged the execution thereof in their presence for the purposes therein expressed and requested that they bear witness thereto. That they signed the same as witnesses thereto in the presence of the Testator & of each other - It is therefore ordered by the court that the said paper writing be and the same is hereby set up and established as the last will & Testament of the said L. W. Sorrell dec'd that same be recorded in "Will Book" & filed

A true copy of original will & probate of same

            Attest; Z. G. Watkins clk.

(P.360)
Last will and Testament) State of Tennessee -
of Mary Ann Fumbanks dec'd(Dyer County -
Probated November Term /85)
& Recorded Feby 9th 1885 (November Term of County Court
              1885
              Monday Nov. 2, 1885

****

I, Mary Ann Fumbanks of Dyer County Tennessee being of sound

(P.360 Cont'd) mind, but feeble in body knowing the uncertainty of life and the certainty of death and desiring to make a disposition of my earthly estate do make, ordain and publish this my last will and testament hereby revoking all others by me at any time made -

First - It is my wish that my executor hereinafter to be named shall as soon as practicable pay my burial expenses out of the money that I have on hand at my death.

Second - As share already given to my children and grand children except my daughter Marthy Ann Cobb all that I desire for them to have of my property I give and bequeath to my daughter the said Marthy Ann Cobb all of my property consisting of my three bedsteads three feather beds and bed clothing one large folding leaf table, one small table one dinning room safe one large and one small wash kettle my two sets of andirons, all of my cooking vessels & all of the money, less my burial expenses, that I have on hand I also give and bequeath to my daughter the said Marthy Ann Cobb all my notes, claims accounts and choses in action &c. I hereby appoint and nominate my son-in-law, Jacob Cobb, my Executor and it is my wish that he be not required to give bond as such Executor - In testimony I have hereunto subscribed my name on this the 15th day of Jany. /85.

          her
       Mary Ann X Fumbanks
          mark

Signed sealed and published in our presence by Mary Ann Fumbanks as her last will and testament and we at his instance and request in his presence and in the presence of each other signed and subscribed our names as witnesses hereto on this the 15th day of Jany. 1885

          J. J. Yates
          I. F. Perry

State of Tennessee) November Term of County Court 1885
Dyer Co.   ) Monday Nov. 2, 1885

In Matter of Last will &) This day a paper writing purporting
Testament of Mary Ann (to be the last will and testament
Fumbanks   ) of Mary Ann Fumbanks dec'd was produced before the court for probate -
Thereupon came (P.361) into open court J. J. Yates, one of the subscribing witnesses thereto who being first duly sworn deposed and said that he was personally acquainted with said Mary Ann Fumbanks in her lifetime. That she was of sound & disposing mind and memory at the time of the execution of said paper writing - That she signed the and published said paper writing as her last will and testament in her presence and in presence of the other witness J. F. Perry, as her last will and testament and requested them to witness same - That he signed same in her presence and in presence of the other witness thereto - Thereupon Jacob Cobb who is named as Executor

(231)

(P.361 Cont'd) of said last will and testament came into open court and was sworn as the law requires, the necessity of his giving bond being waived

A true copy of will & probate

           Attest Z. G. Watkins Clerk.

(P.362)
Last will & Testament of) Know all men by these presents,
W. L. Scott dec'd   (that I, W. L. Scott of the County
Probated Dec. term /85) of Dyer and State of Tennessee do
Recorded Feby. 9 /1886 (hereby ordain and publish this my
Z. G. Watkins clk.   ) last will and testament - First - I
           will all of my personal property,
except what the law allows my wife, be sold and all of my debts be paid -

2nd - I will to my wife during her widowhood and my son Lemuel two hundred acres of land, being the same on which I formerly lived in the 8th Civil District of Gibson County Tennessee, but in the event my wife marries again she is to have a homestead during her life in said land, or if she prefer she may have one half of s'd land during her life - and my son Lemuel the remainder - the division to be made according to quality & quantity.

Third - I will the one hundred and thirty five acres of land that fell to me in the division between myself & Bro. R. H. Scott after the death of our sister Sallie L. Locke to N. R. A. McCorkle in trust, authorizing and empowering him to sell said land at his own option and make deed without ___ or hindrance - and use any or all of the proceeds if needs be in paying my debts and educating my son Lemuel, after my other personal effects have been exhausted and pay any balance that may be in his hands to my son Lemuel when he arrives at the age of twenty one - but if he dies without bodily issue it is to be distributed as hereafter set forth -

4th - Should my son die without bodily issue before my wife, she is to have a life estate in the two hundred acres of land described above and at her death it shall go, one half to my Bro. R. H. Scott and the other half to my niece Lula Moody during her natural life - for her sole use benefit free from the controll of any husband she has or may hereafter have and at her death to her bodily heirs or children if she die without children or issue to R. H. Scott.

5th - If there is any of effects of the sale of said land remaining in my Trustees hands after the foregoing requirements have been complied with it shall be divided equally between R. H. Scott & Lula Woods.

6th - I hereby appoint John E. McCorkle, Executor of this my last will and testament of whom no bond shall be required and he is to have a liberal compensation for the services.

(232)

(P.362 Cont'd)
    Witness my hand and seal this the 12th day of August 1885

Witnesses   W. L. Scott
Jno. E. McCorkle
H. R. A. McCorkle
E. M. Allen, S. A. Dickey

(P.363)
State of Tennessee)   December Term of Dyer County Court 1885
Dyer County   )   Monday December 7th/1885

In the matter of Last will)
& Testament of W. L. Scott)   This day a paper writing purporting to be the last will and testament of W. L. Scott deceased was produced before the court for probate - Thereupon came E. M. Allen and S. A. Dickey subscribing witnesses thereto, who being duly sworn deposed and said that they were personally acquainted with the said W. L. Scott, Testator and that he acknowledged the execution of the said paper writing as his last will and testament in their presence and for the purposes therein contained and requested them to bear witness thereto - That he was of sound and disposing mind and memory at the time of the execution of the same - that they signed their names as witnesses thereto in presence of the testator and at his request - It is therefore, ordered that said paper writing be and the same is hereby set up and established as the last will and testament of said W. L. Scott dec'd and that same be recorded and filed - Thereupon, Jno. E. McCorkle who named as the Executor of said will came into open court with

(P.364)
Last Will & Testament) State of Tennessee -
of Louisa Miller (Dyer County
Probated Jany. Term /86) The last will & Testament of Louisa
Recorded Feby. 10/86 (Miller. First - I give and bequeath
Z. G. Watkins clerk.) to Thos. R. Moss, the sixty five
acres, more or less, lying north of
John Nunn's tract and also Seventy five acres, bought of
W. C. Miller and wife Betty Miller, lying east of the Buck
Nunn tract and west of the first named sixty five acres and
all appurtenances belonging thereto, to hold in fee simple to
him and his children forever -

Second - I give and bequeath unto Betty Miller my "Brit" mule
and buggy and sewing machine - Third - I give and bequeath
unto John Nunn and Buck Nunn each one bed and bed clothes.

Fourth - I give to my relatives and others, who have people
buried in the family grave yard one and one half acres of land
at the grave yard and a pass way thereto to be under the management W. M. Dean, Wilson Frost and John Nunn, or their successors, to be appointed by those who have an interest in said
yard -

Fifth - I, give to John Nunn ten acres, lying west of her tract
being the same length of line north and South as his, and far
enough west to make the ten acres/

Sixth - I give to Sam Turnage (cold) during his lifetime the
old land which lies south of the apple orchard and the fresh
land lying west of the same field and orchard and the "Joe
Thenter" mule to cultivate it with, provided that he shall not
trade said mule -

Seventh - I give to Buck Nunn five acres lying south of his
tract to be the same length of line east & west and far enough
to contain the five acres, provided he completes the clearing
west of Mary A. Stallings.

Eighth - I give to Thos. R. Moss also the remainder of my land
to hold the same, to be his and his children forever

Ninth - I want all my personal property, which is not specified,
consisting of mules, horse-stock, cattle, hogs, sheep, farming
utensils, corn and all other property not herein provided for
or disposed off, to be sold and proceeds applied to the payment
of any debts which I may owe and the building of a good grave
house which I have begun over my husbands grave and mine.

I nominate and appoint W. M. Dean my Executor (P.365) Dec.12th
1885

Witness W. Frost   Louisa Miller
        Jno. B. York

(234)

(P.365 Cont'd)
State of Tennessee) Jany. Term of Dyer County Court 1886
Dyer County   ) Monday Jany. 4th 1886

In matter of Probate of) This day a paper writing purporting
Louisa Miller's   (to be the last will and testament
Last will & testament) of Mrs. Louisa Miller was produced
before the court for probate. Thereupon came into open court Jno. B. York one of the subscribing witnesses thereto, who being first duly sworn deposed & said that he was personally acquainted with the Testatrix in her lifetime - That she was of sound & disposing mind and memory at the time of the execution of said paper writing - That she signed the same & acknowledged the same in his presence as her last will & testament & requested that he bear witness thereto - That he signed the same in the presence of said Testatrix; and also came into court Wilson Frost the other subscribing witness thereto who being first duly sworn, deposed & said that he was personally acquainted with the Testatrix during her lifetime - That she signed said paper writing in her presence but that he did not think her of sound & disposing mind & memory at the time of doing so - The court being of opinion from the proof that said Testatrix was competent to make a will at the time of the execution of said paper writing - It is ordered that the said paper writing be and the same is hereby set up & established as the last will & testament of the said Louisa Miller & that the same be recorded in "Will Book" & filed and thereupon came into court W. M. Dean who is named as Executor of said will together with Jno. C. Miller T. C. Miller & Rufus King his securities and they entered into and acknowledged bond in the penal sum of sixteen hundred dollars conditioned & payable as the law directs for the faithful performance of his duties as such Executor - He was then duly sworn - Let letters Testamentary issue

A true copy of will & probate

Attest Z. G. Watkins   Clerk.

(P.366)
Last Will & Testament of) State of Tennessee, Dyer County,
M. O. B. Gaulden dec'd (March 6 /85 -
Probated March term 1886)
Recorded March 25 /86   (I, M. O. B. Gaulden being of
  Z. G. Watkins clerk   ) sound mind and of body but concious of uncertainty of life and certainty of death desire this to be my last will and testament, to wit: I will all my money, note, bonds or accounts to my wife Margaret F. Gaulden to use and control during her natural life as she will or pleases and at her death to be divided equally between all of my children together with all the household and kitchen furniture, stock farming utensils and all apurtenses of the farm and also will to Robert J. Gaulden Drury's youngest son one tract of land, lying in the 7th civil district, containing 69¾ more or less. I also will to my two daughters Margaret Dickerson & Louisa Thompson, one

(P.366 Cont'd) tract of land lying in the 8th civil district of Dyer County to be equally divided between them - I desire that the above bequeath be faithfully carried out and complied with - I also nominate and appoint my 2 sons J. W. & Drury Gaulden my Ex'tors with full power and authority to act as my legal executors and carry out the the purpose of and design of this my will as set forth and expressed this the 6th day of March A. D. 1885 signed in presence of

Witnesses   M. O. B. Gaulden
J. K. Pursell
L. C. White

    Robert J. Gaulden has forfited his control and have left me and this is nula void.

                                                        M. O. B. Gaulden

In Matter of Last will &   )   County Court of Dyer Co. Tenn.
Testament of M. O. B. Gaulden(March third 1886
deceased   )   On this day the paper writing,
                                                     purporting to be the last will
& testament of M. O. B. Gaulden dec'd was produced before the court for probate (same proven by L. C. White March 1 /86 Monday) Thereupon came into open court Dr. J. K. Pursell one of the subscribing witnesses thereto who being first duly sworn, deposed and said that he was personally acquainted with the said M.O.B. Gaulden in his lifetime - that he was of sound and disposing mind and memory at the time of the execution of the said paper writing as his last will and testament in his presence and for the purposes therein contained. That he the said Pursell) signed the said paper writing as a witness thereto in the presence of the Testator and at his request - It is therefore ordered by the court that the said paper writing be and the same is hereby set up and established as the last will & testament of the said M. O. B. Gaulden dec'd and that the same (P.367) be recorded and filed

A true copy from minutes

                                                        Attest Z. G. Watkins clk.

In the matter of Last   )   County Court
Will & testament of   (March Term 1886
M. O. B. Gaulden dec'd   )   Monday March 1st 1886

           This day a paper writing purporting to be the last will and testament of M. O. B. Gaulden, dec'd, was produced before the court for probate - Thereupon came into open court L. C. White one of the subscribing witnesses thereto who being first duly sworn deposed and said that he was personally acquainted with said M. O. B. Gaulden dec'd in his lifetime. That he was of sound and disposing mind and memory at the time of the execution of the said paper writing - That he acknowledged the execution of the said paper writing as his last will and testament in his presence and for the purposes therein contained and requested him to witness the

(236)

(P.367 Cont'd) same. That he signed the as witness thereto in the presence and at the request of said M. O. B. Gaulden dec'd.

A true copy
        Attest; Z. G. Watkins Clerk.

(P.368)
Last Will & Testament of Rebecca Walker dec'd) State of Tennessee Dyer County -
Probated Sept. 6 /86
Recorded Sept. 13 /86
W. L. Wilkerson Clk.

I, Rebeca Walker do make and publish this as my last will and testament, First I direct that my funeral expenses and all my debts be paid as soon after my death as possible out of my personal property that I die possessed of or may first come into the hands of my executor. Secondly I give and bequeath to A. H. Walker one half of all the land that I am possessed with, and all of my personal property after paying the above named expenses. Thirdly I give to G. W. Walker one half of my land said land shall be divided equally running North and South. Fourthly, the above gift is to be on the condition that A. H. and G. W. Walker pay to J. H. Walker the sum of seventy five dollars each. Fifthly I do hereby nominate and appoint A. H. Walker my executor. In witness whereof I do to this my will set my hand this the ninth day of Dec. eighteen hundred and eighty four.

                                    Rebecca Walker

Signed and published in our presence and we have subscribed our names hereto in the presence of the testator this the ninth day of December eighteen hundred and eighty four

Wilson Frost
T. G. Miller

In the Matter of the last Will & Testament of Rebecca Walker) This day a paper writing purporting to be the last will and testament of Mrs. Rebeca Walker deceased late of Dyer Co. Tenn was produced here before the court for probate. (P.369) Thereupon came Wilson Frost and T. J. Miller subscribing witness thereto who being first duly sworn deposed and said that they were personally acquainted with Rebecca Walker testatrix in her lifetime. That she was of sound and disposing mind and memory at the time of the execution of said paper writing That she signed and acknowledged the same in their presence to be her last will and that they signed the same in the presence of each other and of the testator as witness thereto.

It is therefore ordered by the court that said paper writing be set up and established as the last will and testament of Rebecca Walker dec'd and that same be recorded in Will Book and filed. -

(237)

(P.369 Cont'd)   A true copy of original will & probate of same.

    Attest W. L. Wilkerson Clerk

(P.370)
Last Will & Testament) I, Wm. H. Lanier do make and pub-
of W. H. Lanier Dec'd (lish this my last will and Testa-
Probated Dec. 6th 1886,) ment.
Recorded Dec. 7th 1886,(
W. L. Wilkerson Clerk.) Item 1st   I will and bequeath to my
           wife Pricilla D. Lanier all of my
effects both real and personal of every description except such as hereby mentioned in this will.

Item 2nd   The tract of land lying in district No. 9 of Dyer County which I purchased of O. E. Lanier and wife, at the death of my wife Pricilla D. Lanier I bequeath to my grand sons Ramsy Applewhite son of R. H. Applewhite, Wm. Olly Lanier son of P. T. Lanier and Walter Everett Lanier son of Henry E. Lanier but the said land is to remain the property of my wife Pricilla D. Lanier during her natural life time.

3rd   I, give and bequeath to R. H. Applewhite my watch which I have been in the habit of carrying.

Item 4th   In order to secure my wife Pricilla D. Lanier from any trouble or molestation, and to fully explain my will, I have willed her all my personal property of every description (except the watch) to be hers for her to use and dispose of during her life or at her death as she may choose.

Item 5th   I bequeath to each one of my children the sum of one dollar to be paid to them out of my money that may belong to my estate.

Item 6th   I hereby nominate and appoint my wife Pricilla D. Lanier my Executrix and having full confidence in her integrity, I direct that she be allowed to execute this will without being required to execute or give bond as executrix.

Item 7th   I, W. H. Lanier do further say that I am in my right mind and have calmly considered the subject and have made the above will and have made it as I believe to be my duty.

Witness my hand the 3rd day of August 1883

          W. H. Lanier

(P.371) Signed acknowledged and published in our presence and in testimony thereof we have hereunto set our names in presence of each other and the Testator, this the 30th day of August 1883.

          J. F. Williamson
          J. R. Westbrook
          A. F. Dickson

(P.371 Cont'd)

In the Matter of the)
last will and testa- (This day a paper writing purporting
ment of W. H. Lanier) to be the last will and testament
of W. H. Lanier deceased late a citizen of Dyer County Tennessee was produced here before the court for probate. Thereupon came J. F. Williamson, J. R. Westbrook and A. F. Dickson subscribing witness thereto who being first duly sworn deposed and said they were personally acquainted with W. H. Lanier testator in his lifetime. That he was of sound disposing mind and memory at the time of the execution of said paper writing. That he signed and acknowledged the same in their presence to be his last will and testament for the purposes therein expressed. That they signed the same in the presence of each other and of the testator as witness thereto. It is therefore ordered by the court that the said paper writing be set up and established as the last will and testament of W. H. Lanier deceased and that same be recorded in Will Book and filed.

A true copy of the original will and probate of same

Attest W. L. Wilkerson clerk.

(P.372)

Last will and testament) Know all men by these presents, that
of John Hobday Decd. (I, John Hobday of the county of Dyer
Probated April 5th 1887) State of Tenn. considering the uncer-
Recorded April 5th 1887(tainty of this life and being of
W. L. Wilkerson clk.) sound mind and memory, do make declare and publish this my last will and testament:

First; I give and bequeath after all my just debts are paid; My interest being one half of all the property of Hobday & son to my heirs as follows,

To the heirs of S. M. Hobday Five Dollars $5.00; To the heirs of W. W. Hobday Five Dollars $5.00 and to each of my remaining heirs an equal interest in all my property;

Second; I do nominate and appoint my son T. C. Hobday to be the Executor of this my last will and testament. In testimony whereof I have to this my _my_ last will and testament, subscribed my name and set my seal this 30th day September in the year of Our Lord one thousand eight hundred and eighty six

John Hobday

Signed sealed declared and published by the said John Hobday as and for his last will and Testament in presence of us who at his request and in his presence and in presence of each other have subscribed our names as witnesses hereto

A. B. Pritchard
Wm. Sawyer
G. Chitwood

(239)

(P.373)

In the matter of the) This day a paper writing purporting
Last will & testament of(to be the last will and testament
John Hobday dec'd) of John Hobday dec'd late a citizen
of Dyer County Tennessee, was produced here before the court for probate. Thereupon came Wm. Sawyer & G. Chitwood subscribing witnesses thereto who being first duly sworn deposed and said that they were personally acquainted with John Hobday testator in his lifetime and that he was of sound and disposing mind and memory at the time of the execution of said paper writing. That he signed and acknowledged the same in their presence to be his last will and testament for the purposes therein expressed. That they signed the same in the presence of the testator and in the presence of each other as witnesses thereto.

It is therefore ordered by the court that said paper writing be set up and established as the last will and testament of John Hobday dec'd and that the same be recorded and filed

A true copy of original will and probate of same

Attest W. L. Wilkerson clerk.

(P.374)

Last will & Testament) I, Mary Lou Emma Farris
of Miss. M. L. E. Ferris dec'd(being of sound mind and dis-
Probated April 5, 1887) posing memory, but feeble
Recorded April 5, 1887 (in health hereby make and
W. L. Wilkerson clk.) publish this my last will
and testament hereby revoking all former wills by me heretofore made. Item first - I direct that all my just debts & funeral expenses be paid out of the first money coming into the hands of my executor.

Item second - I give to my brother William Walter Farris all my right title claim and interest in and to the tract of land on which my mother now resides. The tract of land contains seventy three and 3/3 acres and was assigned as Homestead and Dower to my mother Elizabeth E. Farris out of the lands of which my Father W. J. Farris died seized and possessed The land lies in the 9th civil District of Dyer County Tennessee and is bounded on the North by Jessie Pierce East by Tom Green South by R. G. Stockton and west by A. G. Farris and is subject to my mothers homestead and Dower and my interest in the land is undivided. One third of said tract of land I also give to my Brother William Walter Ferris, all my personal property of every kind and description of which I may die possessed.

I hereby appoint Smith Parks as my Executor of this my last will and testament, This 29th day of December 1886

Witness M. L. E. Ferris
R. G. Stockton
J. N. Armstrong

(P.375)

In the matter of the last) This day a paper writing purport-
will and testament of (ing to be the last will and tes-
Miss. L. E. Ferris dec'd) tament of Miss M. L. E. Ferris
dec'd late a citizen of Dyer County
Tennessee was produced before the court for probate. Thereupon
came R. G. Stockton & J. N. Armstrong subscribing witnesses
thereto who being first duly sworn deposed and said that they
were personally acquainted with Miss M. L. E. Ferris Testatrix
in her lifetime and that she was of sound and disposing mind
and memory at the time of the executor of said paper writing.
That she signed and acknowledged the same in their presence to
be her last will and Testament for the purposes therein expressed.
That they signed the same in the presence of the Testatrix and
in the presence of each other as witnesses thereto. It is therefore ordered by the court that said paper writing be set up and
established as the last will and testament of Mrs. M. L. E.
Ferris and that the same be recorded and filed.

A true copy of original will and probate

Attest W. L. Wilkerson clerk

(P.376)

Last Will & Testament of) I, U. C. Hendrix of Dyer County
U. C. Hendrix dec'd (Tennessee being of sound and dis-
Probated June 6 /87) posing mind do hereby make & pub-
Recorded June 6 /87 (lish this my last will & Testament
W. L. Wilkerson clk.) revoking all former wills by me
made at any time.

1st I direct my funeral expenses and all other debts that I
may owe at my death, be paid out of the first money that comes
into the hands of my Executor -

2nd I will to my beloved wife Temperence Hendrix twenty nine
acres of land bought from A. C. Hendrix & being part of the
D. R. Hendrix tract, during her natural life and at her death
my Executor shall sell said 29 acres of land and distribute
as follows;

One sixth to the children of Narsisous Falcum and one sixth to
each of my other children M. R. G. M. A. C. & J. C. Hendrix &
Hattie Wyatte;

3rd I will that the tract of land on which I now live in the
9th District of Dyer Co. and a tract I own in the 15th District
of Dyer County Tennessee, be sold and divided equally between
M. R. Hendricks to G. M. Hendricks & A. C. Hendricks Hattie
Wyatte wife of H. L. Wyatte and the children of (Narsissus
Falcum the children of said Falcum to be one heir & receive one
sixth as their part.

4th I will that my personal property be sold & the proceeds
together with my notes & money on hand after my debts are paid,
shall be equally divided between my wife Temperence Hendrix

(241)

(P.376 Cont'd) J. C. Hendrix, N. R. Hendrix G. M. Hendrix A. C. Hendrix Hattie Wyatte and <u>Narissus</u> Falcum share and share alike. (P.377) I hereby nominate and appoint H. L. Wyatt Executor of this my last will & Testament

Witness my hand & seal this the 13th day of April 1887

Witness;
John E. McCorkle
    her
Eliza X Wyatte
    mark
John E. McCorkle witness
W. L. x Hendrix

        his
U. C. X Hendricks
    mark

In the matter of (This day a paper writing purport-
The Last will & Testament) ing to be the last will & Testa-
of U. C. Hendricks dec'd (ment of U. C. Hendricks deceased
   late a citizen of Dyer County
Tennessee was produced here before the court for probate.

Thereupon came John E. McCorkle and W. L. Hendricks subscribing witnesses thereto who being first duly sworn deposed & said that they were personally acquainted with U. C. Hendrix Testator in his lifetime & that he was of sound & disposing mind & memory at the time of the execution of said paper writing. That he signed and acknowledged the same in their presence to be his last will & Testament for the purposes therein expressed. That they signed the same in the presence of the Testator & in the presence of each other as witnesses thereto.

It is therefore ordered by the court that said paper writing be set up and established as the last will and Testament of said U. C. Hendrix & that the same be recorded & filed

A true copy of original will & probate of same

                            Attest W. L. Wilkerson
                                    Clerk

(P.378)
Last will & Testament) I, Timothy Wilson of Dyer County
of Timothy Wilson dec'd(State of Tennessee being of sound
Probated July Term /87) mind and memory and understandingly
Recorded July 5 /87 (do make my last will & Testament in
W. L. Wilkerson clk.) manner & form as follows, I give &
                        bequeath my house and my lot and all other property personal or real to my beloved wife Ida. Not having but one child Minnie when I took my life insurance policy it was made to my wife and child, I now desire to change, I desire first that my just debts be paid out of it then my dear wife Ida to have one third of the remainder & then the remainder to be divided between my three children Minnie Roy & Asa. I hereby appoint my uncle J. G. Tucker the administrator of my estate & my dear wife Ida I appoint sole Guardian of my children & sole Executrix of this my last will & Testament without her

(P.378 Cont'd) giving any bond or security for same.
This June 10th 1887

                  T. Wilson

D. G. Tucker
F. B. Bryan

(P.379)

In the Matter of the   ) This day a paper writing purporting
Last will & Testament   (to be the last will and testament of
of Timothy Wilson Dec'd)

Timothy Wilson Dec'd late a citizen of Dyer County Tennessee was produced here before the court for probate. Thereupon came D. G. Tucker & F. B. Bryan subscribing witnesses thereto who being first duly sworn deposed & said that they were personally acquainted with T. Wilson Testator during his lifetime & that he was of sound and disposing mind & memory at the time of the execution of said paper writing. That he signed and acknowledged the same in their presence for the purposes therein contained as his last will & testament. That they signed the same in the presence of each other and in the presence of the Testator as witnesses thereto. It is therefore ordered by the court that said paper writing be set up & established as the last will and Testament of the said T. Wilson & that the same be recorded in Will Book & filed.

A true copy of original will & probate of same

                Attest; W. L. Wilkerson clerk.

(P.380) BLANK

(P.381)

The Last Will & Testament) I, Hezikiah Fuller being of sound
of Hezikiah Fuller Dec'd (mind and disposing memory do make
Probated Oct. Term 1887) and publish this my last will and
Recorded Oct. 11th 1887 (Testament hereby revoking all wills
Will L. Wilkerson clerk) by me heretofore at any time made.

Item 1st I direct that all of my just debts be paid by my Executor out of the first monies coming into his hands including my funeral expenses &c.

Item 2nd I give to my beloved wife Nancy all such of my personal property as she may desire to keep for her comfort and subsistence, and after she has selected what she wishes to retain of my personal property, then my Executor will sell the remainder to make assets for the estate. I also give my beloved wife the tract of land on which we reside containing one hundred and fifty acres more or less and bounded North by the Edward Haskins original tract East by my sons Jno. T. & William A. Fuller South by Allen Harris heirs and west by Guy Douglass and J. C. Haskins land purchased from R. E. Johnson to have and to the same for and during her natural life.

Item 3rd I will and direct that my two daughters Ema H. and Nannie S. are to have their home with their mother on the farm

(P.381 Cont'd) given to her in the 2nd item of this will and be supported ~~and~~ by the proceed of the farm as long as they remain single, and their mother lives, all of my children having been advanced by me the sum of two hundred dollars each.

Item 4th In addition to the sum of two hundred dollars mentioned in Item 3rd of this will to each of my children I loaned to George W. Hill the husband of my daughter Sarah E. Hill in his lifetime to wit on the 4th day of December 1867 one thousand dollars for which he executed to me his three notes all bearing interest from that date one for four hundred the other two for three hundred dollars each. I also loaned to Joe. C. Vann the husband of my daughter Susan M. Vann during the lifetime of my said daughter (to wit) on the 20th day of December 1877 six hundred and twenty four dollars and six cents He also owe me the sum of four hundred and forty five dollars forty cents on the first day of January 1880 for which I have his two notes of date above given and on the 19th day of February 1879, I paid to W. C. Doyle Clerk & Master of the Chancery Court at Dyersburg Tennessee, (P.382) twenty one dollars, I also paid (as the security of J. C. Vann, on a prosecution bond in a suit of said Vann, against the Rail Road the sum of twenty six dollars **for which** I have J. A. Odell receipt as Deputy Sheriff showing that I paid said money on the 13th day of April (1878) Eighteen hundred seventy eight. I also have James W. Enochs note (he is the husband of my daughter Ann E.) for three hundred dollars and sixteen cents on the 2nd day of January 1882, and I paid cost in the Supreme Court on Execution against my daughter **Ann E.** Enochs on the 15th September 1883 the sum of one hundred and forty eight dollars eighty five cents for which I have J. G. Wynne Deputy Sheriff receipt I also have the note of my two sons John T. Fuller and William A. Fuller given jointly for eleven hundred and thirty six dollars and seventy five cents on January 1st 1880. Now I will and direct my Executor that in the final settlement of my estate that all the above claims as set forth in this item of my will must be charged up including interest at six per cent to the child or representative of the child who over the said several amounts as set out in this item of my will and the amount in each case will be deducted from the share of such child or its representative from the amt. that may be in the hands of said executor giving to such child or representative of such child, Charging Susan M. Vann's heirs with Jo. C. Vann's amt. of indebtedness and Sarah E. Hill or her heirs with George W. Hill's indebtedness, and then such balance if any there be in the hands of my executor giving to such child, or representative of such child shall be paid over to him her or them as the case may be.

Item 5th: I hereby direct my Executor at the death of my beloved wife Nancy that he sell all my estate real personal or mixed if he deems that the best way to make distribution of the Estate or he may have the Real Estate divided among my heirs the children taking share and share alike in either case. And the representative of **any child** who may be dead at the time of the division taking such share as their parent would have (P.383) received

(P.383 Cont'd) if living and as my daughter Suan M. Vann is now dead leaving children they of course will take their mother's share of my estate after the amount due me from their Father Jo. C. Vann is deducted from such share and my Executor is hereby authorized and empowered to sell any and all of the lands of which I may die seized and possessed and make good and sufficient title to the same without the aid or assistance of any court decree whatever and I leave it entirely at his discretion as to the time he may sell any or all of my other lands except my home place (it is not to be sold until after my wife's death) and he may sell my lands entirely for cash or for part cash and the balance on time as he may deem best for my estate.

Item Sixth; I hereby appoint George R. Fuller my Executor to this my last will and Testament with full power and authority to carry out all its provissions This July 9 /85

Witnesses   H. Fuller
Smith Parks
J. Ira Jones

In the Matter of the last) This day a paper writing purport-
Will and Testament of   (ing to be the last will and Testa-
Hezekiah Fuller dec'd   ) ment of Hezekiah Fuller Deceased
                            late a citizen of Dyer County,
Tennessee, was produced here before the Court for probate. Whereupon came Smith Parks and J. Ira Jones, Subscribing witnesses thereto who being first duly sworn deposed and say that they were acquainted with Hezekiah Fuller Testator during his lifetime that he was sound and disposing mind and memory at the time of the Execution of said paper writing; That he signed and acknowledged the same in their presence for the purposes therein contained as his last will and Testament; That they signed the same in the presence of each other and in the presence of ~~said other~~ Testator as witnesses thereto;

It is therefore ordered by the Court that said paper writing be set up and established as the last will and Testament of the said Hezekiah Fuller deceased and that the same be recorded in Will Book and filed

A true Copy of the original Will and of the probate of the same,

                                    Attest; William L. Wilkerson Clk.
                                    By Wat Sampson D. C.

(P.384)
Last will and Testament) August 25th 1887
T. W. Lanier Dec'd   (
Probated Nov. Term /87) Know all men that I, Thos. W. Lanier
Recorded Nov. 12th /87 (do hereby make make and determine the
                            following as my last will and Testament.

First; I desire that my body shall be decently buried and my

(245)

(P.384 Cont'd)   just debts paid.   And

Second; that it is my will and desire for Thomas D. Applewhite to have and to hold the land on which I now live for which I have all ready executed to him a deed which is registered in Book on June the 10th, 1887 - in case there should be any legal defects in said deed. I hereby give and bequeath the said tract or parcel of land to the said Thomas D. Applewhite his heirs and assigns forever. On condition that he take care of me property during my natural life and pay my Doctors bills and other expenses that may accumilate against me.

Third, that I will and bequeath to the said Thomas D. Applewhite one mule.

Fourth, after my death I will and bequeath to my adopted Son P. F. Lanier all my household and kitchen furniture and farming implements, and one mule in case I have two mules at the time of my death.

Signed and delivered in presence of

J. F. Williamson   Thos. W. Lanier
     and
R. N. Fryer

(P.385)
In the matter of the   ) This day a paper writing purporting
Last will and Testament (to be the last will and testament
of Thos. W. Lanier Dec'd) of Thos. W. Lanier dec'd. late a
                                              citizen of Dyer County Tennessee,
was produced here before the court for probate. Thereupon came J. F. Williamson and R. N. Fryer subscribing witnesses thereto; who being first duly sworn deposed and said that they were personally acquainted Thos. W. Lanier Testator during his natural lifetime. And that he was of sound and disposing mind and memory at the time of the execution of said paper writing. That he signed and acknowledged the same in their presence to be his last will and Testament for the purposes therein expressed. That they signed the same in the presence of the Testator and in the presence of each other as witnesses thereto.

It is therefore ordered by the court that said paper writing be set up and established as the last will and Testament of Thos. W. Lanier dec'd and that the same be recorded and filed.

A true copy of original will & probate of same.

                                    Attest W. L. Wilkerson clerk.
(P.386)
The Last Will & Testament) I, Nannie O. Pate, of Dyer County
of Miss Nannie O. Pate   (Tennessee, recognizing the uncer-
Probated April Term 1888) tainty of life, and the certainty
Recorded April 4th 1888   (of Death and being of sound mind
Will L. Wilkerson Clerk   ) and disposing memory, do make and

(P.386 Cont'd) publish this my last will and Testament, hereby revoking all former wills by me at any time made;

Item 1st; I will and bequeath all money and Cash I may have left at the time of my death, after my burial expenses are paid to Mrs. Nancy Pate wife of Jno. C. Pate and to Mrs. Sallie Pate wife of G. W. Pate to equally divided between them the said Sallie Pate and Nancy Pate.

Item 2nd; I nominate and appoint my friend Allen Rawles the Executor to carry out this my last will and testament

Given under my hand on this 18th day of Nov. 1887

Nannie O. Pate

We the undersigned witnesses have this day signed the foregoing will (written on the reverse side of this paper) at the request of and in the presence of the Testatrix Nannie O. Pate and in the presence of each other.

J. N. Rawles
W. O. Bunnell

(P.387)

In the matter of the Last Will & Testament of Miss Nannie O. Pate dec'd) This day a paper writing purporting to be the last will and Testament of Miss Nannie O. Pate, deceased late a citizen of Dyer County Tennessee was produced here in open court for Probate. Thereupon comes J. N. Rawles and W. A. Bunnell, subscribing witness thereto who being first duly sworn deposed and said that they were personally acquainted with said Nannie O. Pate Testatrix in her lifetime and that she was of sound and disposing mind and memory at the time of the execution of the paper writing; that she signed and acknowledged the same in the presence of ~~each other~~ to be her last will and testament for the purposes expressed therein. That they signed the same in the presence of each other and in the presence of Testatrix as subscribing witnesses thereto. It is therefore ordered by the court that the said paper writing be and the same is hereby set up and established as the last will and testament of the said Nannie O. Pate Deceased recorded and filed

A true copy from the original will and probate

W. L. Wilkerson Clerk.

(P.388)

The Last will and Testament of Mrs. T. E. Boon deceased
Probated June Term 1888
Recorded June 5th 1888
Will L. Wilkerson Clk.

Know all men by these presents that I Frankie E. Boon of Dyersburg Tenn. being sound mind do make publish and declare this to be my last will and testament hereby revoking all others wills that may have been made by me heretofore.

(P.388 Cont'd)

I give to my Sister Martha Turner a portion of my lot beginning at the S. E. Corner of my home place running thence North with the street or alley on my East line North 60 ft: thence west 49 ft; thence South 60 ft. to the line of lot she is now living on; thence East 49 ft. to the beginning. Also my old set of furniture consisting of Beauro Bedstead and wash stand. I give to my niece Vida Earl my home place (except as above) being place bot by me from my Sister Martha Turner and my best feather bed pillows bed clothing &c, for same together with my best bedstead and my Pianow and sewing machine. The balance of my personal property I want sold and applied to the payment of any debts I may owe. If I should owe more than proceeds of sale of my personal property then I want my home place rented out and the rent applied to the payment of my debts untill the same are all paid. After which the rents may go to my said Niece Vida Earl untill she is of age when she shall have possession of the place.

I hereby nominate and appoint my nephew W. D. Roberts Executor of this my will and having confidence in him I hereby waive the necessity of his giving bond in testimony whereof I have this day set my hand this Jan. 27, 1887

                 F. E. B. Boon

Witness
J. W. Tenney
J. A. Foster

(P.389)

In the matter of the last will and Testament of Mrs. Frankie E. Boon dec'd

This day a paper writing purporting to be the last will and testament of Mrs. Frankie E. Boon dec'd late a citizen of Dyer County Tennessee was produced here before the court for probate thereupon came J. W. Tenney and J. A. Foster subscribing witnesses thereto who being first duly sworn deposed and said that they were personally acquainted with the said Frankie E. Boon Testator in her lifetime - that she was of sound mind and memory at the time of the execution of the said paper writing; that she signed and acknowledged the same in their presence to be her last Will and Testament for the purposes therein expressed that they signed the same in the presence of each other and in the presence of the Testator as witnesses thereto. It is therefore ordered by the court that said paper writing be set up and established as the last will and Testament of the said Frankie E. Boon dec'd, and that the same be recorded in Will Book and filed.

A true copy of original will and probate of same.

              Attest; W. L. Wilkerson
                    Clerk.

(P.390)
The Last Will and Testament) I, Sallie R. Penner being
of Mrs. Sallie R. Pinner dec'd (sound mind and disposing memo-
Probated July Term 1888) ry do make and publish this
Recorded July 5th 1888 (as my last will and Testament
Will L. Wilkerson Clerk.) hereby revoking and making
void all others by me at any
time made to wit;

First - I will and devise that all my just debts be paid as soon as practicable after my death -

Second I will and devise that all the real estate of which I shall die the owner be sold by my Executor and to this end I hereby give him the same power and authority to make and complete the sale of said property that I would have if living. And among the powers he would thus have I would specifically designate that he is to determine in his discretion when said property shall be put upon the market or sold or any part of it and whether it shall be divided into smaller parcels and sold or sold altogether and also the place where the terms upon which and the manner in which it shall be sold.

Third - I further will and devise that the net proceeds of said real estate shall go to and be divided between certain of my children and grand children and paid out to them by my Executor as follows; I have three deceased children at this time to wit Mary E. Northington B. E. Pinner and W. W. Pinner and to their children living at my death I devise and bequeath twelve per cent of the net proceeds of said real estate to be divided equally between them and paid out to them if of age and to their regular guardian if under age by my executor and the balance or eighty eight per cent of said net proceeds to be equally divided between my son C. Pinner and my two daughters Margret E. Petty (P.391) and Sallie O. Acree and if either of them be dead at my death then the share intended hereby to go to the deceased shall go to his or her children. By net proceeds I mean what is left after paying all expenses attending the sale of said land and also the debts of the estate and the cost of settling up the estate including $250.00 to my executor for all his services herein except as hereafter shown as my will is that said land or proceeds shall pay all said debts and expenses but if necessary or my Executor thinks proper to do so he may pay said debts and expenses or any part thereof out of any personalty or its proceeds that may come into his hands or out of his own means and then retain the same out of the proceeds of the real estate

Fourth - My further will is that my said Executor shall take charge of said real estate after my death and rent the same out untill sold or otherwise manage it as he may think best for the interest of the parties conserned and the net proceeds of the rents or income from the real estate shall be divided as the proceeds of the real estate are herein directed to be divided -

(P.391 Cont'd)

Fifth - My further will is that no property that I have given to any of my children or grand children or may give them hereafter shall be charged up to them or accounted for by them in the settlement of my estate.

Sixth - I further will devise and bequeath all the rest and residue of my property - that is all except the real estate to my son J. C. Pinner and hereby nominate and appoint him as the executor of this my last will and testament, but excuse him from giving the bond required by law of executor.

Seventh - My will is that said Executor shall be allowed 15 per cent of the original amount for which said land is annually rented, for his services in attending to the renting and taking care of said real estate in (P.392) addition to allowence mentioned heretofore.

Interlineations and additions in different ink made before signing. Witness my hand this the 11 of August 1884

```
Signed by the testator      )        Sally R. Pinner
in our presence and         (
witnessed by us             )
at her request              (
in her presence             )
and in the presence of      (
each other this day 11 of   )
Aug. 1884                   (
Witness E. R. Vernon M. D.  )
   "    N. Coker            (
   "    B. B. Watkins       )
Febry. 23 /1885 L. D. Hargis(
                J. M. Scott )
```

----------Codicil No. One ----------

As all my real estate has been sold since writing the above will I now so change the same and will and devise that all my personal estate of which I may die seized and possessed shall go to and be divided among the parties and as directed in the above third clause in regard to the net proceeds of the real estate and I include herein the rest and residue mentioned in the 6th clause above. And I further so change said will as that my said Executor shall have five hundred dollars instead of two hundred and fifty dollars for his services as such Executor and further no property or effects of any kind that I have or may hereafter give to any of my children or grand children shall be charged up to or accounted for by them as such I intend as a gift and not an advancement and no debt claim or obligation against any of them or effects of any kind received by them up to this time shall be collected off of them or accounted for by them but all such are hereby canceled.

Sally R. Pinner

(P.393)
Signed by the testator
in our presence and
witnessed by us at her
request in her presence
and in the presence
of each other this day
Aug. 9th 1887
J. N. Parker
A. More Stevens
B. B. Watkins

In the matter of the last) This day a paper writing purport-
will and Testament of   (ing to be the last will and tes-
Mrs. Sallie R. Pinner   ) tament of Mrs. Sallie R. Pinner
dec'd, was presented by Joseph C. Pinner the sole Executor nominated therein in open court and asked that same be admitted to probate and set up and established as the last will and testament of said Sallie R. Pinner dec'd and moved the court that the same be done and that he said Joseph C. Pinner be appointed and qualified as sole Executor and there upon came E. R. Vernon and B. B. Watkins two of the subscribing witnesses to the original will and after being duly sworn testify and say that they knew said Sallie R. Pinner in her lifetime; that she is dead and had her usual place of residence in Dyer County Tennessee at the time of her death; that said paper writing is her last will and testament; that said testator signed the same in their presence as her last will and testament and that they signed and witnessed the same in the presence of said testatrix at her request as her last will and testament and also in the presence of N. Coker another subscribing witness who signed and witnessed the same at the same time and in the presence of these witnesses but the ____ to of said Coker is not now known to them; (P.394) and they further testify that said testatrix was at the time of the execution of said original will and testament of sound mind and disposing memory and J. N. Parker and B. B. Watkins subscribing witness to codicil No. one of said original will and testament also came into open court and being duly sworn testify and say that they were personally acquainted with said Sallie E. R. Pinner in her lifetime; that she signed said codicil as the first codicil or codicil no. one of her said last will and testament; and that they signed and witnessed the same in her presence and at her request and as the said codicil no. one of her last will and testament and they further testify that they signed and witnessed said codicil no. one in the presence of A. More Stevens another subscribing witness who signed the same at the same time and that his signature as it so appears is his genuine signature, and further testify that said testatrix at the time of the execution of said codicil resided in Dyer County and was at the time of sound mind and disposing memory.

And it appearing to the court that said last will and Testament of said Sallie R. Pinner properly executed witnessed and proven and should be admitted to probate and set up and established as such.

(P.394 Cont'd) It is therefore ordered and adjudged by the court that said paper writing be and the same is hereby admitted to probate and set up and established as the last will and testament together with the said codicil thereto of said Sallie R. Pinner dec'd and it is ordered to be recorded by the clerk and filed. And in motion of said (P.395) Joseph C. Pinner the executor named in said will and it appearing that he is entitled to be Executor thereof, being so named in the will it is therefore ordered and adjudged that said Joseph C. Pinner into open court and qualified as said Executor as required by law the execution of Bond as such being waived and excused by the terms of the will the same need not be executed by him.

Let Letters of administration issue

A true copy of will & probate of same

Attest W. L. Wilkerson Clerk

(P.396)
The Last Will and Testament) In the Name of God, Amen -----
of Mrs. Martha S. Hood Dec'd(I, Martha S. Hood of Newbern
Probated July Term 1888) Dyer County Tennessee, being of
Recorded July 20th 1888 (sound mind, and disposing memory,
W. L. Wilkerson Clerk) do make and publish this my last
will and testament;

I direct that my just debts, and funeral expenses be paid, And I give, devise, and bequeath to the Trustees of Cumberland University Lebanon Tennessee for the benefit of the Theological Department of said University, all the property real and personal and mixed, that I may die seized and possessed of or that I may own at my death.

In testimony whereof I do hereunto subscribe my name in the presence of H. Parks and Smith Parks whom I request to witness the same on this the 22nd day of November 1886

M. S. Hood

Signed and acknowledged in our presence on this 22nd day of November 1886 and at the request of the testatrix we hereunto subscribe our names.

H. Parks
Smith Parks

Codicil, No. 1.

I, Martha S. Hood do make and publish this as a codicil to my last will and testament, executed by me on the 22nd day of November 1886 and I desire to so change my said will as to give to my two aunts Lucinda Woods and Frances G. Green, my household furniture and wearing appeatal and all the rest and residue

(P.396 Cont'd) of my estate real and personal go as I directed in my said will. Witness my hand this the 9th day of December 1886 in the presence of Hamilton Parks and Smith Parks whom I request to bear witness to the same

            M. S. Hood

Signed and acknowledged in our presence on this 9 day of December 1886
            H. Parks
            Smith Parks

(P.397)   Codicil No. 2.

I, Martha S. Hood being of sound mind do make and publish this as a codicil to my will of November 22nd 1886 to which I added a codicil on December 9th 1886. I have a note for $35.00 executed to me by my cousin J. R. Woods, and aunt Lucinda H. Woods which note if not collected at my death I desire to give and do hereby give to my aunt Lucinda H. Woods and direct the same to be delivered to her. I also give to my Cousin Mrs. Susan Murry of Texas who is now in Newbern - the sum of one hundred dollars which amount I wish paid by Uncle J. R. Green and to be credited on a note for $285.00 which I hold against him.

   I, nominate and appoint Hamilton Parks Jr. of Nashville Tenn. Executor of my last will and codicil thereto;

   In witness whereof I hereunto subscribe my name in the presence of S. H. Brady and W. G. Leonard whom I request to bear witness to same on this 27th day of June 1888,

            M. S. Hood

Signed and acknowledged in our presence on this 27th day of June 1888,
            S. H. Brady
            W. G. Leonard

In the matter of the Last Will &) This day a paper writing
Testament of Mrs. Martha S. Hood) purporting to be the last
              will and testament of Mrs.
Martha S. Hood deceased together with the codicil no's 1 & 2 attached to same was produced here in open court by Hamilton Parks Jr. who is named as executor of said will and codicils thereto and who asked that said will and codicils be admitted to probate and set up and established as the last will and testament of said Martha S. Hood deceased, and thereupon came Smith Parks one of the subscribing witnesses (thereto) to said will and codicil no. 1. to same who being first duly sworn deposed and said that he was well acquainted with said S. Hood in her lifetime that her place of residence was in Dyer County Tennessee, and that she died in said County; That she was of sound mind and disposing memory at the time of the execution of said will and of said codicil no. 1. thereto and that she signed and acknowledged said will and said codicil no. 1 on

(P.397 Cont'd) their respective dates in the presence of witnesses Smith Parks and of H. Parks, the other witness to said will and (P.398) codicil no. 1. and that she requested said witnesses to sign said will and codicil no. 1. as witnesses thereto and that he the said Smith Parks and said H. Parks signed said will and codicil no. 1. in the presence of the Testatrix and at her request and in the presence of each other. That the other witness H. Parks, is very old and feeble and unable to attend this court that he knows the said H. Parks and knows his hand writing, and that said H. Parks signed said will and codicil no. 1. and the same are signed in his hand writing, and thereupon came also S. H. Brady and W. G. Leonard subscribing witness to codicil no. 2. to said will and they both being first duly sworn deposed and said that they knew Mrs. Martha S. Hood in her lifetime and that she signed and acknowledged Codicil No. 2. in their presence and requested them to sign the same as witness thereto that they signed said Codicil No. 2. at her request and in presence and in the presence of each other on the day of its date and that said Mrs. Martha S. Hood was of sound mind and disposing memory at the time she signed and acknowledged said Codicil No. 2. and that her residence was in Dyer County and that she has since died in Dyer County Tennessee.

It is therefore ordered by the Court that the said paper writing be and the same is hereby admitted to probate and set up and established as the last will and testament of the said Martha S. Hood Dec'd and ordered to be recorded and filed.

And upon motion of Hamilton Parks Jr. the Executor named in said will and appearing that he is entitled to be executor thereof. It is therefore ordered that said Hamilton Parks Jr. be and he is hereby appointed sole Executor of said will and thereupon came said Hamilton Parks Jr. into open court brings with him Smith Parks and Jno. N. Parker his securities and they executed and acknowledged bond in the sum of five thousand dollars conditioned and payable as the law directs for the faithful performance of his duties as Executor and the said Hamilton Parks Jr. was then sworn in open court. Let Letters Testamentary issue &c

(P.399)

The last will & Testament) I, Robert M. Drane being in feeble
of R. M. Drane Dec'd (health but of sound mind and dis-
Probated August Term /88) posing memory hereby make and pub-
Recorded Aug. 7th 1888 (lish this my last will and testa-
W. L. Wilkerson clk.) ment hereby revoking all former
wills by me heretofore at any time made.

Item 1st. My will and desire is that all my just debts be paid (including my funeral expenses) out of the first money coming into the hands of my Executor after my death.

Item 2nd. I give to my beloved wife Ella F. Drane the lot of ground on which we live composed of two lots known as the G. W. Parker lot and C. F. Brown lot and I refer to them recorded

(P.399 Cont'd) deed in the Register Office at Dyersburg as to particular as to metes and bounds and quantity I also give her the lot or parcel of land conveyed to me by James S. McCorkle lying just west of the Newbern west corporation line, I also refer to his recorded Deed to me for metes and bounds and other particulars in regard to said lot of land I give these three lots to my beloved wife during her life or widowhood and at her death or marriage then the above described lots are to belong to my youngest son Robt. W. Drane the only child of my beloved wife Ella F. Drane to be his and his heirs and assigns forever and in case of the death of my son Robt. W. Drane Jr. without issue then I give the said three lots to my two children by my first marriage Clide Drane and Nellie Drane to be equally divided between them or their heirs or the survivors of them if either of them die leaving no issue.

Item 3rd:
   I give to my son Clyde Drane and my daughter - Nellie Drane my interest in the brick store house on Main Street in Newbern Dyer County, Tennessee, known as the Wilkerson & Drane store house bounded on the East by Mrs. Lide Clark and on the west by James H. Hamilton & Sons South by main street and north by H. C. Porter. I also give them the Policy on my life issued by the Knights of Honor and for the benefit of my children at the time of the insurance of said Policy I only had two children Clyde and Nellie and it was my intention always that it should go to these two children (P.400) alone I own one half of the brick store house & lot.

Item 4th In the event that my two children Clyde and Nellie should fail to collect or to get the two thousand dollars on my life Policy mentioned in the third item of my will, Then I will and direct that all my property real and personally or mixed be divided between my wife and children as the law directs and divides the estates of persons during intestate my beloved wife taking such part of my estate as the law gives to widow whos husband die intestate -

Item 5th I hereby nominate and appoint Asa Fowlkes Executor of this my last will & Testament. This 11th day of June 1888,

Signed in our presence   R. W. Drane
and witnessed by us
at the request of the
Testator,
W. E. Johnston M. D.
R. B. Wilkerson

(P.401)
In the matter of the last)   This day a paper writing purwill & Testament of R. M. Drane) porting to be the last will
                                                  and testament of Robt. M.
Drane dec'd was presented by Asa Fowlkes in open Court for probate duly signed in presence of witnesses thereupon came into court R. B. Wilkerson one of the subscribing witnesses

(255)

(P.401 Cont'd) thereto who being first duly sworn deposed and said that he was of sound mind and disposing memory at the time of the execution of said instrument of writing that he signed the and published said paper writing as his last will and testament in the presence of himself and of W. E. Johnston the other subscribing witness thereto and request them to sign as witnesses to his act in so doing that he signed same in the presence of said Drane the testator and in the presence of the therefore W. E. Johnston witnessing said paper writing as his deliberate act also came A. B. Tigrett and R. J. Dickey to good and lawful citizen of Dyer County who being first duly sworn deposed and said they were personally acquainted W. E. Johnston in his lifetime whos signature as subscribing witnesses to the said paper writing aforesaid and that they were familliar with the hand writing of said W. E. Johnston having seen him sign his name at various & numerous time and that his name as written as a subscribing witness to said paper writing is in the hand writing of said W. E. Johnston who is now dead -

It is therefore ordered of the Court that said paper writing be and is hereby admitted to probate and established as the last will & testament of said Robt. M. Drane and on motion the said Asa Fowlkes who is named as Executor thereof is hereby appointed and ordained the Executor of said last will and testament. Whereupon came the said Asa Fowlkes into open Court and brings with him H. L. Fowlkes and J. H. Fowlkes, his securities & they entered into and acknowledged bond in the penal sum of six thousand dollars conditioned & payable as the law directs for the faithful performance of his duty as such executor of said will & testament whereupon the said Asa Fowlkes was duly sworn as Executor of and it is ordered that letters testamentary (P.402) issue to him.

The last Will & Testament) I, A. M. Stevens being of sound
of A. M. Stevens Deceased (mind do make and publish this my
Probated August Term, 1888) last will and Testament:
Recorded August 8, 1888 (
  Will L. Wilkerson Clk.)   I hereby will devise and bequeath all my property and effects of every kind as follows, to wit -

First: I will and devise that all my just debts be paid. Second: The remainder of my estate, whether, real, personal or mixed left after the payment of my said debts, I will devise and bequeath as follows, to wit to my Daughter, Georgianna Brackin, wife of J. M. Brackin one fourth thereof to have and to hold the same to her sole & separate use, benefit use and behalf free from the debts, liabilities claim and control of her said husband, J. M. Brackin or any future husband of hers. To my daughter, Fannie Scott, wife of George E. Scott, one fourth thereof to have, to own and to hold the same to her sole and separate use benefit and behalf, free from the debts liabilities claim & control of her said husband Geo. E. Scott or any future husband of hers. To my daughter, Myra Summers

(P.402 Cont'd) wife of Dr. Frank Summers one fourth thereof to have and to own and to hold the same to her sole and separate use benefit and behoof free from the debts liabilities claim and control of her said husband Dr. Frank Summer or any further husband of hers to my daughter Mary King wife of Ed. M. King one fourth thereof to have and to own and to hold the same in her sole and separate use and benefit and behoof free from the debts liabilities claim and control of her said husband Ed. M. King or any future husband of her.

I, further will that my real estate shall be divided in the following manner to wit; That it shall be divided by a committee of five men, who shall be elected and chosen, as follows to wit; Each of my said daughters shall select a man, and the four men so selected shall chose the fifth man, not one of the five men so selected is to be of kin to either of my said daughter or their said husbands, and the said five men when selected shall divide my lands equally between my four daughters as above stated:

It is further my will that in the event any per- (P.403) sonal Estate is left after the payment of my said debts and my said daughters do not agree among themselves as to a division of it by the time said five commissioners are selected to divide my said real estate then that the said five men chosen to divide said real estate ~~then that the said five men~~ shall divide also said personalty equaly between my four daughters as above stated:

And it is further my will that no debt that I have against any daughter of mine up to this date, whether the same is charged upon my books or not shall be collected of her or charged against her as an advancement, nor shall any gift heretofore made by me to any of my said daughters be charged as an advancement unless it is so stated in a conveyance by which the gift was made. It is also my will that no son in law of mine be charged with or be made to account for any board while living at my house. It is further my will that my said four sons in law to wit Geo. E. Scott J. M. Brackin, Ed. M. King and Frank Summers be appointed and act as the executor of this my last will and testament and that they be not required to give bond as such executors they being relieved by me from giving bond.

It is further my will that in the event for any cause any one of my said daughter refuse to select one of the said five men to act as commissioner to divide said real and personal property as required by this will then the Executor who is the husband of one refusing shall select one of said committee.

Witness my hand this January 11th 1888,

            A. M. Stevens

Signed and acknowledged by the testator A. M. Stevens in our presence as his will and signed by us as witnesses thereto in

(P.403 Cont'd) the presence of the Testator, and in the presence of each other. Witness our hands this January 11th 1888

        M.M. Marshall
        T. L. Wells
        B. B. Watkins
        B. L. Thomas

(P.404)

In the matter of the last Will and Testament of A. M. Stevens dec'd) This day a paper writing purporting to be the last will and testament of A. M. Stevens Deceased was presented by Geo. E. Scott, Dr. Frank Summers, J. M. Brackin and Ed. M. King the Executor named therein in open court and asked that the same be admitted to probate and set up and established as the last will and Testament of said A. M. Stevens dec'd and moved the Court, that the same be done and that they (the said Scott, Summers, Brackin and King) be appointed and qualified as said Executors, and thereupon comes T. L. Wells, M. M. Marshall and B. B. Watkins, three of the subscribing witnesses thereto to said paper writing or will, and being duly sworn testify and say, that they knew the said A. M. Stevens in his lifetime, that he is now dead and that his place of residence at the time of his death was in Dyer County that said paper writing is the last will and testament of said A. M. Stevens Dec'd and that the said Testator (A. M. Stevens) signed the same in their presence as his last will and testament and also in the presence of B. L. Thomas another subscribing witness, also that they (said M. M. Marshall, T. L. Wells B. L. Thomas and B. B. Watkins) all signed said paper writing at the instance and the request of said A. M. Stevens as witnesses as aforesaid that they signed it in his (said A. M. Stevens) presence and in the presence of each other, and they further testify that said testator A. M. Stevens was at the time of the execution of said will and testament of sound mind and disposing memory. And it appearing to the Court that said paper writing is proven to be the last will and testament of said A. M. Stevens dec'd - that as such the same has been properly proven witnessed and executed and should be admitted to probate and set up and established as such.

It is therefore ordered, adjudged by the court, that said paper writing be and the same is hereby admitted to probate and set up and established as the last will and Testament of said (P.405) A. M. Stevens deceased and it is accordingly done and it is accordingly ordered to be filed and recorded by the Clerk of this Court.

 And on motion of said Geo. E. Scott, J. M. Brackin Frank Summers and Ed. M. King, the Executors named in said will and it appearing that they are entitled to be the Executor thereof being so named in the will.

 It is therefore ordered and adjudged that said Geo. E. Scott Ed. M. King J. M. Brackin and Frank Summers be and the

(258)

(P.405 Cont'd) same are hereby appointed as the Executors of said last will and testament, and thereupon comes the said Geo. E. Scott Frank Summers E. M. King & J. M. Brackin into open Court and qualified as such Executor as required by law, the Execution of bond by them as such being waived and excused by the terms of the will the same need not be and Executed by them. Let Letters Testamentary issue &c.

(P.406)

The Last Will & Testament)	I, Elizabeth W. Smith of
of Mrs. Elizabeth Smith dec'd(	Dyer County Tennessee, being
Probated August term 1888)	of sound mind and disposing
Recorded August 8th 1888 (	memory but in feeble health
Will L. Wilkerson Clerk)	in body by age recognizing

the uncertainty of life and the certainty of death, do make publish this my last will and testament hereby revoking and setting aside all former wills at any time made by me.

Item 1st I desire my Executor to pay all just debts and charges against my estate out of the first money coming into his hands as executor

Item 2nd I bequeath to my Nephew **Daniel E. Parker** Twenty Six Hundred Dollars with interest on same from February the 8th 1873 until paid

Item 3rd After the payment of the $2600.00 and the interest on same to said D. E. Parker. I bequeath and devise the rest and remainder of my Estate both real and personal as follows, to wit;

One half to my Brother James M. Smith of Martinville Virginia, One fourth to my Nephew D. E. Parker; One Twenty fourth to my grand nephew J. Polk Harris a son of my niece Mary Ann Harris in his own right and the remaining 5/24 to J. Polk Harris interest for his mother my niece Mary Ann Harris for and during her natural life (and direct that he invest the money and rent on the lands) and at the death of my niece Mary Ann Harris, I will and bequeath that the property herein given her for life be divided equally between her five children Mrs. M. E. Parks Bright Harris Mollie A. Harris Daniel Harris and Stonewall Harris

Item 4 : I bequeath my household furniture to my nephew Daniel E. Parker and my niece Mary Ann Harris to be divided between them as I may hereafter direct

Item 5th I nominate and appoint my nephew Daniel E. Parker Executor of this my last will and testament and having full confidence (P.407) in him I direct that he shall not be required to give any bond as my Executor.

In witness whereof I hereunto Subscribe my name This October the 13, 1879, Interlined before signed

E. W. Smith

(P.407 Cont'd) The said Elizabeth W. Smith signed this instrument and published and declared the same to be her last will and testament, and we at her request and in her presence and in the presence of each other have hereunto written our names as subscribing witnesses. This Oct. 13th 1879

M. J. Hart
G. A. Finch

Owing to changes that have occured since writing and publishing the foregoing instrument I, Elizabeth W. Smith hereby execute the following as an alteration of and addition to the foregoing revoking wherein inconsistent and republishing the body of this instrument wherein not conflicting or inconsistent with this codicil Since my brother James M. Smith of Martinville has lately died I desire the portion above bequeathed to him, to be bequeathed to divided among his ~~children~~ and heirs. 2nd Since Daniel Harris has also died I desire his portion to go to his remaining brother and sister and a similar provision to take effect in case of the death of any of the members of said family of children, dying without heirs of the body.

3rd: I further devise that the portion of Mary Ann Harris instead of being committed to J. P. Harris as trustee be given her Mary Ann Harris in her own right

In testimony whereof I have this day subscribed my name
This __ day of __ 1884

E. W. Smith

We witness that the said E. W. Smith Executed and signed the foregoing as an amendment of the foregoing last will and testament at her request in her presence and the presence of each other we hereby subscribe our names as witnesses to the same
This __ day of __ 1884

M. J. Hart
G. A. Finch

(P.408)
In the matter of the last Will and Testament of Mrs. Elizabeth W. Smith dec'd

This day a paper writing purporting to be the last will and testament of Elizabeth W. Smith deceased was produced before the Court for probate by D. E. Parker which paper writing consisted of a will duly signed in presence of witnesses and codicil thereto Thereupon came into open Court M. J. Hart and G. A. Finch Subscribing witnesses thereto who being first duly sworn, deposed & said that they were personally acquainted with the said Elizabeth W. Smith in her lifetime That she was of sound mind and disposing memory at the time of the execution of said paper writing as her last will and testament that she signed and published said paper writing as her last will and Testament in their presence as witnesses thereto and requested them to sign as witnesses to her act in so doing that they signed same in her presence and in presence of each other witnessing said

(P.408 Cont'd)   paper writing as her deliberate act;

Thereupon came D. E. Parker who is named in said paper writing as the Executor thereof into open Court and was sworn as the law directs in such cases without filing or giving any bond the necessity of same being waived in said instrument.

(P.409)
The Last Will & Testament) I, S. A. E. Yancy being of
of S. A. E. Yancy Deceased (sound mind do this day make
Probated at the October term /88) this my "Last Will And
Recorded October 4th 1888 (Testament" I will and be-
William L. Wilkerson Clerk) queath to my son F. J.
Yancy all of my present Tract of land lying on South side of the Road Running East and West in front of my Residence and also Thirteen acres lying on the north side of the road and it being Situated in the North west corner of said Tract of land said Thirteen (13) acres is to be taken out of the north west Corner of said land and to join the other land on the South side of said Road and the remainder of said tract of land named not otherwise disposed of is to go my Daughter E. G. Howell and I also give my Daughter E. G. Howell my Buggy and I also give to my Son J. H. Yancy one Bed Bed clothes and one Bedstead, and the remainder of my household and kitchen furniture Farming Tools and what stock I may have at my death and my personally all of it that I have on hand at my death including crops wheat growing in the field or gathered after all of my debts are paid and all my notes on hand at my death shall go to my Son T. J. Yancy; and I desire this to be my last will and Testament, and I desire that my son T. J. Yancy, shall be my Executor and pay my debts out of my property left at my death, and I desire that he shall carry out this will as Executor without giving any Bond or security this August 3rd 1888

                                        S. A. E. Yancy
Attest
J. J. Yates
U. C. O'Neil

(P.410)
In the matter of the   ) This day a paper writing purporting
Last Will and Testament(to be the last will and testament
of S. A. E. Yancy Dec'd) of S. A. E. Yancy Deceased was pro-
                         duced before the court for probate
by T. J. Yancy, which paper writing consisted of a will duly signed in the presence of witnesses, thereupon came here into open Court J. J. Yates and U. C. Neil subscribing witnesses thereto who being first duly sworn deposed and said that they were personally acquainted with said S. A. E. Yancy in her lifetime that she was of sound mind and disposing memory at the time of the Execution of said Paper writing, That she signed and published the said paper writing as her last will and Testament in their presence as witnesses thereto and requested them to sign as witnesses to her act in so doing that they signed same in her presence and in the pres-

(P.410 Cont'd) ence of each other Witnessing said paper writing as her deliberate act.

(P.411)

The Last Will & Testament of)	In the Name of God Amen; I
Hamilton Parks Dec'd (	Hamilton Parks, of Dyer County
Probated October Term 1888)	Tennessee, being of sound mind,
Recorded Oct. 16th 1888 (	and disposing memory do make
Will L. Wilkerson Clerk)	and publish this my last will
	and testament hereby revoking

and making void all former wills made by me.

Item 1, I direct my Executors to pay all my just debts and funeral expenses, and for such monuments as they think proper for myself and my wife Rebecca Parks.

Item 2, I gave my son Wm. G. Parks and his children $1000.00 and I give to his son E. E. Parks for life, and at his death to his lawful isue my Murray tract of 200 acres of land in 15th district of Dyer County and partly in Gibson County and value it at Five Thousand Dollars, and all my King tract in 15th district Dyer County, except 100 acres on west side of same and south of the creek and value it at Seven Thousand Four Hundred and Twenty Five Dollars. Should E. E. Parks leave no lawful isue at his death the land herein given to him for life is to revert to my estate.

Item 3, I give to my sons Smith Parks and B. R. Parks, or the survivors of them in trust for the sole and separate use and benefit of my son Robert H. Parks one of my brick store houses and lots in Newbern Tennessee fronting on Main Street 26 feet and running North 140 feet, also all of lot No. 3 of my Dougherty & Phillips land in 9th district of Obion County Tennessee, except 20 acre off the west side of same, also also my undivided 7/10 interest in the narrow strip of land 8½ poles wide south of same being in all 160 or 175 acres and I value said store house and lot and said land at Five Thousand Dollars and I also give to them in trust a note on my brother Smith Parks for $2040.00 and interest from Feby 20th 1888 making to Feby 20th 1889 $2162.00 and if I renew the note they are to have the renewal note which note my executors are not to pay until it suits my brother to pay but they may renew the note and collect the interest accruing after my death, and collect rent on the store house and from commencing Jan. 1st after my death and after retaining for taxes expenses and services apply the
(P.412) remainder of the net rents and interests or so much thereof as may be necessary for the best interest of my son Robert H. Parks. This with what I have heretofore given to my son Robert H. Parks is all that he is to have of my estate. If at his death he leaves lawful isue then surviving then the property given to his brothers for his use is to go to his lawful isue in fee - but should he leave no lawful isue living at his death the property herein given is to revert to my estate

Item 4, I have given to my son Smith Parks Twelve Thousand Four Hundred and Twenty Five and 85/100 Dollars, and I give to

(P.412 Cont'd) him an undivided one half of the ___ one of my brick stores & lots in Newbern fronting 20 feet on Main street and running back North 140 feet and I value the half of said house and lot at Eleven Hundred and Twenty Five Dollars.

Item 5 - I gave to my Daughter Mary Jane Cunningham $1650.00 and I now give to her daughters Cora Lee Baker and Mollie Lou Williams for life all my Spencer tract of land in 9th district Obion County Tennessee (except the ell of 137 acres which I have sold) containing about 317 acres which I value to them at Eight Thousand Dollars and as they are well provided for this is all they are to have of my estate, and as their brother Jo. H. Cunningham has had considerable property given, and is inclined to be wild and dissipated, I do not think that he would be benefitted by giving him other property, and as I have heretofore given him some money he is to have no part of my estate left at my death. The land herein given to my grand-daughters for life is leased until 1892 and my executors are to pay the taxes on same until 1892. The land herein given to my grand-daughters for life, is at their death to go to their children in fee - but if at the death of the survivors of them they should leave no isue then living the land herein given to them is to revert to my estate.

Item 6 - I gave to my Son A. S. Parks $3440.00 and I give to his children Harris Hamilton, Andrew S. and Faustina Parks for life the following land in 9th (P.413) district Obion County Tennessee viz Lots No's 1 & 2 and 20 acres off the west of Lot 3 of my Daughty & Phillips tract and my undivided 7/10 interest in the narrow strip of land 8½ poles wide south of same, the whole being about 765 acres which I value to them at Ten Thousand Dollars, Said land to be held in common by them until 1899 At the death of said grandchildren the land herein given to them for life is to go to their lawful isue per ___ but should they leave no lawful isue living at the death of the survivors of them the land is to revert to my estate. I appoint my sons H. Parks Jr. and B. R. Parks guardians of my said grandchildren to act without bond and wish them to have said grandchildren well educated provided they will take an education and to do this said guardians may use the net rents as a common fund to educate those needing an education, and they need not make any settlement until January 1, 1899

Item 7, I have given to my daughter Parina V. Wyatt $8192.00 and I now give to her for life and at her death to her children in fee my H. H. Headen 70 acres in 15th district Dyer County and partly in Gibson County and value same at Two Thousand Dollars also my W. C. Williamson 73 acres in 15th district Dyer County and 100 acres of King tract adjoining the 73 acres lying on the west of the King tract and south of the creek and I value same at Three Thousand Eight Hundred and Ninety Two 50/100 Dollars If she dies before her husband Col. J. N. Wyatt he is to have a life estate in said lands. I have a note on J. N. Wyatt for $394.00 due January 1st 1887 credited same date with $17.20 leaving a balance of $376.80 and I direct my executors so count the interest on said note at annual ___ until January 1st of the year after my death

(P.413 Cont'd) and then to deliver said note to my daughter charging her with the principal and interest due on same

Item 8 I have given to my son H. Parks Jr. Twelve Thousand Eight Hundred and Fifty Five Dollars

Item 9 I have given to my son B. R. Parks Six Thousand Three Hundred Dollars and I now give him my 120 acres in 9th district Dyer County called the McKee place and value it at Three Thousand Dollars and I also give to him (P.414) my Norsworthy Johnston and Herron houses and lots in Newbern and value them at Seventeen Hundred and Fifty Dollars and I give him the middle one of my brick stores & lots in Newbern fronting 20 ft. on Main Street and running North 140 ft. and an undivided half of the ___ one of my brick stores & lots in Newbern joining the middle store and lot, and I value the middle store and lot at Two Thousand Dollars and the undivided half interest in the Eastern store and lot at Eleven Hundred and Twenty Five Dollars

Item 10 I have given to my daughter Lutie A. Tigrett $2150.00 and I now give to her for life, and then to her children in fee the following lands in 9th district Dyer County Tennessee viz. the 224 acres where she lives and value the same at Eight Thousand Five Hundred and Fifteen Dollars, and the 95 acres in my ___ and Turner tracts which I value at Two Thousand Three Hundred and Seventy Five Dollars and my Cox store house and lot in Newbern 30 by 127 feet and value same at Twelve Hundred and Fifty Dollars. Should she die before her husband A. B. Tigrett he is to have a life Estate in said lands.

Item 11 Several of the houses on the lots herein given are insured and should they burn the insurance money collected is to go to the parties who were to get the houses.

Item 12 I direct my executors to collect the rents on all the lands and store houses herein devised until December 31st after my death and use said rents as assets of my estate.

Item 13 I have a number of notes and judgements which I intend to give to my children and grandchildren at my death, and to designate in writing which notes and judgements are to go to my different legatees, and the price or value I charge on same and I direct my executors to deliver said notes and judgements without recourse on my estate and at the price I charge for same

Item 14 I give the following articles without charge viz. to Robert H. Parks my silver watch to Smith Parks my gold watch to H. Parks Jr. my gold headed walking cane (P.415) to B. R. Parks, my silver headed walking cane and writing desk, to J. N. Wyatt my Knights ___ sword and regalia, to A. B. Tigrett my 45 volumes American Tract Society Books and case holding same, and I request my daughters Parina and Lutie or the survivor of them to divide my household furniture and table ware among my children and daughters-in-law according to the wishes

(P.415 Cont'd)   of their mother, all without charges.

Item 15   I give my executors in settling my estate full power and authority without the aid or intervention of any court to buy any land on which I may leave the purchase money or mortgage notes and to compromise any claims or debts for or against my estate in any manner they may deem best in order to avoid the delay expenses and uncertainty of litigation.

Item 16   I have in this will and heretofore given to the following named children and grandchildren as follows.

To Wm. G. Parks and E. E. Parks	$13425.00
To A. S. Parks and his children	$13440.00
To P. V. Wyatt and her children	$14084.50
To L. A. Tigrett and her children	$14290.00
To Smith Parks	$13550.85
To H. Parks Jr.	$12855.00
To B. R. Parks	$14175.00

Making a total to the above named children and grandchildren of Ninety Five Thousand Eight Hundred and Twenty and 35/100 Dollars, and I desire direct that all the parties mentioned in this item be made equal in the final distribution of my estate, giving to Wm. G. Parks and E. E. Parks a childs part, to A. S. Parks and his children a childs part to P. V. Wyatt and her children a childs part to L. A. Tigrett and her children a childs part, to Smith Parks, H. Parks Jr. and B. R. Parks each and every one a childs part, and I give to the above named parties all the rest and residue of my estate both real and personal and if the property herein given to Smith Parks and B. R. Parks in trust or to E. E. Parks or Cora Lee Baker and Mattie Lou Williams (P.416) or to any of my other grandchildren for life should revert to my estate, the same is to go to those parties, above named in this item. And the property herein given to my children and grandchildren is to be divided among them so as to produce perfect equality charging them with the amounts therein charged to them

Item 17   I nominate and appoint my sons H. Parks Jr. and B. R. Parks or the survivor of them executors of this will.

Item 18   I most ernestly request all my children and grandchildren to live honestly and uprightly; to be fair and just in all their dealings with their fellow men; to take the Bible as their great guide in life, to read it, study it and obey its precepts, and to live humble devoted, sincere christian lives, so that, when done with this world, we may all be reunited in a far happier and better world than this, The foregoing eleven pages and eighteen items contain my last will and testament, In witness whereof I do hereunto subscribe my name in the presence of Guy Douglass Jas. W. Hamilton, and M. C. Hamilton, whom I request to witness the same on this the 28th day of August 1888

                                                H. Parks

(P.416 Cont'd) Signed and acknowledged in our presence and we hereunto subscribed our names as witnesses to same in the presence of the Testator, and of each other, and at the request of the testator on this the 28th day of August 1888

                                        Guy Douglass
                                        Joe H. Hamilton
                                        M. C. Hamilton

(P.417)
In the Matter of the   )
Last Will and Testament(
of Hamilton Parks dec'd)

Hamilton Parks Jr. and B. R. Parks produced in open Court a paper writing purporting to be the Last Will and Testament of Reverend Hamilton Parks deceased, in which the said Hamilton Parks Jr. and B. R. Parks are named executors, and thereupon came Guy Douglass, James H. Hamilton and M. C. Hamilton subscribing witnesses to said Will, who being duly sworn said, that they knew the said Hamilton Parks during his life, that he resided in Dyer County at the time of the execution of said will, and that he signed and acknowledged the said paper writing here offered for probate, in their presence, as his last will and testament, and requested them to witness the same, and that they signed said will as witnesses thereto in his presence and at his request, and in the presence of each other, and on the date stated in said will, and that said Hamilton Parks was at the time he signed and acknowledged said will of sound mind and disposing memory, and that he afterwards died at his residence in Dyer County on the 13th day of September 1888, and that they were not interested in the said will, nor in the estate of the said Hamilton Parks and thereupon the said Hamilton Parks Jr. and B. R. Parks moved that said will be admitted to Probate and that Letters Testamentary Isue to them as Executors, and they brought with them into Court E. E. Parks and A. B. Tigrett their securities, and all said parties signed and acknowledged a bond in the Penal sum of Fifteen Thousand Dollars, conditioned and payable as the law directs, to be void in condition that said Hamilton Parks Jr. and B. R. Parks faithfully perform their duty as executors of said will, and account for and pay over the estate of their testator to the parties entitled thereto under said will. It is therefore ordered by the Court, that said paper writing be admitted to Probate and set up and established as the last will and testament of said Hamilton Parks deceased and that the same be recorded and filed. And that Letters Testamentary isue to said Hamilton Parks Jr. and B. R. Parks.

A true copy of original Will and Probate of same

                    Attest
                                        W. L. Wilkerson
                                            Clerk

(P.418 Cont'd)

The Last Will and Testament of W. M. Woodard Dec'd Probated November Term 1888 Recorded November 7th, 1888 W. L. Wilkerson Clerk	The last Will and Testament of W. M. Woodard made in his last Sickness; I will my beloved wife Martha my Tract of land and farm and all belonging thereunto; To have and to hold her lifetime or

while she remains my widow; At her death or should she marry again I will said tract of land and farm to Thomas Trout he being a child in my care, out of my personal property. I will that all of my just debts be paid and I request my Brother in law A. J. Grills to be my Executor and also a Guardian for said Thomas Trout This September the 29, 1888

Witnessed by -   W. M. Woodard
S. S. McCorkle
J. F. Taylor

(P.419)

In the Matter of the Last Will and Testament of W. M. Woodard dec'd	This day a paper writing purporting to be the last will and testament of W. M. Woodard deceased was pre-

sented to the Court by A. J. Grills who is named as Executor in said will and thereupon came S. S. McCorkle and J. F. Taylor Subscribing witnesses to said will who being first duly sworn said that they knew the said W. M. Woodard in his lifetime that he resided in Dyer County at the time of the Execution of said will and that he signed and acknowledged said paper writing here offered for Probate in their presence as his last will and Testament and requested them to witness the same and that they signed the said will as witnesses thereto in his presence and in the presence of each other and on the date stated in said will; and that he W. M. Woodard was at the time of the signing of said will of sound mind and disposing memory and that he afterwards died in Dyer County and that they are of no kin to the said W. M. Woodard Deceased nor in any manner interested in the estate of said W. M. Woodard Dec'd and thereupon the said A. J. Grill moved the Court that said will be admitted to Probate and that letters Testamentary issue to him &c as Executor; And thereupon came the said A. J. Grill here into open Court together with Jno. E. McCorkle and McCorkle & Tipton his securities and they entered into and acknowledged bond in the penal sum of Five Hundred Dollars. Conditioned and payable as the law directs for the faithful performance of his duties as such Executor whereupon the said A. J. Grill was duly sworn let letters issue &c

A true copy of the Original Will and Probate of same

Attest Will L. Wilkerson
Clerk.

(P.420)
The last Will and Testament)   I, B. T. Witt being of sound mind
of B. T. Witt Deceased   (do make and publish this as my
Probated December Term /88)   last will and Testament hereby
Recorded December 4th 1888 (revoking and making void all other
Will L. Wilkerson Clerk   )   wills writings of all ever charac-
                                                                          ter by me at any time made

1st I desire that my funeral expenses and all my just debts be paid as soon after my death as possible out of any moneys that I may die possessed of or may first come into the hands of my executors

2nd I give and bequeath to my beloved wife Elvira Isabelle Witt - all of my real estate consisting of my home and farm in the 7th Civil District of Dyer County Tenn. containing (94½) ninety four and one half acres, be the same more or less - for and during her natural life

3rd I also give and bequeath to my beloved wife Elvira Isabelle Witt - all of my personal property - consisting of household and kitchen furniture horses, cows, hogs sheep &c during her natural life and for her sole use and benefit.

4th I give and bequeath at the death of my beloved wife Elvira Isabelle Witt - To my five youngest children viz - Martha Emaline Witt, Mary Isabelle Witt, Lillie Maud Witt, Albert Sidney Witt and Robert Algie Witt, The use and benefit of the farm and personal property that may be on hand at the death of my wife during their single or unmarried life - share and share alike I mean by this that the above mentioned children are to have the benefit of the rents of said farm during the entire time that any one of the above five mentioned children remain single or unmarried share and share alike in the rents and profits of said farm above and before mentioned

(P.421) 5th I give and bequeath at the death of my beloved wife Elvira Isabelle to my two sons Carter Harrison Witt and William Butler Witt one horse each to be selected by my Executors from any stock on the farm. At the death of my wife Elvira Isabelle Witt.

6th I give and bequeath to my sons Thomas Josephus Witt Clayton Hamilton Witt, Carter Harrison Witt and William Butler Witt the sum of (10) Ten Dollars each to be payed by my Executors out of my money that may come into their hands from my estate.

7th I hereby direct and request that my two sons William Butler Wit and Clayton Hamilton Witt have full controll and management of the farm for their Mother during her life and at her death to continue the management and controll of the farm for the use and benefit of the five youngest children viz. Martha Emaline -Mary Isabelle, Lillie Maud - Albert Sidney and Robert Algie - till each and every one of the above mentioned children are married - as before selected.

(P.421 Cont'd) 8th The property going to my daughters from my estate - or inherited by them from me - I direct that the same go to them free from the debts contracts or controll of their husbands and as a separate estate for their owne use and benefit

9th I direct and request that my Executors after the death of my wife to repair and fix up our graves - and erect tombstones over the same and to pay for the same out of the first money that may come into their hands from my estate.

10th I direct that my Executors after the death of my wife - and the marriage of the five youngest children before mentioned, that they sell the real estate before mentioned, and all the personal property and divide the proceeds of the same equally between all my children share and share alike

(P.422) 11th Lastly I do hereby nominate and appoint my two sons William Butler Witt and Clayton Hamilton Witt my Executors - and waive the necesity of their giving bond as required by law.

Witness my hand, This July 28th 1888

B. X T. Witt

This will was read over to B. T. Witt signed and published in our presence - and we have subscribed our names hereto in the presence of the Testator - and at his request, This July 28th 1888

W. S. Coover
W. C. Winford

In the Matter of the last)
Will and Testament of   (This day a paper writing purport-
B. T. Witt Deceased   ) ing to be the last will and Testament of B. T. Witt deceased was presented by William B. Witt and Clayton H. Witt the Executors named in said will and asked that the same be admitted to probate and set up and established as the last will will and testament of the said B. T. Witt deceased and moved the court that the same be done and that they the said (W. B. Witt and C. H. Witt) be appointed and qualified as executors; and thereupon come W. S. Coover and W. C. Winfred, Two subscribing witnesses to said will and being duly sworn testafied and said that they knew the said B. T. Witt in his life time that he is now dead, That his place of residence was in Dyer County at the time of his death, that the said paper writing is the last will and testament of said B. T. Witt Dec'd and that the said Testator (B. T. Witt) signed the same in their presence; and that they signed the said will at the request and in the presence of the testator and in the presence of each other as witnesses thereto and that the said B. T. Witt was at the time of the execution of said will of sound mind and disposing memory it appearing to the Court, (P.423) that said paper writing has been property proven to be the last will and

(269)

(P.423 Cont'd) testament It is therefore ordered by the court that said paper writing be admitted to probate and set up and established as the last will and Testament of the said B. T. Witt dec'd. and it is ordered to be recorded and filed by the clerk of this court and on motion W. B. Witt and C. H. Witt the executors named in said will and it appearing to the court that they are entitled to the Execution of said estate being so named in said will. It is therefore ordered and adjudged by the Court that the said W. B. Witt and C. H. Witt be and they are hereby appointed Executors of said Last will and Testament. And thereupon come the said W. B. Witt and C. H. Witt here into open Court and were duly qualified as such executors as required by law the execution of Bond being waived and excused by the terms of said Will the same need not be executed by them. Let Letters issue the them &c.

A true copy of original and probate of same
        Attest
        Will L. Wilkerson
          Clerk.

(P.424)
Last Will and Testament) Will and Testamony of Sam'l
of Samuel Fumbanks dec'd(Fumbanks
Probated Dec. term 1888)
Recorded Dec. 6th 1888 (I Sam'l Fumbanks being in my right
Will L. Wilkerson clk.   ) mind do hereby give and bequeath
to my wife Judy Fumbanks all of my property that I may now owne Land and personal property. And all money and notes, untill her death and then to go as stated below, I do give and bequeath to my Daughter Liza Edney 2 and ½ acres of the Harton piece of land on the East end and to my son Jack Fumbank 2 and a ½ west of Lizas; and to my daughter, Lean Brewer the remainer of said track being on the west end. And to my Daughter Betty Smith my house and 2 and a ½ acres on the East end of the first track bought from W. P. Fowlkes, and to my grand-daughter Lindy Smith 2 and a ½ acres west of Betty's Smiths of the same track, and to my great grand child Emily Fumbank the remainer of said track and to my daughter Jane Fowlkes 2 acres on the East end of the sechon track of land bought from W. P. Fowlkes, and to my son Allen Fumbanks 2 acres west of Jane Fowlkes of said track. And to my grand Son Henry Fumbanks the remainer of said track on the west end.

Witness my hand this 16 day of March 1888

        Sam X Fumbanks
    (witness) Sam J. Pierce
    (witness) G. W. Pierce Jr.
    (witness) J. S. Perry

(P.425)
In the Matter of the   )
Last Will and Testament(This day a paper writing purporting
of Sam'l Fumbanks Dec'd) to be the last will and Testament
of Sam'l Fumbanks dec'd was presented by G. W. Pierce Jr. one of the subscribing witnesses

(270)

(P.425 Cont'd) thereto and asked that the same be admitted to probate and set up and established as the last will and Testament of the said Sam'l Fumbanks deceased and moved the court that the same be done; and thereupon come the said Geo. W. Pierce Jr. and Sam'l J. Pierce subscribing witnesses to said will and being duly sworn testafied and said that they knew the said Sam Fumbanks in his lifetime - that he is now dead; that his place of residence was in Dyer County at the time of his death that the said paper writing is the last will and Testament of the said Samuel Fumbanks and that the said Testator was at the time of the Execution of said will of sound mind and disposing memory and that said Testator and in the presence of each other as witnesses thereto, and it appearing to the court that said paper writing has been properly proven to be the last Will and Testament of said Sam'l Fumbanks dec'd - It is therefore ordered by the court that said paper writing be admitted to probate and set up and established as the last will and Testament of the said Sam'l Fumbanks Deceased and it is ordered by the court to be recorded in Will Book and filed by the Clerk.

A true copy of original will and probate of same

                Attest
                Will L. Wilkerson
                      Clerk

(P.426)
Last Will and Testament) Will and Testament of M. T. Bracken
of M. T. Bracken dec'd   (I, M. T. Braken do will, being of
Probated Jan. Term /89   ) sound mind - That my wife Annie M.
W. L. Wilkerson Clerk   (Bracken do pay first my official
debts, if any.

2nd Any other property authenticated debt I may owe to any individual provided always same shall be properly authenticated and legal, All this is to be done out of the proceeds of my policy in the Knight and Ladies of Honor and the balance after such disbursements as mentioned above to go to my wife Annie M. Braken, This February 1st 1887

                M. T. Braken -

In the matter of Probate)
of M. T. Bracken's last (This day came P. J. Weiner and
Will and Testament   ) presented to the Court a paper
writing purporting to be the last Hollographic Last will and Testament of M. T. Bracken dec'd and the said P. J. Weiner being first duly sworn testified that he was personally acquainted with M. T. Bracken dec'd and with his hand writing and that he found the paper writing, here presented to the Court, among the valuable papers of the said M. T. Bracken dec'd and that he verily beleaved that the said paper writing and evry part thereof to be in the handwriting of the said M. T. Bracken dec'd having seen him write

(P.426 Cont'd) and and seen him writing for a number of years and that he has no doubt but that evry word of the paper writing here offered as aforesaid including the signature thereof is in the proper handwriting of the said M. T. Bracken dec'd and thereupon came also into open Court J. T. Boon W. B. Sampson, W. E. Bell and John W. Lauderdale who being duly sworn testified that for many years they were acquainted with M. T. Bracken dec'd and with his handwriting have seen him write and seen him writing frequently and that his handwriting is generally known by his acquaintances the said Bracken having been Cou Court Clk. for number of years (P.427) That they have examined carfully the paper writing here presented to the court for Probate as the Holographic Last will and Testament of M. T. Bracken dec'd and they testify that evry word of said paper writing is in the proper and genuine handwriting of M. T. Bracken dec'd it is therefore ordered by the court that the said paper writing be and the same is hereby set up and established as the last will and Testament of the said M. T. Bracken dec'd and that the same be recorded in the will Book and filed with the Records of this Court and thereupon came P. J. Weiner into open Court with his securities and qualified as Admr. Com Testimento Annexo of the Estate of said M. T. Bracken dec'd. The widow of said Bracken and next of him refusing to qualify as such.

(P.428)
In the Matter of Last Will and Testament of William Fuller dec'd Probated March term /89 Recorded March 6th /89 Will L. Wilkerson Clk.

I, William Fuller being of sound mind & disposing memory but in feeble health do make & publish this as my last Will & Testament, hereby revoking all wills by me at any time made.

First, I desire all my just debts be paid by my Executors out of the first money that comes to his hands or as soon after my death as may be,

Second, I give to my beloved wife Mary A. Fuller my whole estate real personal & mixed during her natural life or widowhood subject to the following restrictions and limitations. She is to manage the same So as that it is not to suffer loss or be permitted to run to waste and is to use the home and farm for the benefit of the family as long as the children remain single unless after they arrive at 21 years of age they choose to remove from their old home. And my beloved wife is also to give my son William a reasonable English Education out of the proceeds of S'd farm stock &c. without any charge to him and my two youngest daughters Louisa Harriet and Lenora are to be educated so as to enable them to read and write well and there is to be no additional charge against them for such Education but the same is to be paid for from the proceeds of the farm stock &c.

Item Third, At the death or marriage of my beloved wife I desire my whole remaining Estate or what is left of my Estate real personal or mixed evry thing that is then or have to be sold by my Executors and the real estate conveyed without the aid of any court on such terms as sd Executors may deem most for the interest of my heirs and the proceeds to be by said Executors equally

(272)

(P.428 Cont'd) divided between my children as follows; Martha C. Jackson one share, Mary Elizabeth Fuller one share Louisa Harriet one share and Lenora one share and William C. one share.

My daughter Stacy Ann Rebecca having married against my wishes and advise and in spite of my remonstrances, I feel it to be my duty to exclude her from the benefits of this (P.429) will. I therefore direct my Executors not to include her in the division of my Estate.

Item Fourth, if my beloved wife should marry again it is not my intentions to exclude her from the benefits of my estate but in the event of her marriage I direct that she have dower in my real estate & a childs part of the personal property just as though this will had not been made.

I hereby appoint Smith Parks and Michail O. King Executors of this my last will and Testament and in the event my beloved wife may think it best to sell part of the stock she may with the consent of my Executors sell such stock and use the proceeds in support of the family if necessary.
Sept. 6 1869
Witness   Wm. Fuller
J. W. Enochs
D. C. Simons

After mature reflection I have determined by this Codicile to change this my last will and Testament in regard to the property herein given to my four daughters Martha C. Jackson, Mary Elizabeth Johnson Louisa Harriet, & Lenora Fuller in so far that I will and direct that all the property of evry kind & discription whatsoever it may be whether real personal or mixed to which my said four daughters may be entitled to under this will I give to them for and during their natural lives, And is not to be subject to the control or liable to the debts of their present Husband, or any future husbands they may marry and at the death of my S'd daughters S'd property shall decend to the heirs of their body   January 31 1872

                                                     Wm. Fuller

(P.430)
In the Matter of the last will)   This day a paper writing pur-
and Testament of Wm. Fuller   )   porting to be the last will
                                    and Testament of Wm. Fuller
dec'd was presented to the Court for probate Thereupon came J. W. Enochs and D. C. Simons subscribing witnesses thereto who being first duly sworn deposed and said that they were personally acquainted with the said Wm. Fuller testator and that he signed and acknowledged the execution of said paper writing as his last will and Testament in their presence and for the purposes therein contained and requested them to bear witness thereto that he was of sound and disposing mind and memory at the time of the execution of the same that they signed their names as witnesses thereto in the presence of the testator and at his request and D. C. Simons a subscribing witness to the Codicile of said will came into open Court

(273)

(P.430 Cont'd) and first being duly sworn testified and said that he was personally acquainted with the said Wm. Fuller testator in his lifetime that he signed said Codicile as a Codicile of his said last will and testament and that he signed and witnessed the same in his presence and at his request as a Codicile of his (Fullers) Last Will and Testament that he was of sound and disposing mind and memory at the time of the execution of said Codicile - And also came M. C. King and Smith Parks who being first duly sworn deposed and said that they were acquainted with the handwriting of Geo. B. Fuller another witness to the Codicile of said will and that they know that the signature of his name to said Codicile is in his (Fullers) proper handwriting. It is therefore ordered by the court that said last will and testament and Codicile thereto be and the same is hereby admitted to probate and set up and established as the last will and testament of the said Wm. Fuller dec'd and ordered to be recorded in Will Book and filed and Smith Parks and M. O. King the Executors named in said will refused to qualify as such and it appearing to the Court that C. L. (P.431) Claiborne is the proper person to administer on said Wm. Fullers Estate. It is therefore ordered by the court that the said C. L. Claiborne be and he is hereby appointed Administrator Com Testamento Annexo of Said Wm. Fuller dec'd Whereupon the said C. L. Claiborne came here into open court together with M. O. King and Manual Johnson his securities and they entered into and acknowledged bond in the penal sum of Twenty five Hundred Dollars conditioned and payable as the law directs for the faithful performance of his duties as such Admr. whereupon the said C. L. Claiborne was duly sworn.

Let Letters issue
A true copy of original will and probate of Same

Attest; - W. L. Wilkerson Clk
By,   R. L. Palmer D. C.

(P.432)
Last Will and Testament) State of Tennessee
of Mrs. S. D. C. Morris dec'd(Dyer County
Probated March Term /89) in the Name of God Amen I
Recorded March 14th 1889 (Susan Delaney Celestial Morris
Will L. Wilkerson Clerk.) Wife of A. J. Morris and daughter of Nathan King dec'd being feeble in health but of sound mind do make and publish this my Last Will and Testament.

Item 1st I give and devise unto my Husband A. J. Morris for and during his natural life all the land and real estate that I now own or may be entitled to as the only living child of my deceased father Nathan King for him my said Husband to have and to hold and use all said land as he pleases during the whole of his natural life and this includes my reversion or remainder interest in the lands of my father which may be allotted to his widow Saluda King (my step mother) as her home stead and Dower interest in same.

(432 Cont'd) Item 2nd After the death of my husband A. J. Morris I will and devise and direct that all my said real estate be divided equally in value between my two children Mary Jewel Morris and John Nathan Morris share and share alike.

Item 3rd I give devise and bequeath unto my said husband A. J. Morris all my personal property of evry kind caracter and discription that I may own or be entitled to from the estate of my late father Nathan King for him my said husband to have own use and controll as he deems best and sees fit for himself and for the benefit of our two children Mary Jewel Morris and John Nathan Morris and I devise him to have both said children well educated while I have full confidence that he will do and at his death I wish him to do a good part by them in giving them personal property if he at that time owns sufficient personal property to do so - but I will and direct that my husband have all my said personal (P.433) property of evry kind caracter and discription that I may own or be entitled to from the estate of my said father Nathan King to have own use and control as he deems best without him being required to give any bond or make any settlement about same leaving it to him as the father of my children without any bond to have them well educated and to do a good part by and for them at his death.

In witness hereof I do hereunto subscribe my name at my residence in Dyer County Tennessee on this the 4th day of February 1885 in the presence of H. Parks Jr. Joseph T. Smith, Mrs. Tommie E. Smith and W. W. Smith whom I request to bear witness to the same.

        S. D. C. Morris

The above will was read over to Mrs. Susan Delaney Celestial Morris and signed and acknowledged by her in our presence to be her last Will and Testament and she desired us to bear witness to the same - and we the said H. Parks Jr. Joseph T. Smith Tommie E. Smith and W. W. Smith do sign this as witnesses in the presence of the Testatrix and at her request and in the presence of each other at her residence in Dyer County Tennessee on this the 4th day of February 1885

        H. Parks Jr.
        Joseph T. Smith
        Tommie E. Smith

I Susan D. C. Morris being of sound mind and disposing memory and being desirous of making some changes (as to the real estate) in the will executed by me heretofore on the 14th day of February 1885 do make and publish this Codicil to said will and hereby revoke any provision in the said will pertaining to my lands and real estate which may conflict with the provisions of this Codicil in any way.

I will direct and bequeath to my beloved husband A. J. Morris, if he shall survive me, all my right (P.434) title and

(P.434 Cont'd) interest in and to all the lands decended to me from the estate of my father Nathan King dec'd to be his in fee simple absolute to sell or dispose of at his pleasure and it is not intended that this Codicil shall effect the disposition of any of my personal effects as made in the foregoing will In witness whereof I hereunto subscribe my name on this April 12, 1885 in the presence of J. B. Turnley & J. W. Turney

In the Matter of the last) This day a paper writing purport-
will and Testament of   (ing to be the last will and Tes-
Mrs. S. D. C. Morris dec'd)   tament of Mrs. S. D. C. Morris
                               dec'd was presented to this Court
for probate and there upon came Joseph G. Smith and W. W. Smith two of the subscribing witnesses to the original will and after being duly sworn testify and say that they knew said S. D. C. Morris in her lifetime that she is dead and had her usual place of residence in Dyer County Tennessee at the time of her death, that said paper writing is her last will and Testament that said Testatrix signed the same in their presence as her last will and Testament and that they signed and witnessed the same in the presence of said Testatrix at her request as her last will and Testament and in the presence of each other and they further testified that said Testatrix was at the time of the execution of said original will and Testament, of sound mind and disposing memory and J. B. Turnley and J. W. Turney subscribing witnesses to the Codicil of said originial will and (P.435) Testament also came into open court and being duly sworn testify and say that they were personally acquainted with the said S. D. C. Morris dec'd in her lifetime that she signed said Codicil as a Codicil of her last will and Testament and that they signed and witnessed the same in her presence and at her request as a Codicil to her last Will and Testament and they further testify that said Testatrix was at the time of the execution of said Codicil of sound and disposing mind and memory. And it appearing to the court that said Last will and Testament and the Codicil thereto as before proven and shown is the last will and Testament of said S. D. C. Morris properly executed witnessed and proven and should be admitted to probate and set up and established as such. It is therefore ordered and adjudged by the Court that said paper-writing be and the same is hereby admitted to probate and set up and established as the Last will and testament together with said Codicil thereto of said S. D. C. Morris dec'd and it is ordered to be recorded by the clerk and filed And on motion and it appearing to the Court that A. J. Morris is the proper person to administer on the Estate of Said S. D. C. Morris. It is therefore ordered by the court that said A. J. Morris be and he is hereby appointed Administrator Com Testamento Annexo of all and singular Goods and Chattles Rights and Credits which ever of the said S. D. C. Morris dec'd Thereupon the said A. J. Morris came here into open Court together with W. A. Hodge and W. J. Miller his securities and they entered into and acknowledged bond in the penal sum of Three Thousand Dollars conditioned and payable as the law directs for the faithful performance of his duties as such

(276)

(P.435 Cont'd) Administrator. Whereupon the said A. J. Morris was duly sworn.

Let Letters issue

A true copy of original will and probate of same

Attest; W. L. Wilkerson Clk.

(P.436)

Last Will and Testament,	I Sallie H. Shelley being of sound
of Sallie H. Shelley dec'd	mind & of good memory & being in
Probated April Term 1889	good health but recognising the un-
Recorded April 9th 1889	certainty of human life do make and
W. L. Wilkerson Clerk	publish this my Last Will and Tes-
By R. L. Palmer D. C.	tament & hereby revoking & annull-
	ing any & all wills that I have

heretofore made.

1st I will that in case of my death that all my personal expenses & all just debts that I may owe shall be paid.

2nd I will and bequeath to my adopted daughter J. Blanch Shelley all of my personal and real Estate the Real Estate consisting of Six offices in the town of West Point Mississippi the same appearing by deeds to me executed to me under the following conditions & Specifications - that said J. Blanch Shelley shall remain in my undisturbed charge & control & after my death the undisturbed controll of the Guardian whom I shall appoint.

The above provision is made for the following reasons to wit; - that is to say in the year 1875 my late husband W. B. Shelley did take from the Orphran Home of the City of St. Louis the said child then known as Blanch Matgove - he executing a bond for her care and maintainance under the assurance of the authorities of said institution that she was an Orphan child & my late husband & myself did proceed to have her legally adopted by the Courts of Clay County State of Mississippi the same appearing of record in said Court. After having kept said child now 10 years one G. W. Margove comes to set up a claim that he is her father & that both Mother & Father are living Now should said parties proceed to establish their claim to said child and take her from me or the Guardian whom I shall appoint - then the devise of the property in this clause of the will shall be null & void & of none effect & should said child die before she becomes 21 years of age & die without bodily issue then the provision is also to be void and my property shall be distributed as hereinafter provided.

3rd I will that in case said child (J. Blanch Shelley) is removed and taken from me or (P.437) the Guardian whom I shall appoint in consideration of my love and devotion for and to said child & in consideration for the love and appreciation which she has ever shown me that she be made equal in the distribution of my property with my six (6) sisters - that is she receiving one seventh (1/7) of my Estate after satisfying the special bequest

(P.437 Cont'd) which I shall make.

4th In case of the removal or death of my adopted daughter from under my controll or the controll of the Guardian whom I shall appoint - then I will my personal property to wit; my furniture bed & bedding & Pianno also my wardrobe to my sister E. J. Williams or to her bodily heirs in case of her death.

5th I will that in the case of the death or removal from my care or the care of my appointed Agent of J. Blanch Shelley before she is 21 years of age - if she have no bodily issue by marriage that my Executor sell all my real Estate collect all notes bonds or other valuables I divide the amount equally between J. Blanch Shelley Mrs. E. J. Williams Mrs. Alice Whiteside Mrs. Kate Knott & Misses Nora, Clifford & Pearl Bowen

6th I will that in case of J. Blanch Shelley remaining under my controll & the controll of her Guardian by me appointed & she should marry & have legitimate issue & should die having a living child - the said child shall be her legal heir and reprasentative

7th I will that Louis M. Williams be Executor to this will and Guardian of my adopted daughter J. Blanch Shelley and that my sister E. J. Williams shall have controll & care of said child directing her education & seeing to all of her personal wants - That said Louis M. Williams & his wife E. J. Williams use as much of my property herein devised as is necessary to comfortably maintain & well educate said child.

8th My said Executor is authorized to sell any or all of my real Estate as he may think best for the interest of the parties concerned & execute deeds for the same & do any and all things necessary to the settling of my business. Made and executed this 26th day of September A. D. 1885

J. M. Senter, Witnesses
M. M. Senter   "

            Sallie H. Shelley

(P.438)
In the matter of the Last) This day a paper writing purport-
Will and Testament of   (ing to be the Last Will and Tes-
Salley H. Shelley dec'd) tament of Salley H. Shelley dec'd
           was presented before the Court
for probate - Thereupon came into open Court J. M. Senter and M. M. Senter subscribing witnesses thereto who first being duly sworn deposed and said that they were personally acquainted with Sallie H. Shelley the Testatrix in her lifetime - That she was of sound and disposing mind and memory at the time of the execution of said Last Will and Testament that she signed and acknowledged the execution of the same as her last will and testament in their presence and that she requested them to bear witness to the same -

That they signed the same as witnesses in the presence of the

(278)

(P.438 Cont'd) Testatrix and in the presence of each other it is therefore ordered by the Court that the said paper writing be and the same is hereby set up and established as the Last Will and Testament of the said Sallie H. Shelley dec'd and that the same be recorded in Will book and filed -

(P.439)
Last Will and Testament) I, Stephen D. Chitwood make and
of Stephen D. Chitwood dec'd(publish this my last Will and
Probated April Term 1889) Testament.
Recorded April 19th 1889 (
Will L. Wilkerson Clerk) Item 1st Let any just debts and
burial expenses be promptly paid out of any money not hereafter specifically bequeathed, that may first come into the hands of my Executor.

Item 2nd I give and bequeath to Everett Bloomingdale son of C. B. Bloomingdale, to be his absolutely and without limitations, all of my live stock that I may have of every description at the time of my death, and all of my farming implements, all of my household and Kitchen furniture, such as beds, bedding, bedsteads, table ware &c. all crops on hand or growing on my home place, all of which property is to be delivered to said Everett Bloomingdale for and during the term of his natural life my home tract of land consisting of about Two Hundred acres, conveyed to me by Dr. Burchett, many years ago. Also to have and to hold the same way one undivided fourth part of a Tract of Six Hundred acres of bottom land in the 8th civil District of Dyer County Tennessee being the same 600 acres entered by Thos. H. Fowlkes and myself, and of which I own one undivided one half, Upon the death of said Everett Bloomingdale, the land herein bequeathed to him for life, shall desend and be vested absolutely in any children that may be born to him, Subject to his widow's dower during her widowhood, If he die without issue born to him and living at the time of his death, then one fourth of the remainder go to his widow, if he leaves one, only (P.440) during her widowhood, and the other three fourths shall revert to his heirs at law. If he die leaving neither widow or issue, then the whole of the land in this item of my will shall revert to my heirs at law.

Item 4th I give and bequeath to Edward Chitwood oldest son of my brother Green Chitwood Forty Nine Acres of land, situated in the 7th civil District of Dyer County Tennessee, and adjoining my home place, the land sold to me by B. T. Witt and to said Witt by Joe Chitwood, also undivided one fourth of the 600 acres of bottom land, to have and to hold for and during the term of his natural life and the remainder, to his heirs at law, Subject to the widows dower, if he should leave one,

Item 5th I have given to Josiah Chitwood $2486.00 for which I have his receipt, This is intended as a gift to him, and my Executor is not to hold him accountable there for.

Item 6th I a note executed to me by my brother Green Chitwood, and his two sons to wit, Creed and Len Chitwood, dated about the 18th day of November 1883 for the sum of $520.00 or near

(P.440 Cont'd) that sum, due five years from date without interest, for which sum I hold a mortgage on the 50 acres of land bought by my brother Green from Patric Henry & Geo. Wright, said mortgage to run 5 years, no interest is to be charged on said note, before the expiration of the 5 years, after five years, If my brother Green should be living, I want him to hold and occupy said land free of charge, during his life, and if his present wife survives him, she may remain and occupy the land as long as she remains a widow, If not redeemed within the 5 years, and at the death of both parties above named, (P.441) or when the widow may marry, should that occur why the said land is to be sold and distributed, the proceeds thereof - to Dora Chitwood only daughter and child of my brother Len, and Charly Chitwood, son of my brother Angiren Chitwood, and Levin Chitwood, the youngest son of my brother Bastie Chitwood now deceased, to and Alex Ray, also, in this item I give and bequeath to the 4 persons above named all the residue of my personal property, not heretofore specially mentioned, I mean all moneys, notes, judgements choses in action &c equally between them.

Item 7th   If Dora Chitwood above mentioned die before arriving at mature age, why her portion shall descend directly to the other 3 just above mentioned.

Item 8th   I hereby nominate and appoint C. L. Nolen Executor of this my last will and Testament, and I hereby revoke all other wills at any time made by me.

Witness my hand and seal this the 7th day of June A. D. 1883
                                his
                        Stephen X Chitwood
                                mark

Signed and published in our presence, In Testimony whereof we have this day here with signed our names in the presence of each other, and in the presence of Stephen Chitwood the Testator, this June 7th day 1883

Witnesses   )
Jas. W. Baker   (
James Swearenger)
R. H. Campbell   (

                    Codicile

I Stephen Chitwood make this codicile No. 1 to this my last will and Testament, this 24th day of May 1887 to wit;

   I will to my Grand Nephew Everet Bloomingdale the Twenty acre tract of land which I purchased from Elias Hall which adjoins (P.442) the lands I have heretofore willed to my Nephew whose recorded deed I refer to for perticular metes & bounds of Sd Land, And I will said land to sd. E. Bloomingdale for and during his natural life and at his death, then to his children or decendants of his children, if they are then living, and to their heirs and assigns forever, On the following conditions to wit; that is provided said Everet Bloomingdale pays

(P.442 Cont'd) to me or to my legal representatives within four years from this date, Five Hundred and Forty Dollars. But if he fail to pay said sum of five Hundred and forty dollars within the time above set forth, then my will is that my Executor will sell said tract of land, and convey the same without the aid of any Court decree, and sell for cash or on strait credit, or for part cash and part on time as he may deem best, and divide the proceeds of such sale share and share alike between my nephew William Chitwood and Levin Chitwood (Bostwick Chitwood's sons) and Dora Chitwood (Len Chitwoods daughter) and Alex L. Ray and Pick Chitwood son of Angerean Chitwood, each of the five taking an equal share, and if my Nephew Everett Bloomingdale pays for said land within the four years above set forth, Then the proceeds of said land will be divided equally between said William Chitwood Levin Chitwood Dora Chitwood Pick Chitwood and A. L. Ray share and share alike

Witness
Smith Parks
J. A. Hall
S. J. Payne

        his
Stephen x Chitwood
        mark

(P.443)
In the Matter of the Last)   This day a paper writing purporting
Will & Testament of   (to be the last Will and Testament
Stephen Chitwood Dec'd   )   of Stephen Chitwood dec'd was
              presented to the Court, for probate, and set up and established as the Last Will and Testament of said Stephen Chitwood, and there upon came Jas. W. Baker & Jas. Swearenger subscribing witnesses, to said will, who being first duly sworn deposed and said that they were personally acquainted with the said Stephen Chitwood Testator in his lifetime, that he was of sound and disposing mind and memory at the time of the execution of said paper writing. That signed and acknowledged the same in their presence to be his last will and Testament, That they signed the same in the presence of each other and the Testator, and at his request as witnesses. And Smith Parks and S. J. Payne subscribing witnesses to the Codicile to said will, being duly sworn deposed and said that they were personally acquainted with Stephen Chitwood the Testator in his lifetime, that he was of sound and disposing mind and memory at the time of the execution of said Codicle to said Last Will and Testament, That he signed and acknowledged the same in their presence to be a Codicile to his said Last will and Testament, and that they signed said Codicile, as witnesses thereto in his presence and at his request.

It is therefore ordered by the Court that said Paper Writing be and the same is hereby set up and established as the Last Will and Testament of said Stephen Chitwood deceased, together with the Codicile thereto, and it is ordered by the Court, that the same be recorded in Will Book (P.444) and filed and C. L. Nolen the Executor named in said Will, approved in open Court refused to qualify as such, and the court being satisfied as to the claims of A. L. Ray to the Administration of said estate. It is therefore ordered by the Court that the Said A. L. Ray be and he is hereby appointed Administrator cum testamento anexo

(P.444 Cont'd) of said Stephen Chitwood deceased.

Thereupon came the said A. L. Ray here into Open Court, together with L. H. Chitwood and Peter Ford his securities and they entered into and acknowledged bond in the penal sum of Five Thousand Dollars, conditioned and payable as the law directs for the faithful performance of his duties as such Executor.

He was duly sworn

Let Letters issue.

(P.445)

Noncupative Will of J. G. Dunivant dec'd Set up and established at September Term 1889 & ordered to be recorded, Recorded Sept. 24 1889, W. L. Wilkerson Clerk	On the 2nd day of September 1889 J. G. Dunnivant deceased in his last sickness at his own habitation in Dyer County declared in the presence of the undersigned whom he especially requested to bear witness thereto that his will was as follows; - That his Daughter M. F.

Dunnivant have all the household and kitchen furniture. That all the rest of his property both real and personal be divided equally between his Eight children or the Heirs of thoes are dead Mrs. Mary A. Wynne, Mrs. Cora Townsend, Mrs. Mary T. Wynne dec'd Miss M. F. Dunnivant, J. H. Dunnivant, W. I. Dunnivant J. B. Dunnivant and F. A. Dunnivant. The said J. H. Dunnivant died on the 4th day of September 1889. Written and signed by us on the 23rd day of September 1889

                                        Guy Douglass
                                        F. A. Dunnivant.

In the Matter of the Noncupative Will of J. G. Dunnivant dec'd   This day a paper writing signed by Guy Douglass and F. A. Dunnivant was produced in open Court and propounded as the noncupative Will of J. G. Dunnivant and it appearing that said Dunnivant has departed this life and was a resident in Dyer County at the time of his death: - and it being proved to the satisfaction of the Court by the Oaths of Guy Douglass and F. A. Dunnivant that said paper writing contains the disposition which the said Dunnivant said he desired to make as to his property and affairs and what he wished done with them after his death and that said verbal directions were given by said Dunnivant during his last sickness at his own dwelling house in Dyer County in the presence and hearing of both of said witnesses and that they were specially called upon by said Dunnivant to bear witness thereto and that he was of sound mind and memory at the time; That said verbal will was reduced to writing and signed by them and it appearing that the heirs have been duly cited to appear here at this day and take such actions as (P.446) they see proper relative to the probate of said will and it further appearing from the Oaths of said two witnesses that said - paper writing contained the verbal noncupative Will of said Dunnivant and that the same

(282)

(P.446 Cont'd) should be established as such. It is therefore ordered by the Court that said paper writing be set up and established as the Last Will and Testament of said J. G. Dunnivant and that the same be recorded in Will Book and filed -

A true copy of Will and probate of same

                Attest; W. L. Wilkerson Clerk
              By   R. L. Palmer D. C.

(P.447)

| The Last Will and Testament of Clem Benton deceased Probated October Term /89 Recorded October 21st /89. W. L. Wilkerson Clerk | Know all men by these presents that I Clem Benton have this day divided my land the sought half is to go to Mariah my wife her lifetime and then go to my daughter Elizer Ann Benton if |

she can be found this half contains 19½ ninteen acres and one half, the whole tract contains 39 Thirty nine acres and one half my wife is to have my Jin Mule and one cow and all of the plunder around the house and in the house. I reserve a Burrying ground on the north west corner of the south half for myself and family,

The north half witch is 19½ of 39 thirty nine acres of witch Mary Benton is to have her part one the north east corner of the North half her part or share is 1 one fourth of the said 19½ ninteen acres and one half and the other three fourths is to go to Richard Benton my son the said three fourths is part of the 19½ ninteen acres and one half of the said North half of the 39 thirty nine acres and that said Richard Benton is to have the same three fourths as long as he lives and then it is to go to his three children Joseph Benton Julia Benton and Lulia Benton this being part of the tract bought of Dr. Thomas Benton of Dyersburg and that Robert Cooper and Scott Brandon is to be my Guardian to see that Mariah my wife gets the rents of the south half of the said 19½ ninteen acres and one half and to see to having the fences is takin care of and to see that the Jeff Mule I bought from W. D. Roberts is paid out of the rent and the balance to go to my wife and that Richard Benton is to build at home and let my wifes part alone and that said Robert Cooper and Scott Brandon is to see that she my wife has her rights.

July 30th /89
                                      his
                                Clem X Benton
                                  mark
                              Robert Cooper
                                    his
                              Scott X Brandon
                                  mark
                              J. M. Koonce

| In the Matter of the last Will and Testament of Clem Benton dec'd | This day a paper writing purporting to be the last will and Testament of Clem Benton deceased was presented to Court for probate |

There upon came into open court J. M. Koonce and Scott Brandon

(P.447 Cont'd) subscribing witnesses thereto who first being duly sworn deposed and said that they were personally acquainted with Clem Benton the Testator in his lifetime that he was of sound and (P.448) desposing mind and memory at the time of the execution of said last Will and Testament, that he signed and acknowledged the execution of the same as his Last Will and Testament in their presence and that he requested them to bear witness to the same, that they signed the same as witnesses in the presence of the Testator and in the presence of each other, It is therefore ordered by the Court that the said paper writing be and the same is hereby set up and established as the last Will and Testament of the said Clem Benton dec'd and that the same be recorded in Will Book and filed

A true copy of Will and probate of same

       Attest; W. L. Wilkerson Clk.
       By R. L. Palmer D. C.

(P.449)

Last Will and Testament of	State of Tennessee
Mrs. Ann Waddy dec'd	Dyer County
Probated Febry Term /90	I Ann Waddy of the County and
Recorded February 5th /90	State aforesaid do make this as
W. L. Wilkerson Clerk	my Last Will and Testament,

First; I direct that my funeral expenses and all my debts be paid as soon after my death as possible out of my moneys that I may die possessed of or may first come into the hands of my Executor.

Secondly; I give and bequeath to my Sister Sarah Gardner of Richmond Virginia my gold frame Spectacles and fifty dollars in money.

Thirdly; I will and bequeath to my Stepson Joseph K. Waddy my house and Lot Lying in the town of Newbern which is bounded on the East by Adams Street, South by G. W. Gregory West by H. Parks 2nd and North by Main Street provided however that the said Joseph K. Waddy Shall pay to his brother John W. Waddy the sum of two hundred dollars as his interest in said Lot. I also bequeath to Joseph K. Waddy my bedstead and Lounge which I have had made and all my household and Kitchen furniture except my bed and bedding that Stands in the North room of my house with the necessary clothing which I will and bequeath to John W. Waddy. I also bequeath To John W. Waddy my gold watch and after the above is complyed with in case there shall be any money Left, then the said John W. Waddy and Joseph K. Waddy divide it equally between them I appoint Jesse F. Williamson my Executor without his being required to give bond as such. I also request that if there should be anything Left unmentioned in this will that the same bed divided between my Step sons John W. & Joseph K. Waddy. In witness whereof I do to this my my will set my hand this the 27th day of April One Thousand eight hundred and eighty eight

           Ann Waddy (seal)

(P.449 Cont'd)
Signed and published in our presence and we have Subscribed our names hereto in the presence of the testator.

This 27 day of April 1888

F. C. Moore
J. W. Willis

(P.450)
In the Matter of the Last Will and) This day a paper writing
Testament of Mrs. Ann Waddy dec'd) purporting to be the Last
Will and Testament of
Mrs. Ann Waddy dec'd was presented to the Court for Probate, Thereupon came into open Court F. C. Moore and J. W. Willis subscribing witnesses thereto who first being duly sworn deposed and said that they were personally acquainted with Mrs. Ann Waddy the Testatrix in her lifetime that she was of sound and disposing mind and memory at the time of the Execution of said Last Will and Testament - That she signed and acknowledged the execution of the same as her last will and Testament in their presence and that she requested them to bear witness to the same, that they signed the same as witnesses in the presence of the Testatrix and in the presence of each other. It is therefore ordered by the Court that the said paper writing be and the same is hereby set up and established as the Last Will and Testament of the said Mrs. Ann Waddy dec'd and that the same be recorded in Will Book and filed

(P.451)
Last Will and Testament   ) I, Will my wife my entire interest
of J. C. Zarecor deceased.(in the land during her life and
Probated March Term /90   ) one note on my Son George for Five
Recorded March 3 rd /90   (Hundred Dollars in addition to
W. L. Wilkerson Clerk   ) what the law allows her 2/11/90

                   J. C. Zarecor

Jno. E. McCorkle
J. H. Charlton
F. E. Scoby

Let this Will be probated and set up March 3 / 90

             W. B. Sampson Chairman

In the Matter of the Last Will   ) This day a paperwriting
and Testament of J. C. Zarecor dec'd) purporting to be the
last Will and Testament of J. C. Zarecor dec'd was presented to the Court for probate. Thereupon came into open Court J. H. Charlton and F. E. Scoby subscribing witnesses thereto who first being duly sworn deposed and said that they were personally acquainted with J. C. Zarecor the Testator in his lifetime, that he was of sound and disposing mind and memory at the time of the execution of the said Last Will and Testament, that he signed and acknowledged the execution of the same as his Last Will and Testament in their presence

(P.451 Cont'd) that he requested them to bear witness to the same, that they signed the same as witnesses in the presence of the Testator and in the presence of each other.

It is therefore ordered by by the Court that the said paper writing be and the same is hereby set up and established as the Last Will and Testament of the said J. C. Zarecor dec'd and that the same be recorded in Will Book and filed

(P.452)
Last Will and Testament) Dyer County Term Mch. 13th 1890
of Jesse Clark deceased,(I, Jesse Clark being sound of mind
Probated April Term 1890) do hearby declair and publish this
Recorded April 18th 1890(my last Will and Testament. First
W. L. Wilkerson Clerk.) I give and bequeath W. T. Joiner
By A. L. Palmer D. C. (and his wife Sarah Abergale and
their children One hundred & Four acres of land known as the Benton place*I now live also my household & Furniture cow & calf Hogs & Waggon.

Second; I give Henderson Humphreys my old place One Hundred Acres lying one mile North of Dyersburg where J. W. Low now lives and this is to be his portion of my Estate.

Third; I want the balance of my lands sold and the proceeds of my lands together with my notes and moneys due me collected and equally divided among the following named parties, first Nancie Vinyard & her children One Eighth part of my personal Estate and the proceeds of the lands to be sold.

Second; Sarah Abergale Joiner and her children One Eighth part of my personal Estate and proceeds of Land to be sold

Third; J. W. Low Jr. child of Alice Humphreys Low One Eighth part of my personal Estate and proceeds of land to be sold.

Fourth; Jessie A. Calvin & children One eighth part of my personal Estate and proceeds of the land to be sold and her part shall be placed in the hands of a Trustee appointed by the Court for the benefit of her and her children for their only use and benefit

Fifth; the children of Mollie Henry One eighth part of my personal Estate and land to be sold

Sixth; Geo. S. Humphreys One Eighth of my personal Estate and land to be sold and the same to be held in trust by J. W. Low for Geo. S. Humphreys use and benefits

Seventh: Fannie E. Bain one Eighth of my personal Estate and land to be sold and the same is to be held in trust for her use and benefit by W. T. Joiner.

Eighth: Macie Humphreys One Eighth part of my personal Estate and proceeds of land to be sold 9th I give to J. W. Low my mule which he now has in possession and I do hereby nominate

*where

(286)

(P.452 Cont'd) and appoint I. Henderson Dawson as my Executor to this my last will and testament and do nominate and empower him to sell and convey all real Estate that I am seized and possessed of not herein disposed of in as full manna as I could do myself after giving ~~going~~ due notice either on time or for cash as may be best. In witness whereof I have hereunto set my hand & seal

Witnesses   Jesse Clerk.
F. Summers
C. P. Clark

(P.453)   ----------   Codicile   ----------

I, Jesse Clark having made my last Will and Testament bearing date the 13th day of March 1890 and desiring to make a change therein do make this codicile thereto to wit: Where as by said Will I have appointed Henderson Dawson Executor thereof and having full confidence in his ability honesty and integrity. I do hereby relieve him from the necessity of giving bond as such Executor. In witness whereof I have hereunto set my hand This 23rd day of March 1890

                                                           Jesse Clark

Signed and acknowledged
by the Testator in our
presence
Witness; F. Summers
       C. P. Clark

In the Matter of the Last Will   (This day a paperwriting
and Testament of Jesse Clark dec'd) purporting to be the
                                                             last will and testament
of Jesse Clark dec'd together with the Codicil No. 1: attached to the same was produced here in open Court by Henderson Dawson who is named as Executor of said Will and Codicile thereto and who asked that said Will and Codicile be admitted to probate and set up and established as the Last Will and Testament of said Jesse Clark dec'd

Thereupon came F. Summers and C. P. Clark subscribing witnesses to said Will and Codicile No. 1 who being first duly sworn deposed and said that they were well acquainted with said Jessie Clark in his lifetime that his place of residence was in Dyer County Tennessee and that he died in said County that he was of sound mind and disposing memory at the time of the execution of said Will and of said Codicile No. 1 thereto and that he signed and acknowledged said Will and Codicile thereto in their presence as his said last Will and Codicile thereto and that he requested them to signe said Will and Codicile No. 1 thereto as witnesses to the same and that they signed said Will and Codicile thereto in the presence of the Testator and at his request and in the presence of each other as witnesses thereto. It is therefore ordered by the Court that the said paper writing be and the same is hereby set up and established as the Last Will and Testament of said Jesse Clark dec'd/ Thereupon Henderson Dawson who is named as Executor of said Last Will and Testament

(P.453 Cont'd) came into open Court and was sworn as the law requires. The necessity of him giving bond being waived by the terms of said Will.

A true copy of Will and probate of same

                          Attest; W. L. Wilkerson Clerk
                         By R. L. Palmer D. C.

(P.454)
Last Will and Testament, of Chas. H. Pate dec'd, Probated July term 1890, Recorded July 29th 1890, W. L. Wilkerson Clerk, By J. A. Paul D. C.

I, Charles H. Pate being of sound mind and good memory do hereby make and publish this my Last Will and Testament.

First; It is my will that all of my just debts be paid as soon after my death as possible.

Second I will and bequeath all of the balance of my property, of every kind, whether real personal or mixed, that may be left after the payment of my just debts, to my beloved wife Julia A. Pate to have and to hold as her own, to her sole and separate use free from the debts, liabilities, use and control of any future husband she may have.

It is my will that my said wife be appointed as Executrix of this my last will and that she be not required to give bond as by law required of Executrix, Witness my hand this December 21st 1889

                                        Charles H. Pate

Signed, acknowledged and published by the testator in our presence as his last will and testament. And signed by us as witnesses at the testators request in his presence and in the presence of each other.

                                  Jno. B. Howell
                                  W. R. Hayes
                                  M. M. Marshall

In the Matter of the Last Will and Testament of Charles H. Pate dec'd

This day a paper writing purporting to be the last will and testament of Chas. H. Pate dec'd, was produced here in open Court by his wife Julia A. Pate who is named as Executrix of said Will, and who asked that said Will be admitted to probate and set up and established as the Last Will and Testament of said Chas. H. Pate deceased. Thereupon came W. R. Hayes and M. M. Marshall subscribing witnesses to said will, who being first duly sworn, deposed and said, that they were well acquainted with the said Chas. H. Pate in his lifetime; that his place of residence was in Dyer County Tennessee and that he died in said County; That he was of sound mind and disposing mememory, at the time of the execution of said Will; (P.455) and that he signed and acknowledged said will and codicile thereto in their presence

(P.455 Cont'd) as his last will and Testament and that he requested them to sign said will as witnesses to the same, and that they signed said will in the presence of the testator, and at his request, and in the presence of each other as witnesses thereto.

It is therefore ordered by the Court that the said paper writing be and the same is hereby set up and established as the Last Will and Testament of said Chas. H. Pate dec'd; that the same be recorded in Will Book and filed. Thereupon Mrs. Julia A. Pate who is named as Executrix of said Last Will and Testament, came into open Court and was sworn as the law requires. The necessity of her giving bond being waived by the terms of said Will.

Let letters issue.

A true copy of Will and probate of same.

       Attest;

(P.456)
Last Will & Testament of Robert E. Johnston dec'd
Probated Sept. Term 1890
Recorded Sept. 4 1890
A. G. Davis Clerk

I, Robert E. Johnston, being of sound mind and memory and considering the uncertainty of life, do make, publish and declare this to be my last will and testament hereby revoking all former wills by me at any time made.

First; - I direct that all my just debts including funeral expenses and the expense of administration be paid out of any money or other assets that may come into the hands of my Executrix.

Second; - I give bequeath and devise all of my property, both real and personal, of which I may die the owner, that may remain after the payment of my debts to my beloved wife Lucy M. Johnston for and during her natural life, to be held by her in trust for her own support and maintenance so long as she may live and for my children and grand children at her death, to be divided among them as hereinafter provided.

 I desire and direct that my said wife shall have a decent, ample and comfortable living and support out of the interest on, and rents and profits of my estate, and if necessary, she may entrench upon the corpus of my Estate for that purpose. She may use annually for the purpose of aiding in paying the salary of her pastor and for other benevelent purposes, and amount which shall not exceed one tenth of the ~~test~~ net annual income on my estate. Such portion of the interest on, and the rents and profits of, my estate as may not be used by my wife for her support and maintenance and for the other purposes herein named shall be a part of my estate and at her death shall be distributed with the balance of my Estate as hereinafter provided.

(P.456 Cont'd) Third; - The only real estate now owned by me is my house and lot situated (P.457) on Main Street in the town of Newbern, Dyer County Tennessee being the house and lot conveyed to me by M. A. Wadlington by deed recorded in the Registers office of said County of Dyer in Book G. page 319. I direct that, in case my wife shall deem it best, said house and lot and any other property that I may own at my death shall be sold and I hereby authorize and empower her as my executrix to sell said house and lot and all other property both real and personal, of which I may die the owner, at private sale on such terms and at such price as she may think advisable and to execute to the purchaser or purchasers a deed or deeds with general warranty of title to the real Estate so sold.

The most of my property being personal property, consisting mainly of money in the bank, notes, bank stock and a policy of insurance or benefit certificate for one thousand dollars issued by the United Order of the Golden Cross on the life of my wife payable to me, and it being probable that at my death my estate will consist largely of the same kind and character of property, I therefore direct that my said wife shall keep all of my funds including the proceeds of said house and lot or other property if the same should be sold, loaned out to good and solvent persons requiring them to execute therefor interest bearing notes with good security; or she may invest such portion of my Estate as she may deem advisable in bank stocks or other good and paying securities.

Fourth: - I desire that and direct that suitable tombstones or monuments for myself and wife be purchased and erected at our graves and paid for out of my estate, the cost of the same not to exceed three hundred dollars. I also direct that if necessary a burial lot in the Newbern cemetery or in some other cemetery be purchased for myself and wife and paid for out of my estate

(P.458) Fifth: - I direct that my wife shall pay out of my estate attorney and counsel fees for necessary legal advice and services rendered for her in the management of my estate.

Sixth: - I desire and direct that my said wife shall pay out of my estate all dues and assessments which it may be necessary to pay to keep said policy of insurance or benefit certificate in force; and I direct that at the death of my wife, said policy or benefit certificate shall be collected and become a part of my estate and be distributed with the balance of my estate as hereinafter directed.

Seventh: - I direct that at the death of my said wife, said house and lot if not previously sold and also all other property, real or personal, that may then belong to my estate, be sold, that that the funeral and other expenses of my said wife be paid out of my estate, and that so much for the corpus of my estate and of the interest on, and rents and profits thereof as may then remain, including the proceeds of said policy of insurance or benefit certificate and the proceeds of said

(P.458 Cont'd) house and lot or other property that may be sold be divided among my four living children and the children of my two deceased sons, James F. Johnston and William E. Johnston, as follows to wit: -

It is my will and desire and I direct that my daughter Katie Wade English, wife of A. D. English have five hundred dollars out of my estate and that the residue and remainder of my estate shall be distributed as follows to wit: - My living sons Daniel B. Johnston, Robert F. Johnston, and Walter E. Johnston and my said daughter Katie Wade English shall each have one sixth thereof the five children of my deceased son James F. Johnston shall have one sixth thereof jointly and equally and the four children of my deceased son William E. Johnston shall have one (P.459) sixth thereof jointly and equally, advancements being accounted for as hereinafter directed.

If any one of my said living children should die prior to my decease or to the decease of my said wife, then the share of my estate to which such deceased child would be entitled if living shall go to and vest in the issue of said deceased child.

Eighth: - I have heretofore made advancements to my children, including my said deceased sons, as follows to wit: -

To James F. Johnston three hundred and seventeen & 96/100 Dollars; to William E. Johnston three hundred dollars; To Daniel B. Johnston two hundred and seventy nine & 85/100 Dollars; to Robert F. Johnston one hundred and thirty three dollars; to Walter E. Johnston one hundred and seventy & 65/100 Dollars; to Katie Wade English sixty seven & 10/100 Dollars. I direct that said advancements be collected and brought into contribution in the partition and distribution of my Estate among my said children and the children of my said deceased sons.

I have heretofore given to my said daughter Katie Wade English a piano which I did not charge to her as an advancement but the same was an absolute gift to her and I direct that it shall not be charged to her as an advancement. I desire that at the death of my wife my said daughter shall have the said bequest of five hundred dollars and in addition thereto one sixth of the residue and remainder of my estate as heretofore provided, accounting only for said advancement of sixty seventy & 10/100 Dollars.

Ninth: - It is my will and desire and I hereby direct that all that my said daughter Katie Wade English shall receive for her sole and separate use, to be used, managed and controlled by her as she may deem proper (P.460) and to be entirely free from the debts and the control and management of her present or any future husband.

Tenth: - It is my will and desire and I direct that the share of my estate herein bequeathed to the children of my deceased son William E. Johnston be held by and vested in a trustee

(P.460 Cont'd) for them who will take charge of said fund and keep it loaned out at interest to good and solvent persons requiring them to execute notes therefor with good personal security. He shall not pay to said children any part of said fund or of the interest and profit thereon until they become twenty one years of age respectively. Each of said children shall receive his or her share of said fund and of the interest and profit thereon upon reaching the age of twenty one but not sooner.

I appoint J. Shumate as trustee for the said children of my deceased son William E. Johnston to take care of and hold and manage said fund for them as herein provided.

Eleventh: - I hereby appoint my said wife Lucy M. Johnston the executrix of this my last will and testament and I direct that she shall not be required to execute a bond as such executrix and that she shall not be required to execute a bond as trustee.

In witness whereof I do to this my will set my hand and affix my seal on this the 31st day of July 1889

        Robert E. Johnston (seal)

Signed, sealed, published and declared by the above named Robert E. Johnston as and for his last will and testament in the presence of us who in his presence and at his request and in the presence of each other have subscribed our names hereto as attesting witnesses

        M. H. Dickey
        Asa Dickey
        J. L. Cawthorn.

I Robert E. Johnston having, on the 31st day of July 1889 made and published my last will and testament do make, publish and declare this as a codicile thereto

It is my will and desire and I hereby direct that, in case my daughter Katie Wade English should die before my decease or before the decease of my wife, the special legacy of Five Hundred Dollars bequeathed to my said daughter in my said will, shall lapse and become a part of my estate, and at the death of my wife my whole estate, including the said legacy, (P.461) shall rest in and belong to and be distributed among my children and grand children as follows to wit: - To Eac each of my living sons, Daniel B. Johnston, Robert F. Johnston and Walter E. Johnston one sixth thereof; to the children of my deceased son James F. Johnston, one sixth thereof, to the children of my deceased son William E. Johnston, one sixth thereof; and to the children of my said daughter, who may survive her one sixth thereof.

I direct that this Codicile be attached to and become a part of my said will.

(P.461 Cont'd)
In testimony whereof I have hereunto set my hand and affixed my seal on this the 12th day of October 1889

        Robert E. Johnston (seal)

Signed, published and declared by the said Robert E. Johnston as and for a codicile to his last will and testament in our presence, and we have in his presence and at his request and in the presence of each other subscribed our names hereto as attending witnesses

        J. S. Cawthorn
        Asa Dickey
        W. H. Dickey

(P.462)
Last Will and Testament of Nat P. Tatum dec'd
Probated Jany. Term 1891
Recorded Jany. 19th 1891
A. G. Davis Clerk, Co. Co.

I, N. P. Tatum do make and publish this as my Last will and Testament hereby revoking and making void all others by me at any time made - First: - I direct that my funeral expenses and all my debts be paid as soon after my death as possible, out of any monies that I may die possessed of, or may first come into the hands of my Executor -

Secondly: - I give and bequeath to Tilda Ann Chitwood wife of S. A. Chitwood Sixteen Hundred and Thirty dollars already paid by me to S. A. Chitwood -

Thirdly: - I give and bequeath to M. B. Webb, wife of G. W. Webb Twenty five Hundred dollars, already paid in land and money -

Fourthly: - I give and bequeath to G. M. Tatum Twenty three hundred and thirty Dollars already paid in money and land -

Fifthly: - I give and bequeath to C. E. Featherston, wife of W. S. Featherston, Twenty two Hundred and seventy dollars - already paid in money to W. S. Featherston -

Sixthly: - I give and bequeath to I. S. Tatum Sixty Two and one half acres of land Known as the Phil Walker place in District No. 8 valued at fifteen hundred and Sixty Two Dollars and fifty cents - and I have already paid I. S. Tatum Three hundred and Thirty seven dollars and fifty cents in money, making in all, Nineteen hundred Dollars.

Seventhly: - I give and bequeath to A. B. Tatum four Hundred and Ten Dollars, already paid in money, and I want A. B. Tatum to have my home place, commencing at G. W. Webbs S. E. corner runs thence west 161½ poles to Witts E. line and Webbs south west corner, thence south 109 poles to E. Bloomingdale's north line and E. Chitwoods south east corner. Thence East 155 2/11 Poles to white oak Tree in Cokers north line, Thence north

(P.462 Cont'd) 89½ poles to a stake with sweet gum pointers. Thence east to a stake with hornbeam gum and ash pointers. Thence north 72 poles to a stake with Elm pointers. Thence west 65½ poles to ___ hackberry in Webbs East line, Then south with Webbs line 52½ poles to the Beginning - containing by estimation 136 1/6 acres more or less valued at thirty four hundred and six dollars & twenty five cents. The said A. B. Tatum is to have this land during his life, and then to his widow - so (P.463) long as she remains his widow, and then to his children if any, if none, To N. P. Tatum's Estate - in all thirty Eight hundred and sixteen Dollars and Twenty Five cents. I think that will be more than his part of my estate, and he is to pay back to the Estate of N. P. Tatum, to make him equal with the rest of the heirs -

Lastly: - I do hereby nominate and appoint G. M. Tatum my Executor. The said G. M. Tatum is to have full right to sell the remainder of my land and make Title to same and the proceeds of same and all other monies that may be collected by him of my estate shall be divided among the heirs to make them all equal - I hold notes of One Thousand Hundred and Ninety five dollars and twenty cents against G. W. Webb - and if said Webb fails to pay said notes - The same is to be deducted from his childrens part of my estate - I hold notes of one hundred and thirty two Dollars and fifty cents against S. A. Chitwood - and if said Chitwood fails to pay said notes the same is to be deducted from his childrens part of my Estate -

In witness whereof I do to this my will set my hand this the 8th day of Aug. 1890

        N. P. Tatum

Signed and published in our presence, and we have subscribed our names hereto in the presence of the Testator - This the 8th day of August 1890

        B. F. Smith
        C. S. Bradshaw

In the Matter of the Last) Jany. 5th 1891
Will and Testament of   (
N. P. Tatum dec'd   ) This day a paperwriting purporting to be the last will and testament of N. P. Tatum deceased - was produced before the Court for probate - whereupon came B. F. Smith & C. S. Bradshaw subscribing witnesses, here into open Court, who being first duly sworn deposed and said that they were personally acquainted with N. P. Tatum the Testator in his lifetime - that he was of sound and disposing mind and memory at the time of the execution of said last will and Testament that he signed and acknowledged the execution of the same as his last will and testament in their presence - and that he requested them to bear witness to the same - That they signed the same as witnesses in the presence of the Testator, and in the presence of each other - It is therefore ordered by (P.464) the Court that the said paper writing be and the same is hereby set up and established

(294)

(P.464 Cont'd) as the last will and Testament of said N. P. Tatum deceased, and that the same be recorded in the will Book & filed

A true copy of Original and probate of same

       Attest H. G. Davis, Clk.
       By H. P. Doyle, D. C.

(P.465)

Last Will & Testament) I, R. D. Bowen, being sound and despos-
of R. D. Bowen dec'd (ing mind, knowing the certainty of
Probated June 8th 1891) death, and the uncertainty of life do
Recorded June 9th /91 (make and publish this my last will and
A. G. Davis Clerk.) Testament revoking all others -

 First: I will and direct that all of my just debts be paid out of my property -

2nd I give and bequeath to my mother R. J. Bowen all of my real and personal property during her natural life. If necessary she may use for her own benefit the corpus of the personal property.

3rd I will and direct that upon the death of my mother the said R. J. Bowen, all my real Estate and whatever personalty may remain in her hands, be divided between my brothers J. L. Bowen H. J. Bowen and Sister Lillie Vernon and the heirs of my deceased sister S. J. Clark per Stirpes

 I appoint my mother R. J. Bowen executrix of this my last will and Testament without bond -

Witness   R. D. Bowen
W. F. Hamner
E. W. Smith

In the Matter of the last will) June 8th /91,
and Testament of R. J. Bowen dec'd) This day a paper writing
              purporting to be the last
will and Testament of R. D. Bowen deceased was produced in open Court for probate: - Whereupon came into open Court E. W. Smith and W. F. Hamner subscribing witness thereto - who being first duly sworn deposed and said as follows That they were personally acquainted with the Testator R. D. Bowen in his lifetime that he is now dead, that his place of Residence at the time of his death was Dyersburg, Dyer Co. Tenn - That said paper writing is the last will and Testament of R. D. Bowen deceased the Testator - That said Testator signed said paper writing in their presence and acknowledged the same to be his last will and testament - and that they at the instance of the tedtator and at his request signed said last will & Testament as witnesses thereto in the presence of the Testator R. D. Bowen and in the presence of each other - And they further testify that at the time of the execution of said last will and Testament the said Testator was of sound mind and dispos--ing memory - (P.466) now therefore it appearing that said

(P.466 Cont'd) paper writing is proven to be the last will and Testament of R. D. Bowen deceased and that as such the same has been properly proven witnessed and Executed and should be admitted to probate and set up and established as the last will and Testament of R. D. Bowen deceased - the same is accordingly done It is ordered that said last will and Testament be recorded in Will Book and filed

    A True Copy
      Attest:
           H. P. Doyle D. C.

The last Will & Testament)   Know all men by these presents,
of H. P. Scott Dec.   (that I, H. P. Scott Sr. of the
Probated June 1st 1891   ) County of Dyer, and State of
Recorded June 9 1891   (Tennessee - considering the uncer-
A. G. Davis Clerk.   ) tainty of this life - and being of
                            sound mind and memory do make, declare and publish this my last will and Testament -

First - After paying all my just debts, I give and bequeath unto my beloved wife Mary Jane, all of my real and personal property together with my Policy on my house and furniture during her lifetime or as long as she remains my widow -

Second - In case of an accident or burning - I want the policy when collected to be used to rebuild at the same place -

Third - I give and bequeath the above unto my beloved wife Mary Jane provided that she gives my daughter Mary Jane Forty Dollars per year if they live together and keep house, but if they have to board I give her one hundred dollars per year as long as she remains single -

Fourth - I give and bequeath to my daughter Mary Jane Lot No. 1 of my land as land off by H. V. C. Wynne the County Surveyor, at the death of her mother

Fifth - I give and bequeath to my daughter H. J. McGee Lot No. 2. of said land as above at her mothers death (P.467) to her during her lifetime, then to her bodily heirs if she has any living at her death - if not to return back to my estate -

Sixth - I give and bequeath to my son R. D. Scott Lot No. 3 of my land as above at the death of his mother

Seventh - My two Sons G. A. Scott and H. P. Scott Jr. are provided for in other lands belonging to their mother - I name G. A. Scott & H. P. Scott Jr. as my executors - in Testimony whereof I have hereunto set my hand seal in presence of the witnesses named below - This April 25th 1891

                                                H. P. Scott (S)

T. H. Vaughn
J. T. Roberson

(P.467 Cont'd) In the matter of the Last will and Testament of H. P. Scott Deceased - This June 1st 1891,

    This day a paper writing purporting to be the last will and Testament of H. P. Scott dec'd was produced in open court for probate - Whereupon came T. H. Vaughan & J. T. Roberson the subscribing witnesses thereto who being first duly sworn - deposed and said that they were personally acquainted with the Testator H. P. Scott in his lifetime. That he is now dead, That his Residence was Dyer County Tenn That said paper writing is the last will and Testament of H. P. Scott Dec'd - That he was of sound and disposing mind and memory at the time of its execution - That the Testator executed and signed said paper writing as his last will and Testament in their presence and requested them to bear witness thereto - and that they signed said paper writing as witnesses thereto in the presence of the testator and of each other -

    It is therefore ordered by the court that said paper writing be admitted to probate - and Set up and established as the last will and Testament of said H. P. Scott dec'd and Recorded in will book and filed

    A true copy
        Attest H. P. Doyle D. C.

(P.468)

The Last Will & Testament of Richard L. Hamilton Probated Jan. 4, 1892 Recorded Jan. 8, 1892 A. G. Davis clerk.	I, Richard L. Hamilton being in feeble health though of sound mind and disposing memory do make and publish this my last will and testament, revoking and annulling any will that I may have made heretofore.

1st I will that my body be decently burried and my soul to God who gave it.

2nd Having full faith in my beloved wife Lillie Hamilton I will and bequeath to her all of my real and personal property including my house and lot in the town of Newbern together with all means arising out of my business with the late firm of M. R. Pace & Co. and any other claim that I may have, and pay first the debt to the Dyersburg Building and Loan Association, and any other just debt that I may owe, and the ballance she shall have, to use for her own support, and the support of our child Biffle Hamilton. I fully authorize her to execute a deed to said house and lot for the above named purposes.

I hereby appoint my wife Lillie Hamilton Executrix to this will, without bond and security. Witness my hand this 12th day of December 1891

                              Richard L. Hamilton

(P.468 Cont'd)
Signed in our presence, and in the presence of each other, this 12th day of Dec. 1891.

    S. S. Ellis)
    M. R. Pace (Witnesses.
    M. C. Hamilton)

In the Matter of the last will and Testament of Richard L. Hamilton deceased. This June 4, 1892.

  This day a paper writing purporting to be the last will and Testament of Richard L. Hamilton dec'd. was presented (P.469) in open court for probate, where upon S. S. Ellis, M. R. Pace, and M. C. Hamilton the subscribing witnesses thereto, who being first duly sworn deposed and said that they were personally acquainted with the Testator, Richard L. Hamilton in his lifetime. That he is now dead. That his residence was Dyer County Tenn. That said paper writing is the last will and testament of Richard L. Hamilton Dec'd. That he was of sound and disposing mind and memory at the time of its execution, that the Testator executed and signed said paper writing as his last will and testament in their presence and requested them to bear witness thereto and that they signed said paper writing as witnesses thereto in the presence of the Testator and of each other.

  It is therefore ordered by the Court that said paper writing be admitted to probate - and set up and established as the last will and Testament of said Richard L. Hamilton dec'd and recorded in Will Book and filed.

  A true coppy.
  Attest - H. P. Doyle D. C.

The Last Will & Testament) I, Ann C. Borum do hereby make and
of Mrs. A. C. Borum   (publish this my last will & Testa-
Probated Jany. 23rd/1892) ment. I hereby give and bequeath
Recorded Jany. 29th /92 (my place in the town of Dyersburg
A. G. Davis Clerk.   ) Tenn. the place on which I am now
            living. The same consisting of
two lots in said town known and designated on the plan of said town as Lots Nos. 72 & 77 and the same conveyed to me by John Skeffington and Mary Amelia Skeffington by deed dated Dec. 20th 1887 to my two daughters Mattie V. Borum and Cornelia A. Nixon, wife of John Nixon, to be by them owned equally as tenants in common.

Witness my hand this the 19th day of September 1888

                 Ann C. Borum

(P.470)
The Last will & Testament)
of Thomas W. Young dec'd (I, Thos. Young do make and pub-
Probated at Jany. term 1892) lish this as my last will and
Recorded Jany. 19th 1892 (Testament - hereby revoking and
A. G. Davis Clerk   ) making void all other wills be
By H. P. Doyle, D. C.   (me at any time made.

(P.470 Cont'd)

I. I direct that my funeral expenses and all my debts if any be paid as soon after my death as possible out of any money I may die possessed of or may first come into the hands of my Executor -

Secondly: - I give, devise and bequeath unto my daughter Nancy Shannon of Perry County and her body heirs all that tract of land on Rocus Creek known as the Pen & Harber land all on the south side of Rocus Creek - bounded on the west by the lands of C. Cotham on the East by the land known as the E. C. Nix land, containing about 425 acres - the same more or less.

Thirdly - I give, devise and bequeath to my daughter Martha said of Perry County and her body heirs a Hundred acres of land on Crooked Creek known as the McKee land -

Fourthly - I give, devise & bequeath to my daughter Mary E. King and her body heirs One hundred and sixty nine acres of land on Tennessee River known as the Denson land. -

Fifthly - I give, devise and bequeath to my grand daughter Sarah E. Carvett and her bodily heirs all of that tract of land known as the E. C. Nix land - bounded on the west by the lands of Nancy and J. J. Shannon on the east by lands of the heirs of Moses Nix - containing about 500 acres - be it the same more or less -

Sixthly: - I give devise and bequeath to my daughters Sarah A. Heard and her bodily heirs One Hundred acres of land 50 acres where she now lives in the state of Kentucky & 50 acres in Dyer County Tenn. known as the Moody Young land -

Seventhly - I give devise and bequeath to my son John S. Young and his heirs one hundred acres of land known as the William A. Warren land where he now lives. -

Eighthly - I give devise and bequeath to my Son Samuel Young and his heirs One hundred and six acres of land known as the John Sanders land -

Ninthly - I give devise and bequeath unto my daughter Margaret Green and her bodily heirs One hundred acres of land known as the Elisha Sanders land.

Tenthly - I give devise & bequeath to my son Charles M. Young One hundred acres of land known at the William White land -

Eleventhly - I give devise and bequeath unto my daughter Manerva A. Young and her (P.471) bodily heirs One hundred and Twenty acres of land be it the same more or less. Beginning on the N. E. C. or 248½ acre tract I purchased from Thomas Ward - runs west with the N. B. line of the same 60 poles to a stake. Thence due south to stake creek, Thence up said creek to the N. E.L. of Benjamine Greens heirs land, thence north to the N. E. C. of the said 248½ acre tract, Thence west to the Beginning.

(P.471 Cont'd) Twelfthly - I give devise and bequeath unto my son B. F. Young and his heirs One hundred and twenty five acres of land be it the same more or less. Beginning on the N. W. corner of 120 acre tract that I have willed to my daughter Manerva A. Young runs thence west 66 poles to a stake in the N. B. L. of the said 248½ acres, Thence due south to Stakes Creek, Thence up said creek to the S. W. C. of the said 120 acres, Thence north to the N. W. C. of the same the beginning -

Thirteenthly - I will devise and bequeath to my Son Thos. W. Young by adoption and his heirs One hundred and Ten acres of land, be it the same more or less - Beginning on the N. W. corner of a 125 acre tract that I willed to B. T. Young - runs due south with the west boundary line of the said 125 acres to Stakes Creek. Thence down said creek 34 poles more or less to the S. E. C. of a 100 acre tract I willed to Margaret Green, Thence north 108½ poles to the N. E. C. of the said 100 acres tract, Thence west 64 poles to the S. W. C. of the said 248½ acre tract, Thence North 100 poles to the N. W. C. of the same Thence East to the Beginning -

Fourteenthly - I give devise and bequeath to my wife E. J. Young 144 acres of land where I am now living during her natural life with all the improvements for the support of her and the minor children

Fifteenthly:- It is my will that the heirs holding the above named land may sell it provided the proceeds is invested in other lands equivilant in value if the proceeds are not invested in other lands the title to be null and void: -

Sixteenthly: - It is my will that the three minor children be paid $260.00 dollars to make them equal with the old ones who have had that amount advanced in property - it is also my will that Manerva B. Young, Benjamine T. Young & Thos. W. Young be each of them paid by Executors $100 one hundred dollars a year from this year until they are of age in Lieu of the rent of this land.

Seventeenthly - It is my will at my decease that my Executors leave a sufficient amount of property for the support of my wife Elizabeth and children - but if they think there is a surplus sell the same, and at her death they may divide the lands that I may be (P.472) possessed of, or sell it and divide the proceeds as they may think best, for the heirs and that immediately after my death my executors collect all my debts and divide the proceeds equally among all after reserving enough in their hands to pay three minor children and an amount sufficient to Educate them equally with the rest, it is also my will that my wife Elizabeth have Two Hundred dollars in cash at my death.

Lastly: - I do hereby nominate and appoint L. A. Williams and Sam Young my Executor to carry out the above as my last will and Testament, in witness whereof I do to this my will set my hand and seal this 27th of March 1873.

            Thos. Young (seal)

(P.472 Cont'd) Signed Sealed and published in our presence and we have subscribed our names hereto in the presence of the Testator March 27th 1873.

J. M. Cochran
J. J. McLemore.

State of Tennessee) On this 18th day of January 1892 Sam Young
Dyer County) and L. A. Williams produced in open court a paper writing purporting to be the last will and testament of Thomas Young and ask that said instrument be probated and set up and established as the last will and testament of said Thomas Young dec'd whereupon came T. A. Green, B. F. Young, T. W. Young and L. A. Williams and all being first duly sworn depose and say: that they were acquainted with the said Thomas Young in his lifetime That he resided at the time of his death in Dyer County Tennessee and died in Dyer County Tennessee That they were well acquainted with the handwriting of the said Thomas Young and that the said instrument or paper writing above named is wholly and entirely in the hand writing of the said Thomas Young and that said instrument or paper writing was found (P.473) after the death of said Thomas Young among his valuable papers L. A. Williams deposing that said paper writing was lodged in his hands by the said Thomas Young (with other valuable papers belonging to said Young) with request to him (said Williams) to take care of it that it was his (Thos. Young's) will.

It is therefore ordered by the court that the said paper writing be admitted to probate and set up and established as the last will and testament of the said Thomas Young deceased and recorded in the Will Book and filed. Thereupon came Sam Young and L. A. Williams who are named as executors in said will together with T. A. Green W. S. Draper, B. F. Young, T. W. Young, R. S. Beaver and their securities and they entered into and acknowledged bond in the penal sum of ____ Dollars conditioned and payable as the law directs for the faithful performance of their duties as said executors and they were then duly sworn and it is ordered by the court that letters testamentary issue to them.

　　　　Monday Jan. 18, 1892
　　　　　A true copy
　　　　　　　Attest A. G. Davis   Clerk.

(P.474)
The Last Will & Testament) I, Ann C. Borum do hereby make and
of Mrs. Ann C. Borum (publish this my last Will and Tes-
Probated Jany 22nd 1892) tament.
Recorded Jany. 29th 1892 (
A. G. Davis Clerk.)　　I hereby give and bequeath my home place in the town of Dyersburg, Tenn. the place on which I am now living - the same consisting of two lots in said town, known and designated on the plan of said town as Lots Nos. 72 & 77. and the same conveyed to me by John Skeffington and Mary Amelia Skeffington by deed dated Dec. 20, 1887, to my two daughters Mattie V. Borum and Cornelia A. Nixon wife of John Nixon, to be by them owned equally as

(P.474 Cont'd) tenants in common. Witness my hand this the 18th day September 1883.

                                        Ann C. Borum

State of Tennessee)   Signed, sealed and published in our pres-
Dyer County   ) ence, and in testimony whereof we have
                      hereunto set our hands in the presence of
each other and the testator this 18th 1888.

                                        S. R. Latta
                                        J. C. Pinner

In the matter of the Last Will) This day a paper writing pur-
and Testament of Mrs. Ann   (porting to be the Last Will
Borum.   ) and Testament of Mrs. Ann C.
                                Borum, late of Dyer County
deceased, was - presented in open court for probate, whereupon
S. R. Latta and J. C. Pinner, the subscribing witnesses thereto came into open court and who being first duly sworn said
that they were personally acquainted with Mrs. Ann Borum, the
testator in her lifetime that she is now dead - that her place
of residence was in Dyersburg Dyer County Tenn. - that said
paper writing was the Last Will & Testament of said Mrs. Ann
C. Borum, dec'd, that she was of sound and disposing mind and
memory at the time of its execution, That the said Mrs. Ann C.
Borum executed said paper writing in their presence, and requested them to bear witness thereto and that they signed the
same as witnesses in the presence of the testator (P.475)
and in the presence of each other.

It is therefore ordered by the court that said paper writing be and it is hereby set up and established as the last will
and Testament of said Mrs. Ann C. Borum deceased and that said
Last Will & Testament be recorded in the Will book and duly
filed

        Attest   A. G. Davis Clerk.

(P.476)
The Last will & Testament) I, T. H. Fitzhugh of the County
of Thos. H. Fitzhugh Dec'd(of Dyer, and State of Tennessee
Probated Febry 22, 1892   )   being of sound mind and memory
Recorded Febry 29, 1892   (considering the certainty of
A. G. Davis Clerk   )   death and the uncertainty of
By H. P. Doyle D. C.   (time thereof do make this my Last
                              will and Testament in manner foll-
owing: that is to say: -

1st My will is that the expenses of my last sickness and funeral be first paid.

2nd All Just debts by me owing at the time of my death

3rd That all my property sold by my administrator which I
shall name hereafter, as soon as he may think best for the
Estate

(P.476 Cont'd) 4th I will that my administrator shall buy a lot at Fowlkes Station and build a house and all necessary buildings on said Lot with the proceeds of the property belonging to me at my death.

5th I give to my beloved wife M. R. Fitzhugh, the said house and Lot to have and to hold during her life.

6th At the death of my wife M. R. Fitzhugh I give and devise to my three youngest children by my wife M. B. Fitzhugh namely O. P. Fitzhugh my son J. B. Fitzhugh and H. A. Fitzhugh, my two daughters the said house & lot to them and their heirs forever.

7th The balance of the money if any from the sale of my property I give to my beloved wife M. R. Fitzhugh.

8th Lastly I do hereby and constitute and appoint T. J. Fitzhugh my son of the County of Dyer and State of Tennessee to be the administrator of this my last will and Testament - revoking and annulling all former wills by me hereafter made. Ratifying confirming this.

In testimony whereof I have hereunto set my and seal the 30 day of Febry 1892,

           his
         T. H. X Fitzhugh.
          mark

Witness
J. B. Turnley
Geo. Viar

In the matter of the Last will and testament of T. H. Fitzhugh dec'd(This day a paper writing purporting to be the last will and Testament of T. H. Fitzhugh deceased was produced in open court for probate whereupon came (P.477) came T. B. Turnley and George Viar subscribing witnesses here into open court, who being first duly sworn deposes and says that they were personally acquainted with Thomas H. Fitzhugh in his lifetime. That he was of sound and disposing mind and memory at the time of the Execution of said Last will and Testament. That he signed and acknowledged the Execution of the same as his last will and Testament in their presence and that he requested them to bear witness to the same, that they signed the same as witnesses in the presence of the Testator and in the presence of each other. It is therefore ordered by the Court that the said paper writing be and the same is hereby set up and established as the last will & Testament of said T. H. Fitzhugh deceased, and that the Bond be recorded and filed

       Attest H. P. Doyle D. C.

(P.478)
Last Will & Testament of)   Oct. 30th 1891
J. O. Sorrell dec'd   (This is my last will and Testa-
Probated April 4th 1892) ment - I, J. O. Sorrell give to my
Recorded April 6th 1892 (sister Mentie One half interest of
A. G. Davis Clerk   ) my place - it being on the North
By H. P. Doyle D. C.   (end, and all the stock I have -
                                        This for her support while she lives
and then to Dollie and his heirs forever.

   Witness   J. C. Sorrell
W. D. Tarkington
J. H. King
W. A. Sorrell

In the matter of Last will   ) This day a paper writ-
and Testament of J. O. Sorrell dec'd) ing purporting to be
                                                     the last will and Tes-
tament of J. O. Sorrell deceased was presented before the
Court for Probate - whereupon came W. D. Tarkington J. H. King
& W. A. Sorrell the subscribing witnesses into open Court, who
being first duly sworn deposed and said that they were personally acquainted with J. O. Sorrell in his lifetime That he was
of sound and disposing mind and memory at the time of the execution of said last will and Testament - That he signed and
acknowledged the execution of the same as his last will and
Testament in their presence and requested them to bear witness
to same, and that they signed same as witnesses in the presence
of each other - It is therefore ordered by the Court that said
paper writing be set up and established as the Last Will & Testament of J. O. Sorrell deceased and same be recorded in Will
Book and filed.

     A True Copy
      Attest H. P. Doyle D. C.

(P.479)
Last will & Testament of)
W. H. Simpson dec'd   (It is my will and wish that if I
Probated May 2, 1892   ) should die while in Middle Tennessee
Recorded May 13th 1892 (that the place belonging to me, known
A. G. Davis Clerk   ) as the Stutts place east of the
By H. P. Doyle, D. C.   (Grave yard shall be given to Ella
                                 Cooper her lifetime and at her death
if she has no (heirs) bodily to revert to my heirs. June 9th
1891
                                                          W. H. Simpson

This is to certify that if I should die before I return from
Dawson, this wish written on the other side must be in full
force until canceled by me -

   JWM Aug 29/91   W. H. Simpson

State of Tennessee) This day a paper writing purporting to be
Dyer County   ) the last will and Testament of W. H. Simpson

(P.479 Cont'd) was produced in open Court for probate - whereupon came Jno. N. Parker and Chamblin Simpson into open Court, who being duly sworn deposed and said that they are and were well acquainted with the handwriting of W. H. Simpson in his lifetime and with said W. H. Simpson - and that each and every part of said paper writing is in the genuine handwriting of said W. H. Simpson - That he was at the date of writing the same of sound mind and memory and that said paper writing was by him delivered to Ella Cooper, and that said W. H. Simpson died before his return from Dawson as mentioned in said paper.

It further appeared to the Court that no will or other paper has been found amongst the papers of the said W. H. Simpson annulling changing or in anywise modifying or altering the said paper here presented to the Court.

It is therefore ordered and decreed by the Court that said paper writing be set up probated and established as the ___ will of said W. H. Simpson - and same be admitted to record.

                      A true copy
                        Attest A. G. Davis Clk.
                            By H. P. **Doyle** D. C.

(P.480)
Last will & Testament	) I, Thomas Watson of the State of
of Thos. Watson dec'd	(Tennessee and County of Dyer do
Probated Oct. Term 1892	) make this my last will and Testament
Recorded Nov. 18, 1892	(and revoke all previous wills and
A. G. Davis Co. Clerk.	) Testaments made by me. I will and
By H. P. Doyle D. C.	(direct

1st That my funeral expenses be fully paid and discharged.

2nd That my debts (if any at that time) be paid.

3rd I give and bequeath unto my wife Narcissa Watson while she is my widow or during her life all of my personal property of every description, all monies that may come into her hands belonging to me at my death or that may come into her hands from claims or debts due me also any and all lands hereafter described which I own for her support. She is empowered to sell any or all of my personal property for the purpose of investing in other property either personal or real, but the property thus purchased by her shall in the event of her marriage be the property of my heirs as hereinafter stated - She is also empowered to sell and convey any and all of my real Estate Consisting of about One Hundred acres lying in Civil District No. 2. and bounded on the East by John E. Bell heirs and J. B. York North by W. M. Dean, west by Stallings heirs and Dave Walker South by Powel and Thurmon and with the proceeds purchase other real Estate to be used by her as before provided but to go to my heirs as herein mentioned at her death or marriage -

5th After the death or marriage of my wife Narcissia Watson I give, bequeath and devise all my property real and personal

(P.480 Cont'd) that may be left by me, or purchased by her as above empowered to my lawful bodily heirs to wit: -

6th I give to Margaret Frances Hughes my daughter by my first wife Five Dollars.

7th I give to Elizabeth Ann, Nancy Hellen, Emma Cellus, Martha Narcissa Matilda Florence, and John Lewis Watson, and the children of Mary T. Hood dec'd, all being children by my wife Narcissa Watson, the balance or residue of all my property of every description, either money, personal or real Estate &c - to be divided equally between them, the children of Mary T. Hood dec'd to have what would be one child's part.

(P.481) 8th I nominate and appoint my wife Narcissa Watson as Executrix of this my last will and testament without Bond or Security.
This Feby. 23rd 1886.   Thomas Watson

Attest
W. M. Dean
W. Frost.

State of Tennessee) This day a paper writing purporting to be
Dyer County   ) the last will and Testament of Thos. Watson
                     dec'd was produced in open Court for probate whereupon came W. M. Dean and W. Frost Subscribing witnesses thereto into open court, who being first duly sworn deposed and said That they were personally acquanted with Thomas Watson the Testator in his lifetime, and that he was of sound and desposing mind and memory at the time of the execution of said paper writing. That he signed and acknowledged the execution of the same in their presence as his last will, and Testament, in their presence, and requested them to bear witness thereto and that they signed the same as such witnesses in his presence and in the presence of each other.

It is therefore ordered that said paper writing be set up and established as the last will and Testament of said Thomas Watson Dec'd and be recorded in Will Book and filed - and it appearing from said paper writing that Mrs. Narcissa Watson was nominated and appointed as Executor of said will without Bond. She was then duly sworn and letters Testamentary issued to her

A true Copy

Attest A. G. Davis   Clerk.

(P.482)
Last Will & Testament of) I, John Kohuman do make and publish
John Kohuman dec'd.   (this my last will and Testament
Probated Oct. term 1892)
Recorded Nov. 17 / 1892 (I Let all my just debts be paid
A. G. Davis Clerk   )
By H. P. Doyle D. C.   (Item 2nd I hereby give and bequeath
                           to my well beloved wife Ida Kohuman
the Ten acres of ground where I now live purchased by me from

(306)

(P.482 Cont'd) S. R. Latta with all the improvements thereon erected. I also give and bequeath to her my Blacksmith Shop, and the Lot of ground upon which it is erected. The same conveyed to me by Tom W. Neal. I also give and bequeath to her all my household effects of every kind, and all the cows and calves I own at time of my death. I also give and bequeath to my wife for and during her natural life or until her marriage my residence and Lot in Town, the same on which I formerly resided, the same to be rented out and the rent applied to the support of my wife and children. My object in giving to my wife the Blacksmith shop is that she may sell the same and use the money in paying the unpaid purchase money due on the above named Ten acres Home place.

    I hereby nominate and appoint my wife Ida Kohuman Executrix of this my last will and Testament and it is my will that she be required to give no bond as Executrix Witness my hand this June 27th 1892.

                                      John Kohuman

Signed Sealed and published in our presence, in Testimony whereof we have hereunto set our hands and seals in the presence of each other and the Testator, June 27 1892

                                       S. R. Latta
                                       A. P. Ford.

State of Tennessee) This day a paper writing purporting to be
Dyersburg   ) the last will and Testament of John Kohuman
                            dec'd was produced in open court for probate, whereupon came S. R. Latta and A. P. Frost subscribing witnesses thereto who being duly sworn deposed and said that they personally acquainted with John Kohuman dec'd in his lifetime, And that he was of sound and desposing mind at the time of the execution of said paper writing, and that he signed the same as his last will and testament in their presence and requested them to bear witness thereto, and that they signed the same in his presence and in the presence of each other. It is therefore ordered that said paper writing be set up and established as the last will & testament of John Kohuman dec'd - and that the same be recorded on Will Book & filed and Ida Kohuman was then duly qualified as Executrix without Bond.

    A true Copy
                    Attest H. P. Doyle D. C.

(P.483)
Last will & Testament of) Dec. 29, 1890
Temperance Hendrix dec'd (Know all men by these presents that
Probated Jany Term 1893) I Temperance Hendrix of the County
Recorded Mch 21 1893   (of Dyer and state of Tennessee being
A. G. Davis Clerk   ) of sound mind and memory, Do this
By G. P. Woollen D. C.   (day publish and declare this my last
                                will & testament revoking all former
wills by me made. viz. First I will that all of my debts be

(P.483 Cont'd) paid including my burial expenses and a set of Tombstones similar to the one at the grave of my husband (M. C. Hendrix) I will Harriett Wyatt one blue coverlet. I will Narcis Forcum and her children all of my wearing apparel, I will Narcis Forcum one blue coverlet, one set of China cups and saucers. I will Delia Cope one dressing table, looking glass two calico quilts and one white ruffled counterpane. I will Daisy Cope one feather bed, pillows and bolster and walnut bedstead. One red calico quilt and one worsted quilt, one counterpane without fringe. I will Ira Cope one large Trunk, I will A. C. Hendricks one large folding leaf table I will Rebecca Bessent five dollars. I will Margaret Leach five dollars. I will to Rebecca Kellare my niece (of North Carolina Davis Co.) Five Dollars. I will to Lou Fulford my niece Five Dollars. I will to Jane Bean col Ten dollars (In care of Lou Fulford of North Carolina). The balance of my property if any after complying with and fulfilling the foregoing bequest, I will to Jeff Bean "colored" of Dyer County Tennessee, I hereby nominate and appoint B. L. Van Eaton Executor of this my last will and Testament of whom no bond is to be required. He is to have what the law allows him for his services. Witness my hand and sealed this the 29th of Dec. 1890.

Witness
Alice Van Eaton)
B. L. Van Eaton)　　　　　　　　　　　Temperance Hendricks

(P.484)
State of Tennessee) This day a paper writing purporting to be
Dyer County) the last will and testament of Temperance
　　　　　　　　　　　Hendricks dec'd was produced in open Court
for Probate.

Whereupon came Alice Van Eaton and B. L. Van Eaton subscribing witnesses thereto who being duly sworn deposed and said that they were personally acquainted with Temperance Hendricks dec'd in her lifetime and that she was of sound and disposing mind and memory at the time of the execution of said paper writing and that she signed the same as her last will and testament in their presence and requested them to bear witness thereto and that they signed the same in her presence and in the presence of each other. It is therefore ordered that said paper writing be set up and established as the last will and Testament of Temperance Hendricks dec'd and that the same be recorded in Will Book and filed.

　　A true copy
　　　　Attest　G. P. Woollen　D. C.

(P.485)
Last Will and Testament of) Recognizing the uncertainty of life
D. E. Parker Deceased　　　(and the certainty of death at no
Probated Mch. 13th 1893　　) distant day while in full vigor of
Recorded Mch. 14th 1893　　(mind and body I make and set up
A. G. Davis Clerk　　　　　) this as my last will and testament
By G. P. Woollen D. C.　　 (revoking all others. I direct that

(308)

(P.485 Cont'd) all of my indebtedness be speedily paid and that my estate real and personal, be divided and disposed of as hereinafter recited -

To my wife Mrs. Robena T. Parker I give the Turney place on which we now reside, containing ninety acres of land and the lands lying directly south of it to Louis Creek containing about twenty acres. Also the North east quarter of my Coon Creek farm (as now divided for purpose of renting and cultivating) occupied now by Mrs. Redd and others, also one hundred acres of hill land lying east of Riley Peels it being a part of the Terrill one thousand acre tract and a nine acre tract adjoining the Light lands on the east granted to Wm. B. Jones also a one half interest in the Coker farm in District No. 12 - recently purchased, also my blacksmith shop at Ro Ellen and some lots of land adjoining it - in all about twenty acres also 40 acres Coker tract, also I have given her the proceeds of Sale of tract of land in western portion of Carroll County known as the Hayes place, The Sale was recently made taking money already turned over to her and notes for balance.

Next I give to my son Daniel G. Parker a citizen of San Bernadino California that portion of my old homestead known as the Fowlkes place lying west of the road to Ro Ellen and north of the Turney and Sharp one thousand and eighty acres East of the Walker lands south of White & Hawks also all of my Anthony Sharp lands lying east of a line running south from a point forty poles east of the G. W. Pritchard south west corner.

(P.486) Next I give my son John N. Parker of Dyersburg Tenn. my old home place, the Turney and Sharp one thousand & fifty acres and that portion of the Fowlkes lands lying east of the Ro Ellen road and South of M. A. Welborn's lands, also a strip forty poles wide off of my Anthony Sharp lands on west side.

Next I give to my daughter Mrs. Mattie R. Carthel of Trenton Tenn. the south west quarter of my Coon Creek farm as now divided among tenants and the bottom lands lying directly west of this tract (one quarter) also the eighty acre tract of the Boon land. Also the one half interest in the Coker farm in District No. 12 - which is to be owned by her and her mother, to be divided in such way as they think best or remain undivided, also a tract of about one hundred acres in Gibson county near Waterford which I advise to sell and reinvest proceeds of said tract and the G. W. Pritchard tract which she may sell, All of the other lands except last two tracts given her are to be used and controlled by her, She receiving all the profits of them and at her death to be equally divided between her children.

Next I give to my daughter Mrs. Hattie C. Green of Dyersburg Tenn. the house and lot in Dyersburg where she now lives also the south east corner of my Coon Creek farm and the bottom lands laying directly west of the Hancock lands owned by me. Also the Booths Point tract of land containing Seven Hundred and eighty four acres. Also my farm west of Dyersburg on the

(P.486 Cont'd) acres - Those lands are to be owned and enjoyed by her. She receiving the net profits of same during her life and at her death to go equally to her children.

Next I give to my daughter Miss Nannie G. Parker the North west quarter of my Coon Creek farm as now divided for renting and the lands adjoining on west and north west (the McIntosh place) containing about five hundred acres in all, also the Moore place of Seventy five acres in the Second district of Dyer County. Also the Mulherin lands and the Sawyer twenty acres and the Sorrell and Pierce lands adjoining the Mulherin lands on the south. Also a house and lot in Memphis on Winchester Street bought of R. C. Binkley I instruct my executor not to collect a note of fourteen hundred dollars and interest on J. P. Harris. Also a claim on Chas. and Mollie Waldron for five hundred dollars - also a small note on J. E. Webb of forty or fifty dollars. I direct my executor to sell at earliest convenient opportunities by private sale the following lands to wit: - the old Smith place in Dist. No. 7 all of same not already sold. The thirty acres sold to R. P. Powell which I have agreed to take back, and the Spraggins place of about forty acres the proceeds of lands sold to become personal property and dispose of by general provision as to personal property. Said Sales are to be made for cash or notes so secured as to be good so as to make most advantageous sale. I direct my executor to set aside my twenty shares of stock in Citizens Bank for and hold it under the rules of said Bank for the benefit of my wife and five children equally accumulating the profits thereon for ten years - said earnings not to be used or applied to the use of the beneficiaries except in case of real need of one or more of them and then only for the necessaries of life. At the end of ten years to be divided together with the earnings on same considerations (P.488) as as other apportionments of personal property herein, My personal property I wish disposed of as follows, I give my wife all the household and kitchen furniture, supplies on hand, stock tools and other property belonging to our present home place.

I also give my daughter Nannie the sum of One Thousand dollars and the Piano to equalize her portion with the other children in past expenditures - I have kept no account of advancements and make only this charge thereof.

I give to my two little grand sons Henry Arthur Green and Daniel Burney Parker the two share of Bank stock purchased of W. D. Roberts one share each to be held and controlled by J. N. Parker as trustee for them till of age & then delivered to them he being cashier of said Bank.

I also give my little grand daughter Robena Carthel my five hundred dollars stock in Exchange Bank at Trenton to be held and controlled by her father J. E. Carthel cashier of said bank as trustee for her until she is of age then delivered to her, and instruct my executor to invest a like amount in Bank stock for Helen. After paying all debts I may owe at my death and providing for the special devises of personal property above specified -and a family monument One thousand dollars, I direct that my

(P.488.Cont'd) remaining personal property be divided equally between my wife and five children. Share and share alike, first deducting five per cent as compensation for my executor -

Should any of my children die without issue or refuse the bequests made herein his her or their portions of the realty and personalty hereinafter specified above set out shall revert to my estate and be divided as other assets, equally be- (P.489) tween the heirs on same conditions as stated in different bequests.

I nominate and appoint J. N. Parker - my son - as executor of this my last Will and Testament and having full confidence in his honesty and integrity - require no bond of him as executor nor of any of the Trustees herein appointed.

Recognizing the uniformity with which estates are depleted after being divided in order to avoid as far as possible a similar result in this case I request and direct the following - that my wife and unmarried daughter Nannie entrust the handling and managing of their interests to J. N. Parker who is hereby directed and required to act as trustee for my married daughter Hattie - to manage and controll her lands and personal property after division is made, and I enjoin upon my Son-in-law J. E. Carthel to carefully advise for Mattie as to her interests and aid her as far as possible to preserve same Having had this my last will and testament written for me at my dictation and having revised and corrected same by erasures and interlineations as appears on face of it. I now sign it in the presence of R. N. Straughan and J. T. Arendall as witnesses hereto - This Sept. 27th 1892

                                                            D. E. Parker.

Witnesses) R. N. Straughn
Witnesses) J. T. Arendall

We hereby certify that D. E. Parker signed the foregoing instrument which he said was his last will and testament in our presence we both being present and signed in each other's presence as witnesses to his act.

                                                            R. N. Straughn
                                                            J. T. Arendall.

In the matter of last will) Be it remembered that on this and Testament of D. E. Parker(the 13th day (P.490) of March deceased.) 1893 a paper writing purporting to be the last will and Testament of D. E. Parker deceased was produced by J. N. Parker named therein - as executor thereof in open court for probate whereupon came R. N. Straughn and J. T. Arendall, the subscribing witnesses thereto into open court, who being first duly sworn deposed and said they were personally acquainted with said D. E. Parker Deceased in his lifetime, that he is now dead that his last place of residence was in Dyer County of this state that

(P.490 Cont'd) he was in sound and disposing mind and memory at the time of the execution of said will, and that Testator signed and acknowledged the execution of said paper writing in their presence as his last will and testament and that he requested them to bear witness thereto and that they signed the same as witnesses in the presence of the testator and in the presence of each other and it appearing to the Court, that said paper writing is the last will and Testament of said D. E. Parker who is now deceased, that same has been property proven witnessed and executed and should be admitted to probate and set up and established as such and on motion said J. N. Parker named as executor or of said will, that it be probated and that letters testamentary issue to him and it appearing that he is entitled to be the executor thereof it is ordered and adjudged by the Court that said paper writing be set up and established as the last will and Testament of said D. E. Parker deceased and that the same be recorded and filed and that letters testamentary issue to J. N. Parker, named in said will as executor therof, without Bond same being waived in said last will and testament which is accordingly done and said Executor is duly appointed, sworn and qualified.

A true copy   Copy from the minutes - Attest -

                     G. P. Woollen
                         Deputy Clerk.

(P.491)
Last will & Testament of Thos. D. Harwell dec'd
Probated May Term 1893
Recorded May 8th 1893
A. G. Davis Clerk.
By H. P. Doyle, D. C.

I desire that Martha Jane Harwell my wife shall have full possession of her part of her fathers estate of whatever she brought with her when we married & I desire her to have the sewing machine for she paid for it. The big chair, the mare Maud, & colt & Buggy a cow and calf (Fikes) Hogs enough to make her meat & the growing crop or enough of it to run her next year and a reasonable lifetime dower in my land.

    The above is a copy of what I give my wife Martha Jane to have if I should die.   Aug. 16, 1891.

                         Thos. D. Harwell

I want the balance of my estate to bury me and pay my Doctors bill and bills with Frank Moore & to be equally divided between J. P. Harwell - L. B. Harwell Thos. T. Harwell & Eddie C. Taylor & I want it all done without a regular administrator. August 16, 1891

                         Thos. D. Harwell.

State of Tennessee) This day a paper writing purporting to be
Dyer County   ) the Last will and Testament of Thos. D.
Harwell dec'd was produced in open court for probate, whereupon came R. L. Beaver, R. H. Clark &

(P.491 Cont'd) L. J. Moore into open court, who being first duly sworn deposed and said, that they are and were well acquainted with the handwriting of Thos. D. Harwell in his lifetime, and with said said Thos. D. Harwell, and that each and every part of said paper writing is in the genuine handwriting of said Thos. D. Harwell - That he was at the date of writing same of sound mind and memory and that said paper writing was among his valuable papers at time of his death, and from the affidavit of L. B. Harwell it appears to the Court that no other paper writing has ever been found purporting to be the last will of Thos. D. Harwell and in any way altering, changing or modefying said paper writing here presented to the Court.

It is therefore ordered and adjudged by the Court that said paper writing be set up and established as the last will and Testament of said Thos. D. Harwell deceased, and that the same be admitted to record.

Attest

May 1893 A. G. Davis Clerk
            By H. P. Doyle D. C.

THE END

www.ingramcontent.com/pod-product-compliance
Lightning Source LLC
Chambersburg PA
CBHW081758300426
44116CB00014B/2159